EVIDENCE AND INFERENCE
IN HISTORY AND LAW

EVIDENCE AND INFERENCE IN HISTORY AND LAW
INTERDISCIPLINARY DIALOGUES

Edited by William Twining and
Iain Hampsher-Monk

 NORTHWESTERN UNIVERSITY PRESS
Evanston, Illinois

Northwestern University Press
Evanston, Illinois 60208-4210

Copyright © 2003 by Northwestern University Press. Published 2003. All rights reserved.

Printed in the United States of America

10 9 8 7 6 5 4 3 2 1

ISBN 0-8101-1893-9 (cloth)
ISBN 0-8101-1756-8 (paper)

Library of Congress Cataloging-in-Publication data are available from the Library of Congress.

The paper used in this publication meets the minimum requirements of the American National Standard for Information Sciences—Permanence of Paper for Printed Library Materials, ANSI Z39.48-1992.

This book is dedicated to Professor Dirk J. van de Kaa, Director of the Netherlands Institute for Advanced Study, 1987 to 1995, with gratitude from the NIAS Fellows (1994–95).

Contents

Acknowledgments   ix

Introduction   3
    William Twining and Iain Hampsher-Monk

1 Evidence and Inferences about Past Events:
  An Overview of Six Case Studies   9
    David A. Schum

2 Reconstructing the Truth about Edith Thompson:
  The Shakespearean and the Jurist   63
    William Twining and René Weis

3 The Last Wedge   122
    M. J. Geller

4 Wigmore Meets "The Last Wedge"   140
    Terence J. Anderson

5 Wigmorean Analysis and the Survival of Cuneiform   216
    M. J. Geller

6 The Mountebank:
  A Case Study in Early Modern Theater Iconography   231
    M. A. Katritzky

7 Schubert *Lieder* and the Guitar:
  Musicological Evidence and Inference   287
    Thomas F. Heck

8 Historical Evidence and Dutch Colonial Labor Relations   311
    V. J. H. Houben

9 Evidence and Inference in the History of Political Thought:
  The Case of Locke's Theory of Property   329
    Iain Hampsher-Monk

Notes on Contributors   355

Acknowledgments

During the preparation of this book we incurred many debts. We wish, in particular, to thank the Netherlands Institute for Advanced Study (NIAS) and its superb staff for creating the context that stimulated this project and for their support and help, NIAS Fellows (1994 to 95) who participated in the early seminars and many informal discussions, the contributors for their cooperation, and Gail Prosser, who undertook the arduous task of harmonizing the various typescripts for publication with diligence, patience, and thoroughness.

Parts of chapter 2 were previously published in William Twining, *Rethinking Evidence* (Evanston, Ill.: Northwestern University Press, 1994) and appear by permission of the publisher.

Mark Geller's drawing (fig. 3.1) of a cuneiform tablet in the Harvard Semitic Museum was previously published in the *Zeitschrift für Assyriologie* 73 (1983), page 116.

The photos in M. A. Katritzky's chapter 6 appear courtesy of Staatliche Museen zu Berlin, Preusssischer Kulturbesitz (plates 3, 4, 11); Christie's, London (plates 7, 9); the Trustees of the Ashmolean Museum, Oxford (plate 8); The Bodleian Library, University of Oxford (plates 12 [Mason C.16(2) T/page], 15, 16); Windsor Castle, Royal Library, © Her Majesty The Queen (plates 2, 6); Wolfenbüttel, Herzog August Bibliothek (=WoBüHAB, plate 14 [Gh 255]).

Parts of Iain Hampsher-Monk's chapter were previously published in Gunther Lottes (Hg.), *Der Eigentumsbegriff im englischen politischen Denken* (1995), and appear by permission of Brockmeyer Verlag.

**EVIDENCE AND INFERENCE
IN HISTORY AND LAW**

Introduction

William Twining and Iain Hampsher-Monk

STARTING IN THE LATE 1970s, the "new evidence scholarship" in law[1] and the writings of Jonathan Cohen and David A. Schum[2] significantly advanced general concepts and techniques of analyzing evidence and inference in several disciplines. The aim of this book is to explore, through detailed case studies, the application of these ideas to other disciplines in the humanities, including argumentation theory, Assyriology, economic history, musicology, narrative, political theory, and theater iconography.

During the academic year 1994–95 the Netherlands Institute for Advanced Study (NIAS) hosted five international groups ("nuclei") of scholars, with each group working on a particular project at the frontier of its field. Other scholars from a variety of disciplines in the humanities and social sciences worked on their own or in smaller groups. Most nuclei included scholars from more than one discipline. The five main projects were (a) history of Dutch political concepts, (b) theater iconography, (c) magic and religion in ancient Assyria, (d) social dilemmas, and (e) forensic expertise in the Netherlands criminal justice system.

At first sight, these five seemingly esoteric projects had almost nothing in common. However, it is the policy of NIAS to encourage multidisciplinary contacts, and over time the initial assumption of the projects' disparity began to be challenged. The current project grew out of the idea that the five nuclei at NIAS had overlapping interests in methodological problems relating to evidence, inference, and interpretation and that a sustained conversation among specialists in the different subject areas could lead to cross-disciplinary fertilization—in particular that concepts, lines of questioning, and techniques of reasoning and analysis developed in one discipline or academic context might fruitfully be applied to problems in one or more of the others. Accordingly, William Twining and Terence J. Anderson suggested that a sixth nucleus be formed to explore these issues.

We began with a series of informal seminars to which all NIAS Fellows were invited. A theoretical framework for planning the project was provided by Schum's recently published *Evidential Foundations of Probabilistic Reasoning*.[3] To provide a focus, Twining suggested the following deliberately provocative hypothesis:

> Notwithstanding differences in (i) the objectives of our particular enquiries, (ii) the nature and extent of available source material, (iii) the culture of our respective disciplines (including their histories, conventions, states of development, etc.), (iv) national backgrounds, and (v) other contextual factors, all of our projects involve, as part of the enterprise, drawing inferences from evidence to test hypotheses and justify conclusions, and the logic of this kind of enquiry is governed by the same principles.

The seminar proceeded informally through presentation of papers and case studies by individual Fellows, including individual scholars from a wider range of disciplines in the humanities and social sciences. In addition, some individuals paired off for more intensive cross-disciplinary discussions. Toward the end of the year, Schum was invited to join the group. He has since advised on the project and contributed a chapter that provides a general theoretical introduction and a review of the six case studies. Members of all five original nuclei and a number of other scholars participated in the 1994 to 1995 period or, as in the case of René Weis, joined at a later date. Sufficient enthusiasm was generated that it was decided to continue the project with a smaller group after we had dispersed. This volume is the result.

The individual case studies are surveyed in Schum's chapter 1, which also introduces general "substance-blind" methods and problems of evidence and inference. It may be useful here to say something about Schum's work. There has, of course, been a long tradition of non-lawyers' finding that law can be a fertile source of examples and ways of thought that are relevant to their own disciplinary concerns.[4] Recently, interest in problems of evidence and inference across disciplines has been given a significant boost by Schum's *Evidential Foundations of Probabilistic Reasoning*.[5] In a masterly survey, which crosses at least eight disciplines and many more different spheres of practical activity, Schum identifies shared problems of evidence and inference, both practical and theoretical. He argues that evidence and inference are of concern to any discipline and practical activity in which conclusions and decisions are reached on the basis of incomplete information. He explores the state of the art in different subject areas with respect to organizing masses of data, constructing and criticizing arguments based on evidence, combining evidence, classifying evidence without regard to its substance or content, and identifying the subtleties of inferential reasoning.

Schum treats law as the pivotal discipline for the study of evidence.[6] He commends it to other disciplines, especially with respect both to dealing with complex bodies of evidence and to some particular aspects of inference, such as ancillary evidence, second-hand evidence (e.g., hearsay), cascaded inferences (inference upon inference), and ways of testing the authenticity and credibility of evidentiary sources. The general theme of his analysis is that the complexity of inferential tasks has often been underestimated in some disciplines or treated with resignation in others, whereas in law we have been forced as a practical matter routinely to grapple with at least some of these difficulties. "Our current methods for gathering, storing, retrieving and transmitting information far exceed, in number and effectiveness, our methods for putting this information to inferential use in the drawing of conclusions from it."[7] Schum is perhaps too generous in giving credit to the contributions of evidence scholarship rather than to the practical context of law in filling what he calls this "methodological gap." If law has been less prone to fall into the trap of underestimating the complexity of most inferential tasks, it is largely because its raw material—real-life cases—regularly forces many such complexities to the surface in the crucible of forensic argument.[8]

It was never our intention here to try to produce general conclusions or an overarching methodology. Rather, our objective was to use case studies to explore in detail the finely nuanced differences among disciplines that involve complex mixtures of culture, tradition, methodology, and focus. David Schum's work points not only to shared analytical concerns that provide channels for cross-fertilization, but also to the complexities that arise from different standpoints and contexts that channel the approaches in different inquiries. On the whole, the original hypothesis stood up quite well, although it needed to be extended to place more emphasis on matters of narrative, interpretation, and the framing of questions—all central concerns in the humanities and social sciences today.

The main aims of this book are to test "Twining's hypothesis" and the applicability of Dr. Schum's thesis about basic concepts of evidence and inference in a variety of disciplines and contexts, and to illustrate in concrete detail their application to a range of types of problem. If there are any general lessons to be drawn from this enterprise, perhaps they are that not only can cross-disciplinary conversations indeed be fruitful and suggestive, but also that local knowledge of the history and culture of a particular academic terrain is an important part of any methodology.

As is implicit in Schum's opening review, the chapters in this book approach the questions posed by "Twining's hypothesis" in different ways. It might be helpful to the reader to be more explicit about their relationship to the hypothesis, and to Wigmorean method, at the outset.

The most dogged and rigorous attempts to deploy Wigmorean analysis are those in the chapters by M. J. Geller and Terence J. Anderson. Anderson in particular deploys the full panoply of technical terminology and devices within the legal method on Geller's arguments in the field of Assyriology. A slightly less rigorous application in an actual legal case is undertaken by William Twining and René Weis. Here the interest lies in the comparison between a legal and a literary scholar's readings of the same material. A legal format—but not a Wigmorean analysis—is used by Thomas F. Heck to present the case for the "authenticity" of guitar-accompanied Schubert *Lieder*. Here the readers themselves might consider reformulating the case in Wigmorean terms. In all of these cases the role of evidence in relation to a particular factual proposition is such that, even if the subject is not itself a legal case, the question can be formulated so as to invite the verdict "proven" or "not proven."

The remaining three cases are rather different in that, for various reasons, the relationship between evidence and conclusion for these cases is not capable of being formulated in quite the same way as for the previous three. M. A. Katritzky, although scrupulous in the gathering and deployment of her evidence, seeks to find out more about mountebanks and their relationship to early theater, rather than to prove any one proposition about them on which we could find a verdict. V. J. H. Houben's case invokes a range of social-science laws, data, and generalizations to understand and illuminate—not to prove the fact of—an episode in economic history. Here the relationship is almost reversed. The facts of the episode might have been taken to be the ultimate probandum, but instead we take the facts as proven; what we want to know is the explanatory contexts in which they can be embedded. Finally, Iain Hampsher-Monk's piece seeks to demonstrate not merely the difficulty of adducing evidence to "prove" interpretative claims, but also to show the dialectic relationship between such attempted demonstrations and the interpretations advanced. Inference and evidence here act in a dynamic and formative way on the ultimate probandum.

It is for the reader to judge the outcome of this exercise—but it is worth making three observations. First, there was no serious disagreement about the proposition that we had overlapping problems of evidence and inference and that we could usefully discuss these across disciplines. Second, the members of the group were all drawn from the humanities and social sciences and all agreed that problems of evidence and inference could not be kept separate from questions about interpretation and narrative. Third, if representatives of the physical sciences, both pure and applied, and of cognate disciplines such as astronomy and mathematics had been represented, there would probably have been little difficulty accommodating them within the group—although there might have been more emphasis on probabilities and statistics and sharper disagreements on some issues. Difficult questions were raised about the relationship between fundamental problems of evidence and inference and the specific contexts and objectives of projects situated in different disciplinary cultures, but overall we had few serious problems of communication. In conclusion, we doubt that this story gives any support to the claim that law is the queen of the inferential disciplines. If we can identify a common mascot, it must be Sherlock Holmes, the fictional character who seems to feature in the literature of almost any discipline that involves inquiry.[9] Perhaps none of this need surprise us, for, as Jeremy Bentham observed: "The field of evidence is no other than the field of knowledge."[10]

Notes

1. For example, M. O. Finkelstein, *Quantitative Methods in Law* (New York: Free Press, 1978); Richard Eggleston, *Evidence, Proof, and Probability*, 2nd ed. (Lon-

don: Weideneld and Nicolson, 1983); Peter Tillers and Eric Green, ed., *Probability and Inference in the Law of Evidence* (Dordrecht: Kluwer, 1988); Terence Anderson and William Twining, *The Analysis of Evidence: How To Do Things with Facts Based upon Wigmore's Science of Judicial Proof* (Evanston, Ill.: Northwestern University Press, 1998); William Twining, *Rethinking Evidence* (Oxford, U.K.: Basil Blackwell, 1990; Chicago: Northwestern University Press, 1994).

2. Jonathan Cohen, *The Probable and the Provable* (Oxford, U.K.: Clarendon Press, 1977); David Schum, *Evidence and Inference for the Intelligence Analyst* (Lanham, Md.: University Press of America, 1987), *The Evidential Foundations of Probabilistic Reasoning* (New York: Wiley, 1994), and, with Joseph B. Kadane, *A Probabilistic Analysis of the Sacco and Vanzetti Evidence* (New York: Wiley, 1996).

3. See note 2.

4. In philosophy, for example, Stephen Toulmin's *Reason in Ethics* (Cambridge: Cambridge University Press, 1950), Cohen's *The Probable and the Provable* (see note 2), and, more recently, Richard Gaskins' *Burdens of Proof in Modern Discourse* (New Haven, Conn.: Yale University Press, 1992) are important works in which legal argumentation about questions of fact has been used to exemplify paradigmatic aspects of general practical reasoning—here, background generalizations, inductive probability, and presumptions. Moral philosophers have often found legal cases a fruitful source of examples for ethical theory, not least (we suspect) because of the number and diversity of problems that a legal system must deal with, and because real life may sometimes be stranger, more complex, or more provocative than fiction. That is, actual cases can be more stimulating than artificial hypotheticals dreamed up by philosophers.

5. In the preface to that work Schum writes, "In any inference task our evidence is always incomplete, rarely conclusive, and often imprecise or vague: it comes from sources having any gradation of credibility."

6. Ibid., 6.

7. Ibid., 4.

8. Argument about disputed questions of fact is, in principle, no less dialectical in inquisitorial than in adversarial systems; whether it is in practice is a separate question. This issue is explored in the following book, produced by the 1994–5 law "nucleus" at NIAS: M. Malsch and J. F. Nijboer, ed., *Complex Cases: Perspectives on the Netherlands Criminal Justice System* (Amsterdam: Thela Thesis, 1999).

9. Schum, *Evidential Foundations*, 477–81.

10. Jeremy Bentham, *An Introductory View of the Rationale of Judicial Evidence*, vol. 6 of *Works*, ed. J. Bowring (Edinburgh: W. Tait, 1838–43).

1 Evidence and Inferences about Past Events
An Overview of Six Case Studies

David A. Schum

IN THIS COLLECTION of essays you will observe eight scholars at work as they draw conclusions about events in the past, based on evidence whose substance is as diverse as anyone could ever imagine. Professors William Twining and René Weis examine certain evidence in a celebrated murder case tried in London more than seventy-five years ago; of particular interest to them are letters written by one defendant to another defendant in this case. Controversy lingers about what interpretation should be placed on the content of some of these letters. Professors M. J. Geller and Terence J. Anderson consider a variety of evidence in inferences about when the Sumerian language became technically extinct (in the sense that it was no longer learned by priests in the scribal schools in Babylonian temples nearly two millenia ago). Dr. M. A. Katritzky's interests concern the characteristics and behavior of itinerant performers and hawkers, termed *mountebanks*, and their possible influence on theatrical productions centuries ago. In her inferences about the behavior and the influence of these interesting characters she employs a variety of pictorial and documentary evidence dating from the early 1500s. Professor Thomas F. Heck considers documentary evidence in a debate about whether Franz Schubert ever wrote arrangements of his *Lieder* (songs) for voice and guitar, in addition to the ones he wrote for voice and piano. Professor V. J. H. Houben's interests concern relations between Javanese contract laborers and their colonial masters in Sumatra eighty years ago. He uses the evidence in one

---

The author gratefully acknowledges the support of the George Mason University School of Law while preparing this chapter.

case of violent confrontation between a Javanese contract laborer and his colonial masters to introduce an analysis of the causes of the widespread discontent among so-called coolie laborers in Sumatra that subsequently led to major social changes in Indonesia. Finally, Professor Ian Hampsher-Monk considers evidential and inferential issues in the history of political thought. To illustrate these issues he draws upon passages from the writings of John Locke on property rights and possession. There is some ambiguity in these passages that he examines.

So, our evidential and inferential journey in this collection of seven essays takes us from the law courts in London in the 1920s, to ancient Babylonian temples, to the theater in the 1500s, to Vienna and Franz Schubert's composing room in the early 1800s, to Sumatra nearly a century ago, and finally back to London in the 1600s. Our guides on these journeys come from the fields of law (Twining and Anderson), Shakespearean studies (Weis), Assyriology (Geller), theater iconography (Katritzky), musicology (Heck), economic history (Houben), and political theory (Hampsher-Monk). Why should anyone wish to take this journey back in time to visit these widely scattered places? One answer is that persons interested in how evidence is used and how conclusions are reached by scholars in different disciplines should be most interested in making this journey. As the French historian Marc Bloch once observed (1953, 18–9): "Each science, taken by itself, represents but a fragment of the universal march toward knowledge. . . . [I]n order to understand and appreciate one's own methods of investigation, however specialized, it is indispensable to see their connections with all simultaneous tendencies in other fields." Without hesitation, I agreed to take this journey for reasons quite similar to those expressed in Bloch's observation. For more than thirty-five years I have been a student of the evidential foundations of probabilistic reasoning. As I have noted elsewhere (Schum 1994), my studies of the properties, uses, and discovery of evidence have taken me on journeys in many fields, including law, history, philosophy and logic, probability, semiotics, artificial intelligence, psychology, and intelligence analysis. I was very pleased when asked by Professor Twining to go on new journeys in the fields of Assyriology, theater iconography, musicology, Dutch colonial history, and the history of political thought.

With one exception, all of the contributors to this volume were visiting Fellows at the Netherlands Institute for Advanced Studies

(NIAS), in Wassenaar, during the academic year 1994–5. One theme that emerged in discourse among the Fellows that year concerned differences and similarities in inferential methodologies across the disciplines represented among the Fellows. This collection of essays is a product of discussions that took place on these methodological issues. One thing the authors have in common is a *historical standpoint*; their inferences all concern events that may or may not have happened in the past. But there are two major differences observable in these essays. As expected, the content or substance of the evidence differs widely across them. The fields of law and history are the only ones known to me in which evidence having every conceivable substance or content is routinely encountered. In these seven essays we consider love letters, cuneiform tablets, illustrations of mountebanks and their companions, printed music, colonial labor records, passages from John Locke's essays, and many other substantive varieties of evidence. A bit later I mention *substance-blind* methods for classifying the evidence in these essays. These methods help us to work our way through differences in evidential substance in an analysis of the inferential methods employed by our authors.

A more important difference emerging in these essays concerns the manner in which the major credentials of evidence are established. These credentials concern the *relevance, credibility,* and *inferential or probative force* of evidence. In each of these essays, the authors faced the very difficult task of drawing conclusions from masses of evidence. The task of trying to make sense out of a mass of evidence can be approached in a variety of ways. Individuals differ considerably in the methods they use for marshaling or organizing their thoughts and their evidence en route to reaching a conclusion. One difference concerns the extent to which they decompose the task of establishing the three credentials of evidence just mentioned. The *decomposition process* involves making explicit arguments or chains of reasoning constructed in defense of the relevance and credibility of evidence. These arguments then provide a specific basis for assessing the inferential force of evidence on the possible conclusions being entertained. The decomposition of arguments can be performed in various ways and to various levels of detail or granularity.

To my knowledge, the first person to perform a systematic study of the process of constructing arguments from a mass of evidence was the American jurist John H. Wigmore. Wigmore (1913, 1937) developed an *analytic* and *synthetic* method for marshaling thoughts and evidence in probabilistic reasoning. He was more than sixty years ahead of his time in studying complex and interrelated chains of reasoning, which are now termed *inference networks*. Wigmore's methods provide the best examples I know concerning the microscopic decomposition of arguments based on a mass of evidence. Each link in a chain of reasoning from evidence to hypotheses (or matters to be proved) exposes a source of doubt or uncertainty. Often, many sources of doubt lurk between our evidence and our hypotheses and our arguments can thus become stunningly complex, particularly when they are based upon a *mass* of evidence. Wigmore argued that we ought to identify as many sources of doubt as we can, lest an opponent or critic identify them for us. I return to Wigmore's methods a bit later.

It happens that two of the contributors to this collection of essays, along with Professor Peter Tillers (Cardozo School of Law), are the world's authorities on Wigmorean methods for the analysis of masses of evidence. In their *Analysis of Evidence: How to Do Things with Facts Based on Wigmore's Science of Judicial Proof* (1998), Anderson and Twining provide many examples of the virtue of laying out arguments in detail so that they can be examined critically before they are to be defended at trial or in some other forum. So, it is not a surprise that two of the essays in this volume—the essay by Twining and Weis and the one by Anderson—make use of Wigmore's methods or modifications of them. Scholars and practitioners in law and in other disciplines have been slow to recognize the virtues of Wigmore's methods for constructing arguments, in spite of the fact that no one ever questioned Wigmore's basic logic. There are some striking similarities between Wigmore's methods for argument construction and those provided years later by Stephen Toulmin (1964). Reasons that Wigmore's methods were not enthusiastically received have been discussed at length elsewhere (e.g., Twining 1985, 164–6; Anderson and Twining 1998, 117–31; Tillers and Schum 1988; Stein 1992). Today we are witnessing a renewed interest in Wigmore's methods in law and in other fields, partly because of the discipline they enforce on our probabilistic reasoning based on masses of evidence. As one example, Professor Joseph B. (Jay) Kadane (Carnegie Mellon University) and I employed Wigmore's methods in our recent (1996) probabilistic analysis of the mass of trial and posttrial evidence in the celebrated American law case *Commonwealth v. Sacco and Vanzetti*.

The authors of the other five essays in this volume employ other, less detailed methods for marshaling their thoughts and evidence. Wigmore's methods are not to everyone's taste and, in fact, they have been be criticized for being overly *atomistic* (e.g., Twining 1985, 183–6). As far as the decomposition of complex probabilistic reasoning tasks is concerned, the other end of the continuum is represented by *holistic* analysis. On this view, the whole of our evidence is always viewed to be different than the sum of its parts. Our conclusions should therefore be based on assessments of bodies of evidence, *taken in the aggregate*, with due attention being paid to any interactions in the processes we are investigating as they are revealed by our evidence. There is fear that very detailed analyses such as Wigmore's will somehow prevent us from capturing the extraordinarily wide array of evidential and inferential subtleties that reside just below the surface of even the simplest of probabilistic reasoning tasks. This raises an interesting set of issues now taken very seriously in what has been termed the *science of complexity* (e.g., Waldrop 1992; Coveny and Highfield 1995).

As you will observe, another thing these seven essays have in common is the *complexity* of the inferential problems they address. In the Twining and Weis essay the relationship among Edith Thompson, her husband Percy, and her lover Freddie Bywaters shows great complexity. In the Geller and Anderson essays, who knows how many factors actually combined to cause the extinction of the Sumerian language in Babylonia. In the Katritzky essay, mountebanks and their companions seem to have played complex roles in influencing theatrical productions. Many factors combine to influence our beliefs about whether Schubert wrote for guitar as well as for piano. In the Houben essay, many societal and other elements must have combined to influence the relations between Indonesian laborers and their colonial masters nearly a century ago. John Locke's thoughts on property rights and possession raise complex issues concerning the context in which he offered them. Study of all of these very complex matters is made even more difficult by the nature of the evidence we have about events that occurred so long ago.

One element that emerges in this new science of complexity is the importance of considering *interactions* or *nonindependencies* among individual factors or variables judged to be relevant and important. Another way of stating the matter is to say that the processes investigated in these essays are *nonlinear;* wholes are never merely equal to the sum of their parts, as they would be if the processes were linear. Consider all the factors that any of our authors mention in their essays. We cannot simply add together their separate influences and hope to reach conclusions that are defensible and persuasive. In a recent work (Schum 1999), I have discussed this new science of complexity and what it reveals about the complexities of probabilistic reasoning. As it turns out, Wigmore's atomistic methods, carefully implemented, *do not* induce linearity in our inferences in spite of their focus on argument decomposition. Indeed, as Kadane and I illustrated in our work on the Sacco and Vanzetti evidence, these methods, together with some modern probabilistic concepts, allow us to capture a wide assortment of evidential interactions or nonlinearities in reasoning based on masses of evidence. In short, Wigmore's detailed analyses can help us perform better holistic analyses.

A Substance-Blind Look at Evidence

I first became interested in the study of evidence during my years in graduate school at Ohio State University. At the time, I was studying probabilistic expressions involving chains of reasoning from evidence to hypotheses or matters to be proved. I quickly realized that I needed to know more about evidence and the many forms it might take. My searches through literature in philosophy, logic, probability, and statistics were not very fruitful. When I went on to Rice University in 1966 I decided to expand my search into the field of law in the belief that centuries of experience with evidence in our courts should provide a legacy of information about the properties and uses of evidence. In law-related literature on evidence I found exactly what I was searching for, and so much more. The legacy of experience and scholarship concerning evidence is richer in the field of law than in any other field known to me. As Twining has noted (1994, 181–2), the complexities of probabilistic reasoning surface in the crucible of adversarial argument that takes place as real-life cases are tried in our courts. In any event, I encountered the works of Wigmore and other evidence scholars, which I consumed with great interest. This scholarship strongly influenced the direction that all of my subsequent probabilistic studies have taken.

The other major benefit I received from my studies of evidence in law was contact in the late 1970s with many prominent legal-evidence scholars themselves, including Professors Twining and

Anderson. Their wisdom, patience, and good humor made my further studies of evidence in law so interesting and enjoyable. We share an interest in Wigmore's proof-related works, especially his analytic and synthetic methods for constructing defensible arguments from a mass of evidence. As our joint interests in such matters expanded, researchers in other disciplines such as decision theory, computer science, and artificial intelligence began to take interest in complex probabilistic reasoning and in the analysis of the inference networks I mentioned earlier. I was always happy to be able to assert Wigmore's precedence in this work (e.g., 1980, 1990, 1994, 156–73). One of the many enjoyable and productive associations I have had with Twining and Anderson occurred at several of the seminars that took place at NIAS in 1994–5, where I met most of the other authors of essays in this volume. Some of our discussions involved evidential matters I presented in my 1994 work *Evidential Foundations of Probabilistic Reasoning*. I mention a few of these matters here because they arise in my overview of the essays in this volume.

I begin by mentioning again the historical standpoint taken by the authors of these essays. In our own case study involving the Sacco and Vanzetti evidence, Jay Kadane and I adopted a mixed standpoint, one element of which was historical in nature. We took some care to consider what taking a historical standpoint seems to entail (Kadane and Schum 1996, 34–48). In the process we discovered some very fine works on the use of evidence by historians, including the works by Bloch (1953), Collingwood (1956), Carr (1961), Winks (1969), Fischer (1970), and especially Lichtman and French (1978). Some of the evidential distinctions I now make are already known among historians; others may not yet be recognized.

Given the very wide diversity of substance or content of the evidence in the seven essays in this volume, how could anyone analyze and compare them in any systematic way? Such analyses and comparisons are indeed possible if we ignore the *substance* of evidence and focus instead on its *inferential properties*. When we do this we see that the evidential materials in all of these case studies have many common properties. Figure 1.1 is a *substance-blind* categorization of evidence having two dimensions; one involves the credibility of evidence and the other involves the relevance of evidence. The credibility dimension arises in response to the question, how does the user of the evidence (the person drawing conclusions from it) stand in relation to the evidence? The relevance dimension

A SUBSTANCE-BLIND CATEGORIZATION OF EVIDENCE

	DIRECT RELEVANCE		Indirect Relevance
	Direct*	Circumstantial*	Ancillary*
TANGIBLE [+ or −]			
TESTIMONIAL UNEQUIVOCAL [+ or −]			
TESTIMONIAL EQUIVOCAL			
MISSING TANGIBLES OR TESTIMONY			
AUTHORITATIVE RECORDS [Accepted Facts]			

* These distinctions are relative as explained in the text.

FIGURE 1.1. A taxonomy of evidence

involves the question, how does the evidence stand in relation to hypotheses of interest or matters to be proven? This classification scheme was stimulated by Wigmore's work but differs substantially from the categorization scheme he offered (e.g., Wigmore 1937, 11–3; Anderson and Twining 1998, 56–62).

Consider the rows in figure 1.1, which identify different forms of evidence. The dimension relating to these forms of evidence involves credibility, a *multiattribute* characteristic or credential of evidence. Which credibility attributes we find necessary to establish for an item of evidence depends on what form this evidence takes. As I note later, evidence can take more than one form. It happens that the user of evidence stands in a somewhat different relation to each of these forms of evidence. The user can examine *tangible evi-*

dence directly in order to judge what event(s) it reveals. In other words, the user of tangible evidence can make a direct observation to judge what the tangible item reveals. In other instances, a person confronted with a tangible item needs an expert to explain what it reveals. There are many types of tangible evidence, including objects, documents, images, measurements, and charts. One major credibility issue for tangible evidence concerns its *authenticity*, where the question is, is the item of evidence what it is represented to be? An important element in establishing the authenticity of tangible evidence concerns the *chain of custody* through which it passed before a user observes it. If the tangible item is a sensor image (such as a photo or radar image) or a measurement of some kind, we are also concerned about its *accuracy* or *sensitivity* and its *reliability*.

In many cases we are not ourselves privy to events of interest and must rely upon other persons for information about these events. Their reports to us are termed *testimonial evidence*. One trouble with this kind of evidence is that there are different species of testimony that can be discerned. Testimony in some cases may be *unequivocal* in the sense that a person asserts that a particular event definitely occurred. In other cases, a person may *equivocate* in various ways, which I shall mention momentarily. Note in figure 1.1 the plus (+) and minus (−) signs under tangible and unequivocal testimonial evidence; these signs indicate whether the evidence is positive or negative. *Positive evidence* records the occurrence of an event or events; *negative evidence* records the nonoccurrence of an event or events. In any inference, it may be just as important to know which events have not occurred as to know which events have occurred.

Suppose a person P testifies, unequivocally, that event E occurred. We ask this person, "How did you obtain this information about E?" One possibility is that P made a direct observation of E; in this case, P might be termed a *primary source*. Another possibility is that P received this information about E from another person, Q; in this case we would say that P obtained this information at secondhand. We might, as in law, say that P's testimony to us is *hearsay*. In many situations we observe that information passes through numerous sources before we obtain it ourselves. If we cannot identify the primary source of this information, we say that it is *rumor* or *gossip*. In assessing the inferential force of secondhand evidence we must consider the credibility of every recognized source in the chain of sources through which it came. This process can become wretchedly difficult, as I have described elsewhere (Schum 1992). The use of hearsay evidence in historical studies is not uncommon. However, Bloch (1953, 51) noted that historians relying on hearsay are "as if at the rear of a column, in which news travels from the head back through the ranks. It is not a good vantage point from which to gather correct information." Finally, person P's testimony that E occurred might be based on information about events other than E. For example, P might assert, "I received information that events C and D occurred and so I inferred that E also occurred." In law, testimony about events based on such inferences is said to be *opinion evidence*.

Not all testimonial assertions are unequivocal. In some cases a witness may hedge or equivocate in various ways. An extreme form is *complete equivocation*, when a witness may respond by saying such things as "The event might have happened or not, but I don't remember [or I don't know, or I'm not sure]." Such testimony may represent honest self-impeachment on the part of the witness. Unfortunately, another explanation is possible: the witness does know or does remember but refuses to reveal what he or she knows or remembers. Testimony can be equivocal in probabilistic ways; for example, a witness might say, "It was probably X whom I saw fleeing from the scene." In other situations this equivocation may be expressed numerically. For example, a witness might say, "I am seventy percent sure that it was X whom I saw fleeing the scene." In such probabilistic equivocation, the witness essentially comments on his or her own credibility.

Assessing the credibility of persons who provide testimony is usually a difficult matter. Testimonial evidence involves different credibility attributes than does tangible evidence. People are known to testify against their beliefs, and so we have their *veracity* to consider. We could not say a person is untruthful unless this person told us something that he or she did not believe. People are also known to form beliefs against the evidence of their senses. They may believe what they expect or wish to observe regardless of what their senses tell them. In this case we have their *objectivity* to consider. Beliefs are elastic and may change over time. Recalling a belief held in the past involves important memory-related factors. Suppose a person does form a belief based on sensory evidence rather than upon expectations or desires. The next question is, How good was this sensory evidence? Answering this question involves assessing a person's *observational sensitivity* or *accuracy* as well as the conditions under which the observation was allegedly made. There is much more to be said about these three credibility attributes (e.g., Schum 1989, 1992, and 1994, 100–9). Another characteristic of human sources of evidence is their *competence*. We are obliged to ask whether a witness did in fact make the observation he or she alleges and whether this person has any understanding of what was observed. Credibility and competence do not necessarily covary. Not all credible persons are competent and not all competent persons are credible.

In some cases, expected evidence cannot be found or is not produced by those from whom it is requested. In either case, *missing evidence* (whether tangible or testimonial) may be evidence itself. When evidence is missing, some obvious explanations are that it does not exist, that it was lost or destroyed, that we looked in the wrong place, or that we asked the wrong person. There is another explanation, however: The evidence exists but someone is keeping it from us. In our legal system an adverse inference is often permitted to be drawn from the nonproduction of evidence by the person from whom it is requested. The argument is that this evidence, if produced, would be unfavorable to the interests of the person who fails to produce it. As we know, missing evidence and negative evidence are sometimes confused. *Evidence of absence* is not the same as *absence of evidence*. I will examine an interesting case of missing evidence in my comments on Professor Heck's chapter on Schubert's *Lieder*.

A further category of evidence in figure 1.1 concerns information we extract from records taken as accepted facts or matters we may accept without further proof. In short, certain kinds of evidence we are willing to accept as credible. As John Locke noted centuries ago, we accept certain matters whose probability, he said, rises to near certainty. As examples, Locke cited "That Fire warmed a man, made Lead fluid, and changed the colour or consistency in Wood or Charcoal: that iron sank in Water and swam in Quicksilver" ([1689] 1991, 662). We now accept as fact that strychnine in sufficient amounts is toxic to human beings, that New York has a larger population than Omaha, and that heroin is a narcotic substance. We also accept as facts information we receive from tide tables, celestial tables, and other authoritative records. Behind accepted facts there always resides a universal generalization such as "If a thing is iron, then it will sink in water."

One trouble is that these forms of evidence can occur in combination, and so we often have difficult and extensive credibility assessments. Testimonial assertions may be required to explain the significance of tangible evidence. Furthermore, there are complex mixtures of these forms of evidence. Here is a tangible document that records testimony given by a witness on some past occasion. We have the authenticity and accuracy of the document as well as the credibility of the witness to consider. In more extreme cases, we may have document trails containing descriptions of tangibles as well as accounts of testimony obtained through a chain of sources. In such instances, the credibility-related issues become very difficult and interesting. Establishing the credibility of evidence provides the foundation upon which all subsequent inferences from the evidence are based.

Now consider the three columns in figure 1.1 and the question, How does the evidence stand in relation to matters to be proven? The issue here is one of *relevance*. Credibility issues concern the question, can we, as users of an item of evidence, believe what the evidence reveals? Relevance issues concern the question, so what? A datum or item of information becomes evidence only when its relevance to some material issue is established by plausible argument. It happens that evidence can be relevant in two essential ways, as figure 1.2 illustrates. In figure 1.2, evidence is indicated by the filled circle at the bottom of the chain of reasoning. Evidence is said to be *directly relevant* if we can form a plausible chain of reasoning that links the evidence to some major hypothesis or matter to be proved. Evidence is said to be *indirectly relevant* if it bears upon the strength or weakness of links in chains of reasoning set up by directly relevant evidence. Indirectly relevant evidence is often said to be *ancillary* or *auxiliary* evidence. Some of these links in a chain of reasoning may concern the credibility of directly relevant evidence. In this case ancillary evidence is evidence about other evidence. Thus, the term *meta-evidence* might also be used in such cases. To illustrate the distinction between directly relevant and ancillary evidence, I draw upon some testimony in the Sacco and Vanzetti trial.

A witness named Lewis Pelser testified that he saw Nicola Sacco at the scene of the crime (a robbery and shooting) at the time it happened. This testimonial assertion is directly relevant to whether Sacco did the shooting, since, if Sacco was at the scene of the crime when it happened, he might have participated in committing this crime. Another witness, named Dominic Constantino, later testi-

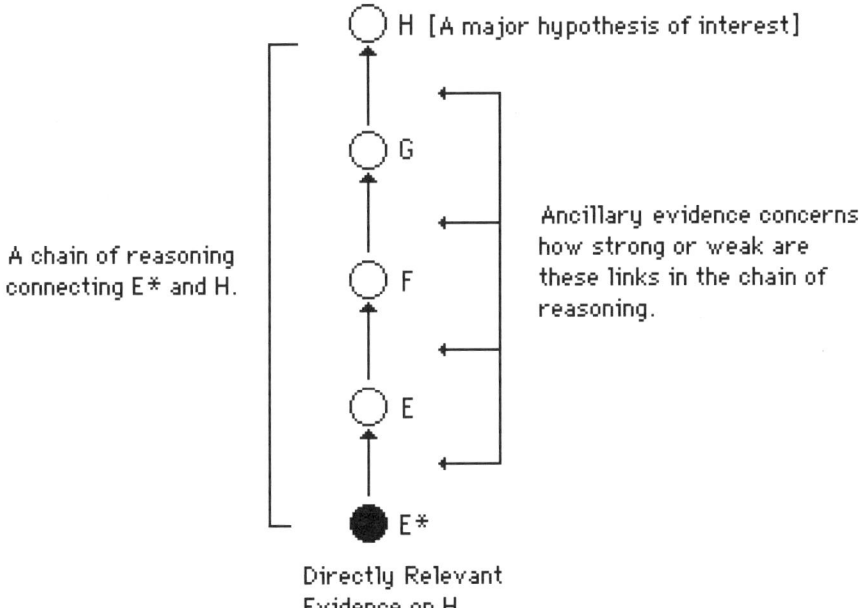

FIGURE 1.2. Illustrating directly relevant and ancillary evidence

fied that, when the shooting began, Pelser immediately ducked under a workbench in the factory building where he and Constantino worked. On its own, Constantino's testimony has nothing whatever to say about Sacco's being involved in the crime. Evidence about what Pelser was doing, by itself, says nothing about Sacco. However, Constantino's testimony acquires relevance since it bears on Pelser's credibility. If Pelser was indeed under a workbench, he cannot have seen the events to which he testified. In other words, Constantino's testimony, if credible, acts to undermine Pelser's credibility.

Now observe in figure 1.1 that there are two species of directly relevant evidence that have been identified: *direct* and *circumstantial*. Evidence is said to be direct if it goes in one stage of reasoning to some hypothesis. One common form of direct evidence is an eyewitness assertion about some event. For example, Pelser's testimony that Sacco was at the scene of the crime when it happened *seems to be* direct evidence on the event that Sacco was actually at the scene of the crime when it happened. If Pelser is credible, that apparently settles it: Sacco was at the scene of the crime when it happened. But there is trouble with the concept of direct evidence. As Wigmore noted (1937, 13–5) any link in a chain of reasoning can be decomposed into two or more other links. We might, for example, decompose this allegedly direct link into other links that capture the following specific, credibility-related uncertainties: (a) Did Pelser believe what he testified? (b) Was Pelser's belief formed on the basis of sensory evidence or on other matters such as his expectancies, desires, or instructions? and (c) If Pelser did form this belief on the basis of his sensory evidence at the time, how good was this evidence? Thus, an apparently direct inferential linkage can be decomposed by adding new links that reveal additional uncertainties.

Circumstantial evidence is that which, even if credible, supplies only some but not complete grounds for believing in the occurrence of a certain event or hypothesis. Thus, Pelser's testimony that Sacco was at the scene of the crime when it happened is only circumstantial evidence that Sacco participated in the crime. Sacco could have been an innocent bystander who simply happened to be in the wrong place at the wrong time. I note in figure 1.1 that these relevance distinctions are always relative; they are relative to context and to time. They are context-relative because an item of evidence can be relevant in one inference but not in another. The letters from Edith Thompson to Freddy Bywaters in the Twining and Weis essay have no relevance (that I can see) to the inferences in the Geller and Anderson studies involving the extinction of the Sumerian language. In addition, evidence can occupy different relevance status at different times in work on an inference problem. Some evidence might be viewed as ancillary at one stage of work and directly relevant at another. For example, at an early stage of some investigation, person A supplies ancillary evidence regarding the credibility of person B. However, at a later stage of investigation, we may discover that what A said about B is directly relevant to some issue of interest to us.

Recurrent Combinations of Evidence

As the holists and complexity theorists I mentioned will argue, we never consider evidence items in isolation, as I did in forming the taxonomy in figure 1.1. Two or more items of evidence, taken together, may mean something quite different than they would if considered separately. It happens that there are some recurrent or generic combinations of evidence that can be recognized, regardless of the substance of the evidence. Study of these evidence combinations reveals some interesting subtleties that can be exploited in inferences if they are recognized.

Taken together, a collection of evidence items may reveal various patterns of *dissonance*. Some of the evidence seems to point in one direction and some of the evidence seems to point in another. Two forms of evidential dissonance need to be recognized. The first, termed *contradictory evidence*, occurs when two or more items of evidence report mutually exclusive events—that is, events that cannot occur jointly. Evidence that defendant D was in Miami at 4:00 P.M. on February 4, 2002, and evidence that D was in Chicago at this same time are contradictory, because D cannot have been in both of these places at the same time. There is an interesting history of attempts to resolve evidential contradictions. In former times the solution was to "count heads" on each side of a contradiction and resolve it by majority rule. We now see that what counts is the aggregate credibility on each side of a contradiction, regardless of how many heads there are on each side. Contradictions are thus resolved entirely on credibility grounds.

A far more difficult form of dissonance involves evidence that seems to point in different directions but involves events that are not necessarily mutually exclusive. In a medical context, for example, we may be interested in an inference about whether a patient P, facing open-heart surgery, will survive this experience. Suppose it is known that patients under forty years of age have a greater chance of survival than do those over forty years of age. Patient P happens to be thirty-two years of age and so we believe his age favors his surviving the surgery. But we also know that patients who have had one or more prior episodes of open-heart surgery have less chance of surviving a new episode of open-heart surgery than do those who have never had any previous episodes. Patient P has had two prior episodes of open-heart surgery and so we believe this favors his nonsurvival of his coming open-heart surgery. The events revealed in these two items of evidence are certainly not mutually exclusive. There are, unfortunately, many patients under forty years of age who have had one or more experiences of open-heart surgery.

The two items of evidence in this medical example can be called *divergent* or *conflicting* since they point in different inferential directions. Contradictions also exhibit divergence or conflict, but the difference involves whether the events reported in the evidence can occur jointly. Not all evidential divergence or conflict involves a contradiction. Resolving evidential divergences or conflicts that do not involve contradictions are as difficult as they are interesting. They may be resolved on credibility-related grounds, but not necessarily so. Perhaps with better knowledge of the meaning of the evidence, and by considering the joint occurrence of the evidence, we may be able to resolve the conflict. There are many instances in which we may have patterns of evidential contradictions that are embedded in other patterns of evidential divergence or conflict. Resolving these complex patterns is a difficult inferential exercise, as I have noted elsewhere (Schum 1994, 412–7).

Other recurrent evidential combinations are *harmonious* in the sense that the evidence seems to agree in favoring the same hypotheses. Two species of harmonious evidence need to be considered. One is *corroborative evidence*, from two or more sources, all of which or whom report the same event. As I note later, there is a bit of inferential danger here involving the possibility that we will double-count this corroborative evidence and accord it greater inferential mileage than it may deserve. The other form of harmonious evidence—*convergent evidence*—occurs when evidence about different events seems to converge in favoring the same hypothesis. There is an important inferential subtlety lurking here. Convergent evidence can also be synergistic in the sense that one item of convergent evidence seems to enhance the inferential or probative force of another item. This is a particular instance of situations in which two or more items of evidence, taken together, mean something different than they do if considered separately. In other words, such *evidential synergism* is just one form of a nonlinear aggregation of evidence. Consider the following example of evidential synergism.

Defendant D is on trial for the murder of victim V. First, we have evidence that defendant D fired a weapon at the scene of the crime, but this does not mean that D hit V with the bullet he fired. Second, we also have evidence that the bullet that killed V came from a revolver said to be owned by D. This evidence, by itself, this does not mean that D was the one who fired the shot. Taken together, however, these two items of evidence seem stronger in pointing toward D as the killer of V than they would do if we considered them separately or independently.

Certain combinations of evidence exhibit other interesting subtleties associated with *inferential redundancy*. Consider the corroborative evidence mentioned above in which two or more sources reveal the occurrence of the same event. If we believe the first source, then it seems that further evidence about this event is superfluous or redundant. We may call this species of redundancy *corroborative redundancy* because the same event gets reported over and over again. This situation becomes interesting when none of the sources is perfectly credible. In these situations we must determine how much inferential value remains as we receive each new corroborating report. If we treat all reports as if they were equally valuable, we are ignoring their redundancy and are double-counting the significance of this evidence.

Another form of evidential redundancy occurs when two or more sources report different events, but what one source tells us reduces the inferential force of what another source tells us. As an example, I return to Lewis Pelser and his testimony in the Sacco and Vanzetti case. Pelser testified that he saw Sacco at the scene of the crime when it occurred. Then, another witness, Lewis Wade, testified that he saw *someone who looked like Sacco* at the scene of the crime when it occurred. If we believe Pelser, Wade's testimony has no inferential force because, if Sacco was at the scene of the crime when it occurred, this entails that someone who looked like Sacco was there at the time. In legal terms, the testimonies of Pelser and Wade might be said to be *cumulative*; so, I have termed this form of evidential redundancy *cumulative redundancy*. On ancillary evidence given at trial by other witnesses, Pelser's credibility was severely challenged. This makes Wade's testimony have potential inferential force. However, Wade's credibility did not go unscathed during his cross-examination and by the testimony of other witnesses.

In another work (Schum 1994) I have examined all of the forms and combinations of evidence just mentioned and have shown how inferential subtleties can be captured for study and analysis by different formal systems of probabilistic reasoning, including the *Bayesian* system, the *Baconian* system (Cohen 1977, 1989), and the system of *Belief Functions* (Shafer 1976). All of these systems of probability allow us, in different ways, to capture the interactions, nonlinearities, or nonindependencies associated with so many interesting evidential subtleties. Linear aggregations of evidence (the whole equals the sum of its parts) produce no subtleties or surprises. But an abundance of subtleties or surprises lurks in various combinations of evidence that can indeed be captured in probabilistic analyses, provided we structure arguments in such a way that these subtleties can be recognized. This leads us to Wigmorean methods for marshaling or juxtaposing our thoughts and an emerging mass of evidence.

Wigmore and Masses of Evidence

Part 5 of Wigmore's *The Science of Judicial Proof: As Given by Logic, Psychology, and General Experience, and Illustrated in Judicial Trials* (1937) carries the title "Mixed Masses of Evidence in Trials for Analysis." In this section Wigmore begins by contrasting two methods for making sense out of a mass of what he termed *mixed evidence*. I have always supposed that, by the use of the term *mixed*, Wigmore was thinking of the various recurrent, generic, and substance-blind forms and combinations of evidence I just mentioned. He did not make all the distinctions I have made and would, perhaps, have disagreed with some of mine. In any case, Wigmore begins his part 5 by contrasting two methods that he called the *narrative method* and the *chart method* (821). He says that the narrative method ". . . rearranges all the evidential data under some scheme of logical sequence, narrating at each point the related evidential facts, and at each fact noting the subordinate evidence upon which it depends; concluding with a narrative summary." The chart method, he says, ". . . using the same logical scheme, represents the evidential data by symbols signifying their probative kind and effect, and arranges these symbols in a chart, enabling the practitioner to study on a single sheet the entire mass of data."

What Wigmore described as the narrative method has always seemed to me to be essentially a *holistic* process designed to capture important spatial and temporal relations among events revealed in evidence. The *Oxford English Dictionary* (OED) tells us that a narrative tells a story and is "An account of a series of events, facts, etc., given in order and with the establishing of connections between them." Attorneys tell stories in their opening and closing arguments; historians offer us many narrative accounts of past events. Wigmore sneered at the narrative method, saying that it is simple and readily used by "the beginner" (1937, 821). He went on to argue that his chart method is the "only thorough and scientific method," even if it "may not commend itself to some types of mind" (858). Wigmore's chart method is an *atomistic* process in which one attempts to lay out specific links in arguments or chains of reasoning connecting evidence and major hypotheses or probanda (matters to be proved). By such a detailed analysis we attempt to expose

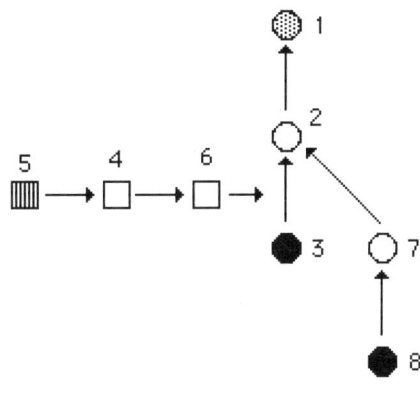

FIGURE 1.3. A simple Wigmorean analysis

sources of doubt or uncertainty we believe to be interposed between our evidence and what we are trying to prove from it. If we can express the magnitude of these uncertainties, we then have a basis for assessing the probative force of our evidence. However, Wigmore also emphasized that we must consider all the evidence we have, whether it is directly relevant or ancillary in nature.

In modern terms, Wigmore's chart method describes a process for constructing an *inference network*. In such networks we lay out arguments in defense of the three necessary credentials of evidence: relevance, credibility, and inferential (probative) force. As mentioned elsewhere (Tillers and Schum 1988, 936), Wigmore might be more than surprised to learn that the evidence charts he described are, in current language, "directed acyclic graphs whose nodes are propositions and whose arcs are fuzzy probative force qualifers." By means of figure 1.3, I provide a very simple example of the analytic and synthetic elements of Wigmore's chart method; this example involves the three witnesses I mentioned earlier: Pelser, Wade, and Constantino in the Sacco and Vanzetti case. In figure 1.3, I show just a portion of the trial evidence involving testimony from these three witnesses. A complete account of this evidence is given elsewhere (Kadane and Schum 1996, 92, 290–1). In figure 1.3 the two filled circles indicate directly relevant evidence. The filled square (5) shows an item of ancillary evidence. Item 1 represents a major hypothesis (probandum) at issue.

Wigmore frequently used the term *probanda* with reference to "propositions to be proved," which is the Latin translation of this word. The *analytic element* of Wigmore's chart method consists of a *key-list* containing propositions describing *evidence* (directly relevant or ancillary), *major probanda*, and *interim probanda* that represent propositions identifying sources of doubt one imagines to exist between the evidence and the major probanda. In addition, a key-list might also contain *generalizations* that support or license particular links in a chain of reasoning. As Wigmore realized, the construction of an evidence chart, or inference network, is a distinctly creative act and is always particular to the person doing the charting. Different persons might discern different sources of uncertainty and different chains of reasoning linking evidence and hypotheses. The *synthetic element* consists of a chart on which, using various symbols, we lay out what we believe to be logical connections among the propositions included on a key-list. In short, a Wigmore evidence chart is a pictorial representation of a complex argument we construct in order to connect our evidence with what we are trying to prove from it.

The key-list in figure 1.3 shows eight propositions concerning two items of directly relevant evidence (Pelser's and Wade's), one item of ancillary evidence (Constantino's), four interim probanda (the open circles and squares), and one major probandum. I might also have included generalizations on this key-list. For example, I might have included the following (common-sense) generalization to license a reasoning step between propositions 2 and 1. This generalization might read, "People who are at the scenes of crimes when they are committed are *frequently* the ones who have committed these crimes." Note the italicized hedge in this generalization. I might encounter disagreement with this generalization if I had said "*always*."

The chart in figure 1.3 has two basic ingredients: *nodes* representing propositions from the key-list (the circles and squares) and *arcs* (arrows) representing probabilistic linkages. This chart, like all Wigmore charts, is a *directed* graph or network because it shows reasoning from evidence to a major probandum. It is *acyclic* because you cannot follow a reasoning path from any node that returns you to this same node. If this happened you would be in an inferential "loop" that brings you right back to where you started. Note that Pelser's and Wade's testimonies are directly relevant since they can be connected by a chain of reasoning to the major probandum, shown as node 1. Constantino's testimony, however, is only indirectly relevant or is ancillary in nature. Here we expose an interesting fact about inference networks.

As I mentioned earlier, ancillary evidence bears on the strength of links in chains of reasoning set up by directly relevant evidence. Notice that we have a chain of reasoning from Constantino's testimony that is directed at the arc linking Pelser's testimonial assertion (node 3) with the event he asserted (node 2). By such means we indicate that Constantino's evidence bears on the credibility-related linkage between Pelser's testimony and the event to which he testified. Wigmore was most insistent that we always distinguish between evidence about an event and the event itself. There is certainly a distinction to be made between Pelser's telling us that Sacco was at the scene of the crime when it occurred and Sacco's actually being there at the time. Wigmore says that failure to make this distinction would be "like a bridge with the bolts left out of the truss angles" (1937, 859–60). Now, however, we observe that we have one inference network (the argument from Constantino's testimony) embedded in another inference network (based on Pelser's and Wade's testimonies). In another work (Schum 1994, 187–92) I have explored some of the complexities in probabilistic reasoning that these embedded networks reveal.

I now return to Wigmore's comment, noted earlier, that we can show a mass of evidence on a single page. Wigmore did not tell us how large this page might be. One reason is that he confined his illustrations to fairly simple collections of evidence. In our work on the Sacco and Vanzetti evidence, Kadane and I considered 395 items of trial and posttrial evidence. Our Wigmorean analysis of this mass of evidence requires a page that is eighteen feet in length. Of necessity we broke this evidence chart down into twenty-eight sectors or fragments, each representing a particular substantive issue in the case. But this is no size record for Wigmore evidence charting. William Twining reports receiving a Wigmore chart from a student that measured thirty-seven feet in length (1984, 31). What virtue is there in constructing such detailed pictures of our arguments based on masses of evidence?

Twining (1984, 31) has noted that Wigmore's method ". . . lays a foundation for a systematic approach to analyzing disputed questions of fact; it sets forth a disciplined approach to charting the overall structure of a case, to digging out unstated, often dubious propositions, and to mapping all the relations between all relevant evidence." I noted earlier that Wigmore's methods, as atomistic as they appear, can actually assist more holistic analyses such as narrative methods. Wigmore's methods may seem atomistic, but they do not induce "linear thinking" in which wholes are always just the sum of their parts. As Twining has noted, Wigmore's methods require us to map all relations we perceive among the items of evidence whose relevance we are attempting to establish. By such means we capture evidential interactions, nonindependencies, or nonlinearities. A complex Wigmore chart can be presented in a way that greatly facilitates its explanation to persons seeking to understand what the chart reveals. The top-level nodes or major probanda in an argument reveal the essence or major elements of an argument. The major elements of one's arguments can usually be presented on a single page. As the occasion demands, arguments on each of these major elements can then be further decomposed to reveal detailed chains of reasoning from evidence to each major element.

In exploring further connections between Wigmore's atomistic chart method and the holistic narrative method he dismissed, I draw upon a recent work entitled *Anchored Narratives*, written by our Dutch colleagues Willem Wagenaar, Peter van Koppen, and Hans Crombag (1993). In the Dutch legal system there are no jury trials; cases are decided by panels of judges or tribunals. The authors argue that judges in Dutch courts are too often persuaded by "good" stories that are not always anchored on evidence. Wigmore's methods provide some very good ways to anchor stories on evidence. If our arguments from evidence are not defensible, the anchors will not hold and we are set adrift in stories we tell from this evidence. Wigmore's methods expose our arguments to criticism and allow us to gauge their strength before we anchor narratives on them.

There is another, often overlooked, virtue of Wigmorean evidence charting; this method is an elegant *heuristic device* for generating new evidence and, perhaps, new hypotheses. In charting an argument from an item of evidence to some major hypothesis or probandum we identify potential evidence whose probative force on this probandum may be greater than the force of the evidence item that initially set up the argument. Each interim probandum or link we insert in a chain of reasoning identifies a proposition that may be instantiated by evidence. As an illustration, consider figure 1.3 again. Suppose that all we had at the moment was Wade's testimony that there was someone who looked like Sacco at the scene of the crime when it occurred. We would then naturally try to find someone who could testify that, indeed, this person was Sacco.

I suspect that some of the resistance to applying Wigmore's methods in areas other than law stems from a considerable advantage that occurs in legal arguments based on evidence. Inference networks constructed in evidence-based legal arguments tend to be very well structured at the top of the network; here is an example. In the Sacco and Vanzetti case, the *ultimate probandum* U may be stated as follows: "Sacco and Vanzetti are guilty of first-degree murder in the slaying of Alessandro Berardelli during a robbery that took place in South Braintree, Massachusetts, on April 15, 1920." To prove U beyond reasonable doubt, substantive law required the prosecution to prove, beyond reasonable doubt, each one of the following three *penultimate probanda*:

> Probandum 1: Berardelli died of gunshot wounds he received on April 15, 1920.
> Probandum 2: At the time he was shot, Berardelli was in possession of a payroll.
> Probandum 3: It was Sacco who, with the assistance of Vanzetti, intentionally fired shots that took the life of Alessandro Berardelli during a robbery of the payroll Berardelli was carrying.

These three penultimate probanda, specified by substantive law, supplied the essential relevance "hooks" on which must be hung, by argument, all evidence introduced at the trial of Sacco and Vanzetti. In legal terms, these three penultimate probanda list the material elements of U, each of which the prosecution was obliged to prove beyond reasonable doubt.

Now compare this situation with the inferential task faced by historians such as the ones we meet on our journey throughout this volume. There appear to be no corresponding "substantive historical rules" that our authors must satisfy in reaching conclusions about matters in their areas of interest. As Twining notes in the first essay, historians have no existing lists of material elements they must satisfy in their inferences on a matter of interest. For example, no one has told Professor Geller exactly what he must prove in order to justify a conclusion that the Sumerian language became extinct at some particular time in the past. But these difficulties are certainly no impediment to the employment of Wigmore's chart method in any area in which probabilistic inferences are based on evidence. These methods simply require an analyst to be specific about what probanda he or she judges to be material in drawing conclusions about major matters at issue in the inference task at hand. In short, Wigmore's ideas require no external materiality prescriptions.

My final comments about Wigmore's chart method concern probability. Wigmore recognized that the links in a chain of reasoning (like the arcs or arrows in figure 1.3) are fundamentally probabilistic in nature. For all his other talents, Wigmore was no probabilist; this would have been asking too much of him. He chose to grade the strength of these links or arcs in verbal terms, using what today we call *fuzzy probabilities*. For example, he used terms such as *strong force*, *provisional force*, and *weak force* to indicate the strength of reasoning links. Trouble arose immediately because Wigmore offered no procedures or algorithms for combining his fuzzy gradations in order to determine the overall force of a mass of evidence. It was not until 1965, twenty-two years after Wigmore's death, that Professor Lotfi Zadeh began to develop rules for combining what we now term fuzzy probabilities (Zadeh 1965). But the probabilities on the links in chains of reasoning can be expressed in other ways and combined by rules quite different than the ones Zadeh developed. In our work on the Sacco and Vanzetti evidence, Kadane and I employed Bayesian methods for combining ingredients called *likelihoods*, which can also be used to grade the strength of links in a chain of reasoning. I have also noted (Schum 1991, 1994, 257–60) how Jonathan Cohen's system of Baconian probabilities (Cohen 1977) can be applied to chains of reasoning.

Six Case Studies: A Travel Guide

Here is an overview of what you can expect to see when you read the seven essays in this volume. You will notice in my brief tour through each of these essays that I do not evaluate or criticize the final conclusions reached by any of the authors. To do so would require substantive credentials I do not have. Come to think of it, no one I know holds valid substantive credentials in *all* of the areas of research described in these essays. My purpose in this travel guide, or overview, is to comment on the inferential methodologies employed by the authors, noting interesting evidential difficulties they encounter. I give special attention to the forms and combinations of evidence the authors employ in their studies and to the means by which they marshaled their thoughts and evidence en route to reaching their conclusions. Along the way, I will occasionally interject ideas about evidence and inference I have encountered in my visits to fields other than the ones described in these essays. I do so partly out of respect for Marc Bloch's observation I mentioned in my opening remarks. In complex inferential reasoning we all need all the help we can get; such help can come from many directions.

To begin, I will comment on five general elements of the evidential complexity faced by each of the essays in this volume. The conclusions in each one are reached on the basis of a mass of evidence. These particular masses of evidence, like all others I have ever encountered, have five common characteristics that, when taken in combination, help characterize the complexity of the inference tasks faced by our authors. They also show why our conclusions from masses of evidence are necessarily probabilistic in nature.

First, regardless of how massive is any collection of evidence, it is always *incomplete*; we never have all of it. This seems an obvious point, but it is one not always recognized. We frequently hear a person say, "I will wait to decide, or to draw a conclusion, until I have all the evidence [or all the 'facts']." This person is condemned to perpetual inaction because we never have all the evidence. Just one way of showing that this is so involves the directly relevant and ancillary evidential distinctions I illustrated in figure 1.2. We may have an item of directly relevant evidence, such as Pelser's testimony in the Sacco and Vanzetti trial. Then we have ancillary evidence, from Constantino, about Pelser's evidence. This is "evidence about evidence." But then we also have evidence about Constantino's evidence; this is evidence about evidence about evidence. There is an infinite regress here. The trial of Sacco and Vanzetti would still be in progress, and would continue forever, if our courts did not stop this regress at some point. So, all of our masses of evidence are truncated. We draw conclusions from the evidence we have at the point when we run out of time, resources, and patience to generate further evidence. None of the authors of the seven essays in this volume claim evidential completeness.

The second characteristic of evidence in some mass is that it is commonly *inconclusive*. This means the evidence items, taken alone or in combination, are consistent with the truth of more than one hypothesis, possibility, or probandum. What we should all like to have, but so rarely do have, is conclusive evidence on some major hypothesis. In the field of intelligence analysis such evidence would be called a *nugget*. Lacking such nuggets, we are forced to mine lots of lower grade ore in the form of inconclusive evidence, hoping to find patterns of consistency in this evidence that will favor some hypothesis being considered. In short, in our inferences we are so frequently forced to trade off quality for quantity in the evidential foundations of our inferences. In none of these seven essays will you find authors claiming to have found true nuggets. All face the task of refining a great deal of ore having various grades of quality.

Third, the evidence we collect is commonly *dissonant* in the two ways I mentioned previously. Some of it seems to favor one hypothesis and some of it seems to favor another. Few masses of evidence are entirely harmonious. When they appear to be, perhaps we should look to our evidence-gathering processes to insure that we have been unbiased in the steps we took to discover new evidence. Were we looking only for evidence that would favor some hypothesis to which we may have been committed? All the essays in this volume rest on various patterns of evidential dissonance.

A fourth characteristic of evidence is that it is frequently *ambiguous*. In such cases we cannot say with any precision what the evidence is telling us. Some of the finest examples of evidential ambiguity I have ever seen occur in the Twining-Weis essay. There is also ambiguity in Locke's writings, as Hampsher-Monk discusses. Finally, evidence is *never perfectly credible*. We commonly ground our conclusions on the basis of evidence coming from sources having any possible gradation of credibility shy of perfection. As I noted above, credibility-related issues are compounded in historical studies because we must so often consider chains of sources through which our evidence may have come. With these five evidential characteristics in mind, I now take you on a tour of the seven essays in this volume.

TRIANGULATING CALAMITY: EDITH, PERCY, AND FREDDY

In their essay, Twining and Weis first tell stories about how they discovered their mutual interest in a celebrated English murder trial and its outcome. Edith Thompson and Frederick Bywaters were tried, convicted, and executed in 1923 for the murder of Percy Bywaters, Edith's husband. There seems little doubt that Edith and Freddy were lovers, so we have a classic love triangle in this case.

Twining and Weis are members of the faculty of University College London, Twining in the faculty of laws and Weis in the English department. What they discovered was that they had each told stories about the fairness and rectitude of Edith's conviction in this case (Twining 1990a, 262–307; Weis 1988). Learning of their mutual interest, Twining wrote another story comparing their respective views about Edith's conviction (1990b, 308–31). The present essay is a continuance of their dialogue about Edith. Both Twining and Weis have reached similar conclusions about Edith; they both believe that she was wrongly convicted. Neither argues that the conviction of Freddy was unfair or incorrect. But Twining and Weis took quite different methodological and inferential routes in reaching their conclusions. My comments concern these differences as well as certain characteristics of the evidence they both considered.

I have learned many things from Professors Twining and Anderson, one of the most important being how necessary it is to clarify one's *standpoint* before reporting inferences based on evidence. This seems like such a little thing, but failure to do it can produce serious trouble for the person reporting the inference as well as for the audience hearing or seeing this report. How a person has judged the relevance, credibility, and inferential force of evidence depends on this person's standpoint. Unless this standpoint is made clear, these judgments may be at least mystifying to an audience. Some measure of how much importance I have attached to standpoint clarification can be observed in my work with Jay Kadane on the Sacco and Vanzetti evidence. We devoted an entire chapter to a declaration of our standpoint (Kadane and Schum 1996, 28–65). This careful declaration may be vexing to readers but we believed it necessary, in part because we adopted the standpoints of historians, trial attorneys, probabilists, and psychologists at various points in our analysis.

A declaration of standpoint involves answering three questions (Anderson and Twining 1998, 120–1): (a) Who am I? (b) At what stage in what process am I? and (c) What am I trying to do? Answering the first question involves more than merely stating your name. Persons play different roles, or "wear different hats." Differing roles provide different perspectives and a person reporting an inference is obliged to make clear the perspective from which he or she generated evidence and drew conclusions from it. The second question acknowledges that a person may play different roles, and have different perspectives, at different times and in different contexts. A person answers this second question by being specific about any temporal or contextual factors that have influenced his or her perspective in the inference being reported. Answering the third question involves being forthcoming about what objectives were being entertained throughout the life cycle of the inference task being described. Twining and Weis approached their analyses from apparently different standpoints, although they shared an interest in questioning whether Edith was guilty as charged. The fact that they reached similar conclusions about Edith does not diminish the importance of clarifying these standpoints because they bear directly on the methods each employed in his analysis. Readers in doubt about the importance of standpoint declaration will certainly profit from reading this essay.

The trial and execution of Bywaters and Thompson produced strong public outrage, as did the trial and execution of Sacco and Vanzetti. From the standpoint of a historian today, and from available evidence, it seems beyond reasonable doubt that Freddy stabbed and killed Percy outside the Thompson home in Ilford, and in the presence of Edith, who was walking with Percy at the time. A major issue in the trial of Edith and Freddy concerned whether Edith had conspired with Freddy to commit this act (i.e., whether the stabbing on this particular occasion was premeditated on their part), or whether Edith had simply incited Freddy to commit an act such as the one he seems indeed to have committed. As framed by the prosecution, either of two routes could be taken by jurors in convicting Edith. She would be guilty whether she *conspired* with Freddy in planning the attack on Percy whether she simply *incited* Freddy to perform a murderous act on Percy on some unspecified occasion, and he acted upon this incitement.

I have mentioned a property of evidence called *ambiguity*. This characteristic is nowhere more apparent than in the major evidence against Edith that was presented at trial. Freddy worked aboard a ship and was frequently gone. Edith and Freddy carried on an extensive correspondence by mail. Edith kept only a few letters she received from Freddy, but Freddy kept nearly all the ones he received from Edith. A selection of these letters from Edith to Freddy was entered at trial as evidence against Edith. As I noted earlier, evidence is ambiguous to the extent that we cannot tell what it says. I have never encountered better examples of ambiguous evidence than exist in these letters from Edith to Freddy. Some of the letters mention broken glass and poison; had Edith herself tried to kill Percy? Other letters describe certain plans; did these plans concern the murder of Percy? There seem to be more innocent interpretations that can be placed on such details in these letters. I will let Twining and Weis tell you what they believe these letters say about Edith, Percy, and Freddy. One thing clear is that these letters had an effect on the jury, who convicted Edith for either planning or inciting the murder of her husband.

In this essay, Twining tells us about the "modified Wigmorean analyses" he employed in an effort to make sense of Edith's letters and the other evidence in this case. The major modification of Wigmore's methods apparent in Twining's discussion is that he dwells on the analytic elements of these methods. In other words, Twining presents key-lists of propositions but no charts showing their relationships. My own feeling is that this is like listing all the elements of an electric circuit without showing how they are connected. The more complex and interrelated are our arguments, the more we stand in need of a "wiring diagram" that shows these connections. This is an issue of presentation and not of substance, since pictorial charts simply assist in conveying the essence of one's complex arguments to other persons. The strictly analytic method employed by Twining does preserve the idea of decomposing elements of an argument.

Anderson and Twining have added several stages to Wigmore's methods, including clarification of standpoint, framing the ultimate probanda, and stating a theory of the case as a whole (1998, 120–31). Twining attends to these matters and, in the process, uses his analytic methods in order to show how some of the content in Edith's letters bears upon four different case theories involving Edith; two favor the prosecution and two favor the defense. The prosecution theories are *conspiracy* (that the specific attack on Percy was planned by Edith and Freddy, or that Edith and Freddy agreed to try to kill Percy when the opportunity arose) and *incitement* (that there was a protracted and continuous incitement of Freddy by Edith to get rid of Percy and Freddy eventually acted on this incitement). The defense theories are *fantasy* (that Edith only fantasized about Percy's death and harbored no real intention to kill Percy or to have him killed) and *a broken chain* (that there was no connection between Edith's behavior and Freddy's act).

There is a clear difference in the objectives entertained by Twining and Weis as they began their studies of this case. Twining initially focused on the Thompson and Bywaters case in order to show how Wigmore's atomistic methods of analysis could be applied to even the most complex and ambiguous evidence. But Weis tells us that his book about Edith Thompson, *Criminal Justice: The True Story of Edith Thompson*, is a *narrative biography* written with two objectives: (a) to clear Edith's name, and (b) to secure a posthumous pardon for her. On evidential matters, Weis's study is unique among all those presented in this volume. It is the only one that makes use of testimonial evidence from live witnesses. Weis found persons who were alive during the trial of Edith and Freddy and who either had some association with them or recalled events during their trial. Having read Weis's riveting book, I can testify to the care he took in assembling many different forms of evidence bearing on Edith's behavior and state of mind. Both Twining and Weis make use of documentary evidence provided by the trial transcript and Edith's letters to Freddy.

The major contention offered by Weis is that if we knew more about Edith's entire life, we would draw a different conclusion about the meaning of her incriminating letters to Freddy than the one drawn by the jurors at her trial. His analysis consists mainly of a meticulous chronological account of all he could find out about Edith, including what is revealed in her letters to Freddy. A major objective he entertained was to establish an appropriate context for establishing the meaning of some of the crucial passages in these letters. He notes that the prosecution was quite selective in determining which of these letters they would introduce as evidence in her trial. Had they introduced all of these letters, Weis believes the trial outcome might have been different. Weis believes his analysis shows that the damaging passages in Edith's letters were manifestations of her fantasy life and that no real conspiracy or incitement should be inferred from them.

I close my comments on this fascinating essay by noting how both authors make use of counterfactual statements. They both seem to agree that "If Edith had not taken the stand in her own defense, she would probably not have been convicted." Twining, in closing his work *Anatomy of a Cause Célèbre: The Case of Edith Thompson* (1990a, 295), lists no fewer than twenty counterfactual statements, which, if true, might have changed the trial outcome or might have kept Percy alive. I am reminded of the very admirable contemporary work of Philip Tetlock and Aaron Belkin (1996) on the various uses made of counterfactual statements by persons seeking to defend or to explain their analyses of situations in light of how these situations actually played out.

WHEN DID THE SUMERIAN LANGUAGE DRAW ITS LAST BREATH?

I found the Geller and Anderson essays especially interesting for several reasons, one of which is their subject matter. Being interested in the history of science and mathematics, I was eager to see what conclusions they would draw concerning when a very old and widely used language became technically dead. One of the earliest, perhaps the earliest, form of writing emerged in Babylonia and Sumeria. As far back as 8000 B.C., people in these areas began to use clay tokens of various shapes to keep records of the number of items involved in their business transactions. Tokens of different shapes represented different items such as loaves of bread, jars of oil, or sacks of grain. As the centuries passed, people began to develop an accounting system for business transactions by collecting the tokens in a transaction and storing them in hollow clay vessels, each of which would be marked by impressions made on these vessels. At a later time the individual clay tokens themselves came to be marked to indicate the items to which they referred. From such markings emerged, between 3500 and 3000 B.C., a system of writing called *cuneiform* (from the Latin *cuneus*, meaning *wedge*).

As we know, the ancient Egyptians came to write on papyrus, made from the pith of a reed common in Egypt and now called the *tall sledge (Cyperus papryus)*. There being an abundance of clay in Babylonia and Sumeria, it was natural for persons in these areas to record their writings on clay tablets. Scribes and others who knew the language made their markings on these clay tablets using a tool made from wedge-shaped reeds; hence the name for the script in which they wrote. The clay, of course, had to be kept moist until the writing was completed. Many thousands of cuneiform writings on clay tablets survive and tell us much about these ancient peoples.

Among their other accomplishments, the Babylonians were very skilled in mathematics and employed decimal (base-10), duodecimal (base-12), and sexagesimal (base-60) number systems. Figure 1.4 shows two examples of numbers expressed in cuneiform script; the second example shows a positional number system very similar to the one we use today. Examples of cuneiform writings on mathematics can be found in works by Smith (1958, vol. 1, 36) and

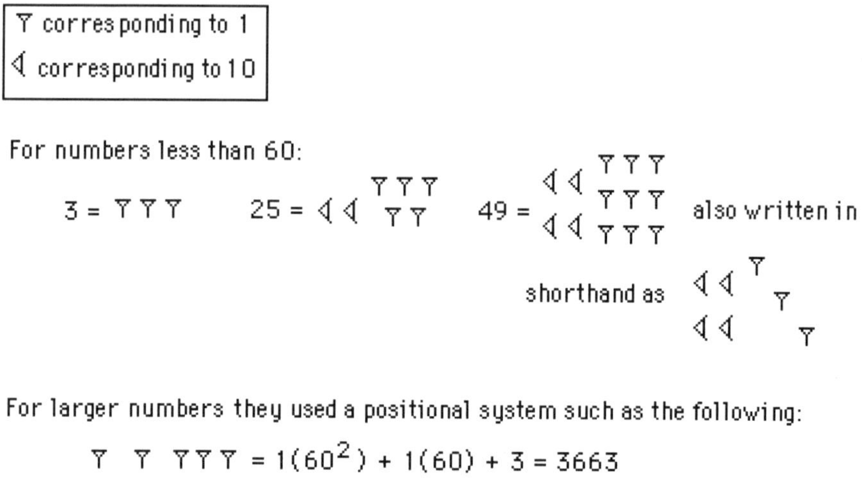

> ⊤ corresponding to 1
> ◁ corresponding to 10

For numbers less than 60:

3 = ⊤⊤⊤   25 = ◁◁ ⊤⊤⊤/⊤⊤   49 = ◁◁ / ◁◁ ⊤⊤⊤/⊤⊤⊤/⊤⊤⊤   also written in

shorthand as ◁◁ ⊤/⊤/⊤ / ◁◁ ⊤

For larger numbers they used a positional system such as the following:

⊤ ⊤ ⊤⊤⊤ = $1(60^2) + 1(60) + 3 = 3663$

FIGURE 1.4. Numbers in cuneiform script

by Gellert et al. (1975, appendix figure 11). Additional examples of cuneiform and an assessment of the significance of early Babylonian mathematics are found in the work by Resnikoff and Wells (1984, 25–8, 69–89). In fact, an entire treatise is devoted to mathematical texts written in cuneiform script (Neugebauer and Sachs 1945). My point in dwelling upon these matters is that cuneiform script is still understood quite well today.

What is accurate to say is that the Sumerian language, based on the reading of cuneiform script, is not in common use today. Geller and Anderson wish to know when this language ceased to be commonly used and have stated as their criterion the time at which this language ceased to be learned by priests in scribal schools in Babylonian temples. Geller argues that this date, which he places in the third century A.D., is more recent than has commonly been believed. As evidence in his inference about this date Geller employs tangible evidence in the form of surviving cuneiform tablets that can be dated with reasonable accuracy. He also considers various items of documentary evidence bearing upon which languages were in use at times surrounding the one he infers for the demise of the Sumerian language.

Professor Geller was in the process of completing a paper he had titled "The Last Wedge" when, at the NIAS seminars in 1994–5, he encountered a hardened and shameless Wigmorean named Terence J. Anderson. Anderson convinced Geller that he should apply Wigmore's analytic and synthetic methods to the arguments

Geller was forming regarding his inferences about when the common use of Sumerian was finally extinguished. Together, Geller and Anderson decomposed Geller's arguments on this matter. Anderson's essay contains an extensive key list of propositions in Geller's decomposed arguments and an evidence chart he constructed. As Geller notes, he was disappointed when his decomposed arguments did not seem to favor the same conclusions he was preparing to offer in "The Last Wedge." In his essay, Geller wonders whether the Wigmorean methods exposed flaws in his earlier undecomposed arguments or whether the skimpy and very inconclusive evidence Geller was able to gather requires a different logic than the one reflected in Wigmore's methods. For reasons I now mention, I was quite sympathetic to Geller's predicament, since I have had very many similar experiences.

In my studies of the inferential force of the forms and combinations of evidence I mentioned earlier, I decomposed arguments from examples of these forms and combinations of evidence to certain hypotheses or possible conclusions. In many cases my studies involved abstractions of evidence and hypotheses, but in some cases I studied evidence drawn from actual situations and actual hypotheses to which this evidence was taken as relevant. My decompositions led to nonlinear mathematical expressions that, on a conventional view of probability, allow me to grade the inferential force of evidence when particular probabilistic ingredients of these statements are supplied. In most cases the resulting equations are very complex because they have many ingredients; in some cases they have dozens of ingredients. Using these equations I am able to tell different stories about the force of evidence depending on which ingredient probabilities I supply. Jay Kadane and I provide many examples of these stories told by numbers in our work on the Sacco and Vanzetti evidence (1996). Different stories about the force of evidence items are told by different combinations of probabilistic ingredients. The equations I use simply show how each one of these stories about the force of evidence should end in a manner consistent within the conventional probability system we employed. All of our stories can then be translated into words.

I can now be specific about how my studies of the inferential force of evidence led me into the same predicament that Geller describes in his essay with Anderson. On very many occasions, the ending of a story told by numbers, based on my decomposed arguments, was not the ending I expected. In short, my intuition about how the story should end was violated, often drastically. As an example, I might expect that, given certain probabilistic ingredients in an equation, the evidence should favor hypothesis H over not-H by a factor of, say, 10 to 1. However, my equation might have told me that the evidence favors not-H over H by a factor of 100 to 1. In short, my intuition was off by a factor of 1,000. Here are some of the possible explanations for this divergence between my subjective or intuitive holistic judgments and the results of my decomposed analysis:

- My decomposed argument was faulty.
- My equation was incorrectly derived.
- I made an arithmetic error in combining ingredient probabilities.
- My intuition was incorrect.

In all but a very few cases among the many thousands I have studied, the fourth explanation turned out to be the appropriate one. Few of us can take a complex nonlinear equation containing many variables or ingredients and accurately predict what result this equation will provide in response to these many ingredients. No requirement in mathematics states that the equations we construct will always supply us with results that match what we expect on intuitive grounds. Geller's inferential problems are orders of magnitude more complex than ones I have ever studied. It does not surprise me at all that his decomposed analysis resulted in a conclusion at variance with what he expected using other methods for combining his thoughts and his evidence. I have not read Geller's original version of "The Last Wedge," and so I cannot comment on either the inferential methods he used or on the specific points in his and Anderson's Wigmorean analysis that may offer explanations for the divergence Geller mentions in his essay.

Geller notes that Wigmorean analyses may not address all the problems historians and others encounter in inferences in nonlegal contexts. Wigmore was a jurist who wrote for an audience of attorneys faced with the task of preparing arguments to be offered at trial. In my view, Wigmore's methods are every bit as substance-blind as the categories of forms and combinations of evidence I described earlier. His analytic and synthetic methods are essentially abstract and apply regardless of context. I believe they are as useful to the historian as they are to the physician, the auditor, the intelligence analyst, or anyone else faced with the task of making sense, in defensible ways, out of a mass of evidence. In fact, some graphical representations of arguments, very similar to Wigmore's, are discussed by the historians Lichtman and French (1978, 38). Nothing I have ever found ties Wigmore's methods exclusively to the field of law. Indeed, as I have noted elsewhere, Wigmore's views about the construction of complex inference networks contain many valid ideas that have not yet been recognized in current studies that focus on computer-assisted analyses of these networks in many different fields of study (Schum 1994, 156–92).

We are told by Geller that historians must so often deal with propositions that are *possible* or *plausible* and not necessarily *provable*. This fact is mentioned as one reason Wigmore's methods may not be so useful in historical research. Historians so often find evidence that suggests new, interesting lines of inquiry about past events that are always difficult if not impossible to prove. There are of course no standards of proof, explicit or implicit, in Wigmore's methods. The comments made by the author suggest another term and another form of reasoning associated with the author's terms *possible* or *plausible*. I read into this comment the fact that evidence can often be *heuristically* valuable in generating new ideas and new evidence. The form of reasoning that has been associated with such generation or discovery was termed *abduction* by Charles S. Peirce (e.g., [1898] 1992, 140; [1901] 1955, 151). Peirce noted that abduction and induction are frequently mixed together, a mixture Peirce called *abductory induction* (Houser and Kloesel 1992, 197).

Historians are not at all innocent of Peirce's work on these matters. One historian has even coined the term *adduction* to refer to mixtures of abduction and induction (Fischer 1970, xvi). The construction of an argument is an exercise in abductive reasoning, as explained elsewhere (Kadane and Schum 1996, 74–5). Wigmore's methods are among the most valuable ones known to me for facilitating abductive reasoning because they require us to generate chains of explanations for the evidence we have. These chains of reasoning may of course lead us to entirely new possibilities and new evidence. That inferences in history so often involve abduction or adduction is no reason for being averse to Wigmore's methods. Indeed, these methods rest upon, encourage, and assist these forms of reasoning.

MOUNTEBANKS, CHARLATANS, AND QUACKSALVERS

Before I met Dr. Katritzky at the NIAS seminars I knew next to nothing about her area of research, theater iconography. As she explains in her essay, theater iconography is an interdisciplinary field that draws upon art-historical methods and that makes use of extant visual or iconic materials such as drawings and paintings, as well as documentary evidence, in reaching conclusions about events in the history of theatrical performances. I was captivated by her essay for two major reasons. The first is the care she has taken in stating what conclusions can justifiably be drawn from the tangible visual and documentary evidence available to her. Earlier, I mentioned the authenticity, accuracy, and reliability attributes of the credibility of tangible evidence. Katritzky's assessment of these credibility attributes for the evidence she presents is remarkably thorough and perceptive. I could find nothing to add to her assessment of the credibility of her evidence. The second reason is the very interesting characters she has chosen to study—performers and salesmen called *mountebanks* (also called *charlatans* or *quacksalvers*). She provides a very interesting and enjoyable look at these characters and their behavior, as well as the roles they may have played in the history of theatrical productions. My first comments concern the evidential issues she addresses.

Theater history is certainly interesting in its own right, but it is also valuable in providing glimpses of people and societies at various times. As Katritzky notes, there are some very difficult evidential issues encountered in theater history. Historians can study only what has been left behind as peoples and societies come and go. Theater historians of the future will have tangible evidence, in the form of films, photographs, and videotapes, of what the theater was like in our own era. Historians such as Katritzky have no such advantages in their studies of actors, costumes, stage settings, gestures, and other elements of theatrical productions centuries ago. As she notes, theatrical productions in the past were ephemeral phenomena, most evidence of which disappeared as soon as the curtain fell. All that has been left behind are documents and artistic representations, images, or icons of actors and stage settings drawn by persons who allegedly attended these performances. Issues of *authenticity* of these icons immediately arise. To what extent are they faithful representations and not just products of artistic imagination?

The visual images of interest in theater iconography are products of persons having various levels of artistic talent. Katritzky has included some examples of these images, the study of which brings historical studies of the theater in contact with methods employed by art historians. Katritzky notes a certain tension between conventional art historians and theater iconographers. The visual images of interest to the latter do not necessarily qualify as "great art" and, as a result, might be ignored by some art historians. However, these images, together with certain documentary materials, form the only extant evidence we have about characters, costumes, and stage settings in theatrical productions of the past. In addition, of course, these images provide valuable information about past societies and individuals. Katritzky observes that there is little correlation between the aesthetic value of an image and its historical significance as far as cultural, economic, or political factors are concerned. Whether an image has profound artistic merit is incidental to its value as a historical record.

The mountebanks, charlatans, or quacksalvers appearing in Katritzky's studies are certainly fascinating, even though many of them may have been outright scoundrels. In Samuel Johnson's ([1773] 1978) *Dictionary* he defines a *mountebank* as "A doctor that mounts a bench in the market, and boasts his infallible remedies and cures." In the *OED*, the word *charlatan* appears as a synonym for the word *mountebank*. A *quacksalver* is one who makes exaggerated claims of salves, remedies, and the like. Who knows for how long a time persons such as mountebanks have appeared to offer their fellow beings, for a price, cures for every conceivable human ailment or discomfort. My favorite example comes from Joseph Addison's *The Tatler*. As he records (*The Tatler*, no. 240, October 21, 1710):

> I remember when our whole island was shaken with an earthquake some years ago, there was an impudent mountebank who sold pills which (as he told the country people) were very good against an earthquake.

I have often wondered how many earthquake pills this wretch actually sold. By some accounts (e.g., Stalker and Glymore 1989), mountebanks are still with us in various forms.

Mountebanks mounted benches (hence their name) in order to peddle their remedies or nostrums, and also, later, performed on so-called *trestle stages*. These were portable stages supported by trestles resembling large sawhorses. Mountebanks also employed varying numbers of assistants in performances designed to attract the attention of people wandering about in the markets. As Katritzky notes, these performances were often of a comedic and occasionally lewd nature designed to appeal to a variety of tastes. Assistants, who played roles of buffoons or zanies, were eventually given colorful names such as "Merry-Andrews" and "Jack-Puddings." Partridge (1972) tells us that these persons were clowning assistants to mountebanks and that the term *Merry-Andrew* came from the name of one Andrew Boorde, who was a traveler and author in the early sixteenth century. The significance of these matters is that mountebanks put on performances of various sorts and possibly employed professional actors in staging these performances. Katritzky dwells on the nature of these mountebank performances and the extent to which they may have influenced other theatrical productions. It seems that many professional actors in these times had a singular aversion to being associated with mountebanks.

Katritzky provides a wide assortment of interesting information about mountebanks, their companions, and their performances. She first considers the venues, stages, and audiences for performances by mountebanks and their companions. Major cities throughout Europe were favored by these performances, which often attracted as many as a thousand people. She next describes the astonishing array of alleged remedies, potions, trinkets, and other wares hawked by mountebanks. I could not help wondering how many of the miraculous substances offered by mountebanks three or four hundred years ago are still being peddled in stores and on the Internet. Katritzky next considers the chief mountebanks' personal appearances and performance routines. Their costumes varied, but all wore costumes designed to attract the notice of the crowd. Many performed what appeared to be life-threatening acts in order to illustrate the effectiveness of the remedies being offered. Mountebank companions are next described. Usually a mountebank was accompanied by two companions, one being a zany, or fool, and the other being an attractive woman. Of considerable interest to Katritzky are the types of entertainment offered by mountebanks and their companions, who provided comedy routines, acrobatics, and all sorts of other entertainment. It also appears from the evidence that mountebank companies were capable of putting on full-length plays.

Katritzky offers no Wigmorean decompositions of the arguments she makes based on the visual and documentary evidence she presents. One of her objectives, she notes, is to provide new lines of evidence rather than to dissect the meaning of evidence already known to be inconclusive and ambiguous. She certainly does not need any argument decompositions to enhance the value or interest of her analysis.

SONGS FOUND AND MANUSCRIPTS MISSING: A SMATTERING OF PROBABILITY

Our next journey takes us to Vienna during the short but very productive lifetime of the composer Franz Schubert (1797–1828). In his very interesting and enjoyable essay, Professor Heck obeys the spirit of this volume connecting the fields of law and history by contriving a legal hearing involving a European magistrate and himself, as an expert musicological witness. It seems that in the case being judged by this magistrate, the plaintiffs—a fictitious "Franz Schubert Society"—have lodged a complaint alleging that certain modern musicians are besmirching Schubert's reputation by substituting guitars for pianos as accompaniment in their vocal performances of some of Schubert's *Lieder*. Plaintiffs further allege that Schubert wrote his *Lieder* only for piano and voices and that any existing transcriptions of Schubert's *Lieder* for guitar and voices must be both inaccurate and unauthorized. The magistrate puts a series of questions to Professor Heck regarding his knowledge of these matters.

As the interrogation of Heck by the magistrate proceeds, we find specific examples of some of the forms of evidence I mentioned earlier. I hope Professor Heck will not object to my putting some of the evidence he mentions to a Wigmorean analysis, which I will then use as the basis for a mathematical argument concerning the inferential or probative force of this evidence. The affinity between music and mathematics is so strong that I believe Heck would not object to my inserting a bit of mathematics, which, I believe, bolsters the case he presents to the magistrate.

The magistrate begins by asking Heck whether the guitar was even in existence in Schubert's day and whether Schubert himself ever had any contact with guitars. Heck satisfies the magistrate that guitars were indeed in existence at the time and that Schubert knew the guitar well enough to compose and arrange music for it. Then the magistrate asks Heck whether there are any surviving manuscripts in Schubert's own hand of songs he wrote or arranged for guitar and voices. Heck replies: "No. And here we are confronted with the obvious truism that the lack of evidence proves nothing either way." This brings to mind the missing tangible evidence I mentioned in my account of the various substance-blind forms of evidence (see fig. 1.1). One major virtue of Wigmorean analysis is that we can often expose something that may seem obvious to alternative explanations that make it not so obvious. A truism is something taken as self-evident. In a moment I will offer a Wigmorean argument that it is *not* self-evident that lack of evidence says nothing one way or the other.

In later stages of his interrogation by the magistrate, Heck presents a variety of documentary evidence showing that guitar arrangements of some of Schubert's *Lieder* were actually written, by someone, shortly after the time that Schubert wrote the original piano arrangements of these same *Lieder*. Heck argues that, even if Schubert did not write these guitar arrangements, he knew of their existence and sanctioned them. Heck offers further evidence about who these other persons might have been. He also comments on the musical merits of these guitar arrangements and how they compare with Schubert's original piano arrangements.

I wish to return to the missing evidence concerning guitar arrangements of *Lieder* that may have been written by Schubert himself. On Heck's testimony, none are to be found. Our failure to find evidence we expect to gather does not mean that it does not exist. Several possibilities come to mind, including the following: (a) We have looked in the wrong places; (b) we have queried the wrong sources; (c) the evidence was lost or destroyed; or (d) someone is hiding the evidence from us. The fact that we cannot find the evidence we seek is a form of evidence itself, and we must ask what our failure to find evidence may mean. In short, we can construct arguments from testimony about missing evidence to hypotheses of interest in our inferences. Here is where Wigmore comes to our assistance.

Figure 1.5 shows an argument we could construct from Heck's testimony about the missing evidence to the hypothesis that Schubert never actually made any guitar arrangements himself. Beginning at the bottom of the reasoning chain, we have Professor Heck's testimony to the magistrate about missing evidence of any *Lieder* guitar arrangements written by Schubert himself; I give this testimony the symbol M*. Now, however, two possibilities come to mind that bring us to the first link in this chain of reasoning. The first, indicated by the symbol M, is that there is no existing evidence that Schubert himself made guitar arrangements of cer-

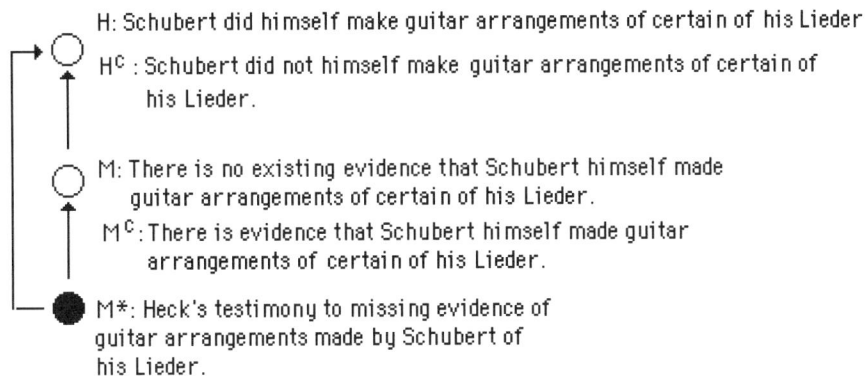

FIGURE 1.5. An argument concerning missing evidence

tain of his *Lieder*. We lack evidence simply because none exists. But there is another possibility indicated by the symbol M^c (read *M-complement* or *not-M*), which means that there is evidence that Schubert himself made guitar arrangements of certain of his *Lieder*. The evidence exists someplace but no one has found it. So, at this first stage we simply note that our failure to find evidence does not mean that none exists.

Now, at the second stage, first suppose that event M is true: There is no existing evidence that Schubert himself made guitar arrangements of certain of his *Lieder*. This does not entail that Schubert himself did not make any guitar arrangements of certain of his *Lieder*; this possibility is indicated by the symbol H^c (read *not-H*). He could have written some but they were lost or destroyed. Suppose instead that M^c is true: There is evidence that Schubert himself made guitar arrangements of certain of his *Lieder*. The truth of M^c does not entail that hypothesis H is true, where H is the hypothesis that Schubert did himself make guitar arrangements of certain of his *Lieder*. It is possible that any existing but undiscovered arrangements of Schubert's *Lieder* for guitar are not authentic. So, at this second stage we are concerned about what we could infer from the known actual occurrence or nonoccurrence of existing evidence that Schubert himself made any guitar arrangements of certain of his *Lieder*.

The argument I have just constructed reveals two sources of uncertainty suggested by Professor Heck's testimony to the magistrate: (a) How sure are we that there is no existing evidence that Schubert made these guitar arrangements himself? and (b) how good would the actual existence or nonexistence of this evidence be in an inference about whether Schubert did himself make these guitar arrangements? Our inferences about whether H or H^c is true, based on Heck's testimony M*, can only be probabilistic in nature. I now part company with Wigmore in order to cast the chain of reasoning in figure 1.5 in mathematical form. I do so in order to form an expression that tells us how strong Professor Heck's testimony M* might be in an inference about whether H or H^c is true. My purpose is to show that the alleged truism "a lack of evidence proves nothing either way" is not at all self-evident. In fact, as I will demonstrate, Heck's testimony about the lack of evidence can have *any degree of probative or inferential force*, depending upon how we assess the uncertainties at each of the two stages of reasoning in figure 1.5 that I just mentioned.

In the conventional view of probability that we all learn about in school, there is a consequence known as *Bayes's rule* that tells us how we might determine the probability of hypotheses we entertain, in light of evidence we have. In our present case, we have two hypotheses H and H^c, and one item of evidence, Heck's testimony M*. Using this rule, we ask: How likely is hypothesis H, that Schubert himself made guitar arrangements of certain of his *Lieder*, given Heck's testimony M*, that we have no evidence that he did? In conventional symbols this probability is $P(H|M^*)$. The vertical bar (|) represents the words "given," "in light of," "conditional upon," or "assuming." Under the rules of conventional probability, once we have determined $P(H|M^*)$ we automatically have another probability $P(H^c|M^*)$, which in words says: How likely is it that Schubert did not himself make any guitar arrangements of certain of his *Lieder*, given Heck's testimony that we lack any evidence that he did? The reason is that, because H and H^c (not-H) are mutually exclusive and exhaustive events, $P(H|M^*) + P(H^c|M^*) = 1.0$. In other words, $P(H^c|M^*) = 1 - P(H|M^*)$.

Now, in Bayes's rule there appear ingredients called *likelihoods* that grade the inferential or probative force of Heck's evidence M* on our two hypotheses H and H^c. In symbols, these likelihoods are $P(M^*|H)$ and $P(M^*|H^c)$. These two likelihoods do not have to sum to 1.0 as do the probabilities $P(H|M^*)$ and $P(H^c|M^*)$. The reason is that these two likelihoods involve the same event M*. By means of these two likelihoods we answer the following question: Is Heck's testimony M* more likely if we assume H (that Schubert did himself make the guitar arrangements) or if we assume H^c (that Schubert did not himself make these guitar arrangements)? What matters is the ratio of these two terms, $P(M^*|H)/P(M^*|H^c)$, which is called a *likelihood ratio*. I give this ratio the symbol L_{M^*}. I decomposed the argument from Heck's testimony M^* to hypotheses H and H^c by inserting the events M and M^c. I thought this to be necessary since Heck's testimony, or anyone else's testimony, that there is no evidence does not logically entail that there is actually no evidence. Thus, I must also decompose the two likelihoods $P(M^*|H)$ and $P(M^*|H^c)$ in their ratio L_{M^*}. There are specific rules in conventional probability for doing these kinds of decompositions. In another work I dwell on these rules and how they apply to chains of reasoning such as the one in figure 1.5 (Schum 1994, 290–342).

When we apply these decomposition rules, we can express L_{M^*} as follows:

$$L_{M^*} = \frac{P(M^*|H)}{P(M^*|H^c)} = \frac{P(M|H)[P(M^*|MH) - P(M^*|M^cH)] + P(M^*|M^cH)}{P(M|H^c)[P(M^*|MH^c) - P(M^*|M^cH^c)] + P(M^*|M^cH^c)}.$$

The probabilities in this expression are all likelihoods and represent our uncertainties regarding stages in the chain of reasoning shown in figure 1.5. First consider the two likelihoods $P(M|H)$ and $P(M|H^c)$. These probabilities, relevant to the second stage of reasoning in figure 1.5, force the following question: Would the actual nonexistence of any evidence that Schubert himself made guitar arrangements of Lieder (M) be more likely if Schubert himself never made any (H^c) or if he did himself make one or more (H)? Perhaps we can all agree that $P(M|H)$ is not zero, since some guitar arrangements that Schubert might have made are lost or have been destroyed. Perhaps we can also agree that $P(M|H^c)$ is greater than $P(M|H)$. In words, the present nonexistence of evidence that Schubert made any guitar arrangements seems more likely if he never made any than if he did.

The remaining four likelihoods in the previous equation concern Heck's testimony M^* that no evidence exists that Schubert himself ever made any guitar arrangements of his *Lieder*. Notice in figure 1.5 that his testimony M^* is connected to the hypotheses H and H^c in two ways: (a) through propositions M and M^c, and (b) directly to H and H^c. Bayes's rule requires us to consider both possible connections. In doing so it allows us to capture a very wide assortment of interesting and inferentially valuable subtleties associated with the sources of our evidence, Heck in this instance. What these four likelihoods ask us to consider is whether Heck's testimony that there is no existing evidence depends not only on whether there is such evidence or there is not (i.e., on propositions M and M^c), but also upon whether indeed Schubert himself ever made guitar arrangements (hypotheses H and H^c). It seems natural that we should take all of these possibilities into account, as Bayes's rule requires of us. Here is what these four likelihoods ask us to consider. In all of these expressions, symbol combinations such as "MH" mean "M and H."

The likelihood P(M*|MH) asks: How likely is Heck's testimony M*, given that there is no such evidence presently existing (M) *and* that Schubert actually made some guitar arrangements himself (H)? Stated differently, the question is: How likely is Heck's testimony, given that Schubert's guitar arrangements were either lost or destroyed? The likelihood P(M*|M^{c}H) involves the question: How likely is Heck's testimony, given that there is existing evidence of Schubert's having made guitar arrangements *and* that Schubert actually made some? Stated in other words: How likely is Heck's testimony, given that we have simply looked for Schubert's guitar arrangements in the wrong places? Together, these two likelihoods ask: Given that Schubert himself actually made some guitar arrangements, is Heck's testimony more likely if these arrangements were lost/destroyed or if we simply have not looked in the right places for them?

The remaining two likelihoods ask the same questions under the assumption that Schubert did not himself make any guitar arrangements for his *Lieder*. The likelihood P(M*|MH^c) asks: How likely is Heck's testimony, given that there is no existing evidence that Schubert made any guitar arrangements *and* that, indeed, Schubert never made any? In this case, there is no existing evidence for the simple reason that Schubert never provided any. The likelihood P(M*|M^{c}H^c) is quite interesting. It asks: How likely is Heck's testimony, given that there is existing evidence that Schubert himself made guitar arrangements for his *Lieder*, *and* that Schubert himself never wrote any? In this case we capture the possibility that evidence existing somewhere is not authentic. So, taken together, these two likelihoods ask: Given that Schubert himself did not make any guitar arrangements for his *Lieder*, is Heck's testimony more likely if there is no existing evidence that he did, or if there is inauthentic evidence that he did?

I close this probabilistic discussion by telling a story using numbers in the form of the six likelihoods in the previous equation. The story I will tell illustrates how, using a Wigmorean argument and the previous equation, Heck's testimony that we have no evidence that Schubert ever wrote guitar arrangements for his *Lieder* can indeed have significant probative force. Suppose the magistrate in Heck's fictitious hearing knew of my equation and assessed some numerical values of each of the six likelihoods it combines. Here are the ones the magistrate assessed. First, based on Heck's very informative account of the literature in this matter, the magistrate assesses $P(M|H) = 0.05$ and $P(M|H^c) = 0.75$. The magistrate believes that the lack of existing evidence that Schubert himself ever made guitar arrangements for his *Lieder* is twenty-five times more likely if Schubert never wrote any than if Schubert did write some but they have been lost or destroyed.

Now, in assessing the likelihoods involving his expert witness's testimony, the magistrate is very impressed by the thoroughness of Heck's scholarship. The magistrate first assesses $P(M^*|MH) = 0.4$ and $P(M^*|M^cH) = 0.01$. These assessments indicate the magistrate's belief that Heck's testimony is forty times more likely if Schubert actually made some guitar arrangements for his *Lieder* that were lost or destroyed than if Heck and his colleagues had simply looked in the wrong places. The magistrate believes that if the evidence was there, Heck would have found it. Finally, the magistrate assesses $P(M^*|MH^c) = 0.9$ and $P(M^*|M^cH^c) = 0.001$. The magistrate thinks Heck's testimony very likely, given that there is no evidence of Schubert's guitar arrangements of his *Lieder* because Schubert never wrote any. This magistrate thinks Heck's testimony preposterously unlikely, given that evidence exists somewhere but is inauthentic (i.e., that there are some forged copies of Schubert guitar arrangements somewhere).

When these six numbers are inserted in their proper places in the equation, the calculated result is that $L_{M^*} = P(M^*|H)/P(M^*|H^c) = 1/22.89$. This means that Heck's testimony is nearly twenty-three times more likely if Schubert himself never made any guitar arrangements for certain of his *Lieder* than if he did. Professor Heck never claimed that Schubert made any of these guitar arrangements himself but only that Schubert knew other persons wrote them with his approval. Well satisfied with Heck's account of these matters and impressed by Heck's thoroughness, the magistrate adds a generous bonus to the fee Heck and the judge had previously negotiated.

I can now justify my earlier remark that Wigmore's methods for decomposing arguments do not induce linear thinking, in which we regard a whole as merely the sum of its parts. The equation I used to grade the probative force of Heck's testimony rests on the decomposition shown in figure 1.5. Observe that this equation is a *nonlinear* combination of the probabilistic likelihood ingredients figure 1.5 suggests. The force of Heck's testimony in this hypothetical case is not a simple linear aggregate of the various uncertainties suggested by his testimony. In analyses such as the one I have just discussed, wholes are always different than the sums of their parts, and they so often produce surprises.

My dwelling on this matter of missing evidence should not at all detract from the excellence of Heck's analysis. I simply found a good and fairly simple example of how Wigmorean analysis, together with some probabilistic ideas, can change our minds about matters that may seem obvious to everyone. Evidence of the absence of evidence can indeed be probative when we consider various possible explanations for our failure to find evidence. In our Wigmorean and probabilistic analysis of the Sacco and Vanzetti evidence, Kadane and I found hundreds of sources of reasonable doubt arising from the trial evidence in spite of the fact that a jury had found the defendants guilty *beyond reasonable doubt*. There are so many subtleties or complexities residing just below the surface of even the simplest of inference tasks. In complex reasoning tasks, such as those faced by all of the authors in this volume, there are subtleties or complexities all over the place. These subtleties can be exploited in probabilistic reasoning if they are recognized. Wigmore's methods, together with modern probabilistic methods, can help us recognize and exploit these subtleties in drawing conclusions from masses of evidence.

THE CASE OF SI DOEL: INDENTURED LABOR TROUBLES IN A FORMER DUTCH COLONY

In the Twining-Weis essay we observe how complex the interactions among only three persons can be. When the interactions of interest concern several large groups having conflicting objectives, the complexity of these interactions becomes positively baroque. Fortunately, there are persons such as Professor V. J. H. Houben with enough persistence and insight to try to sort out elements of the complexity of these interactions in the hope of identifying possible causes of events having significant historical interest. Houben's announced task is to explore various ways of explaining the unrest among indentured laborers eighty years ago in the former Dutch colony of Indonesia. This emerging unrest led to widespread acts of violence against the overseers of these laborers. One of Houben's goals in this study is to shed additional light on controversial and painful episodes in the history of Dutch-Indonesian relations. Following a period of military confrontation in the years 1945 to 1949, Indonesia gained its independence from the Dutch.

As Houben tells us, the economy of Indonesia changed rather importantly around 1870. Prior to this time, the Indonesian economy centered on the island of Java and involved traditional tropical products such as coffee, tea, and sugar. By degrees, this economy shifted to the outer islands of Sumatra and Kalimantan and involved the production of new items such as oil, coal, rubber, and tobacco. Such production required a sizeable labor force, which, before 1900, consisted of Chinese laborers who were referred to at the time as *coolies*. The OED tells us that the word *coolie* is a racially offensive term used with reference to non-European laborers, mainly (but not exclusively) from China and India. Apparently, there were not enough Chinese laborers to meet the increasing demand for oil, coal, rubber, and tobacco. Thus, a new labor source had to be identified. The obvious local source was the Island of Java, which was overpopulated at the time. The use of Javanese laborers on the outer islands increased drastically between 1911 and 1929. The means by which these laborers were induced to work on the outer islands can be looked upon as a significant influence on the labor unrest that followed.

Houben tells us that a system of forced labor was introduced to supply labor needs in the outer islands. The so-called Coolie Ordinances of 1880 established work contracts between laborer and employer. According to these ordinances it was a criminal offense for a laborer to run away from his job. Houben tells us that such forced labor was thought of at the time as a middle ground between slavery and free labor. Any distinctions between forced labor and slavery, if there are any, were probably lost among these laborers. Not unexpectedly, the treatment of these forced laborers by their overseers was not always humane. Houben tells us about the magnitude of the unrest that emerged and how it eventually resulted in widespread attacks by laborers on their overseers.

As an example of how unrest among indentured laborers in Sumatra was generated, Houben invites us to consider the case of one Si Doel, a Javanese man who was serving as a watchman on a plantation in Sumatra in May of 1918. Briefly, Doel was late in responding to calls from his manager, a Dutchman named De Koningh. Asked to account for his tardiness, Doel admitted that he was asleep on duty, which his manager told him was a serious offense. As punishment, the manager told Doel that he would be demoted to an inferior position. A bit later, the manager asked Doel if he would prefer a beating to being demoted. Doel initially seemed to indicate that he would prefer being beaten to being demoted; but then he changed his mind and accepted the demotion. The manager then told Doel that he would presently receive a beating and then receive a demotion the following day. As the beating took place a struggle ensued in which Doel used a knife to stab three of the persons who were trying to punish him. Houben provides an account of the explanatory significance of cases such as this one.

Houben quotes the historian E. H. Carr, who said that the study of history is the study of causes. Such studies would be so much easier in any field of research if agreement could be reached about what it means to say that A has *caused* B. Many works have been written on this subject by philosophers (e.g., Mackie 1974; Eells 1991) and by legal scholars (e.g., Wigmore 1940, 406–514; Hart and Honore 1985). To my knowledge, there is no account of causal associations that satisfies everyone. In fact, the philosopher Brian Skyrms has argued that it might be more useful to talk about conditions of *necessity* and *sufficiency* than to talk about causes and effects (Skyrms 1986, 84–8). In most cases people using the term *causality* never specify whether the association of interest is one of necessity, sufficiency, or both.

A most interesting element of Houben's analysis involves his observations of how the causes of this unrest were viewed at the time by the laborers themselves, their employers, and Dutch government labor inspectors. He provides a tabular account of possible causes for the labor unrest as they were actually asserted by two groups of labor officials and by employers. The labor officials cited various forms of maltreatment by overseers. The employers cited a variety of laborer deficiencies and a lack of appropriate law enforcement. In all, this table records thirty-two possible causes. Although Houben presents no specific model of how these possible causes might be combined, he does allow that they would combine in distinctly nonlinear ways.

LOCKE ON PROPERTY RIGHTS: ANOTHER CASE OF AMBIGUITY

The preceding essays have all concerned inferences about particular people and events in the past. Professor Hampsher-Monk's essay concerns inferences arising in the history of an *idea*, namely, what justifies an individual's saying that he or she has a right to own property in the form of goods and land. One person whose thoughts about property rights have been most influential is John Locke (1632–1704). In commenting on the Twining-Weis essay I dwelled upon the ambiguity of the letters Edith wrote to Freddy, which formed the most damaging evidence against her at their trial. In Locke's writings on property rights we have another instance of ambiguity because different interpretations can be and have been placed on these writings. Hampsher-Monk considers this apparent ambiguity and suggests that it is a consequence of the ambiguity of the context in which Locke was writing on property rights. However, Locke wrote on other matters that are of present concern to us.

In this collection of works concerning evidence and inference in law and history, and now in considering the history of ideas, I thought it important to note that Locke's important thoughts on evidence and probability are not always recognized. In tracing the linkage between probability and evidence, some writers, such as Keynes ([1921] 1957, 90–1) and Kneale (1952, 9–13), begin their account of this linkage after Locke's time and without considering his important thoughts. Earlier, in discussing an evidence taxonomy shown in figure 1.1, I gave some examples from Locke concerning accepted facts as a form of evidence. In his *Essay Concerning Human Understanding* ([1689] 1991), however, Locke dwells upon what he termed *degrees of assent*—what we now term the *inferential force* of evidence, a concept that involves probability. In the process, he considers a variety of the forms and combinations of evidence (which I included in figure 1.1) and also considers matters concerning the task of assessing the credibility of different forms of evidence. So, we are in Locke's debt in more than one way in this collection of essays.

Hampsher-Monk's essay is a very important contribution to this collection since he carefully considers the task of interpreting the evidence we have. As we all know, different people frequently arrive at different conclusions from the same body of evidence.

There is nothing in any structural categorization scheme, such as in figure 1.1, or in any formal system for probabilistic reasoning that tells us how to interpret the significance of any item or body of evidence we encounter. In part, the interpretation we place on evidence depends on the standpoint matters I mentioned earlier together and whose importance Anderson and Twining emphasize. Two important standpoint-related matters concern the context in which some analysis is given and the objectives being served by the person or persons performing this analysis. Hampsher-Monk asks us to consider such matters as we attempt to understand what Locke said about the property rights of individuals. Hampsher-Monk argues that there are two important contexts within which to examine Locke's writings. One is intellectual and concerns the essential basis for the property rights of individual persons; the other is political and concerns Locke's time and the form of government then in power. Perhaps some of the ambiguity in Locke's writings could have been removed or reduced if Locke himself had been more careful in articulating the standpoints from which he wrote on property rights.

In Locke's time, the Stuarts (Charles II and James II) were in power in England and were most concerned about defending their rights as absolute monarchs. Taken seriously, such absolute rights would allow them not only to tax lands and goods held by others but even to take possession of these lands and goods if they sought to do so. As Hampsher-Monk explains, some writers attempted to justify these royal rights using, in some cases, references to biblical scriptures (e.g., God gave land to Adam; present kings, ruling by "divine right," are the natural inheritors of God's grant to Adam). Other writers, including Locke, wrote in defense of individual persons who maintained that they could themselves own certain lands and goods and could decide who should inherit these lands and goods, and that these property rights were inviolable. Yet Locke seems to have faced a dilemma. On the one hand, he appreciated the importance of private ownership of property. On the other hand, he also appreciated the needs of persons who owned little or no property and the importance of having orderly and efficient governments. How was he to reconcile individual property rights with the rights and needs of others as well as with the requirements of the monarchical form of government then in existence in England?

Hampsher-Monk gives an account of the sources of Locke's apparent ambiguity in writing about property rights. He first gives an account of Locke's case for unrestricted individual property ownership. Basically, on this argument, people came to say they owned land because they developed this land by their own labors or paid others to do so, in which case they could say that they owned this labor. Locke describes how the continued community ownership of land would have been maladaptive as far as the survival of our species is concerned. As Hampsher-Monk explains, Locke was writing to defend individual property rights against absolute rulers, but he was also attentive to certain social issues that gave rise to ambiguities in Locke's writings on property rights.

As Hampsher-Monk explains, Locke's writings are permeated by a *law of nature*, according to which the human species is to be preserved. Our instincts toward self-preservation come from God, but they must also be accompanied by equal concern for the survival of others. In Locke's writings there is evidence of his belief that the property rights of individuals are not absolute or inviolable but are conditional on social factors such as the needs of indigents, who also have the right of survival. Individual property rights, then, leave off where they begin to infringe upon the survival of others. Here, however, Locke faced another dilemma concerning the possible redistribution of property, an issue still with us today. Locke believed it a major duty of governments to protect property rights. If this is so, how could a government then be called upon to take property claimed by one person and distribute it among others? Perhaps we all ponder this same question when our taxes are due.

One thing clear is that the questions of concern to Locke have not yet been answered definitively. We have found it a far easier task to put people on the moon than we have to settle upon an uncontroversial way for the equitable distribution of the resources of our nations. Debates between capitalists and Marxists involve this question, and Locke's writings have formed an important part of this debate. As Hampsher-Monk explains, historians studying the development of political thought over time encounter a range of activities as they consider the assumptions, context, and other elements present in the interpretation of thoughts expressed by others, perhaps (as in Locke's case) more than 300 years ago. Hampsher-Monk's thoughts on the interpretation of evidence should be of considerable interest to scholars in other fields.

Bon Voyage!

Drawing conclusions from a mass of evidence is a marvelously rich intellectual enterprise that involves far more than just the balancing of probabilities. The evidence, possible conclusions, and arguments linking them must all be generated or discovered by imaginative thought. No better examples of such intellectual richness can be found than in the essays included in this volume. As expected, the authors of these seven essays approach their inference tasks in different ways. Some of this methodological variance may simply reflect differences in the academic cultures to which our authors belong. Certain inferential methods may be expected (or enforced) in one discipline but not in others. Awareness of alternative inferential methods may not be uniform across all disciplines. However, as Marc Bloch noted, this is one of the reasons we should wish to examine the work of colleagues in disciplines other than our own. No one discipline holds the repository of all useful ideas regarding complex reasoning based on evidence. We can all learn much about evidence and inference from our colleagues in different disciplines.

I have thoroughly enjoyed my journeys to the places and times mentioned in these essays. On each journey I found myself wanting to know more about the events and situations of interest to the authors. My only regret is that I had made no previous visits in many of these places and times. I thank the authors for sharing their wisdom with us, and close by wishing the readers of this volume as pleasant a journey through these very interesting times and places as I have had.

References

Anderson, T., and W. Twining. 1998. *Analysis of evidence: How to do things with facts based on Wigmore's science of judicial proof.* Evanston, Ill.: Northwestern University Press.

Bloch, M. 1953. *The historian's craft.* New York: Vintage Books.

Carr, E. 1961. *What is history?* New York: Vintage Books.

Cohen, L. J. 1977. *The probable and the provable.* Oxford, U.K.: Clarendon Press.

———. 1989. *An introduction to the philosophy of induction and probability.* Oxford, U.K.: Clarendon Press.

Collingwood, R. 1956. *The idea of history.* Oxford: Oxford University Press.

Coveny, P., and R. Highfield. 1995. *Frontiers of complexity: The search for order in a chaotic world.* New York: Fawcett-Columbine.

Davidson, J., and M. Lytle. 1992. *After the fact: The art of historical detection.* New York: McGraw-Hill.

Eells, E. 1991. *Probabilistic causality.* Cambridge: Cambridge University Press.

Fischer, D. 1970. *Historian's fallacies: Toward a logic of historical thought.* New York: Harper Torchbooks.

Gellert, W., H. Kustner, M. Hellwich, and H. Kastner. 1975. *The VNR concise encyclopedia of mathematics.* New York: Van Nostrand.

Hart, H. L. A., and T. Honoré. 1985. *Causation in the law.* 2nd ed. Oxford, U.K.: Clarendon Press.

Houser, N., and C. Kloesel. 1992. *The essential Peirce: Selected philosophical writings.* Vol. 1, 1867–1893. Bloomington: Indiana University Press.

Johnson, S. [1773] 1978. *A dictionary of the English language.* 4th ed. Facsimile reprint, Beirut: Librairie Du Leban.

Kadane, J., and D. Schum. 1996. *A probabilistic analysis of the Sacco and Vanzetti evidence.* New York: Wiley.

Keynes, J. [1921] 1957. *A treatise on probability.* 1st. ed. Reprint, London: MacMillan.

Kneale, W. 1952. *Probability and induction.* Oxford, U.K.: Clarendon Press.

Lichtman, A., and V. French. 1978. *Historians and the living past.* Arlington Heights, Ill.: Harlan Davidson, Inc.

Locke, J. [1689] 1991. *An essay concerning human understanding.* Reprint, ed. P. Nidditch. Oxford, U.K.: Clarendon Press.

Mackie, J. L. 1974. *The cement of the universe: A study of causation.* Oxford, U.K.: Clarendon Press.

Neugebauer, O., and A. Sachs. 1945. *Mathematical cuneiform texts.* Vol. 29 of *American Oriental Series.* New Haven, Conn.: American Oriental Society.

Partridge, E. 1972. *A dictionary of slang and unconventional English.* 7th ed. New York: Macmillan.

Peirce, C. S. [1898] 1992. *Reasoning and the logic of things: Cambridge conferences 1898*, ed. K. Ketner. Cambridge, Mass.: Harvard University Press.

Peirce, C. [1901] 1955. Abduction and induction. In *Philosophical writings of Peirce*, ed. J. Buchler, 150–6. New York: Dover.

Resnikoff, H., and R. Wells. 1984. *Mathematics in civilization.* New York: Dover.

Schum, D. 1980. Current developments in research on cascaded inference processes. In *Cognitive processes in choice and decision behavior*, ed. T. Wallsten, 179–210. Hillsdale, N.J.: Lawrence Erlbaum Associates.

———. 1989. Knowledge, probability, and credibility. *Journal of Behavioral Decision Making* 2:39–62.

———. 1990. Inference networks and their many subtle properties. *Information and Decision Technologies* 16:69–98.

———. 1991. Jonathan Cohen and Thomas Bayes on the analysis of chains of reasoning. In *Probability and rationality: Studies on L. Jonathan Cohen's philosophy of science.* ed. E. Eells and T. Maruszewski, 99–145. Vol. 21 in Poznan Studies in the Philosophy of the Sciences and the Humanities. Amsterdam: Rodopi Press.

———. 1992. Hearsay from a layperson. *Cardozo Law Review* 14 (1):1–77.

———. 1994. *The evidential foundations of probabilistic reasoning.* New York: Wiley.

———. 1999. Probabilistic reasoning and the science of complexity. In *Decision science and technology: Reflections on the contributions of Ward Edwards*, ed. J. Shanteau, B. Mellers, and D. Schum, 183–209. New York: Kluwer.

Shafer, G. 1976. *A mathematical theory of evidence.* Princeton, N.J.: Princeton University Press.

Skyrms, B. 1986. *Choice and chance: An introduction to inductive logic.* 3rd ed. Belmont, Calif.: Wadsworth Publishing Co.

Smith, D. 1958. *History of mathematics.* New York: Dover.

Stalker, D., and C. Glymore, eds. 1989. *Examining holistic medicine.* Buffalo, N.Y.: Prometheus Books.

Stein, J. 1992. The quest for Colonel Wigmore. *Litigation* 19 (1):43–6.

Tetlock, P., and A. Belkin. 1996. *Counterfactual thought experiments in world politics: Logical, methodological, and psychological perspectives.* Princeton, N.J.: Princeton University Press.

Tillers, P., and D. Schum. 1988. Charting new territory in judicial proof: Beyond Wigmore. *Cardozo Law Review* 9 (3):907–66.

Toulmin, S. 1964. *The uses of argument.* Cambridge: Cambridge University Press.

Twining, W. 1984. Taking facts seriously. *Journal of Legal Education* 34:22–42.

———. 1985. *Theories of evidence: Bentham and Wigmore.* Stanford, Calif.: Stanford University Press.

———. 1994a. Anatomy of a cause célèbre: The case of Edith Thompson. In *Rethinking evidence: Exploratory essays,* 262–307. Evanston, Ill.: Northwestern University Press.

———. 1994b. Thompson and Wigmore: Fresh evidence and new perspectives. In *Rethinking evidence: Exploratory essays,* 308–31. Evanston, Ill.: Northwestern University Press.

———. 1994c. *Blackstone's Tower: The English Law School.* The Hamlyn Lectures. London: Stevens and Sons.

Wagenaar, W., P. van Koppen, and H. Crombag. 1993. *Anchored narratives: The psychology of criminal evidence.* Hemel Hempstead, Hertfordshire, U.K.: Harvester Wheatsheaf.

Waldrop, M. 1992. *Complexity: The emerging science at the edge of order and chaos.* New York: Simon and Schuster.

Weis, R. 1988. *Criminal justice: The true story of Edith Thompson.* London: Hamish Hamilton.

Wigmore, J. 1913. The problem of proof. *Illinois Law Review* 8 (2):77–103.

———. 1937. *The science of judicial proof: As given by logic, psychology, and general experience, and illustrated in judicial trials.* 3rd ed. Boston: Little, Brown.

———. 1940. *Wigmore on evidence.* 3rd ed. Vol. 2. Boston: Little, Brown.

Winks, R. 1969. *The historian as detective: Essays on evidence.* New York: Harper Torchbooks.

Zadeh, L. 1965. Fuzzy sets. *Information and control* 8:338–53.

2 Reconstructing the Truth about Edith Thompson
The Shakespearean and the Jurist

William Twining and René Weis

Introduction: Two Stories

THIS CHAPTER LINKS two stories, each with subplots. The first concerns one of the most famous cases in English legal history, the story of Edith Thompson and Frederick Bywaters, who were hanged in 1923 for the murder of Edith's husband, Percy. The second is the story of two scholars in different departments in the same institution who over several years had worked on the case and had each completed a substantial study before they learned of one another's interests. The first story is both a human tragedy and a historical mystery; the second exemplifies the fragmentation of learning and illustrates contrasting approaches to history by two scholars from different academic cultures. This chapter is a case study of the methods of a jurist (William Twining) and a Shakespearean (René Weis) in approaching the question: Was Edith Thompson guilty of the murder of Percy Thompson? We shall start with the more modest tale.

THE JURIST'S TALE
William Twining

Early in the 1970s I began to use original trial records as a vehicle for teaching evidence to undergraduate law students, first at the University of Warwick and later at the University of Miami. I was concerned with both the theory of proof in legal contexts and certain practical techniques of inferential reasoning, as part of what is known as the logic of proof. In particular, I was interested in how to construct and criticize complex arguments based on evidence in legal contexts.

After a time, I settled on the case of *R. v. Bywaters and Thompson* as the best vehicle for my purposes simply because the evidence was both extremely complex and ambiguous. The case had the additional advantages of having real human interest and a secondary literature that was radically divided on the question of Edith Thompson's guilt. The key point, however, was the complexity and the intractability of the material. As one student put it, "If you can analyze Edith Thompson's prose you can analyze anything." In 1982 I gave a public lecture about the case. The main purpose was to illustrate a particular method of analyzing evidence, modified Wigmorean analysis, which I shall introduce later.

I moved to University College London in 1983, and continued to use the case in teaching, but it was not until 1987–88 that I revised and expanded my lecture into a long essay. I was making final revisions to my essay when I first heard that René Weis, a colleague in the UCL English Department who is a Shakespearean scholar, had finished a book on the same case. When I read the book, which I greatly admired, I decided not to revise my original essay. Instead I wrote a second essay comparing our general approaches, our treatment of detail, and our conclusions.[1] Since then we have discussed the case both publicly and in private on a number of occasions. This chapter continues the conversation.

THE SHAKESPEAREAN'S TALE
René Weis

In the early 1980s judicial issues featured prominently on the parliamentary agenda. In the wake of the House of Commons debate on the death penalty in July 1983, I read Arthur Koestler's polemical study *Reflections on Hanging*,[2] which paved the way for the abolition of the death penalty in Britain. It was Koestler's remarks about Edith Thompson that first aroused my interest in the case of Bywaters and Thompson.

After reading *The Trial of Frederick Bywaters and Edith Thompson* (one of the volumes in the "Notable British Trials" series),[3] which also reproduces Edith Thompson's letters, I decided to write a biography of her. I was convinced that an account of Edith Thompson's life and death would make an effective contribution to the case against the death penalty. Although there now seemed to be almost universal agreement on her innocence, she remained a convicted felon in the eyes of the law. Furthermore, the manner of her death and the rumors about it had caused great controversy at the time, the repercussions of which were felt as late as the 1950s when Koestler's book appeared.

I was impressed by Edith's minute detailing in her correspondence of life in London in the early 1920s, and by her vivid discussions of books, plays, and music-hall shows. As a professional reader of literature, I was intrigued by the extent to which the boundaries between fantasy and reality were blurred in Edith Thompson's mind. As well as being a successful career woman with a good head for business, she was an Emma Bovary figure capable of losing herself in countless romantic novels. Her imaginary escapes from an unfulfilling marriage and the boredom of everyday life might never have translated into reality, if Frederick Bywaters had not appeared on the scene. He seemed to offer everything that Edith's husband had failed to deliver, and Edith grabbed the opportunity.

In *Criminal Justice: The True Story of Edith Thompson*,[4] I argue that in the course of her relationship with Bywaters, Edith Thompson's tenuous grip on vital distinctions between reality and imagination slipped altogether. Not only did she discuss the fates of heroes and heroines as if they were real people, but she began to fantasize along similar lines about ridding herself of her husband. Rather than seeking a divorce, Edith Thompson preferred to toy with thoughts of her husband's death.

Her claims to have attempted to kill him, specifically with poison and glass, were demonstrated by the Crown's own pathologists to be false. I interpreted these protestations as rhetorical flourishes, a way of assuring Bywaters that she would go to any length to prove her love for him. Imaginary murder, it appears, seemed preferable to the real social stigma and difficulty of divorce. To the extent that Edith Thompson failed to walk out on her marriage and set up home with Bywaters, she was a prisoner (probably) of her temperament, and (certainly) of her class and time.

Whether or not her declared intent to kill her husband influenced Bywaters' murder of Percy Thompson late one night in Ilford has been debated ever since Edith Thompson and Freddy Bywaters were jointly charged with murder. I argued that the two were not linked, and that Bywaters had begun to drift away from Edith Thompson in the months before the murder. I maintained that Edith Thompson was innocent of the charges brought against her, and that she was the victim of a moral climate that cast her as the sirenic temptress of a young, infatuated hothead.

Criminal Justice is anchored in a contextual reconstruction of Edith Thompson's life, from her primary school records to a study of the books and plays she read and saw. I analyzed the newspapers of the period, and I gained access to closed Home Office and Prison Commission files on the case. At the time of my research in the mid-1980s there were still people living who had known the protagonists of the story (one of them was Bywaters' best childhood friend). They shared their memories and their photographs of Edith, Freddy, and Percy with me. This enabled me to flesh out their story in ways that are acceptable, and indeed expected, in a biography. By exploring the locations in which Edith and Freddy grew up I could, for example, establish that on the night of the murder Edith and Percy Thompson returned to their home *on the usual and most direct* route, an important point in view of the statements in court to the contrary. My narrative strategy was to offer a prospective, day-by-day account, which took the shape of a narrative "diary" for the eighteen months of Edith Thompson's involvement with Bywaters.

Part 1. Anatomy of a Cause Célèbre
William Twining

THE FACTS

About midnight of Tuesday/Wednesday, October 3/4, 1922, Percy Thompson and his wife, Edith, were returning from a visit to a West End theater to see a Ben Travers farce. They were within 100 yards of their home in Kensington Gardens, Ilford, when a man in a raincoat and hat came from behind them, pushed Mrs. Thompson aside, and approached Percy Thompson. After a struggle Percy Thompson collapsed on the pavement fifty feet further on and the man ran away. Edith's voice was heard by a neighbor crying, "Oh, don't; oh, don't." Shortly afterward she ran up to a group of people, also returning from Ilford Station, and cried out, "Oh, my God! Will you help me; my husband is ill, he is bleeding." When a Dr. Maudsley arrived from a nearby house some five to eight minutes later, he found that Percy Thompson was dead. He had been propped up against a wall by his wife. Mrs. Thompson was in a confused and hysterical condition. When told that Percy was dead, she said: "Why did you not come sooner and save him?" Blood was gushing from the mouth of the deceased, but it was only after he had been taken to the mortuary that several knife wounds were found in his body. There were several slight cuts in the front of the body and two deep stab wounds in the back of the neck.

When the police called at the Thompsons' house at 3:00 A.M. Edith Thompson was in a very distressed state. She said that all she knew was that her husband dropped down and screamed out, "Oh." She said that she had thought that it was one of his attacks. She denied that either she or her husband had a knife. The following morning the police learned of Edith's friendship with a young merchant seaman called Frederick Bywaters and, having found out that he had spent the evening with Edith's parents, the Graydons, some two miles from the scene of the crime, the police detained him for questioning at 6:00 P.M. on October 4. In Bywaters' room in his mother's house they found two notes, five letters, and a telegram, all from Edith Thompson. Bywaters made his first statement, after caution, denying both knowledge of the crime and owning a knife. Mrs. Thompson was arrested on the evening of the same day. On the following day she was shown some letters from her to Bywaters. She then made a statement in which she denied seeing anyone at the time her husband fell; she acknowledged her relationship with Freddy Bywaters, admitting that they had corresponded on affectionate terms. Immediately after making a statement she was taken past a room in which she saw Bywaters. She said, "Oh God, Oh God, what can I do? I did not want him to do it." After caution, she made another statement in which she said that on the night of the incident a man had rushed out and pushed her away. She saw the man and her husband scuffling. She recognized the man as Bywaters by his coat and hat. Bywaters made a further statement on October 5, after being told that he and Edith Thompson were to be charged with murder. He admitted to killing Percy after a struggle. "Mrs. Thompson must have been spellbound for I saw nothing of her during the fight."

The police found the murder weapon, a knife, on October 9, as a result of statements made by Bywaters. On October 12, they found a box on Bywaters' ship, the SS *Morea*, containing sixty-two letters and telegrams from Edith to Frederick, together with fifty clippings from newspapers enclosed in the letters and a photograph of Edith. A number of the cuttings dealt with murder, mainly by poison. Three letters from Bywaters to Edith were found at her place of work. More than half of the letters and a selection of the cuttings were put in evidence by the prosecution. Much of the interest of the case centers on Edith's letters and the cuttings, which constituted the main, but not the only, evidence against Edith.

It is universally accepted that it was Bywaters who killed Percy Thompson. It is also not disputed that Edith and Freddy were lovers and that they both had a prima facie motive for killing Percy. Freddy pleaded not guilty on the ground that he had killed Percy in self-defense. Since Percy was unarmed at the time, it is hardly surprising that this defense failed. The interesting question was whether Edith was also guilty, either on the ground that she incited Freddy to kill Percy or that they jointly planned to kill him. It is clear from the letters that Edith and Freddy had been lovers for nearly two years; that Edith was very unhappy; that she wished to end her marriage; and that she had expressed the view that she would not be sorry if Percy were dead.

Edith Thompson and Frederick Bywaters were tried at the Central Criminal Court on December 6–11, 1922. They were both charged with the murder of Percy Thompson, Bywaters as principal, Edith as a principal in the second degree, because she was present at the killing. A second indictment containing a number of counts, including charges against Edith of administering poison and broken glass with intent to murder, was not proceeded with. The jury found both accused guilty, after barely two hours' deliberation. They were sentenced to death; ten days later the Court of Appeal rejected their appeals; and on January 9, three months and six days after the death of Percy, Bywaters and Thompson were hanged.

The full transcript of the trial has been published in the "Notable British Trials" series; this includes all the evidence presented in court, together with a complete transcript of letters from Edith Thompson that were not put in evidence at the trial and the judgments of the Court of Criminal Appeal in the case (two appeals). We thus have available to us what Wigmore called "a mixed mass of evidence." This includes statements made by the two accused, the testimony of witnesses who were nearby at the time or immediately after the attack, and a limited amount of circumstantial evidence—including the report of Sir Bernard Spilsbury that there were no traces of either glass or poison discovered in the post mortem examination. The exhibits included the murder weapon, three letters from Freddy to Edith, and Edith's letters to Freddy. There is also the evidence given by both accused at the trial. Some additional information not given in evidence at the trial will be ignored for present purposes. I shall concentrate on those of Edith's letters that were put in evidence, but it is worth mentioning briefly that the other evidence establishes beyond reasonable doubt that it was Freddy who killed Percy; that there is almost nothing to support, and a good deal to confute, Freddy's claim that he acted in self-defense; that under cross-examination Edith admitted that she wished to give Freddy the impression that she had tried to make her husband ill; and that, although the testimony of both accused is an important aid to interpretation of some passages in the letters, there is little outside the letters to support the prosecution case and nothing that might be taken as determinative or dispositive in regard to the other main theories. Accordingly, let us treat the letters as the main evidence against Edith and consider the other evidence presented at the trial as supplementary.

A striking feature of the extensive secondary literature about the case is that the commentators have been almost equally split on the question of Edith's guilt. By and large these comments belong to the literature of popular entertainment, although some are very competent examples of this particular genre—carefully researched, often perceptive, usually readable. Since the main objective is to arouse interest or to make a case, detail tends to be sacrificed to readability and more emphasis is placed on amateurish psychological speculation than on the more mundane aspects of meticulous analysis of evidence.

What can a more scholarly or scientific approach add to our understanding of a complex case such as this?

MODIFIED WIGMOREAN ANALYSIS

In this case study I shall apply a modified version of Wigmore's chart method of analyzing evidence. The original method is extensively described and discussed elsewhere in this volume (see fig. 1.3 in chap. 1 by Schum, and chap. 4 by Anderson). Here it is modified in three ways: First, no use will be made of symbols and charts. Second, clarification of standpoint will be treated as an essential ingredient in macroscopic analysis of the case as a whole. Third, there will be much more emphasis on the idea of "theories" of the case.

The analysis will involve the following steps:

1. Clarification of standpoint;
2. Definition of the ultimate probanda;
3. Outlining of the four main theories of the case, with some variant subtheories, stories, and themes;
4. Testing of one of these theories, by way of illustration, through detailed analysis of only two items of evidence: the

facts about the knife and one passage in Edith's last letter (exhibit 60; see appendix 2); and finally,

5. Suggestion of some provisional conclusions on the basis of this partial analysis.

This will not resolve the mystery; but I hope it will show that even this selective and relatively straightforward exercise in analysis significantly narrows the possibilities and throws some light on the particular case and on some of the general themes that it illustrates.

Clarification of Standpoint

The first step is to clarify the standpoint from which the analysis is to be undertaken. For present purposes, I shall adopt the standpoint of a historian in 1988,[5] confronted with a finite body of data—the record of the trial—and concerned with answering the narrow question, "Does the available evidence support beyond reasonable doubt the allegation that Edith Thompson was legally responsible for planning or inciting the murder of her husband?"

Adopting the standpoint of the historian enables us to pursue the truth about Edith Thompson on the basis of analysis of the available evidence (the data) without regard to the procedural complexities, multiple objectives, and "noise" factors that concern participants in actual trials.[6] However, in order to keep matters simple and to maintain a close connection with the actual trial, I shall impose two artificial constraints on our inquiry. First, I shall confine my analysis to the evidence in the trial record. A real historian normally would not accept such a limitation. Second, I shall concentrate on the single question whether Edith was guilty as charged. This question is, of course, by no means the only question about the case that might interest historians—but it is a standard one that is very close to the question posed to the jury in the case.

Framing the Ultimate Probanda

The next step is to identify the ultimate probanda—the material allegations on which our judgment of the case as a whole must rest. Historians have no concept of materiality.[7] They are free to frame their questions as they wish without formal constraints. When arguing in court about disputed questions of fact, lawyers have no such freedom. The questions arising from the indictment (or other pleading) are defined in advance by law. Where the law is clear this can greatly simplify the tasks of analysis and argument, for it lays down clear and fixed touchstones of relevance. Evidence is relevant if it tends to support or tends to negate the facts that must be proved beyond reasonable doubt. Where the law is unclear, however, the task becomes much more difficult.

With respect to Bywaters the law was clear enough. The prosecution had to prove beyond reasonable doubt that he had intentionally, with malice aforethought and without lawful justification, caused the death of Percy Thompson. The only points in dispute were whether Freddy acted in self-defense or under immediate provocation. The jury apparently had no doubts on this matter; nor should it unduly trouble a historian. Bywaters' defense was that he accosted Percy to ask him to agree to a separation or divorce, the argument developed spontaneously into a fight, and he stabbed Percy in self-defense because he thought Percy was about to draw a gun. Two of the stab wounds were in the back and there was no evidence to suggest that Percy had a gun on this or any other occasion, nor that Freddy had any reason to think that he did. The evidence supporting provocation is almost as thin. It is not surprising that Freddy's story was not believed.

The case against Edith was less simple. She was charged as a principal in the second degree. What this meant was that the prosecution had to prove (a) that Bywaters murdered Percy Thompson, (b) that Edith was physically present at the murder, and (c) that she aided and abetted the murder. The first two requirements are relatively unproblematic, but the third contains the seeds of some genuine difficulties. Aiding and abetting, conspiracy, and incitement are three areas of criminal law that involve notorious problems of interpretation and application. In the trial and on appeal these difficulties barely surfaced, although a careful reading suggests that the trial judge took a much narrower view of the law than had been assumed by the prosecution or than the authorities at the time probably warranted. He directed the jury that they must be satisfied that Bywaters and Thompson had planned this attack, an interpretation that was surprisingly favorable to Edith.[8]

In order to succeed on the charge of murder against both of the accused, the prosecution had to satisfy the jury that the truth of the following propositions had been established beyond reasonable doubt:

> 1. That Frederick Bywaters deliberately and with malice aforethought killed Percy Thompson; and

2. Either
   a. that Edith Thompson conspired with Frederick Bywaters to kill Percy Thompson, on this occasion or whenever opportunity arose; or
   b. that Edith Thompson intentionally incited Frederick Bywaters to kill Percy Thompson and that the killing was within the scope of that incitement.[9]

These three propositions were the facts in issue—that is, the material allegations that the prosecution had to prove beyond reasonable doubt in order to succeed. The test of relevance of any item of evidence in this case is whether it tended to support or to negate one of these propositions.

In order to convict Freddy it was sufficient for the prosecution to prove the first proposition only. As we have seen, this was not difficult. Although it was relevant to prove intent and motive to show that this attack had been planned or that there had been earlier attempts by either or both of them to kill Percy, these were not strictly necessary for the prosecution's case. At the trial there was no dispute about the cause of death or the identity of the killer; it was not even necessary for the prosecution to show that the attack was premeditated, as they claimed, so long as they established that it was intentional.

The case against Edith was more complex. In order to succeed, the prosecution had to show that Bywaters was guilty of murder (proposition 1) *and* that Edith had either planned Percy's death with Freddy or had been responsible for inciting Freddy to kill him. In argument the prosecution, while presenting a story of continuous incitement leading to an attack that had been planned in advance, rather blurred the distinction between incitement and conspiracy—not surprisingly, for either was sufficient.[10] Mr. Justice Shearman, however, in his charge to the jury implied that they should convict Edith only if they were satisfied that this particular attack had been planned in advance. There is an ironic contrast between the unequivocal sententiousness of tone of the judge's charge and his insistence that Edith should be convicted only on the basis of what I hope to show is by far the weakest of the possible theories of the case that are consistent with her guilt.

The judge exuded generalized disapproval, indicating his belief in her guilt, but then analytically posed the issue in such a way as to make conviction of Edith much more difficult, at least in theory.

If, as seems likely, both the jury and nearly all subsequent commentators reacted more to the general attitude of the judge than to his precise words, that is doubly ironic.

Theories of the Case as a Whole

The next step is to consider, from the point of view of an historian, the range of tolerably plausible hypotheses about the case as a whole, and the general lines of argument for and against each hypothesis—what we may conveniently refer to as the main theories of the case. The aim here is to provide a broad framework of competing general hypotheses and strategic arguments within which all the relevant evidence can be organized and weighed.

In adversarial criminal proceedings the prosecution typically presents its case against the accused in the form of a coherent story of what happened.[11] In order to succeed the prosecution must prove each of the material allegations beyond reasonable doubt. Typically, but not necessarily, this involves persuading the trier of fact to accept their account of the story as a whole. The theory of a case is an internally consistent collection of hypotheses that form a coherent argument, which supports the story.

In order to counter the prosecution's case the defense has three main options available to use either independently or in combination: *to deny* the prosecution's story, either in toto or in some material particular(s), without offering an alternative (e.g., by submitting that there is no case to answer); *to explain away* the prosecution's story (e.g., by admitting most of the hypothetical facts, but interpreting them in a manner consistent with the innocence of the accused—Freddy admitted killing Percy, but claimed that it was in self-defense); or *to present a rival account* of what happened with respect to one or more material facts (e.g., by presenting an alibi). In practice many defenses involve a combination of all three strategies, but sometimes these are incompatible with each other.

A *theory* in this sense relates to the case as a whole. It can serve a number of functions: It helps to organize the material; it provides a basis for selecting some of a mass of potentially relevant evidence for inclusion or emphasis—a subsidiary test of relevance; it may serve to fill in gaps in the available information with more or less plausible hypotheses; and it provides a general basis for testing internal coherence and consistency. From the point of view of counsel, each side's theories provide a strategic framework that guides, and often determines, many specific tactical choices.

In trials, when there are disputed questions of fact, the trier of fact is usually being asked only to do one of two things: to select between competing theories of the case, or to assess whether, on the basis of the evidence presented, the proponent has proved his or her version to the applicable standard. Historians do not have the law's elaborate devices for guiding decisions in situations of uncertainty in adversary proceedings; they do not have concepts such as materiality, conclusive or rebuttable presumptions, standards of proof, or burdens of proof or production.[12] However, the notion of competing theories or accounts fits a dialectical view of historical inquiries into truth. One way of proceeding is to test a series of competing hypotheses against the available evidence and to select the most plausible one. In the present context, a series of alternative theories of the events in *Bywaters and Thompson* serves much the same function as they would in a real trial. Part of the interest of the present case is that even at this general or strategic level, there is room for considerable doubt and disagreement.

Four Theories of the Case. To simplify matters, of the many different theories about the case which can be advanced, each with possible variants, let us outline four main theories, two favoring the prosecution (or the thesis that Edith was guilty as charged), and two favoring the defense.

1. *The conspiracy theory:* This particular attack was planned by Edith and Freddy on the day before. Freddy set out carrying a knife with the intention of killing Percy as the Thompsons returned home from the theater. Edith expected this attack because she had planned it. In most versions of this theory Edith was the mastermind, Freddy the instrument. The actual attack was the culmination of a long series of attempts to kill Percy. This was one of the theories advanced by the prosecution and the one that was emphasized by the judge in his charge to the jury. An important variant of this theory is that Edith and Freddy had agreed to try to kill Percy whenever opportunity arose, but that Edith had not necessarily planned or expected this attack.

2. *The incitement theory:* Edith may not have known of or expected this attack, but she had over a long period deliberately tried to persuade Freddy to kill her husband—working on him by direct incitement, by innuendo, by suggesting different ways of getting rid of Percy, and by claiming (whether truthfully or not) that she was prepared to risk trying to kill him herself and that she had indeed

made several unsuccessful attempts to do so. There was, in short, a protracted and continuous incitement of Freddy by Edith to get rid of her husband. The particular timing and method of the attack were immaterial; Edith deliberately influenced Freddy to kill Percy. One variant is that there was some specific act of incitement that influenced Freddy on this occasion.

3. *The fantasy theory:* The attack on Percy probably was unpremeditated and certainly was totally unexpected so far as Edith was concerned. At no stage had Edith tried to kill her husband; nor had she deliberately, recklessly, or even inadvertently incited Freddy to do so. In this view many of the key passages had an innocent explanation, and even the potentially most damaging statements merely represent the outpourings of a vivid imagination and were so interpreted by Freddy. When Edith wrote to Freddy she entered a world of daydreams and make-believe, and nothing that she said constitutes evidence of intent to kill or to incite Freddy to kill in the real world. Her letters were, as Freddy unromantically put it, mere "melodrama." A variant is that although some of the passages are to be interpreted as references to attempts to kill Percy, they were merely part of a game, possibly a sexual game, designed to give spice and excitement to their relationship—and again, this is how they were interpreted by Freddy.

4. *The broken chain theory:* This theory denies any connection between Edith's behavior and Freddy's act. At one or more points the alleged chain of connection is broken. The theory takes two main forms: One version consists of a straight denial of one or more key points in the prosecution's theory or theories without advancing an alternative account of what happened. An obvious example is a denial that the attack was premeditated. An alternative version is to present a rival account of the attack (and of preceding events), which serves the same function. For example, Edith lived in an imaginary world of passion, daring actions, and desperate measures, a world in which fact and fiction and fantasy were inextricably mixed. She gave full rein to her imagination in her letters, pretending, perhaps even imagining, that she had tried to kill Percy. All the possibly damaging passages are in the earlier letters, which represent a particular phase in her relationship with Freddy. In this view it is unnecessary to reach any firm conclusion as to what these passages might mean—whether, for example, she was claiming (truthfully or not) to have put broken glass in Percy's food. Even if the most damaging interpretation is put on the key passages relat-

ing to incitement, conspiracy, and attempted murder there is no sufficient connection between the actual killing and the letters because of one or more of the following: (a) Freddy did not take them seriously; (b) the relationship had entered a quite different phase in the period before the killing; all the passages that might bear a damaging interpretation were written six months or more before Percy's death; or (c) the actual attack was spontaneous rather than premeditated. Any one of these is sufficient to break the connection between Edith's letters and Freddy's act.[13]

To recapitulate briefly: the *conspiracy theory* suggests that this attack was either planned shortly before by both of the accused or was the culmination of a more general plan; the *incitement theory* suggests that this attack, regardless of whether it was planned or premeditated, was the direct result of a continuous and protracted campaign of incitement by Edith; the *fantasy theory* suggests that all the potentially damaging passages in the letters are either open to alternative, innocent interpretations or were merely figments of Edith's heated imagination and were interpreted by Freddy as "melodrama." The *broken chain theory* suggests that whatever interpretation is put on the letters there was no direct connection between the killing of Percy and the letters (or Edith's other actions).

It is worth making some points about these general theories of the case. First, they are not all of the same kind. The first three each involved advancing a coherent account of what happened—constructing an integrated story that hangs together as a whole. So does the second version of the broken chain theory. There is scope for a few loose ends or ambiguities or gaps, but the overall plausibility or credibility of each theory depends in part on its internal coherence. Does the story *as a whole* form a unity and fit the available evidence?

The first version of the broken chain theory lacks this positive quality. Essentially it consists of a series of negative assertions about key elements in the other theories. It does not necessarily involve constructing an internally consistent story about what happened. One of the notable features of the trial is that, contrary to the strong advice of her counsel, Edith Thompson insisted on going into the witness box. This had several catastrophic results. It gave the prosecution the opportunity to extract some damaging admissions from her in cross-examination; and she had to advance a single coherent account of what happened and to give her interpretation of key passages in the letters and to have these positive assertions challenged by the prosecution. She thus gave the prosecution a specific target to attack and made it difficult for the defense to cumulate doubt about different elements of the prosecution's case. The broken chain theory allows what amounts to a series of arguments in the alternative along such lines as these:

1. None of the relevant passages in the letters supports the view that Edith either tried or pretended to try to kill her husband.
2. Even if she had tried, the chain is broken because Freddy did not believe her.
3. Even if Freddy believed her, the chain is broken because he did not act on that belief at the time and there is no evidence of a connection between the letters and his behavior on the night.
4. The evidence does not support the proposition that the attack was premeditated—that Freddy set out with the intention of attacking Percy; but even if the attack was premeditated the evidence does not support the contention that Edith had inspired Freddy's plan.

By giving evidence, Edith Thompson gave the jury a chance to choose which of the two competing stories they found to be plausible, rather than to judge whether each of the key elements in the prosecution's case was established beyond reasonable doubt on the basis of the evidence. Or again, instead of arguing that a particular passage might mean A or B or C or D rather than E, as the prosecution suggested, the defense was committed to giving a single interpretation to each key passage and to having that interpretation challenged. Almost all commentators agree that it would have been much more difficult to convict Edith if she had not given evidence.

Of course, historians do not have the option of deciding not to call a witness. That is a matter of legal procedure. However, the broken chain theory could well provide a sufficient answer to our historian's question—for if one or other version of that theory is accepted as correct, according to whatever standard is thought appropriate, then it establishes that Edith was not guilty as charged.

Each of these theories is a sketch of a complex argument. I have noted only some of the more obvious variants of each of these four main lines of argument. The range of possibilities is immense. There is considerable potential overlap among several of them.

Enough has been said to illustrate how, even at this stage of general strategy, judgment and choice are unavoidable in constructing and criticizing this kind of argument. There is nothing mechanical about the art of analyzing evidence. This is one reason for doubting Wigmore's claim that his chart method "is the only . . . scientific method."[14]

Experience suggests some useful working rules of thumb in exercising the art of analysis at this strategic stage:

1. *Strategy first, tactics later.* Despite the kinds of complexities that have been illustrated, strategic theories are powerful simplifying devices: They are a means of structuring, managing, and selecting material, however extensive and complex it seems.
2. *Proceed dialectically.* The historian and the lawyer need to recognize the weak as well as the strong points in their own and rival theories.
3. *Construct the strongest version that you can of each theory and identify its weakest points.* What constitutes strength may, of course, be rather different for a trial lawyer and a historian.
4. *Go for the jugular.* That is to say, select one or two or a few key points in an argument and concentrate on those.

Such precepts are commonplaces of advocacy and, perhaps less explicitly, of analysis of evidence by historians and others. They are essentially heuristic techniques for making complex problems more manageable. All presuppose a reflexive view of the process. One cannot construct theories, judge their strength, and identify key points without regard to detail. On the face of it the advice may seem to suggest moving from the general to the particular; in fact, familiarity with the particular is almost always a precondition for clarifying the general.

Subtheories, subplots, and characters. Each theory is dependent to a significant degree on one or more subtheories. First, an assessment of Edith's character, or at least some important aspects of it, is relevant to each of them. For example, the fantasy and incitement theories depend very largely on the view one takes of Edith, and a view of her character is relevant, though less important, to the conspiracy theory. It is not so important to the first version of the broken chain theory, which depends much more on an interpretation of Freddy's likely reactions to the letters and whether the attack was spontaneous or premeditated. Here the focus is more on Freddy, but an assessment of Edith's character is important for all the theories both as an aid to interpreting the letters and as part of interpreting the nature and course of their relationship. For example, both Edith and Freddy claimed that the phrase "only three and three quarter years left" in Edith's very last letter (exhibit 60; see appendix 2) referred to a suicide pact. That phrase is relevant to all four theories. Whether there was in fact such a pact, whether Edith had suggested it but Freddy had not taken it seriously, or whether this is an example of Edith's alleged fantasizing depends in part on one's views of Edith's and Freddy's characters, in part on one's view of their relationship, and in part on other evidence (e.g., other passages ostensibly referring to the same topic).

The main facts about the three principal protagonists and of their relations with each other are not seriously disputed. However, there is room for different interpretations of their characters (especially that of Edith) and of Bywaters' attitude toward Edith at the time of the killing.

Percy Thompson had married Edith Graydon, who was four years his junior, in January 1916. There were no children of the marriage. Percy appears to have been a steady, respectable, dull, and not particularly successful shipping clerk. There is evidence that he was suspicious and jealous of Edith's relations with Freddy. She expressed fears that he would be violent and there is some evidence that he assaulted her on at least one occasion. She speaks of "submitting" to him sexually on a number of occasions but also of refusing him without repercussions.

Edith Thompson had a striking personality. The undisputed facts about her include the following: She had worked as a bookkeeper and manager for a wholesale milliner's in Aldersgate for several years and was well-regarded by her employers. She earned slightly more than her husband. She had several male admirers in addition to Freddy, but there is nothing to suggest that she had had extramarital sexual relations with anyone but him. At the time of the murder Percy Thompson was thirty-two, Edith twenty-eight, and Freddy twenty. It is clear that Edith's marriage to Percy was not happy; it is less clear what price she was prepared to pay to escape from the security, comfort, and respectability of her domestic situation. We have plenty of material on which to base judgements about Edith Thompson's character, but it is open to a variety of interpretations.

Frederick Bywaters has been described as "a clean-cut, self-possessed, attractive-looking youth of twenty with a good character and record."[15] He had gone to sea before he was sixteen, and at the time of the murder was variously described as a ship's writer, a clerk, and a laundry steward. During the period of his relationship with the Thompsons he was at sea for well over half of the time, and this was the occasion both for the protracted and intense correspondence between Freddy and Edith and for the possible fluctuations in their relationship. During the trial he instructed his counsel to conduct the case so as not to prejudice Edith's chances of acquittal. This won him a lot of sympathy from public opinion, as reflected in the popular press, but it may possibly have damaged Edith's case, as he appeared as the dignified, loyal lover, whereas she was seen by some to be solely concerned with saving herself.

The variety of interpretations of Edith's character to be found in the literature is both fascinating and bewildering. The prosecution, backed by the judge and seemingly by the Home Secretary and most public opinion, saw Edith as an immoral, scheming, manipulative older woman—a sorceress, who insidiously and persistently worked on an impressionable, inexperienced younger man to kill her husband or to help her kill him. Other writers have compared Edith to Madame Bovary, and even to Marilyn Monroe. What these various interpretations have in common is that they are highly speculative, confidently asserted, impressionistic judgments by amateur psychologists. There are passages in the letters taken singly that can be used to support each of these and no doubt many other interpretations. Nowhere in the literature is there any attempt to build up a careful picture of Edith's personality and behavior on the basis of considering the evidence as a whole using any method other than impression. It may be possible for psychologists (or psycho-historians) to construct a less speculative profile of Edith on the basis of the available evidence.

Another subtheory concerns Freddy's character, which, apart from points already mentioned, is relevant to assessing his credibility as a witness and to the question of whether the attack was premeditated or spontaneous (crucial to all but the fantasy theory, important for the broken chain theory, and relevant to the other two).

Some sort of picture of the nature and course of the relationships between the main actors is also relevant at least as background to all the theories of the case; it is crucial to parts of the broken chain theory, which is greatly strengthened if one can show a cooling off on the part of Freddy after the most damaging letters were written (there is quite cogent evidence in favor of this) and a calmer, less frenetic reaction on the part of Edith. However, even if it were accepted that at one stage Freddy had tried either to break off or to cool down the relationship ("Can we be pals, only," he had suggested in September), there is a counter-theory, to the effect that there was a revival of passion later, backed not least by the fact that Freddy killed Percy. Without going further into detail here I wish to suggest that in order to assess the credibility of the broken chain theory in toto and responses to it, it is important to consider in meticulous detail the precise nature of the relationship at a number of stages in the story and to test the hypothesis that the early letters belong to a distinct phase that was significantly different from the state of the relationship in the days immediately before Percy's death.

Macroscopic Analysis: A Preliminary Stock-Taking

One of the main claims made for Wigmore's method is that it provides a powerful tool for organizing and mapping complex arguments based on *masses* of evidence. The guiding rule of thumb is to begin with the conclusions (the ultimate probanda, facts in issue) and to work down or back to the evidence. The ideal type of an argument of this kind is pyramid-shaped, with the apex being simpler than the base. In adjudication, there is typically only one apex (guilty/not guilty; liable/not liable), but usually multiple facts in issue are involved; these are the "ultimate probanda." It is almost always essential to define each fact in issue *before* proceeding to analyze the evidence relevant to it.

At first sight, the preliminary stages of the analysis of the case of Edith Thompson may not seem to be a good advertisement for Wigmorean analysis as a simplifying device. The first stages have not been simple, but this is due to the nature of the case rather than the method. The case is usually considered to be complex because of the volume of the evidence and the difficulties involved in interpreting Edith's letters. The first stage in our analysis has revealed a number of further complications.

First, the ultimate probanda are more than usually complex. Many famous trials involve ultimate probanda in which the prosecution had to prove $A + B + C + D$, when only one element (e.g., identity or criminal intent) has been the subject of serious doubt or dispute. In the case of Edith Thompson, the facts in issue exhibit a more complex form: The prosecution's case involved a mixture of necessary and sufficient conditions that can be represented as follows:

A (Freddy murdered P) + B {(i) or (ii) or [(i) or (ii) or *possibly* (iii)]}.

Second, some doubts surrounded the law governing the facts in issue: Was it sufficient to prove a general conspiracy to murder Percy (B [i]), or did the prosecution have to prove that this attack was planned? What precisely is the scope of the proposition "E incited F"? Is the scope of "incitement" a question of law, of fact, or of mixed fact and law? Furthermore—although it was not raised at the trial—would Edith be responsible, if the prosecution established the "exploding bomb" theory?[16] This merely illustrates the general point that to the extent that the interpretation or application of the governing law is unclear, the task of constructing or evaluating arguments about disputed questions of fact becomes correspondingly more difficult.

Third, the complexity of the ultimate probanda is reflected in the multiplicity of potential theories of the case, each of which has variants. What this means is that there are several potential possible lines of argument both for and against Edith. A "comprehensive" analysis of the case would need to map and evaluate each of these arguments.

Fourth, some of the lines of argument overlap. For example, as we shall see, the fantasy theory may represent both a sufficient argument for exonerating Edith (with respect to both conspiracy and incitement) and a substantial prop for the broken chain theory. This is not uncommon in disputed cases involving multiple lines of argument.

Fifth, in many causes célèbres the sole or main disputed issue relates to some relatively "hard fact," such as identity or alibi or the death of the victim. In this case we are dealing with the mental state of not one, but two, people: Did Edith intend . . . etc.? Was Freddy's act caused/inspired/done in furtherance of Edith's incitement or plan? Proof of mental states is notoriously more elusive than proof of "simple facts."

Finally, as we have seen, some of the intermediate probanda that are potentially important in most of the theories involve interpreting the characters of and the relationship between the two main characters.

The case clearly illustrates how complications can arise at the top of the pyramid as well as at other points. Nevertheless the first steps in the analysis have imposed some order onto the material. Our standpoint has been clarified; the range of potential ultimate probanda, albeit unusually complex, has been laid out; four main theories of the case have been articulated, with scope left for dealing with variants of these where appropriate. We are now ready to proceed to the next stage.

Microscopic Analysis: Premeditation

All Wigmorean analysis involves selection; completeness and comprehensiveness are only relative matters in this context. However, the purpose of this essay is to illustrate the application of this method to a particularly complex case. Accordingly, I propose to proceed highly selectively by concentrating on one small sector of potential arguments about the case as a whole.

First, let us look at just one element in the broken chain theory—the proposition (intermediate probandum) that "Freddy's attack on Percy was spontaneous/unpremeditated" and the main evidence used by the prosecution to support premeditation. I shall use this to illustrate a number of points about Wigmorean analysis (e.g., generalizations, prejudice, and the use of emotive language); but there is another reason for selecting this as a focal point. It is a maxim of advocacy that one should "go for the jugular." If a reasonable doubt is established about the proposition that the attack was premeditated, it breaks the connection between Edith's thoughts and actions and all the prosecution theories, except possibly the legally dubious and highly speculative "exploding bomb" theory. This is one potential "jugular" that could be sufficient to destroy all versions of the case against Edith. Regardless of whether the analysis achieves this result here—which I leave to the reader to judge—it may illustrate the potential value of careful microscopic analysis of one or more key points in a highly complex argument the main outlines of which have been firmly set by careful preliminary macroscopic structuring.

Let us start, then, by constructing the strongest possible argument based on the available materials, that Freddy's assault on Percy was unpremeditated. This subtheory might be constructed in outline as follows:

1. When Freddy set out from the Graydons' he did not plan to meet Edith and Percy.
2. A planned murder would probably have (a) been carried out

in the absence of Edith; (b) been executed without a struggle; and (c) been carried out in some other place.
3. Edith was genuinely surprised by the attack.
4. Freddy's purpose in meeting Percy was to ask him to grant Edith a divorce. The stabbing occurred during an unexpected struggle when the confrontation misfired.
5. Freddy's carrying of the knife was innocent.

All five props in this argument are consistent with Bywaters' conviction for murder and the rejection of his self-defense theory. These five theses are separable, but can be combined in various ways. I shall concentrate on (5), which was treated as crucial in the case. Suffice it to say, in my judgment, that there is quite strong support for (3) and that there is little or nothing in the record to negate (1), (2), and (4), but there is little beyond Freddy's story to give them direct support, either, except some speculative generalizations that give weak support to (2) and (4).

To convict Edith, the prosecution had to establish not only that Freddy murdered Percy but also that the attack was premeditated. The two main props for the latter proposition are (a) that the carrying of the knife was not innocent, and (b) that there is clear evidence that this attack was planned. Establishing (a) or (b) or (a + b) beyond reasonable doubt would be sufficient for this purpose. Let us look at (a) and (b) in turn.

(a) *The knife.* Reconstruction of the actual arguments used at the trial with respect to the knife is particularly revealing. The prosecution's argument was, in effect, that Bywaters had purchased the knife with the intention of killing Percy and that he had put it in his overcoat pocket on the day of the murder for the same reason. The defense claimed that Freddy had bought the knife a long time previously, that he had taken it abroad with him on his last voyage, that he regularly carried it around with him, and that it was natural that he should do so. In the process of the arguments about premeditation, the weapon was variously described as an ordinary sheath knife, an English hunting knife, a deadly weapon, a dagger, a stabbing instrument, and a dreadful weapon. Interestingly, some of the more emotive terms were used by the judge.

There were also some striking differences in the generalizations invoked in the context of considering this issue. Counsel for the prosecution suggested that possession of a knife of this kind is in itself suspicious. In order to cast doubt on the suggestion that

Bywaters had possessed the knife for some time, the prosecution suggested that if this were true "it would have been a subject of jocular remarks"; the judge said, "It is suggested that no reasonable man living in London carries a knife like that about in his pocket." Defense counsel, on the other hand, in the course of a single paragraph said, "It is not strange for a sea-faring man, visiting foreign countries, to purchase a knife," and "There are few sailors who do not possess a knife." The editor of the record in the "Notable British Trials" series commented on the last remark in a footnote: "Bywaters was not a 'sailor' in the technical sense. He was a clerk on board a ship, and had more use for a fountain pen than for a knife."[17]

In the preceding examples not only is Bywaters variously categorized as a sailor, a seafaring man visiting foreign ports, a clerk, and a man living in London, but quite different generalizations are also invoked about the purchase, possession, and carrying of knives. At the trial the jury had the opportunity to inspect the knife itself and thus could form their own judgment on its description and on the specific issue of whether it would fit conveniently in the pocket of Bywaters' coat. They could also check the accuracy of the various categorizations of Bywaters: For example, it is arguable that he was both someone living in London and a seafaring man, who visited foreign countries, but the jurors were probably only slightly better placed than the modern reader for making confident judgments about the contemporary habits of merchant seamen or ships' clerks with respect to knives or to the likelihood that if someone possessed a knife of this kind for a considerable period it would be the subject of jocular remarks.

The example of the knife in *Bywaters and Thompson* is a simple example of the leeway for choice in selecting and formulating generalizations as part of an argument about a particular issue of fact. It shows how there is room for the use of emotive terms, for distortion, and for selection by emphasizing different aspects of the same situation. Moreover, it is an example of invoking commonplace generalizations—such as those about the normality of carrying knives about London and of sailors' possessing and carrying knives—about which the jury is expected to rely on its own version(s) of general experience in order to come to a conclusion. Clearly there is scope in this kind of context for the intrusion of bias, prejudice, and sheer speculation. Moreover, it is doubtful whether all the relevant background knowledge can ever be fully articulated. However, as Wigmore might have argued, what better basis is there for making such judgments?

The date of purchase of the knife and the issue of whether Freddy was carrying it with the purpose of attacking Percy were perceived by the main participants to be significant. Almost all the available information about it can be gleaned from the explicit arguments advanced in the case. To this can be added a few further propositions. Mr. H. W. Forster of Osborne and Co., tool merchants of Aldersgate, testified that his business sold identical knives for six shillings and had stocked them for about seventeen years. Neither the defense nor the prosecution attempted to adduce evidence corroborating or negating Bywaters' statement that he had purchased the knife in November 1921—that is, almost a year before the attack. If the defense had managed to find one or two of Bywaters' shipmates who would testify that he had owned a knife for a long time and that he regularly carried it about with him, this could have significantly strengthened Edith's case.

A key-list of propositions relating to the propositions that (a) the purchase and (b) the carrying of the knife were both innocent, based on the available evidence, and constructed from the point of view of a relatively detached historian, might read as follows:

The purchase of the knife was innocent. The carrying of the knife was innocent.
1. The knife was bought in November 1921.
2. Freddy Bywaters (testimony, 53).
3. Freddy Bywaters carried the knife everywhere in England.
4. Freddy Bywaters (cross-examined, 71).
5. It was handy at sea and handy at home.
6. Bywaters (70).
7. Bywaters bought the knife from Osborne and Co.
8. Knives of this kind were sold by Osborne and Co.
9. Such knives had been stocked for about seventeen years.
10. H. W. Forster (director of Osborne's) testified to points 8 and 9 (42).
11. Defense called no witness to corroborate Freddy's possession of knife since November 1921.
12. Shearman J (137).
13. "It was difficult to put the knife into any kind of pocket, except the side pocket."
14. Shearman J (137).

15. Generalizations about the normality of carrying such a knife about.

Prima facie this key-list adds little to the arguments presented in the case. However, it can be used as the basis for some other propositions that further weaken the premeditation thesis:

16. There is no evidence that Freddy Bywaters bought the knife on the day of the killing.
17. If Bywaters already owned the knife (1 + 16), he had it with him when he left home.
18. Bywaters carried the knife about with him from the time he left home until after the killing.
19. Bywaters had the knife on him during at least three social engagements (morning coffee and afternoon tea with Edith; visit to the Graydons).
20. The knife fitted easily in his coat.

All of this helps to bolster Freddy's claim that the purchase and carrying of the knife were both innocent. Furthermore, (17) suggests that the premeditation thesis requires that Freddy had formed the plan to attack Percy before he left home. Yet none of the several witnesses who saw him during the course of the day observed anything strange or unusual about his demeanor. The net effect of all this, I would suggest, is to give some (albeit weak) support to this part of Freddy's story; it suggests that there is nothing in the evidence about the knife (other than the fact of its possession and use in the killing) that supports the premeditation thesis.

For the prosecution to convict Edith, they had to prove that Bywaters' attack was premeditated. Even if one totally discounts Freddy's evidence about the events of the evening (and his story of the period up to 11:00 P.M. was generally consistent and was largely corroborated by the Graydons), there is almost nothing to support the proposition that the attack was premeditated. There was no evidence to support the proposition that the knife was purchased recently in order to attack Percy; there was no evidence in support of the proposition that Bywaters put the knife in his pocket that morning because he planned to attack Percy—the best that the prosecution could do was point out that there was no corroboration for his claim that he was in the habit of carrying it. The alternative hypotheses about his state of mind (planned attack, loss of control in the heat of the moment) are essentially speculative. The evidence relating to the wounds may support an inference of intent, but it is about evenly balanced (and weak) with respect to the question of premeditation versus spontaneity. More information about the date of purchase of the knife, whether Bywaters did regularly carry it about, and its size in relation to the pockets of the overcoat might have helped one side or the other. However, on the basis of careful scrutiny of the available evidence, my conclusion is that it gives only weak support to either side and, on balance, it marginally favors Edith. Accordingly there is considerable doubt about this crucial aspect of both prosecution theories.

b. *Edith's last letter: the "tea-room" passage (exhibit 60; see appendix 2).* The other specific prop of the premeditation thesis was the closing passage in Edith's last letter to Freddy. In presentation, the prosecution did not subject this to close scrutiny, preferring to concentrate on building up a general impression of a continuous process of encouragement and stimulation ("by precept and example, actual or simulated"). Edith incited Freddy and plotted Percy's death with him and this led directly to Percy's death. In the case, Edith's letters were admitted as evidence of motive and intent but were used for other purposes, including as direct evidence of conspiracy. Since the judge ruled that it was necessary to establish that Edith incited or planned *this* attack, the last letter in fact formed a crucial part of the prosecution's case.

I shall argue that the letter at most gives only very weak support to the prosecution and that there is almost no other evidence to support the proposition that this attack was planned. It is worth subjecting one key passage to detailed scrutiny as an illustration of the potential methods and value of microscopic Wigmorean analysis.

There is some uncertainty about when this letter was written and when it was received;[18] let us, for the sake of argument, take the timing most favorable to the prosecution: that it was written on the day before the killing (that is, on October 2) and received before Freddy left his mother's house on October 3. It is reproduced in full in appendix 2. The whole letter was the main evidence used by the prosecution in favor of the conspiracy theory. Let us focus on the following words, on which *both* sides relied to support their case: "Don't forget what we talked in the Tea Room, I'll still risk and try if you will—we only have 3¾ years left darlingest. Try & help." The prosecution theory was that "what" referred to killing Percy; the defense claimed that "what" referred to Freddy's trying to find Edith a post abroad so that they could elope.

If, from the standpoint of a historian, we take a fresh but careful look at this passage, it is clear that it is susceptible to quite elaborate textual analysis. Here I shall only sketch a possible approach. One might, for example, start by listing a series of propositions about possible referents of "what" (also of "risk and try," "try and help"—risk what? try what?—(and so on) as follows:

1. "What" could refer to almost anything (i.e., there is no clear referent).
2. "What" could refer to killing Percy.
3. "What" could refer to getting a post abroad.
4. "What" could refer to eloping.
5. "What" could refer to a secret assignation.
6. "What" could refer to asking Percy for a divorce.
7. "What" could refer to a general conversation covering several or all of the above and possibly much else besides.
8. "What" could refer to whether to use poison or a dagger (Shearman, 151).

This probably covers the main possibilities, though the list is not exhaustive. There are a number of potential aids to interpretation that might give support to one or more of these hypotheses and eliminate others. Such aids include the immediate context of these twenty-seven words; the context of the letter as a whole; the context of the whole corpus of letters and of particular passages in other letters (e.g., Edith often uses the words "risk" and "try"); one or another subtheory about the state of the relationship between Edith and Freddy; extraneous evidence from people who saw (or possibly overheard them) in the tearoom; and the conduct of Edith and Freddy before and after the meeting. One might also investigate the occasion for writing the letter, and, of course, Edith and Freddy could be asked about the meaning of the passage.

Both the prosecution and the defense, in a very crude fashion, used something akin to textual analysis of the "tearoom" passage in their arguments; but, in my view, they both cheated.

This passage is the main evidence in favor of the proposition that this particular attack was planned—that is, the conspiracy theory. The prosecution emphasized the words "risk," "try," "help," and "only" in the passage itself to bolster the idea that they referred to a sinister conspiracy. Then, by taking a number of other words and phrases out of context ("great big things," "he was suspicious," "do something tomorrow night") and linking them to the fact of

Percy's death and other letters, some of which were ambiguous and written more than six months before, they suggested that the conversation in the tearoom was the culmination of a continuing conspiracy.

The defense emphasized "only 3¾ years" (strange if one were planning something immediate) and the fact that Edith and Freddy *both* testified that "what" referred to eloping and risking her future with Bywaters; but then counsel used the fact of the prosecution's misuse of this passage to cast doubt on their interpretation of all other passages, while carefully skipping over any explicit reference to any of the most damaging ones.

Even more remarkable is Mr. Justice Shearman's treatment of the passage; for he asserts, with no basis whatsoever and going well beyond what the prosecution had argued, that "what" refers to whether it was better to kill Percy by means of poison or a dagger.

A more careful analysis using the aids mentioned above can take us some way beyond this. First, we can quite confidently eliminate some of the possible hypotheses. For example, the judge's suggestion can be attacked on the following grounds:

1. It is sheer speculation, with no evidence to support it.
2. It involves a petitio principii in that it assumes what it seeks to prove.
3. It does not make sense of the passage, "Don't forget what we talked in the Tea Room [about whether to use poison or a dagger], I'll still risk and try if you will—we only have 3¾ years left darlingest."

Again, we can fairly confidently discard the first hypothesis that "what" could refer to almost anything. The context of the letter as a whole, the context of the sentence, the general background of their relationship, and the testimony of both Freddy and Edith all support the proposition that "what" concerned some aspect of their relationship, rather than something else. It seems unlikely that it referred to buying a motor car or that morning's world news, for example.

Of the remaining six hypotheses (2–7), only (2) favors the prosecution thesis that they were conspiring in the tearoom to kill Percy. Number (7) (general conversation about their situation) hardly constitutes evidence of conspiracy. The other four hypotheses all positively support the defense contention that the conversation had nothing to do with murder. Even if we totally discount testimony of both accused that it referred to eloping (the "risks" being financial or of social stigma), the context of the letter as a whole and the words "3¾ years left" both tend to support the judgment that an innocent explanation is a good deal more likely than the prosecution's interpretation. At the very least, such factors seem to me to cast a reasonable doubt on that interpretation, yet this passage was the main item of evidence in support of the conspiracy theory. The passage supports the proposition that they met and talked seriously about their relationship, but it gives no significant support to the proposition that they were conspiring to kill—it tends to negate it.

Undertaking such analysis and reading about it can appear wearisome to most people. It is much more entertaining to play with stories and let Edith go hang. This kind of approach, however, can and does yield results. In this particular instance I do not think it can do more than eliminate some of the possibilities and cast doubt on the wisdom of making any confident judgment about what was said in the tearoom; but in regard to other passages, including some that played a key role in the case, meticulous analysis can lead to the conclusion that one particular interpretation is very probably (or almost certainly, or even beyond peradventure) the correct one. However, in this particular case one's conclusions about different individual passages in Edith's letters tend to point in different directions. For example, the more carefully one studies the "Marconigram" passage (appendix 1, page 113), the less easy is it to believe that Edith was merely fantasizing or playing games, or that Freddy was not actively involved in whatever was being transacted between them at that time. On the other hand, some of the other apparently damaging passages either become hopelessly ambiguous in the light of careful scrutiny or else seem to help Edith in one way or another. In short, it is unlikely that this kind of analysis will ever conclusively resolve all the doubts about Edith Thompson's guilt. In my view, however, it strongly substantiates the judgment that there is at least a reasonable doubt about it.

Conclusion

I have suggested that careful analysis of even such unpromising material as Edith Thompson's allusive, ambiguous, inconsequential love letters can at least reduce the range of plausible interpretations, even if it cannot resolve all doubts. I would further suggest that such analysis is the best available way of getting as near as possible to the truth, but it was not the method used at the trial—nor is it a method that is well suited to our system of adversarial proceedings and oral presentation of evidence. In my view, the prosecution used selected passages unfairly by taking them out of context, attributing particular meanings to them on the basis of innuendo, impression, and bare assertion rather than analysis and argument. The reading aloud of the letters in court could create only a general impression, which is no substitute for careful study of the texts. Even if the defense had been handled more skillfully and if the emotional atmosphere and the pressure of time had been less, the basic flaw would have been the same: The oral presentation of such material, whether to twelve laypersons or to an experienced professional, cannot provide a satisfactory basis for the careful analysis and evaluation of the evidence. Thus my conclusion is that dispassionate, logical analysis of even such unpromising material as Edith Thompson's letters is a possible, indeed even a necessary, method of trying to work toward the truth, but that such a method is incompatible with oral presentation of the material—as much in a public lecture as in a courtroom.

Part 2. Edith Thompson: Fresh Evidence and New Perspectives
William Twining

One hazard of academic life is to learn of an important work on one's subject shortly before or after completing a project. I was making final revisions to "Anatomy of a Cause Célèbre" (hereafter "Anatomy") in June 1988 when I learned of the publication of *Criminal Justice: The True Story of Edith Thompson* by René Weis. This is by far the most substantial study of the life and death of Edith. Remarkably, Weis and I are colleagues at University College London, yet over a period of five years neither of us knew that the other was working on the case. Dr. Weis's is a scholarly contribution to the general literature on causes célèbres and is the first full-scale biography of Edith.

Criminal Justice contains much new information and many insights about Edith Thompson. I share many of Dr. Weis's values and I agree with some, but not all, of his interpretations and judgments.[19] We both conclude that Edith was probably wrongly convicted, but for somewhat different reasons. However, this section deals only indirectly with the "truth" about Edith Thompson.

Rather, its concern is methodological. It is a case study of the differences in approach of a jurist using modified Wigmorean analysis and a specialist in English literature using a sophisticated version of the narrative method to reconstruct and present the "True Story of Edith Thompson." My objective here is to explore quite briefly and report as honestly as I can what I think a first reading of Dr. Weis's account has added to my understanding of the case with respect to the question "Was Edith guilty as charged?" and, second, what modified Wigmorean analysis might have added to his account. This is a sort of "thought experiment." In order to reach for relative detachment I shall refer to both authors in the third person.

Criminal Justice is a substantial book of over 300 pages. It is presented in a form designed to attract the general reader. It is based on extensive and meticulous original research and contains some conventional scholarly furniture: a table of contents, a preface, two pages of acknowledgements, a list of illustrations, a "cast of main characters," an appendix on sources, and an index based almost exclusively on proper names. Significantly, it has almost no footnotes. Even more significantly for present purposes, it is presented as a story: The arrangement is chronological, starting with a description of Edith's parents and ending with a harrowing reconstruction of the execution of Edith and Freddy and a brief account of the subsequent lives of Edith's closest relatives. The whole forms a readable, coherent, and moving narrative biography. Weis states, "My readers will be the final arbiters of whether or not . . . I have successfully allowed Edith Thompson to argue her innocence."[20]

Criminal Justice differs from "Anatomy" in respect of, for example, purpose, length, style, source material, comprehensiveness, literary form, and intended audiences. They are contrasting products of significantly different enterprises. There is, however, a solid basis for comparison, for both works focus on the question of Edith's guilt, using her letters as the main, but not the only, evidence. One can thus compare and contrast two different ways of treating selected matters bearing on this question, with particular reference to the relationships among narrative, analysis, and argument.

STANDPOINT

The first step in any such analysis is to clarify standpoint by asking "Who am I? At what stage in what process am I? What am I trying to do?"[21] Partial answers to these questions in respect of *Criminal*

Justice and "Anatomy" have already been indicated. However, posing the questions more sharply suggests some further affinities and contrasts. Both authors purport to adopt the standpoint of a historian exploring the question of Edith's guilt from almost the same vantage point: University College London, in the 1980s.[22] Neither is a professional historian; both are liberal academics with a humanistic bent. They have produced works for publication at the end of rather different processes of research. Personal factors apart, some of their differences in perspective might be attributable to the kinds of differences one might expect between a legal and a literary mind: Twining more drily analytical, Weis more practiced in the interpretation of literary texts and character. However, one may ask: Is it sensible to think in such terms or to draw sharp distinctions between legal and literary historical truth? Are not the similarities in standpoint much greater than the differences, given that they have both been addressing essentially the same central question?

Weis's story is based on extensive original research.[23] He has located an impressive range of materials in newspapers, official records (some made publicly available for the first time); "evidence" to two Royal Commissions; parliamentary debates; and, of course, the record of the trial (edited by Filson Young); and numerous secondary works, few of which, he says, add much to Young's volume. Weis can claim some notable coups: He has unearthed some new letters from Edith, Freddy, members of their families, and others. Apart from their intrinsic interest some of these are directly relevant to the question of Edith's guilt. He has also interviewed a number of people who knew some of the actors or who were able to throw light on the environment of the main characters and the central action of the story. Almost as significantly, Weis reports that some potentially crucial documents are missing (including the originals of Edith's letters) and some official files are still closed. Weis uses his material to give the fullest account to date of the background, biographies, and personalities of the main actors, but both authors use the published version of Edith's letters as their primary source for the events leading to Percy's death.

THE FACTS IN ISSUE: ELUCIDATING THE QUESTION

Weis interprets the charge of murder against Edith almost exclusively in terms of conspiracy,[24] as did Mr. Justice Shearman in his charge to the jury.[25] However, he interprets the relevance of conspiracy rather differently from both Shearman and Twining. The former directed that the jury should convict only if they were satisfied beyond reasonable doubt that the lovers had planned this attack. Twining suggests that it would have been sufficient to convict Edith if the jury was satisfied that Freddy acted in pursuance of a continuing conspiracy to kill Percy whenever opportunity arose. Weis tends to gloss over this distinction. He also treats the question of whether Edith and Freddy had conspired to poison Percy in the period up to May as central to the question of Edith's guilt.[26] Twining, on the other hand, argues that under the broken chain theory, even if Edith were held to have attempted to poison Percy or to have conspired with Freddy to do so, these acts were too remote from the fatal attack to be sufficient to implicate her in the murder. As the prosecution tried to argue, some of the early letters could be interpreted to support the theory of a protracted and continuing conspiracy, but the defense countered that the evidence failed to support the hypothesis that, if there ever was a conspiracy, it was continuing or that Freddy had acted because of it. Twining differs from Weis in being much less confident that all the early letters are susceptible to an innocent interpretation, but believes that far less turns on them than Weis thinks.

Weis pays relatively little attention to the significance of incitement, both in respect of the murder and of interpreting some of the potentially most damning passages in the letters. Twining, on the other hand, argues that Edith was more vulnerable in respect of incitement than conspiracy, even without resort to the legally dubious but psychologically plausible "exploding bomb" theory.[27] However, in his analysis the chain was also broken in respect of incitement.

It might be argued that since the trier of fact was a jury of laypersons charged with rendering a general verdict, they would not in practice be concerned with such legal niceties. They made an undifferentiated (holistic?) judgment about Edith's legal (and moral) responsibility for Freddy's act, and this is what society expects of juries. Accordingly, this should also be adequate for an historian. On this view, Twining's differentiations are unduly legalistic and academic. Twining dissents. Such an argument is not qualitatively different from the judgment, which may well be historically correct, that Edith was "hanged for adultery."[28] Insofar as our enterprise is rationally reconstructing the strongest possible arguments concerning Edith's legal responsibility for Percy's death, precision is very important indeed. The crucial point is that under Twining's interpretation of the law the prosecution had several alternative routes open to them, and Edith's defenders need to deal with all of the main alternatives. Wigmorean analysis requires as precise a clarification of the legal issues as legal interpretation will admit; and where, as in this case, there are multiple facts in issue, some of which are open to more than one interpretation, arguments have to be constructed about each of them.

THEORIES OF THE CASE

In "Anatomy" Twining outlines four main theories of the case, each with several possible variants and subvariants: the conspiracy theory, the incitement theory, the fantasy theory, and the broken chain theory. A statement of a theory in this context means a summary statement of a general argument about the facts in issue. A theory in this sense is an analytic device of macroscopic analysis: For advocates, such theories typically form the basis of a strategy of argumentation; for historians and the like they are similarly a useful instrument for organizing complex material. In analyzing the present case, outlining four main theories and their variants helps to clarify how each side had several different routes open for reaching the conclusion for which it was arguing. Twining suggests that the broken chain theory is the most plausible of the four. It has the special advantage that it can be used to cumulate doubt about opposing theories without necessarily claiming to advance a fully coherent account of the truth about Edith Thompson. This theory was the main basis for the defense strategy at Edith's trial, but was undermined by her insistence on testifying and therefore being compelled to advance one account of key events and one interpretation of some passages in her letters. Most secondary writers who are sympathetic to Edith, including Weis, rely heavily on the fantasy theory. This has the most human interest and fits in with the function of general literature on causes célèbres, which tend to be judged by their entertainment value as well as—or more than—by their contribution to knowledge. Twining, however, believes that the fantasy theory is very difficult to sustain by evidence and argument. It is both highly speculative and difficult to reconcile with some of the data. It is in his view the least cogent of the four main theories, although it is not as weak as the tearoom conspiracy theory.

Weis does not use the concept of "theory" to differentiate lines of argument. It is reasonable to interpret *Criminal Justice* as being based primarily on a version of the fantasy theory with a few broken chain points used to supplement his case.²⁹ As noted above, Weis does not differentiate very clearly among the competing theories and their variants. This blunts the force of his negative attack on rival hypotheses and leads him to underestimate the importance of incitement in building up the case against Edith, especially in providing alternative interpretations of some of the letters.

On the positive side, it is probably fair to say that Weis, by sustained and careful interpretation of Edith's letters, constructs the most plausible and best supported version of the fantasy theory yet published. Most secondary writers assert (rather than try to prove) the fantasy theory and, in so doing, commit or come close to committing the fallacy of *petitio principii*. Weis, through skilful use of Edith's letters to document the theme of the constant intermingling of fact and fiction, at least provides an impressive number of texts to ground the thesis. His subtle reconstruction of Edith's character, not least through a perceptive use of her reactions and commentaries on the novels she has been reading,³⁰ lends support to the fantasy theory. At the very least he provides a coherent and plausible interpretation of the letters read as a whole that is consistent with this line of argument. However, as will be argued below, his interpretations too often involve assertion rather than argument. Moreover, the fantasy theory is by its nature heavily dependent on "soft" psychological speculation, which is in danger of foundering at crucial points when compared with rather "harder" data.

A first reading of *Criminal Justice* suggests a further, ironic, twist. Weis's version of the fantasy theory, even if true, does not necessarily absolve Edith from legal responsibility. Even if those passages of her letters which suggest that Edith had tried to poison Percy or that she is "dreaming" of Percy's death are indeed mere fantasy, she is still responsible for communicating those thoughts in a form which might reasonably be interpreted as being factual reports of her acts or desires—for example, that she had tried to poison Percy or that she wished him dead.³¹ Absent a positive defense of insanity, such acts could legally ground a finding of incitement or conspiracy. There are some hard facts that need to be explained away: Edith did make these statements; she admits to having tried to manipulate Freddy on a number of occasions, as lovers do; she did send at least nine cuttings about cases of murder by poison;³² she did ask Freddy to send her "things" which might be interpreted as poisons;³³ Freddy did supply her with some medicines;³⁴ Edith more than once expressed a wish that Percy were dead;³⁵ Freddy did kill Percy. The fantasy theory has a lot of explaining to do; it is inevitably speculative and fantasy can spill over into fact as easily as fact can spill over into fantasy—even if such a distinction can be maintained in legal or other discourse.³⁶ This is not to say that the fantasy theory is untrue nor to suggest that it has no explanatory power. As an argument, however, it is not very cogent.

SUBTHEORIES, SUBPLOTS, AND CHARACTERS

In "Anatomy" Twining argues that an assessment of the characters of the main protagonists and of their relationships to each other is relevant to each of the main theories of the case. He reports a number of different interpretations of these matters that were implicit in the arguments at trial or that have been advanced in the secondary literature, but he does not seek to develop them in detail.

Criminal Justice, on the other hand, adduces a wealth of new biographical and background facts, and builds up in fascinating detail a picture of Edith, Freddy, and Percy, as well as many other members of the cast of characters. It contains a rich, perceptive, and plausible account of all these matters which cannot but add to our understanding of the story, even if one does not accept all of the interpretations. At the macro level, Weis's most striking achievement is to piece together a coherent and detailed chronological account of the course of a number of key relationships—not only between Edith and Freddy, but also between the lovers and members of their families and their circle of friends and contacts. Of particular interest is the detailed account of the course of the relationship between Edith and Freddy, including some significant new information about their attempts to communicate with each other after the trial.³⁷ Some of the detail may be irrelevant or tangential to the question of Edith's guilt, but the story is well worth telling at length for its own sake and Weis tells it very well. The final chapters have been justly praised as a devastating depiction of the horrors of capital punishment.

Not surprisingly, this meticulous reconstruction has implications for all of the main theories of the case. Although it is presented as an argument in favor of Edith's innocence, it also provides material that could be used for and against each of the main theories. To take but one example: Weis's account of the relationship between Freddy and Edith (which had even more ups and downs than had previously been noted)³⁸ supports the general thesis that the early letters are of very limited value in interpreting the events immediately preceding Percy's death. It strongly negates any suggestion of either continuing conspiracy or protracted incitement. It gives some support to the contention that the prejudicial effect of the early letters outweighed their probative value and that they ought not to have been admitted at all.[39] On the other hand, given time, one could argue that some parts of Weis's account could be used to argue that Edith was probably guilty of some of the lesser offenses charged in the second indictment (which was not proceeded with) in the early phase of the relationship.[40] However, that is beyond the scope of this essay.

Weis's reconstruction of characters, relationships, and subplots (including some new ones) is very helpful in interpreting and making sense of many passages in Edith's letters. One does not need to accept all of his particular interpretations to recognize the value of these intermediate generalizations and of a coherent narrative as aids to developing well-grounded, mutually supportive interpretations of the meaning and significance of these elusive texts. The process is, of course, reflexive: One constructs a picture of a character, or incident, or sequence of events from the letters or other sources and uses these constructs to interpret the letters. This is quite compatible with a Wigmorean approach and Weis is arguably at his best at this level of analysis.

Microscopic Analysis

Two main values are claimed for Wigmorean analysis: At the macro level it helps clarify the central issues and impose order on a mass of mixed evidence or data through the development of carefully formulated hypotheses, theories, and subtheories; at the micro level it provides tools for sharply focused and detailed analysis of selected phases of an argument that have been identified as potentially crucial or otherwise deserving special attention. At each level the main claim is that it helps to clarify what precisely is being argued as a preliminary to evaluating its cogency. In "Anatomy" some particular examples were chosen to illustrate the application of microscopic analysis. We have already looked at the treatment of just one of these in *Criminal Justice*, the last letter (exhibit 60) with particular reference to the "tearoom passage."[41]

Twining concludes that the passage does not give any significant support to the conspiracy theory; if anything, it tends to negate it. Furthermore, the analysis suggests that the prosecution, the defense, and the judge all used the passage in ways that do not stand up to close scrutiny.

Weis reaches a similar conclusion by a different route.[42] He reconstructs the context of the letter and the events to which the key passage refers. He argues plausibly, partly on the basis of new evidence, that the letter was written before 5:00 P.M. on Monday, October 3 (i.e., a few hours before the killing), and that the meeting in the tearoom took place on Friday, September 29, and not on October 3, as the prosecution had suggested.[43] He states, "The Crown will mistakenly assume that the tea room conversation occurred on Monday afternoon, the day before the murder and that it ought to be *causally* linked to the tragedy."[44] This is a partial non sequitur. If it were accepted that Edith and Freddy had been conspiring to kill Percy a few days before his death, that would have been sufficient to implicate Edith. It is only marginally more damaging to claim that the meeting took place a few hours before the murder, rather than a few days. The dating of the letter and of the meeting involves only a minor and immaterial adjustment in the prosecution's version of the events. In this instance textual analysis is more helpful than contextual analysis, because the point at issue is what the passage means.[45]

The other specific points analyzed by Twining can be dealt with briefly. Weis's account of Freddy's movements in the twelve hours before the murder is much more detailed but, like Twining's, casts doubt on the proposition that the attack was premeditated.[46] Weis produces some new information about the knife:

> Getting a knife under the circumstances was hardly prima facie evidence to be used to convict, although his carrying it on this night was a different matter. The dagger itself consisted of a double-edged blade, which measured five and a half inches and protruded from a four-inch long, chequered pattern handle. The weapon caused a stir when it was produced in court, not least among the jury. The police might never have found it, had Bywaters not told them precisely where to look, unaware of the damage its visual impact would inflict on his case.[47]

Weis's account of Freddy's movements also supports the proposition that the knife fitted easily and inconspicuously in Freddy's coat pocket: Freddy left home about noon (a crucial moment in the premeditation thesis), met Edith twice, completed a few errands in the city,[48] dined with the Graydons, went out for a drink at a nearby hotel with Avis Graydon (Edith's sister), and made several journeys by public transport.⁴⁹ There is no evidence to suggest that anyone noticed he was carrying a knife. All this in turn is at least consistent with Freddy's claim that he always carried it with him.⁵⁰ Weis invokes the defense's generalizations about merchant seamen carrying knives in foreign parts, but implicitly acknowledges that this does not in itself dispose of the proposition that possessing and carrying such a knife in London is in itself suspicious. It was a quite formidable instrument. Weis confirms that there is no evidence to support the suggestion that Freddy had purchased the knife recently for the specific purpose of threatening or attacking Percy.⁵¹ All in all, this corroborates Twining's contention that the evidence about the knife gives little support to the premeditation thesis; however, its nature and size (Weis follows Shearman in calling it a "dagger") is damaging to Edith as well as to Freddy in the context of the premeditation argument because that bears on the conspiracy and broken chain theories.

Perhaps because he underestimates the significance of incitement, Weis never squarely addresses the crucial but complex question "Was Edith the dominant partner in respect of significant phases of the story?" If she was, it is suggested, this could ground a different interpretation of some key passages in her letters from those advanced by Weis. To put the matter crudely: If one sees Edith as a manipulative, scheming, or forceful woman who exerted or tried to exert influence over her younger, less experienced lover, this supports the thesis that several passages constitute incitement or solicitation to murder either by direct exhortation or by more or less subtle innuendo. This could significantly change the texture and emphasis of Weis's story, although Edith might still be rescued from responsibility for murder by the broken chain argument. Before applying this to a specific example, it is necessary to consider Weis's method of interpreting the letters.

INTERPRETING THE LETTERS

René Weis's enterprise is to reconstruct and present "the true story of Edith Thompson." He is openly sympathetic to Edith and explicitly claims to argue her case in her own terms.⁵² *Criminal Justice* is, in an important sense, Edith's story and is presented in a form which serves literary, humanistic, and publishing values as well as the pursuit of a mundane kind of truth. It is a good read. In considering Weis's method it is accordingly important to distinguish between analysis and presentation and between narrative and argument. This is especially significant in the present context in that the main values claimed for the Wigmorean approach relate to analysis rather than presentation (e.g., it is more useful in pretrial preparation than in presentation at trial). Furthermore, although narrative may legitimately form part of a rational argument—stories may constitute arguments as well as be vehicles for presentation—narrative may also be used to sneak in irrelevant or invalid factors, to gloss over weaknesses in an argument, to obscure what is being argued, or to serve other functions such as attracting attention, sustaining interest, or winning sympathy.[53] It might be the case that while Weis's treatment of the case is more readable and eloquent, Twining's argument is more cogent.

In *Criminal Justice* Weis uses the letters as the main vehicle for presenting a coherent account of the story of Edith. Only exceptionally does he explicitly discuss alternative interpretations of these texts. If he had done so, it would have broken the flow in ways which not only would have reduced readability, but also would have impaired the coherence of his presentation. This is not to suggest that as a meticulous and fair-minded scholar he did not analyze and consider some competing interpretations and the arguments for and against them. It is fair to say, however, that in dealing with the letters he generally reports his conclusions and only occasionally considers competing interpretations in detail. This opens up a whole range of issues that will not be pursued here. Rather, let us illustrate some quite simple points with reference to a single passage.

Appended to a long letter, dated April 1, 1922[54] but possibly written over several days, is a separate note which begins: "Don't keep this piece." The text of the note is reprinted in full in appendix 1, page 113. It is worth reading carefully at this point. It has been widely regarded as the most damaging part of all Edith's correspondence by the lawyers in the case, by commentators, and by several dozen intelligent law students, most of whom were sympathetic to Edith.

After summarizing the passage rather less scrupulously than usual, Weis comments as follows:

> That this piece of fantasy could ever be construed as part of a premeditated murder plot defies belief. Bywaters knew it was fiction and that she had herself tasted the quinine in the tea to be able to

give an accurate account of Percy's complaint.⁵⁵ In the court the jury was told that "the passage is full of crime." Yes, as long as it is understood that crime means "imaginary crime." It is never easy to separate fact from fiction in Edith Thompson's extensive and intense correspondence, and though outside evidence is available to help distinguish one from the other, the more intimately acquainted the reader becomes with the correspondence, the more complex its rash interweaving of fact and fiction is bound to appear. In most of our lives such a blurring is not uncommon. It is not always harmless. But it is seldom the matter of life and death into which it is developed here.⁵⁶

This contrasts sharply with Twining's report of his reactions to the passage. He states, "the more carefully one studies the 'Marconigram' passage, the less easy is it to believe that Edith was *merely* fantasizing or playing games or that Freddy was not actively involved in what was being transacted at the time."⁵⁷ This merely reports a considered judgment reached after quite lengthy discussion in several classes. Rather than attempt an elaborate analysis of the whole passage, which prima facie contains several damaging statements, let us focus on one sentence and outline a strategy for construing it: "I wish we had not got electric light. . . . [I]t would be so easy." To what might "it" refer in this context? Nearly everyone who reads this for the first time concludes, in the context of the rest of the note, that "it" means killing Percy (using gas; interpretation 1). A strong case for this can be built up solely from the internal evidence of the passage. Other possibilities include making Percy ill, but not killing him (interpretation 2),⁵⁸ but the talk of death in the previous sentence casts doubt on that. Some commentators have suggested that this—and some other passages—refers to Edith's trying to perform an abortion on herself (interpretation 3). Even if these other passages support the subtheory that Edith was pregnant by Freddy (as Weis argues) or even that she experimented with unconventional methods of contraception, these interpretations do not make sense in this context. For example, how can one reconcile them with the *timing* of these actions ("I'm not going to try any more until you come back," "I'm going to try the glass again occasionally")? And what of "if we are successful in our action" (what action?) or the need to be careful in what Freddy says to Dan, and so on?

If "it" does refer to killing Percy, can this meaning be explained away? One possibility is that Edith was *pretending* to try to kill Percy.⁵⁹ If so, why would she do this except to urge Freddy to try, too? Or could this all be a joke—a form of black humor, an April Fool—or a more elaborate game of make-believe? The last is the most common version of the fantasy theory; its application seems pretty dubious in this context. First, it seems likely from the context that Dan existed, that the "Sunday morning escapade" actually did occur,[60] and that Freddy did supply quinine and other drugs to Edith. It stretches one's credulity to suggest that the harmless elements are true but the damaging ones are fantasy. Second, whose fantasy is it? If only Edith's, how do we explain the passages that imply Freddy's participation ("About the Marconigram?—do you mean . . . what you said about Dan")? If this is a joint fantasy, how does this square with our general picture of Freddy as the down-to-earth young fellow who dismisses Edith's "vapourings" as "melodrama"? The reader is invited to construct an argument that explains away this note as evidence which supports any of the following propositions: (a) that at that time, Edith and Freddy were in fact conspiring to kill Percy; (b) that Edith was pretending that she had been trying to kill Percy in order to incite Freddy to risk and try, too; or (c) that Edith, on this and other occasions, was telling Freddy that she wished Percy's death.

I return now to Weis's method. In this instance, he asserts rather than argues that the whole note is a "piece of fantasy" and that Freddy knew that.[61] This is tantamount to a petitio principii. Furthermore, it is not clear what precisely he is arguing when he says that "in most of our lives such a blurring [of fact and fiction] is not uncommon. . . . But it is seldom the matter of life and death into which it is developed here." Blurring of fact and fiction about the death of one's husband is not so very common, and the coincidence of harmless fantasizing about such a death with the actual murder of the recipient of such fantasies is unique in my experience. On reconsideration, in my judgment the Marconigram note does lend support to several elements in the incitement and conspiracy theories; it also raises some doubts about the fantasy theory itself, for the reasons stated. However, the timing of the note (six months before the attack) still leaves ample scope for the broken chain theory.

Many of Weis's interpretations of Edith's letters help to make sense of them and are much more convincing. However, he generally advances an interpretation on the basis of assertion or implicit argument without considering alternatives.[62] To have done otherwise with the great majority of letters would probably have been unrewarding as well as tedious. However, closer textual analysis of competing interpretations of selected key passages would almost certainly have refined his argument, and might also have changed it.

FRESH EVIDENCE AND NEW PERSPECTIVES

Weis has collected a mass of new data and revealing insights and has skillfully woven them into a coherent whole which, for most readers, is greater than its parts. Much of the new material fleshes out the background; some has a direct bearing on the central issue. Most of the new information helps build a quite sympathetic picture of Edith; some of it could be used against her. Some of the facts are "hard"—such as the dimensions of the knife; other data are more difficult to evaluate. What, for example, is a historian to make of the following judgment of Margery Fry, who visited Edith in prison and afterward became a committed abolitionist? According to Fry's biographer, Edith struck her "as a rather foolish girl who had romanticised her sordid little love affair and genuinely thought herself innocent, discounting her own influence on her lover."[63] For an historian, is this evidence that bears on the question of Edith's guilt?

The central themes of this book—the interplay of law, fact, and value, of reason and imagination, of narrative coherence and atomistic analysis—have all resurfaced in this essay. What, if anything, does it suggest about the uses and limitations of Wigmorean analysis? My personal conclusion is as follows: *Criminal Justice* has added immeasurably to my knowledge and understanding of a case with which I already had an intimate acquaintance. It is an outstanding example of what Wigmore called the "narrative method." The book's argument in respect of the issue of Edith Thompson's guilt would almost certainly have been sharpened and refined by the application of modified Wigmorean analysis—first, in respect of clarification of the precise issues of law and fact, differentiating several distinct theories of the case and the broad lines of argument that bear on them; and second, in respect of selecting and subjecting to detailed microscopic analysis key phases of these arguments. Wigmorean analysis would have supplied a firmer foundation and clearer lines of argument around which to build Weis's detailed edifice. Finally, René Weis has reconstructed a version of events which contains the most careful, cogent, and coherent case for Edith's complete innocence that has yet been made. His narrative also contains a good deal of material that could be used for several other lines of argument. For me, the effect of reading, reflecting upon, and reacting to Weis's account has been to strengthen my belief that although some of Edith's letters could reasonably be construed as involving acts of incitement, Weis's account strengthens the case for the broken chain theory.

Part 3. The Biographer's Response to a Wigmorean Analysis of "Thompson and Bywaters"
René Weis

NARRATIVE BIOGRAPHY AND METHODOLOGY

Although William Twining and René Weis agree about Edith Thompson's innocence to the extent that both writers believe her to have been wrongfully convicted, Twining's analysis of much of the same evidence at first seems to differ strikingly from Weis's, even though both writers take their cue from the same material, Edith Thompson's correspondence.

It will be the purpose of the ensuing pages to offer some reflections on these two approaches, particularly on the methodology of a narrative account of the case and how it bears on details of the evidence. The strategies of a narrative history are bound to differ from those deployed in an analysis such as Twining's, which is embedded in a structured approach whose intermediate conclusions are set out at every turn.

Different audiences respond differently to various expositions of the same material, and it will be argued here that the audience the writer has in mind may determine the differences in methodology. Weis's study was conceived as a biographical work from the cradle to the grave. It aimed to evolve chronologically from Edith Thompson's birth and childhood in the 1890s to her death at Holloway in 1923. Although this seems in many ways the obvious course to follow, it was in fact a decision by the author which conflicted with the wishes of the publishers, who preferred a stronger opening in the death cell at Holloway. Such a narrative strategy would have been legitimate in view of the obiter dicta about what it is, above all, that renders Edith Thompson's life a legitimate, albeit painful, subject of study. The long-term effect of a "dramatic" opening, however, would have been the opposite of the one intended by Weis, which was to take the reader into the recesses of Edith Thompson's inner and outer life without at first framing her entire existence by the end in the manner of a Sophoclean tragedy.

It seemed preferable to chart the mundane details of the life of a reasonably affluent London housewife who was also an urban professional, and to pretend that nothing sinister lay in store for her, rather than to distort our perspective on the case by setting the whole life in the context of violent death.

The "plot" of the narrative of *Criminal Justice* consisted in minutely detailing the course of Edith Thompson's life in order to enlist the reader's empathy, to get the reader to identify with or at least understand (while not necessarily condoning) Edith Thompson's every move. Weis was greatly assisted in the task of charting Edith's movements by Edith Thompson's own practice in her letters of recreating her days in a kind of subdocumentary writing, as a way of tying Bywaters to her (or attempting to do so). In Twining's earlier analysis of Edith's letters, he quotes a law student's saying that "If you can analyze Edith Thompson's prose you can analyze anything" to describe the problems posed by what Twining perceives to be the "stream-of-consciousness quality" of her letters. Coming to these letters from a slightly different tradition, Weis does not quite take this view, although it is certainly the case that the letters often ramble, freely associate, and at times seem to be the product of an undisciplined imagination. On the other hand, the same prose which can be described as "deathly" by Twining often sounds colorful notes that more refined and self-conscious writers in the period do not always achieve in spite of striving to do so.

The main object of the first part of *Criminal Justice* was therefore to make Edith Thompson's life happen as a life, and it is this which decided Weis to write the bulk of the book in the present tense. There were a number of reasons for this, but the clinching one was the extent to which the narrative use of the past tense forecloses reality, whereas the use of the present, in theory at least, leaves everything open: The future is never less anticipated than in a present-tense narrative, whereas in a past-tense story the future has already happened at the time of its telling. To that extent the biographical narrative proposes a "fiction" of the case which, in its own terms, agrees with Twining's strategic emphasis on the need to assess the evidence in the case independently from its interpretations in court.

It is of course true that the story of Edith Thompson had emphatically happened by the time *Criminal Justice* was written in the 1980s (and to that extent, the use of the present tense might be seen to be a sleight of hand), but it would *not* have happened for an audience of the book. The intention behind the book was twofold:

(a) to clear Edith Thompson's name through putting her case to the jury of a contemporary British audience, and (b) to convince the Home Secretary of the day that a posthumous pardon would be appropriate. The use of tense could therefore be interpreted as a legitimate forensic strategy.

Weis's training as a textual scholar provided some of the pasting-up and collating expertise required for documenting Edith Thompson's life from sources. This involved the sorting of Edith's published (and some of her unpublished) correspondence into a correct chronological order, reading the novels she read, and finally collating all this with further information gleaned from several newspapers (including her own preferred *Daily Sketch*) to form a *comprehensive diary*. Eventually Weis was in a position to tell, almost to the hour, what Edith was doing at particular times on any given day. This allowed Weis to decode much of Edith's rhetoric (particularly as it relates to her sexuality) and to formulate the kind of contextual hypotheses which he deemed to be crucial for refuting a number of charges relating to incitement that counted heavily against Edith at her trial.

THE LETTERS

If the case in law against Edith Thompson was based on the evidence provided by the letters, then it should have stood to reason that *all* the letters ought to have been submitted, that counsel for the defense ought to have either (a) insisted on their inclusion from the start, or (b) demanded that the trial judge set the record straight on the Solicitor-General's prevarication when he falsely claimed that crucial evidence about the time and place of the actual murder was to be found in the letters.

The jury, who had access to only half the evidence appealed to, could not know that this was not the case. If anything, they may well have been suspicious of the contents of the withheld letters, since it was the defense who elected not to submit them. Whatever finer legal points were involved in the end, the jury's opinion was greatly influenced by the correspondence; and thirty years after the events the foreman of the jury described their contents as "nauseous" and noted that "Mrs Thompson's letters were her own condemnation."

It was Weis's firm belief that the microcosmic account of Edith Thompson's life would assist in the search for the "truth" about the death of Percy Thompson, and that Edith Thompson's innocence could be proven best through the telling of the story of her life and milieu and through a scrutiny of her fantasies—particularly where those can be measured against texts which inspired them, in this case romantic novels from the period.

THE FANTASY THEORY

Twining notes that Weis's study is largely predicated on the fantasy theory. This is a fair assessment. It need not, however, open the study to the charge of evolving in an area where the writer could therefore be thought to be selecting at random what he likes (if it assists Edith's case) and discarding what he dislikes (material prejudicial to Edith's innocence). It is of course the case that Weis never appears to entertain the idea of Edith Thompson's guilt, and that this certainly results in a number of shortcuts through some of the evidence that is open to hostile interpretation. Weis's defense against this would be to maintain that the burden of proof did (and does) rest with the prosecution, and that the Crown never produced the conclusive evidence that would have convicted Edith Thompson in a fairer trial.

Twining also stresses the widely held view (by Marshall Hall, among others) that if Edith had not taken the stand she almost certainly would not have been convicted of the charges brought against her, notwithstanding strong suspicions on the other counts which were not pursued. In view of this it does not seem entirely illogical of Weis "to suggest that the harmless elements [in Edith's letters] are true but the damaging ones are fantasy."[64] If Edith Thompson was innocent, then that would logically be the case: The potentially damaging passages could be innocently explained, and the innocent ones would be either true or untrue, but it would not greatly matter.

Furthermore, Weis believes that the narrative method can contextually prove that "the most damaging part of all Edith's correspondence," the Marconigram,[65] is open to an innocent reading as long as the principle of the presumption of innocence is respected.

THE TEAROOM AND THE MARCONIGRAM

Before proceeding to the Marconigram,[66] it is worth turning to the tearoom passage (exhibit 60; see appendix 2), which Weis analyzes at some length,[67] as does Twining.

The two different approaches here coincide in their conclusion, but arrive there from very different directions. Weis was concerned to establish that the (potentially) most incriminating sentence in the letter, "Don't forget what we talked in the Tea Room, I'll still risk and try if you will," referred to a conversation five days before the murder. The Crown suggested that it took place a mere twenty-four hours before the murder with a view presumably to linking the sentence temporally, and therefore, in the minds of the jury, causally, to the murder of October 3.

Twining rightly queries the usefulness of Weis's attempt to restore the time span to its true chronology because the two lengths of time are not ultimately different enough to matter. Instead Twining demolishes, by a closely argued *textual* rather than contextual analysis, the probative value to the prosecution of Edith's statement. The judge did not, however, have such scruples and bluntly told the jury that the "what" in the sentence referred to "whether it was better to kill Percy by means of poison or a dagger."[68] Here again it seems that the judge's anxieties and Weis's almost coincide, albeit from opposite ends of the spectrum.

It is a measure of the difference between the approaches of Weis and Twining that Edith's question about the Marconigram (exhibit 17; see appendix 1), starting with "Don't keep this piece," should be found so damaging by some (the Crown, the judge, Twining, and—Twining reports—students in law classes), but dismissed as fantasy by Weis.[69]

Twining's particular objection to Weis's treatment of the passage is Weis's refusal to entertain the idea that this passage ought to be treated differently from any other of the various passages in Edith's correspondence that recklessly touch on the idea of murder. Weis fully accepts Twining's stricture that a blurring of fact and fiction, when it relates specifically to the death of a spouse, "is not so very common, and the coincidence of harmless fantasizing about such a death with the actual murder of the recipient of such fantasies is unique in my experience." The fact that it is unique in our experience (though probably not in life) does not by itself invalidate Weis's point, but it stresses the challenge that the defense faced in court.

The reason Weis passed over this passage was not so much because of "soft"-fact speculation, but because the hardest of all facts unambiguously seemed to him to argue against taking the passage as conclusive evidence of an attempt on Percy Thompson's life by Edith. The "hardest" fact here refers to Sir Bernard Spilsbury's autopsy report (independently corroborated by a second Home Office pathologist) that there were no traces of poison or glass in Percy's body. To argue, as the Crown did, that the passage is "full of crime," flies in the face of the pathologists' reports (there was no poison, no glass, and no attempt even to use gas, which is mentioned here as a *possibility*).

Within days of sending the Marconigram letter, Edith wrote again and, presumably to protest her good faith, announced that she had now "used the light bulb three times but the third time—he found a piece—so I've given it up—until you come." The "light bulb" in question was the "electric light globe" that she referred to in the last sentence of the Marconigram letter.

It seems to Weis that although one may well be legitimately troubled by the business of "Dan," wonder about the "Sunday morning escapade," and be dismayed by Edith's dallying with fanciful ideas of murder, these are presumably fanciful in law, unless the concept of incitement makes no allowance for a period of "penitence" in the five-month gap between the letter and the murder; and incitement would legally (presumably) be the only way the Marconigram would come into play, since the methods of killing discussed here were scientifically proven not to have been carried into effect. It seems to Weis, as narrative biographer, that the Marconigram is an instance where hard facts bear out soft facts such as psychologically speculative interpretations.

That Edith Thompson was economical with the truth is undeniable. That she was capable of embellishing her untruths with shrewd authenticating touches is also true, and Weis at least suspects that Percy's rather colorful claim in the Marconigram to be "like a cat with nine lives" may well be attributed to him by his wife.

From time to time in this essay Weis's and the judge's responses to the case have been seen to share common ground. Although this is a state of affairs that originally rather discomfited Weis, Twining's pointing this out helped to shape the approach of the preceding pages.

The judge in the case has received a poor press, not least for his notorious antifeminism, which suggests that Edith suffered twice at the hands of male ideas about gender, due to the judge's misogynism and the Home Secretary's alleged feminism. More to the point perhaps may be the fact that the judge's intellectual and legal limitations led him to simplify the facts for the lay jury too crudely, although a careful perusal of his summing up does not quite bear this out. However, it is almost certainly the case that his blunt pro-

III

Reconstructing the Truth about Edith Thompson

nouncements on sordid affairs and marriage, along with his clear moral disapproval, carried more weight than his ultra-fair legal point about the time and place of the murder as explained above.

The jury, Weis would submit, listened to the facts, their interpretations, and the law. A combination of all three could be expected to sway them, but it would appear that in the end it was the immorality of the letters which above all convicted Edith Thompson. The defense's repeated attempts to refocus the case away from damaging moral considerations failed. It probably had as much chance of succeeding as judges' directions have when they instruct juries to "un-hear" a piece of counsel's strategically planted indiscretion. Once the damage is done it cannot be undone. It was Weis's conviction that if the truth about Edith Thompson were to be told within the boundaries of the possible, it would inevitably become invasive and intrusive and would have to move far beyond the legal hard evidence that was used at her trial. A deeper knowledge of the law would have been helpful. It would have resulted in a better, and a more dispassionate book.

Conclusion
William Twining and René Weis

In this chapter Twining and Weis address the same question of Edith Thompson's innocence and wrongful conviction. Their approaches differ widely. Twining rigorously and exclusively focuses his analysis on the evidence provided by the trial record, while Weis, using the same material, contextualizes it in the interest of a biographical history.

The logical criteria by which evidence is evaluated ought to be the same in both cases. The fact that through a study of the same evidence Twining and Weis arrived independently at the same conclusion on the question of guilt, and by such different routes, would appear to bear this out. That is, it could be claimed that the Wigmorean jurist and the literary biographer *demonstrate* that Edith Thompson was wrongly convicted, just as two independent experts, be they pathologists or statisticians, might. Although Twining and Weis differ in some of their microscopic analyses, as for example in the readings of the Marconigram, the overall picture is one of broadly based agreement. They draw the same conclusions from a substantial body of disparate raw material.

Even at the level of strategy where the gulf between the two authors seems to be widest, they share some common ground of history and narrative. Whereas Weis avails himself of a number of rhetorical devices that are commonly associated with storytelling, such as the manipulation of tense, Twining also tells a "story," as indeed did the Crown and the defense at the original trial. The filleting of the available material by both parties at the trial, with a view to constructing coherent cases, is echoed by Twining's focus on selected key issues, such as the knife, the Marconigram, and the meaning of the word "what." The jurist's story is differently conceived, but its moral is the same as the Shakespearean's.

Appendix 1
Exhibit 17: Enclosure in letter dated 1/4/22[70]

Dont keep this piece.

About the Marconigram—do you mean one saying Yes or No, because I shant send it darlint I'm not going to try any more until you come back.

I made up my mind about this last Thursday.

He was telling his Mother etc. the circumstances of my "Sunday morning escapade" and he puts great stress on the fact of the tea tasting bitter "as if something had been put in it" he says. Now I think whatever else I try it in again will still taste bitter—he will recognise it and be more suspicious still and if the quantity is still not successful—it will injure any chance I may have of trying when you come home.

Do you understand? I thought a lot about what you said of Dan.

Darlint, don't trust him—I don't mean don't tell him anything because I know you never would—What I mean is don't let him be suspicious of you regarding that—because if we were successful in the action—darlint circumstances may afterwards make us want many friends—or helpers and we must have no enemies—or even people that know a little too much. Remember the saying, "A little knowledge is a dangerous thing."

Darlint we'll have no one to help us in the world *now* and we musnt make enemies unnecessarily.

He says—to his people—he fought and fought with himself to keep conscious—"I'll never die, except naturally—I'm like a cat with nine lives" he said and detailed to them an occasion when he was young and nearly suffocated by gas fumes.

I wish we had not got electric light—it would be easy.

I'm going to try the glass again occasionally—when it is safe Ive got an electric light globe this time.

Appendix 2
Exhibit 60: Plain envelope[71]

Darlingest lover of mine, thank you, thank you, oh thank you a thousand times for Friday—it was lovely—its always lovely to go out with you.

And then Saturday—yes I did feel happy—I didn't think a teeny bit about anything in this world, except being with you—and all Saturday evening I was thinking about you—I was just with you in a big arm chair in front of a great big fire feeling all the time how much I had won—cos I have darlint, won such a lot—it feels such a great big thing to me sometimes—that I can't breathe.

When you are away and I see girls with men walking along together—perhaps they are acknowledged sweethearts—they look so ordinary then I feel proud—so proud to think and feel that you are my lover and even tho' not acknowledged I can still hold you—just with a tiny 'hope.'

Darlint, we've said we'll always be Pals haven't we, shall we say we'll always be lovers—even tho' secret ones, or is it (this great big love) a thing we can't control—dare we say that—I think I will dare. Yes I will 'I'll always love you'—if you are dead—if you have left me even if you don't still love me, I always shall you.

Your love to me is new, it is something different, it is my life and if things should go badly with us, I shall always have this past year to look back upon and feel that 'Then I lived' I never did before and I never shall again.

Darlingest lover, what happened last night? I don't know myself I only know how I felt—no not really how I felt but how I could feel—if time and circumstances were different.

It seems like a great welling up of love—of feeling—of inertia, just as if I am wax in your hands—to do with as you will and I feel that if you do as you wish I shall be happy, its physical purely and I can't really describe it—but you will understand darlint wont you? You said you knew it would be like this one day—if it hadn't would you have been disappointed. Darlingest when you are rough, I go dead—try not to be please.

The book is lovely—it's going to be sad darlint tho', why can't life go on happy always?

I like Clarie—she is so natural so unworldly.

Why aren't you an artist and I as she is—I feel when I am reading frightfully jealous of her—its a picture darlint, just how I did once picture that little flat in Chelsea—why can't he go on loving her always—why are men different—I am right when I say that love to a man is a thing apart from his life—but to a woman it is her whole existence.

───────

I tried so hard to find a way out of tonight darlingest but he was suspicious and still is—I suppose we must make a study of this deceit for some time longer. I hate it. I hate every lie I have to tell to see you—because lies seem such small mean things to attain such an object as ours. We ought to be able to use great big things for a great big love like ours. I'd love to be able to say 'I'm going to see my lover tonight.' If I did he would prevent me—there would be scenes and he would come to 168 and interfere and I couldn't bear that—I could be beaten all over at home and still be defiant—but at 168 it's different. It's my living—you wouldn't let me live on him would you and I shouldn't want to—darlint its funds that are our stumbling block—until we have those we can do nothing. Darlingest find me a job abroad. I'll go tomorrow and not say I was going to a soul and not have one little regret. I said I wouldn't think—that I'd try to forget—circumstances—Pal, help me to forget again—I have succeeded up to now—but its thinking of tonight and tomorrow when I can't see you and feel you holding me.

Darlint—do something tomorrow night will you? something to make you forget. I'll be hurt I know, but I want you to hurt me— I do really—the bargain now, seems so one sided—so unfair— but how can I alter it?

───────

About the watch—I didn't think you thought more of that— how can I explain what I did feel? I felt that we had parted—you weren't going to see me—I had given you something to remind you of me and I had purposely retained it. If I said 'come for it' you would—but only the once and it would be as a pal, because you would want me so badly at times—that the watch would help you not to feel so badly and if you hadn't got it—the feeling would be so great—it would conquer you against your will.

Darlint do I flatter myself when I think you think more of the watch than of anything else. That wasn't a present—that was something you asked me to give you—when we decided to be *pals* a sort of sealing of the compact. I couldn't afford it then, but immediately I could I did. Do you remember when and where we were when you asked me for it? If you do tell me, if you don't, forget I asked.

How I thought you would feel about the watch, I would feel about something I have.

It isn't mine, but it belongs to us and unless we were differently situated than we are now, I would follow you everywhere—until you gave it to me back. He's still well—he's going to gaze all day long at you in your temporary home—after Wednesday.

Don't forget what we talked in the Tea Room, I'll still risk and try if you will—we only have 3¾ years left darlingest.

Try & help

PEIDI.

Notes

1. Both essays were published in William Twining, *Rethinking Evidence* (Evanston, Ill.: Northwestern University Press, 1994 [hereafter RE]), chaps. 8 and 9. Parts 1 and 2 of this paper are abbreviated versions of the originals. A great deal of detail, including bibliographical material, has been omitted, but the original text is reproduced almost verbatim except where otherwise indicated.

2. Arthur Koestler, *Reflections on Hanging* (London: Victor Gollancz, 1956).w

3. Filson Young, ed., *The Trial of Frederick Bywaters and Edith Thompson*, part of the "Notable British Trials" series (Edinburgh: W. Hodge and Co., 1923).

4. René Weis, *Criminal Justice: The True Story of Edith Thompson* (London: Hamish Hamilton, 1988; London, Penguin, 2001), hereafter CJ.

5. I.e., before the publication of CJ.

6. In my experience, law students find it difficult to separate the original event (in this case the killing of Percy) from the subsequent legal proceedings dealing with that event. Hence they sometimes conflate two separate ideas involved in a miscarriage of justice: the fairness of the proceedings and the strength of the evidence about the original event. There is a third intermediate meaning: Given the evidence before the court, the decision to convict or acquit was not justified. For example, some lawyers believe that O. J. Simpson was as a matter of historical fact guilty of the murder of Nicole Brown Simpson and Ronald Goldman, but that the evidence adduced at the criminal trial did not satisfy the standard of proof beyond reasonable doubt. Many laypersons find it difficult to understand how Simpson could be acquitted in the criminal case but be found to have committed the murder in the subsequent civil action. Surely one of the verdicts must have been wrong. From a legal point of view, it may be that both verdicts were correct: The standards of proof are different, the evidence adduced was

not identical, and it is the duty of the jury to decide on the evidence presented to them. In respect of Edith Thompson we are concerned here with her historical guilt independently of what happened at the trial, which is mainly relevant as a *source* of evidence—for example, Edith's and Freddy's evidence on oath.

7. What has to be proved by the prosecution in a criminal case is prescribed by substantive law. For example, the law of murder prescribes the ingredients of the crime, each of which has to be proved beyond reasonable doubt. The facts to be proved are variously known as "material facts," "facts in issue," or facta probanda. In the present context, these terms are interchangeable.

8. "You will not convict her unless you are satisfied that she and he agreed that this man should be murdered when he could be, and she knew he was going to do it, and directed him to do it, and by arrangement between them he was doing it. If you are not satisfied of that you will acquit her; if you are it will be your duty to convict her" (Young, *Trial*, 133–55, esp. 155). Cf. p. 127, where Mr. Justice Shearman interrupted the closing speech for the prosecution to say, in respect of incitement, "It is necessary, of course, to be careful of words, and I do not feel inclined to take the matter at large." In the context this was interpreted by the Solicitor-General to mean that the "persuasion" lasted right up to the murder (128), but both gloss over the distinction between planning this attack and killing when an opportunity arose.

9. For some legal doubts about the meaning of "incitement" at the time, which further complicate the analysis, see RE, 272–3.

10. At several points the Solicitor-General made it clear that either incitement or conspiracy was sufficient (e.g., Young, *Trial*, 17, 132–3).

11. On the distinction between "stories" and "theories" and their relationship, see RE, 222–5.

12. See, generally, Richard Gaskins, *Burdens of Proof in Modern Discourse* (New York: Yale University Press, 1992).

13. One may note in passing that there is a possible countertheory to the broken chain argument—what one might call the unexploded bomb theory. Briefly, this theory holds that, even if only the early letters are evidence against Edith of conspiracy or incitement or attempted murder, and that at the time Freddy did not consciously take them seriously, nevertheless they had the effect both of sowing the idea and working on his emotions at the level of his subconscious so that he was like an unexploded bomb which was detonated in a moment of stress some time later. This theory raises some interesting questions about Edith's legal responsibility, if it is correct; but since it was neither raised at the trial nor has it been seriously canvassed in the literature, I shall not pursue it further here.

14. J. Wigmore, *The Science of Judicial Proof: As Given by Logic, Psychology, and General Experience, and Illustrated in Judicial Trials*, 3rd ed. (Boston: Little, Brown, 1937), 858.

15. Young, *Trial*, xvii; see now CJ, passim.

16. See n. 13.

17. Young, *Trial*, n. 110.

18. See p. CJ, 171–2.

19. The most relevant shared values are that we are both opposed to the death penalty (Weis emphasizes that his book is not primarily a polemic against capital punishment; CJ, xii). We would firmly uphold the criminal standard of proof beyond reasonable doubt and have a general sympathy for Edith.

20. CJ, xi.

21. W. Twining and D. Miers, *How To Do Things with Rules*, 3rd ed. (London: Weidenfeld and Nicolson, 1991), 64–74, 185–9. (Note that there is a more recent 4th ed. of this book published by Butterworths in 1999.)

22. On the dangers of generalizing "about the historian" see RE, chap. 4. Twining's standpoint in "Anatomy" could be characterized as that of a student of Wigmorean analysis who is adopting the vantage point of a historian (i.e., operating in a context of free proof) and considering the question, "Was Edith guilty as charged?" Weis adopts a similar vantage point with regard to this question, but without the explicit methodological concern.

23. On sources, see CJ, x and 313–6. By comparison, Twining's efforts hardly count as historical research. He has read most of the secondary literature (but only a few newspaper reports), and he has focused almost exclusively on the published versions of the proceedings (trial and appeal) and of Edith's letters. He has had access to some additional primary and secondary legal sources, but agrees with Weis's judgment that most of the prior secondary literature (with one possible exception—Fenton Bresler's *Reprieve* [London: Harrap, 1965]) adds little to Filson Young's volume. He also agrees that "[t]he most authentic tribute to Edith Thompson remains F. Tennyson Jesse's *A Pin To See the Peepshow*" (London: Heinemann, 1934) (CJ, 320), although he is more skeptical than Weis about its closeness to the likely historical truth. The potential significance of some of Weis's new evidence will be considered below. Weis relies heavily on Spilsbury's testimony (and notes) to support the thesis that if Edith had tried to poison Percy that fact would have emerged in the postmortem (CJ, 215–6, 223, 226–7). He does not consider Bresler's argument that Spilsbury's case card contains the statement "no substance found to account for the fatty degeneration of organs." This implies that Spilsbury suspected poison. Twining is skeptical of Bresler's thesis and, on the basis of the "broken chain theory," argues that even if Edith had really attempted to murder Percy this would not lend other than indirect and weak support to the prosecution's case on the first indictment. The proposition that Spilsbury suspected poison would not, however, be entirely irrelevant, for it could be argued that Edith had attempted to murder Percy because (a) she wished Percy's death; (b) she was capable of intent to murder; or (c) there was a continuing series of attempts to murder Percy (see p. 74, above). Browne and Tullett (1951, 10) suggest that Spilsbury believed Edith to be innocent (259, 267).

24. CJ, 316.

25. Young, *Trial*, 133 ff., discussed above, p. 72.

26. CJ, ix–x, 215–6. Edith's supporters believed that Spilsbury's testimony would be sufficient to exonerate her (e.g., 216, 226–7, 271). Even if this testimony is given the most favorable interpretation, however, it does not on its own destroy either the conspiracy or incitement theories.

27. RE, 276. Some support for the exploding bomb hypothesis can be found in CJ's sources, e.g., 39–40 (impulsive action of Bywaters in jumping ship); 177–87; 289 ("I lost my temper. . . . I just went blank and killed him"—Bywaters to his mother just before his execution).

28. RE, 264. Cf. Weis on Shearman (CJ, 246), the jury (247–8), the Court of Criminal Appeal (260–1), et passim.

29. See especially CJ, x, 58–9, 104–8, 112–3, 141, 148.

30. Especially on *The Fruitful Vine* (see CJ, 147–50) and *Bella Donna* (see CJ, 140–1). These were romantic novels written by Robert Hichens in 1911 and 1909, respectively. They were not generally perceived as trashy at the time, notwith-

standing the judge's view of them. Henry James, for example, admired Hichens, and the novels were regularly reviewed in prime spots in the *Times*.

31. It would still be necessary to show that these communications were made with criminal intent.

32. Exhibits 15a, 15b, 15c, 15d, 20a, 21a, 22a, 22b, 55a. Those relating to the death of the parson, Henry George Bolding (15a, 15b), had a local interest because suspicion fell on Dr. Preston Wallis, a ship's surgeon, who had lived at Manor Park and treated Edith (CJ, 4, 83–4, 89). The others do not have such specific explanations but need to be set in the context of a significantly greater number of clippings dealing with other topics. The innocent explanation of the Wallis clippings might be challenged by Edith's comment: "It might prove interesting, darlint I want to have you only I love you so much try and help me Peidi" (Young, *Trial*, 171, exhibit 15); the same letter includes two clippings about poisoned chocolates being sent to the vice chancellor of Oxford (15c). See also n. 55.

33. Exhibit 15. Weis acknowledges that in this letter Edith hints how easy it would be to murder her husband (84–5), but dismisses her remarks as "silly."

34. Weis's version of events includes the thesis that Edith twice became pregnant by Freddy, she suffered a miscarriage, and that some of the passages about poisons or medicines refer to abortifacients (68 ff., 101–2, 124). If these interpretations are true this disposes of more sinister readings of some, but not all, of the early letters. The arguments for and against Weis's readings are too complex to deal with here.

35. See n. 31.

36. Cf. Weis's use of the fact/fantasy theme, discussed at page 97.

37. Chap. 6.

38. E.g., CJ, 75–8, 110–1, 132, 136, 143, 161.

39. The argument for excluding some of the early letters was put by Curtis-Bennett (Young, *Trial*, 3–6). This was rejected by Mr. Justice Shearman and by the Court of Criminal Appeal. The lord chief justice pointed out, rightly in Twining's view, that there was "more than one ground on which the use of these letters could be justified" (259). It is a matter for speculation whether a court today would be willing to exclude some of the early letters on the basis that their prejudicial effect outweighed their probative value (see Police and Criminal Evidence Act, 1984, s. 78).

40. On the second indictment see Young, *Trial*, 296. Edith seems most vulnerable on the second and third counts (Soliciting to Murder and Inciting to Commit a Misdemeanour), especially in respect of exhibit 15 (February 10, 1922), and exhibit 17 (April 1[?], 1922), especially the "Marconigram" passage, discussed below (317).

41. Exhibit 60, quoted in full in Young, *Trial*, 297.

42. CJ, 168–72, 241, 246–7.

43. Ibid., 171–2.

44. Ibid., 172.

45. Weis also makes some valid points about more serious misuses by the Crown of other passages in exhibit 60 and of other evidence, e.g., CJ, 171, 241, 245–6.

46. Ibid., 174–87.

47. Ibid., 179. The fact that the sheath was not recovered may have contributed to the impression that this was a "dreadful weapon" (CJ, 207).

48. Ibid., 174.

49. Ibid., 177–8.
50. Young, *Trial*, 70.
51. *CJ*, 178–9, 206–7, 224.
52. Ibid., xi.
53. "Lawyers' Stories," *RE*, chapter 7.
54. Exhibit 17 was dated April 1 (Young, *Trial*, 179). Weis convincingly argues that it is more likely to be April 10 (personal communication) because the earlier date does not fit in with his reconstruction of events of this period. The letter is prima facie one of the most damaging to Edith, so incorrectly dating it is particularly significant.
55. Weis points out that quinine was considered an abortifacient, but not a poison, although Edith may not have known this (*CJ*, 86, 92). Another possibility is that "quinine" was a code word for something more sinister, but this is conjectural. I find it difficult to make sense of the quinine passages.
56. *CJ*, 105.
57. Ibid., 290 (cf. 312).
58. See Young, *Trial*, 95–6, where the most damaging passage in Edith's cross-examination occurs:

> "It would be so easy darlint—if I had things—I do hope I shall."
> What would be easy?—I was asking or saying it would be better if I had things as Mr. Bywaters suggested I should have.
> What would be easy?—To administer them as he suggested.
> "I do hope I shall." Was that acting or was that real?—That was acting for him.
> You were acting to Bywaters that you wished to destroy your husband's life?—I was.
> By MR. JUSTICE SHEARMAN—One moment, I do not want to be mistaken. Did I take you down rightly as saying, "I wanted him to think I was willing to take my husband's life"?—I wanted him to think I was willing to do what he suggested.
> That is to take your husband's life?—Not necessarily.
> *Cross-examination continued*—To injure your husband at any rate?—To make him ill.
> What was the object of making him ill?—I had not discussed the special object.
> What was in your heart the object of making him ill? So that he should not recover from his heart attacks?—Yes, that was certainly the impression, yes.
>
> The Court adjourned.

59. See Edith's admission above, n. 42. Weis places great weight on Spilsbury's pathological evidence that there was no evidence of poison having been administered to Percy. Assuming that this is correct, this does not dispose of the hypothesis that Edith was claiming to have been trying to poison him in order to persuade Freddy to "risk and try" too (60, 63, 79, 94). Weis does not deny this.
60. Young, *Trial*, 183 and testimony of Edith and Freddy. It seems that Weis does not doubt that these incidents occurred, but gives them an innocent interpretation.
61. *CJ*, 105.
62. E.g., 104–5.

63. CJ, 293.
64. Above, 104.
65. Above, 102.
66. Young, Trial, 183.
67. CJ, 168–72.
68. Above, 90.
69. CJ, 105.
70. From Young, Trial, 183.
71. Ibid., 214–5. The date of this letter is stated in Trial to be October 3, 1922, the day before the murder. The prosecution suggested that the meeting in the tearoom took place on Monday, October 2. Weis (CJ, 171–2) argues convincingly that it was written before 5:00 P.M. on the Monday and that the meeting in the tearoom took place on Friday, September 29.

3 The Last Wedge

M. J. Geller

I HAVE OFTEN HEARD it said, although I cannot document it, that when the early pilgrims first came to America the suggestion was made that in the New World—the New Canaan, where religion could flourish—the official language should be Hebrew rather than English. I cannot vouch for the truth of this suggestion, but it is useful speculation for us nevertheless. Can you imagine that I would have moved to England from America as a native speaker of Hebrew? That Mark Twain and Thomas Jefferson would have written in Hebrew? That Duke Ellington, James Cagney, and Marilyn Monroe would have spoken Hebrew? What a profound difference such a simple change in language would have made in our world. A change of language affects our politics, our identity, our alliances, and sometimes even our economic status and feelings of well-being.

Yet, how can this story possibly be true, since by the sixteenth century biblical Hebrew was technically a dead language? Hebrew had not been spoken for centuries, and even in Hellenistic Palestine, Hebrew was probably no longer spoken; Jesus, as we all know, spoke Aramaic, as did almost everyone else. This story raises in-

---

Editors' note: This chapter is the text of an inaugural lecture that Mark Geller, an Assyriologist, delivered at University College London in December 1994. That text was the "evidence" that Terence Anderson, a legal theorist, analyzed using a chart method of analysis developed within the discipline of law. In chapter 4, Professor Anderson describes the difficulties he encountered in conducting such a cross-disciplinary analysis and presents the products of that analysis and his comments (an "outsider's" comments) on the uses and limitations of that method of analysis outside the discipline of law. In the succeeding chapter, Professor Geller, the "insider," presents his view of and comments on the exercise.

triguing questions about how we define a dead language, and whether a language no longer spoken for centuries ought to be considered living or dead.

Languages can, as the epitaph says, be gone but not forgotten. I was always taught in school that Latin was a "dead language," but I know of some cardinals in the Vatican who might hotly dispute such an idea. They read Latin, they write Latin, they speak Latin. The language seems to be alive—perhaps not well, perhaps not even thriving, perhaps even arguably on its last legs—but still alive. Somewhere a scholar is burning the midnight oil poring over the old the classical texts and teaching them to his few students. This is an important process which must not be overlooked.

Death is not always what it seems—the heart may still be beating when the patient is brain dead. We can use this same analogy: The language is no longer being spoken, nor are new texts being written in it, but one can still read it; the heart is still beating, but the brainwaves are gone. *Death can be determined when the script or written form of the language can no longer be read.* This is the crucial difference: A language no longer spoken may still be legible to some few scholars, students, or priests who can read the script, but only when the script can no longer be read by anyone is the language really dead. This process may take longer than one thinks; languages can linger for quite a time. When the script of a language is no longer legible, however, nor the language spoken, a remarkable event unfolds—we witness the death of a civilization on the world stage, a clearly definable historical boundary which is almost impossible to determine by any other objective means.

A dead language can of course be resurrected through decipherment, which is what happened with the great civilizations in Sumer and Babylonia, as well as peoples such as the Hittites. Once the cuneiform scripts were lost, the process of decipherment took nearly two millennia to revive them, long after the civilizations were virtually forgotten. People have often asked why such complex societies did not survive. In fact, this is wrong; they did survive. The people survived, their cities and homes continued to be occupied, their history carried on in somewhat different forms, but in fact, they survived. So what did die? The answer is simple: Their script died. The ability to read their own classical literature was lost. A civilization is lost when its successors no longer have access to its ideas or written legacy, and hence to its language.

Let us clear up a misconception regarding scripts and alphabets. One script does not drive out another. People often think that somehow a simple calculation is made: This script has 600 characters, the other has 30 characters, we should all use the simpler script. It makes good sense; the simpler script is easier to learn to read and write, which means that more people can learn to read and write easily, that society will become more literate, and so on. If such were actually the case, the Chinese would certainly not be using their script today, some 3,500 years after the invention of the alphabet. Even closer to home, in the Near East itself (where the alphabet first appeared) it took nearly two millennia for the alphabet to replace the old syllabaries. The fact is, scripts usually change when one language replaces another. If the new language uses a different script, that script becomes dominant. Examples are numerous: Arabic replaced Aramaic and Greek and other languages in many parts of the Near East and Europe, and in those lands Arabic script was used universally. In the same way, the alphabet became popular in Mesopotamia when Aramaic was introduced as the popular and later official language of the region. At that point cuneiform gradually gave way to an alphabet, not as the victory of one script over another, but because Aramaic took the place of Akkadian.

Thus, our description of a dead civilization is based upon very specific symptoms. The script is dead. The country may still be inhabited by the same peoples, who now speak a different language, but they cannot read their ancient script. They may even speak the language and not be able to read its script. I was once in Turkey, visiting a small village on the Black Sea, and only I and one old man in the village square could read the inscription on the fountain. The Turkish inscription was written in Arabic script, but since the days of Ataturk no Turkish children had learned to read this script in school. Within two generations the access to their own literature was lost by peoples who still speak the language. There are inherent dangers in tampering with a nation's script, which is of course why the Chinese and Japanese and others cling to their traditional systems of writing and avoid the Latin alphabet; but my fear is that, with the increasing use of computers, this too might change.

Mesopotamian culture actually survived far longer than anyone has previously realized. Much depends, of course, on how one defines survival. In my opinion, *as long as a priest in a temple in a city in Mesopotamia could still read cuneiform script, the language was still alive.* This is a somewhat extreme position, of course; one priest cannot preserve an entire civilization, but we are defining here the minimal limits of survival. However few such priests there might have been, the process of survival of cuneiform lasted at least into the third century A.D. This statement runs counter to the impressions of almost any other Assyriologist one might meet. Most cuneiform specialists assume that the language had more or less died out by the second or first century B.C. They know about the latest tablet, an astronomical diary which is actually dated to 75 A.D., but that tablet is usually considered a curious aberration, and by 76 A.D. the language was surely dead and gone.

If we could only date our cuneiform tablets more precisely, we would probably be surprised at how late the cuneiform corpus really is. The scribe who actually wrote the astronomical diary tablet in 75 A.D. obviously knew what he was doing: He was composing his text in Akkadian. There are many other undated fragments in the British Museum which are written in a very late script, but how late? At the moment we have no way of knowing how many of these tablets could have come from 75 A.D., or even later. What is more, these late tablets are the last representatives of large archives of cuneiform tablets written and even composed in Hellenistic Babylonia. The Pergamon Museum in Berlin, for example, has an impressive collection of hymns and prayers in both Sumerian and Akkadian, reflecting the contemporary temple liturgy. The language of these tablets is extremely conservative and archaic, but the colophons of the text say they were written down (or copied) around 250 B.C. The collection is extensive, and points to a great flourishing of scribal and literary activity in this late period, when we least expect it. Historians will often refer to the use of Aramaic in Babylonia at the time, as well as to the increased Hellenization of the country under the Seleucids, but the texts indicate something else entirely—the tenacity of ancient Babylonian culture, as expressed in the continual use of cuneiform, especially in the temples.

More than ten years ago, I became interested in a small group of tablets known as *Graeco-Babyloniaca*. Most of the twenty or so examples of these tablets come from the British Museum, although there is also one in the Harvard Semitic Museum, one in Berlin, and one in St. Petersburg. These tablets are unique because they were all written with cuneiform on one side and in the Greek alphabet on the other side. The same text is repeated, written once in Sumerian or Akkadian, and on the reverse a transliteration is written in Greek letters (see fig. 3.1.) Note that this is a transliteration, not a translation. The Greek script was intended to show how the

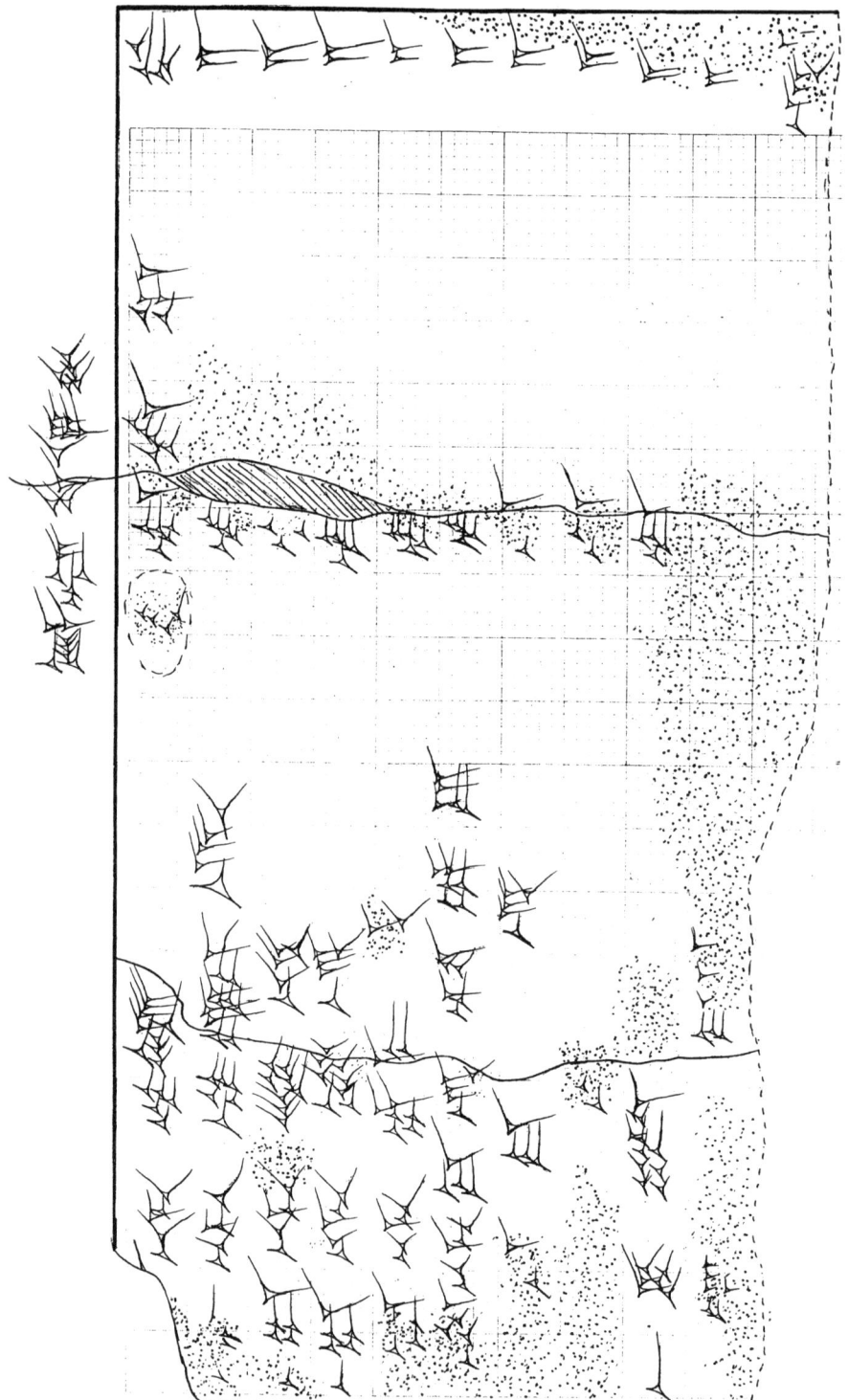

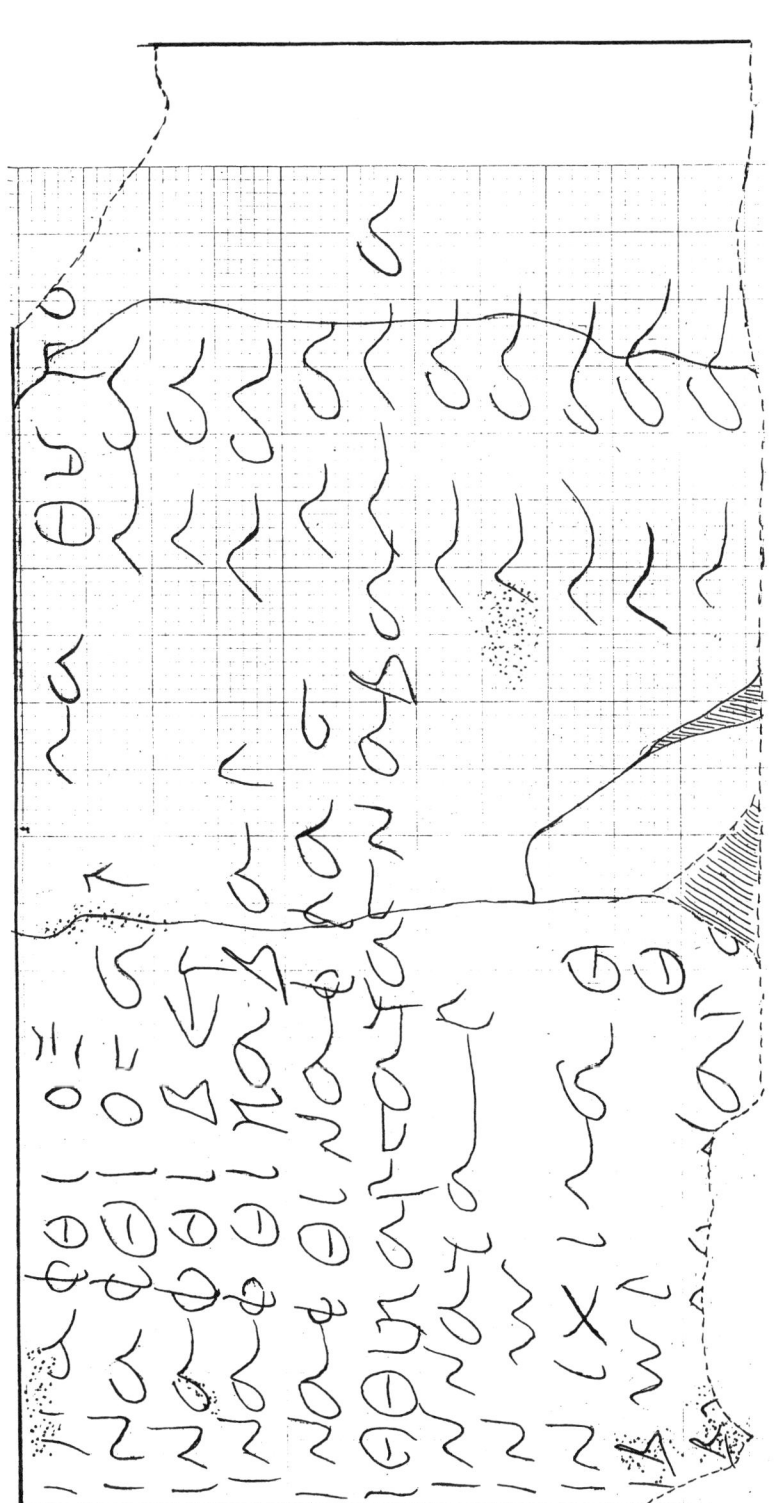

FIGURE 3.1. Samples of Graeco-Babyloniaca tablets: panel A (top), in cuneiform; panel B (bottom), in Greek

Note: This cuneiform tablet in the Harvard Semitic Museum dates from at least the second century A.D. and is probably the latest known tablet from the scribal school of Babylon. The text is an Akkadian incantation, written in cuneiform on the obverse and in Greek letters on the reverse.

Source: Drawn by the author. Previously published in the Zeitschrift für Assyriologie 73 (1983), p. 116.

cuneiform is to be read—probably read aloud. It is very similar to writing down in Latin letters the Kaddish, the memorial prayer in a synagogue, for the benefit of those who want to recite it but cannot read the Hebrew. These Graeco-Babyloniaca texts are striking, because they prove beyond any doubt that someone in Babylon in a very late period could still read Sumerian and Akkadian; this in itself is remarkable, since Sumerian by that time had not been spoken or used conversationally for some 2,000 years. Even Akkadian, the Semitic language of Mesopotamia, was most likely no longer spoken, but could still be read and understood.

So who wrote these tablets, and why? Either a Greek speaker who wanted to learn cuneiform wrote them, or a Babylonian speaker who wanted to learn Greek; there are good arguments on both sides.

The first thing noteworthy about our Graeco-Babyloniaca tablets is that they come from an ancient school. They are typical samples of the school curriculum, texts copied by Babylonian schoolboys. We have samples of a hymn to Shamash, or incantations, or Sumerian-Akkadian glossaries which are typical of school texts. In this case, a Babylonian student writes his lines on the back of his tablet—a sort of crib sheet, just as students today would make when preparing for classes in Akkadian or Sumerian. Our Babylonian student, however, writes only a transliteration—no translation. The Mesopotamian schools, in fact, were always translating, usually from Sumerian into Akkadian, but of the few scraps of Graeco-Babyloniaca we find, none is translated into Greek. There is no evidence here that anyone is learning Greek from these tablets.

The second possibility is that a Greek speaker is learning cuneiform. Here we have the evidence of the script itself to help us. The cuneiform on these tablets looks exactly the same as on school texts written as far back as the Late Babylonian period, from around 600 B.C. Although our knowledge of cuneiform paleography is still at a relatively primitive stage, we can detect certain earlier or later features in the cuneiform writing of the Seleucid period as distinct from the Persian period. The cuneiform writings on these school texts are exact copies of tablets from earlier periods, much like those medieval scribes in Europe made of earlier manuscripts. There is no suggestion that there is anything at all unusual about the handwriting on the Graeco-Babyloniaca tablets: The cuneiform looks the same as that of any other Late Babylonian school text, and if one had only the obverse of the tablet surviving without the Greek, one would not really know how very late the tablet was. We cannot say, then, that a Greek scribe was taking rudimentary lessons in cuneiform, because the Akkadian appears to be the same as for any other Babylonian pupil. There is no obvious reason that the need for transliteration into Greek script ought to have arisen during a period of both literary and administrative scribal activity. Never mind whether the scribe may have spoken Aramaic to his children or Greek to his tax official.

One other interesting feature of the Graeco-Babyloniaca tablets is the system of transcribing cuneiform into Greek: The very same system of transliteration was used by the church father Origen to transliterate Hebrew and Aramaic into Greek in the third century A.D. Origen's Hexapla was a monumental six-column tome, incorporating a transliteration of the Hebrew Bible into Greek along with several competing translations. Our Graeco-Babyloniaca tablets suggest that Origen's system of transliteration was inherited intact from Babylonia. However, it is worth remembering Origen's dates—he flourished in the mid–third century A.D., when cuneiform may still have been alive. The same patterns of transliteration were used both by Origen in Caesarea and priests in Babylon, and perhaps even at the same time.

These problems have been occupying me for the past several months. For those readers who do not know, I am spending the 1994–5 academic year on sabbatical at the Netherlands Institute for Advanced Studies in the Humanities (NIAS). I am pleased to report that although scholars come from as far away as Novosibirsk in Siberia, the only institution from outside Holland which has two visiting fellows is University College London. My other colleague at NIAS is William Twining from the UCL laws faculty. I have rather benefitted from his legal perspectives on these issues, and I have decided to approach the death of cuneiform as a type of coroner's inquest. We would like to know the time of death, and the cause of death, and whether anyone saw it happening.

I call as my first witness one Iamblichus, a writer who appears in The Library of Photius. Iamblichus was a Syrian who composed erotic tales in Greek in approximately 200 A.D. He was conversant with Babylonian magic but had been educated as a Greek. The scholiast add that Iamblichus "was a native Syrian, and not a Greek-Syrian, who knew Syriac, but also had a tutor who taught him the Babylonian language, as well as (Babylonian) customs and history." The source in Photius goes on to say that Iamblichus later continued his career as a writer in Rome, residing there in the reign of Septimus Severus, circa 200 A.D. So here we have an independent record of a Syrian who already speaks the *glossa Syriaca*, or the local dialect of Aramaic, and wishes to learn the *glossa Babyloniaca*, which in my view is most likely to be Akkadian, and during the reign of Septimus Severus. Who, though, was Iamblichus's tutor? How and where did he find a teacher for cuneiform in, say, the mid–second century A.D.? The scholiast adds this important detail: Iamblichus's teacher was a Babylonian who was taken prisoner by the Romans during Trajan's campaign there and later sold into slavery in Syria. The teacher had obviously got on well as a pedagogue or scribe in Syria, since he had been well educated. The scholiast is clear on this point: Iamblichus's teacher was skilled in "barbarian learning," having served as a royal scribe in Babylon. "Barbarian learning" never refers to Greek culture; Iamblichus's teacher was a scholar who most likely knew cuneiform. He had served as a royal scribe, being conversant in cuneiform, in Babylon in the beginning of the second century A.D. before being captured by the Romans, and he remembered cuneiform well enough to teach Iamblichus later in the century.

I would like to call as our next witness the Roman emperor Elagabalus. It is probably understating the case to suggest that this emperor was, by imperial standards, somewhat eccentric. Although actually named Varius Avitus Bassianus, he was widely known by the sobriquet "Elagabalus," a Semitic term for "Mountain God" which became applied to the sun god. Everything about the emperor Elagabalus was strange and foreign to the historians of the period, such as Cassius Dio and Herodian. As a priest of the sun god, Elagabalus insisted on wearing Syrian dress, which earned him the nickname "the Assyrian." Even more shocking to the Roman historians was the fact that Elagabalus lived with (or married) a vestal virgin; Dio quotes the emperor as saying, "I did it in order that godlike children might spring from me, the high priest, and from her, the high priestess."[1] From a Babylonian perspective, this behavior would be understandable; the traditional sacred marriage ceremony consisted of the Babylonian king's having sexual relations with a priestess to insure all manner of fertility in the land. We cannot extract very much from Elagabalus, except for this: that he was a Roman emperor in the third century A.D. who attracted critical comment from his contemporaries for introducing Near Eastern practices to the office of Roman emperor. The practices certainly hark back to Syria, but may also reflect Babylonian cults still currently being used in temples in Mesopotamia.

It is rather well documented by now that cults and shrines of Mesopotamian gods proliferated in neighboring Syria, to a surprising extent; paganism survived side by side with Christianity, even in a Christian city like Edessa, until at least the sixth century A.D. The cults of the Babylonian gods Bel and Belti, as well as Nabû, Nergal, Shamash, Tammuz, Nanai, and Adad, are all represented. The cults of Bel and Nabû were particularly strong in Palmyra: The temple of Bel was constructed in 32 A.D., roughly contemporary with a Nabû temple which was also built in Palmyra in the first century A.D. The cult of the moon god Sin was still prominent in Parthian Harran, as it had been already for many centuries. Hatra also demonstrates Babylonian influence in the cult, although the city became prominent only at the end of the second century A.D. Many of these same Babylonian gods occur in theophoric personal names in inscriptions and records from Syria in the second and third centuries A.D. Many such persons with good Babylonian names are known from Palmyra and Dura-Europus, Edessa, and elsewhere. Of course, this proves very little; Babylonian proper names do not prove that Babylonian culture still existed, because names can live on well after a civilization is gone. Nevertheless, it is not preposterous to think that Babylonian cults in Syria might flourish alongside the continuation of these cults in their original homes in Mesopotamia. However, we need to have a closer look at the evidence for cults in Mesopotamia itself in the third century A.D.

The crucial point is whether the temples in Babylon were still in use. The evidence of the earlier Seleucid period suggests that they may well have been. Not only were the older temples of the major cities of Babylon, Borsippa, Uruk, Kish, and Nippur still in use, but in Uruk two new large temple complexes were built in the Seleucid period, along traditional lines. These new building programs indicate enormous investment in Babylonian religion during the Hellenistic period, although it was previously thought that after the third century B.C. local religions were on the wane.

However, there is some important counterevidence based upon eyewitness testimony. Both the Roman emperors Trajan and Septimus Severus visited Babylonia, and it may be worth hearing what they had to say about it. When Trajan stayed in Babylon during his

Parthian campaign of 115 A.D., he found the city in ruins, and Septimius Severus reported in 199 A.D. that Babylon looked deserted; most historians consider these statements to be a confirmation of Babylon's early demise. This conclusion certainly runs counter to every argument we have been putting forward.

Such evidence from classical sources does require some rethinking. Although Trajan and Severus both viewed Babylon as a deserted ruin, it is conceivable that the very presence of the Roman legions may have persuaded the locals to abandon the city. Furthermore, the mud-brick fabric of Babylon may have been a great disappointment to a Roman general, accustomed to the more durable and ornate architecture of Hellenistic cities, built in stone. To an aristocratic Roman, Babylon may well have looked like a ruin (but not necessarily to one Dioskurides, who left a neatly engraved dedicatory Greek inscription on the amphitheater at Babylon in the late second century A.D.).

Some later evidence also suggests that the temple cults were still functioning in third-century A.D. Mesopotamia. We have a well-known group of important inscriptions from Assur, all in Aramaic. These dedicatory inscriptions give us some idea of the cults, since they are dedications to the local gods of Assur, including the chief god Assur himself and his spouse Sherua, as well as the gods also known from Syria in this period, such as Nannai, Nabû, and Nergal. The suggestion has been made that since so many of these votive plaques were offered during the first half of Nisan, they reflect the continuation of the Akitu ceremony, the Babylonian new year festival. The stone inscriptions offer hints and intimations at the continuation of the cult; the archaeological information supports Andrae's idea that the Assur temple in Assur was still in use throughout the Parthian period, at least up until the Sassanian conquest—but why, then, were no tablets found on the site? Surely, had the temple been in use—and these Aramaic votive inscriptions do exist—would it not be implied that Aramaic had fully replaced Akkadian as the language in the third-century Assur temple, thus demolishing our argument that cuneiform and the use of the temples went hand in hand? As you can expect, the answer is a firm "no."

Most of the Aramaic inscriptions found are written in stone, not on clay tablets; one group of images decorates a pithos or vase. The inscriptions are given by devotees of the cult—the "parishioners," in modern parlance. They no doubt spoke Aramaic. The tablets, which have not been found, would have represented the school of the temple, kept by the priests and not for the use of ordinary people. The fact that such an archive has not been found is not all that surprising; archaeology is a science guided by accident and coincidental discovery, and one never knows when a new archive or find of tablets will appear in Mesopotamia that overturns all of our previous theories and ideas. Incidentally, one fact which is easily missed is that one of the Assur temple inscriptions on a stele actually has the remnants of a cuneiform inscription on the edge of the stone, although it is apparently no longer legible. This particular statue is quite early, dating from 12 or 13 A.D., but the presence of a cuneiform inscription on the stele is nonetheless striking.

We must not ignore literary as well as inscriptional evidence during our inquest. For this we call upon the second century A.D. writer Lucian, who wrote in Greek about his native Babylonia. Lucian writes about a man named Menippos who wishes to travel to the Netherworld, presumably to learn about the future. Lucian himself may or may not have realized that his hero Menippos bears a good Akkadian name, already known centuries earlier in Babylonia: Mina-eppush, literally meaning, "What did I do (to the god)?" In Lucian's story, Menippos goes to Babylon to get charms and rites from a Magus to open the gates of Hades. Menippos soon finds the Chaldean Mithrobazarnes, a Magian with a good Persian name, who prescribes a complicated ritual for Menippos to get to the Netherworld and back again. First of all, he has Menippos bathe in the Euphrates for each of twenty-nine days, beginning with the new moon. On each occasion the Magian invokes demons in a language Menippos does not understand (which Lucian interprets as foreign-sounding meaningless words) and then spits in Menippos' face three times, after which they eat a simple vegetarian meal and sleep outside. After these preparations comes the final ritual: Menippos is bathed again, this time in the Tigris, and is purified from head to foot with torches and accompanying incantations. Menippos is dressed in a special costume consisting of a lion's skin, with a lyre and cap. After the purification, Menippos has to walk home backward, and not look at anyone he meets.

The importance of this passage is simply that Lucian is describing what appears to be an Akkadian purification ritual, known also from very late Seleucid-period texts. The process of bathing in the Tigris during the lunar month, and even of being dressed in a lion's skin and carrying a musical instrument for ritual purposes, is reminiscent of Akkadian ritual practice, which was normally accompanied by incantations and invocations to gods or demons. The other interesting details of the account, such as eating unusual foods of nuts and milk and sleeping out on the grass, not greeting anyone, and walking home backward, are also indicative of special rituals associated with the Netherworld. When the Mesopotamian hero Enkidu is preparing to go to the Netherworld, Gilgamesh warns him not to indulge in normal human behavior. Enkidu is warned against wearing a clean garment or shoes, carrying a staff, being anointed, or kissing his wife or son. Furthermore, the Netherworld was known in Mesopotamia as "the Place of No Return"; this name may have inspired the Magian to instruct Menippos to return home walking backward, as if not returning at all, and avoiding greeting anyone on the way. None of these details are to be found in either Homer or Vergil, but belong exclusively to the world of Mesopotamian ritual texts, such as Namburbî rituals.

Now, what of this Magian? We had better have a closer look at him and his fellow magi to see how they operated and from where they derived their authority and reputation. Tacitus associated the term "Magian" with Chaldeans, and Arthur Darby Nock makes one surprising comment about the magi: that there is "nothing to suggest that any of them were familiar with the Persian language."[2] So who were they? The overwhelming impression from all of our sources is how little we know about these Magi. Everything about them is slightly ambiguous; their very name, Magian or magus, can simply mean "magician," a term that equally applies to the famous first-century A.D. wonder-worker Apollonius of Tyana, who contributes some important information about the magi. Thus we call upon Apollonius's testimony, which arises from a trip that he made to India to consult the philosophers there. En route he passed through Babylon, where Apollonius interviewed the magi to learn about "the wisdom which is indigenous among you and is cultivated by the Magi, and of finding out whether they are such wise theologians as they are reported to be."[3] This statement is very revealing because it recognizes that the magi inherited the ancient local wisdom of Babylonia (which provided the basis for their reputations as wise men, and maybe even, by extrapolation, as magicians). Apollonius's testimony has one other contribution to make: He noted that the king in Babylonia was making sacrifices in company with the magi, because "religious rites are performed under their supervision."[4] What is intriguing about this eyewitness report is that we have no evidence here of separate Magian or even Persian temples in Babylonia, from which the king would have made his sacrifices.

The best evidence we have from classical sources is that contemporary writers in Greek and Latin confused the Chaldeans and magi, without being able to distinguish clearly between them. Both types of priests were known for their interests in astrology and magic. The emperor Julian refers to the Chaldeans as "a sacred race, skilled in theurgy" (or magic).[5] The third-century writer Diogenes Laertus writes that the Chaldeans "apply themselves to astronomy and forecasting the future,"[6] while the magi spend their time in worshiping the gods, in sacrifices and prayers, but also practice divination and forecasting the future. Ammianus Marcellinus also referred to the occult arts and divination among the Chaldeans, to which Zoroaster added his own ideas which were kept by the magi.

There is one inference which must be drawn: The magi and the Chaldeans were often considered to be one and the same, at least perhaps during the Parthian rule of Mesopotamia in the second and third centuries A.D. It is the magi who may have kept the ancient Babylonian temples in use and maintained the traditional forms of sacrifice. Moreover, the magi may have gained their reputation for esoteric wisdom and knowledge of magic and divination by carrying on the traditional learning of those of the Babylonian temples, the so-called Chaldeans. Where would the Magi have gained such knowledge? Directly from the tablets. It is they who may still have been reading cuneiform, and using the ancient script.

We know that cuneiform script was used primarily by professional scribes, usually operating out of temples; priests also were often scribes, and the scribal schools belonged to the temples. The obvious proposition must be that *as long as the ancient temples were in use in Mesopotamia, then it is likely that cuneiform script survived as well.* Hence, our lonely priest is important, because he bears the sole responsibility for preserving the language.

There is further evidence of priests in Babylonian temples being consulted when the tablets were needed. The most noted example of such was the third-century rabbi in the Talmud, Mar Samuel, who is remembered for his knowledge of the calendar and astronomy. The Talmud specifically states that Mar Samuel went to a Babylonian temple to consult with the priest regarding a question of astronomy. In my view, the priest looked up the information on a tablet and translated it for Mar Samuel. This story in the

Talmud serves as a good example of how, in this late period, the temple cuneiform archives could still have been used. The Talmud gives no information about the Babylonian priest or the temple. Was the priest a Magian? I think he was. Mar Samuel's great academic rival was another rabbi known as "Rab," and many arguments are recorded between these two Talmud scholars. It was Rab who was reported to have said, "He who learns a single word from a Magian is worthy of death."[7] Nevertheless, the case of Mar Samuel and the objections of his colleague Rab point in the same direction, namely that *cuneiform script was in use so long as the temples were in use*. Our priests are still keeping cuneiform alive.

We have by now heard the testimony of several witnesses, all of whom attest to the survival of cuneiform up to the third century A.D. We have seen Iamblichus looking for a teacher, Elagabalus violating Roman sensibilities by marrying a vestal virgin and celebrating the Babylonian-style new year festival in Rome; Menippos finding his way into the Netherworld and back, with the help of a Magian who knew his Akkadian ritual texts; and finally Apollonius of Tyana interviewing the Magians to find out how much they knew of local wisdom in Babylonia. Babylonian cults survive both in Assur and in cities of Syria, as do people bearing Babylonian names. Most important of all, however, we not only have an eyewitness, but we also have a body. We have found a small number of tablets, mostly from Babylon, which show very late Greek writing on them, together with the cuneiform, which indicates that death was a long time in coming.

But death it certainly was. Probably by the fourth century our victim was both gone and forgotten. The Aramaic magic bowls found in many archaeological sites in Babylonia betray no signs of Babylonian personal names, but only good Persian names born by Jews, pagans, and perhaps Christians. The archaeological record shows little evidence of survival of Babylonian temples into the Sassanian period after the mid–third century. The question is, was this death from old age, or murder?

Much of our archaeological data point to the destruction which occurred in 256 A.D., during the Sassanian conquest of Babylonia. From the early Sassanian conquest onward, the new rulers pursued a policy of religious intolerance and persecution. This is partly reflected in the fact that Mani, the so-called Apostle of Babylon, was executed during this period. One of the main reasons for religious intolerance was that the formulation of the Sassanian state was largely based upon a new religious ideology which did not allow for competing religious systems in the new Iran; this was in stark contrast to the previous Parthian regimes, which were characterized by syncretism and tolerance of local religions. We must not overstate the case: Both Judaism and Christianity survived under Sassanian rule, as did paganism as well, judging by Christian Syriac writers. Nevertheless, the survival of Babylonian temple cults may have been fragile at best, without much provocation needed to close their doors forever. It is impossible to be definite about this, but the evidence looks consistent—that cuneiform culture did not long survive the advent of the Sassanian Empire.

The last remaining question in any postmortem is of Nachlass—who inherited what, and when? This is a vital matter for us, because it may well change our perception of how basic ideas were transmitted from one culture to another, and from one period to another.

Of the tablets that survived into late periods in Mesopotamia, there is little evidence of the use of cuneiform for everyday-life transactions. These functions were most likely now carried out in Aramaic or Syriac, which can partly be demonstrated by legal documents that survive in those languages, and their similarities with earlier Akkadian documents. The tablets that survive into the first century B.C. and onward tend to be directly related to the temple, such as the astronomical diaries written by the priests, as well as incantations and prayers. The interests were in a sort of ancient "science," using that term loosely; the Roman perception of Babylonian priests interested in forecasting the future and in countering demons was somewhat accurate. This is the legacy that we should look for in later literature.

As it happens, Jewish texts preserve a great deal of material that appears to be based upon Babylonian science. Two recently published Aramaic texts from among the Dead Sea Scrolls shed light on the Babylonian Nachlass. One text is astronomical, charting the course of the moon through the heavens, reflecting the Akkadian text known as MUL.APIN, which partly charts the same heavenly phenomena. The second text consists of omens taken from the physical appearance of a man and based upon a well-known genre of physiognomic omena from Babylonia. I would like to stress that the parallels in these texts are mostly Babylonian; colleague Bob Sharples (professor of classics at UCL and an expert on

Greek science) assures me that Theophrastus knew nothing similar. Other astronomical-omen texts with similar Babylonian prototypes have appeared, surprisingly enough, even in the Cairo Genizah, another recent discovery. However, other parallels are much nearer at hand, and the texts have been known for a very long time.

Much of the thrust of nineteenth-century Jewish scholarship in Talmud and rabbinic literature represented attempts to identify Greece and Rome as the primary contributors to ancient Jewish culture. Comparative studies such as "Jewish and Roman Law" and "Hellenism in Jewish Palestine" began to appear, and other works on Jewish magic and Jewish medicine sought analogs in Greek for every obscure word in the Talmud, with the underlying assumption being that the rabbis learned their science from the Greeks, as all civilized Westerners must have done. The results have not always been successful; many obscure Aramaic words were compared with equally obscure Greek ones, and many misinterpretations have resulted. In their enthusiasm to prove the connections between rabbinic and Hellenistic thought, they seem to have forgotten that most of the rabbis mentioned in the Babylonian Talmud knew no Greek. In Parthian and Sassanian Babylonia, Greek was a foreign language, and the few Greek words which filter through came from the early literary strata of the Mishnah, which was edited in Roman Palestine.

The rabbis did develop systems of science, however, such as medicine, divination, and magic, based primarily upon the age-old and respectable traditions of Babylonia. The Talmud scholars, like their counterparts in India, used a value of 3 for pi long after the true value was discovered in Greece, but they chose to preserve the traditional numerical value learned from Babylonian mathematics. The rabbis knew little about the internal workings of the human body because they allowed no autopsies—but then again, neither did the Hippocratics.

In my view, both Hippocrates and his school inherited most of their knowledge of symptom recordings and diagnosis from Babylonia, as did the rabbis in the Talmud; the similarities reflect the fact that both early Greek medicine and Talmudic medicine derive from the same source, from Babylonia. This transmission is possible as long as the tradition of learning in Babylonia was preserved, through the survival of cuneiform script. It is not now, nor has it ever been, possible to translate an entire culture from one script or one language to another, and Babylonia was no exception. The similarities are likely to have been based upon a living transmission—an active and breathing Babylonian priest reading from a tablet, providing information that partially ended up in other literatures, in Greek, in Aramaic, in Syriac, and even later in Arabic.

This changes our perceptions of antiquity in the Near East. It survived longer than we think, and had more influence than we think. Those who study the Talmud must now reckon with it, as well as anyone who wants to tackle the Syriac Book of Medicine, or Hippocrates. New vistas are opened to us, and new ways of thinking about antiquity, because of the presence in the British Museum of a small collection of some twenty tablets, which may show that some of our basic notions of antiquity need to be rethought and revised.

There is a lot of work to do here. We need Assyriologists, Talmudists, classicists, and papyrologists, to collaborate and compare notes. Let us get on with it.

Notes

1. Cassius Dio, *Roman History*, vol. 9, sections 3–4.
2. A. D. Nock and Z. Stewart, ed., *Essays on Religion and the Ancient World*, vol. 1 (Oxford: Oxford University Press, 1972), 311.
3. Philastratus, *Life of Apollonius of Tyana*, Loeb Classical Library, book 1, pp. xxxiii, 91.
4. Ibid.
5. Julian, *Orations*, vol. 4, 156C.
6. Diogenes Laertus, *Prologue*, book 1.
7. See Nock and Stewart, *Essays*, 325.

4 Wigmore Meets "The Last Wedge"

Terence J. Anderson

MARK GELLER DELIVERED his inaugural lecture, "The Last Wedge," in December 1994.[1] In the longer, published version, he summarized the arguments that he had first presented in that lecture:

> The ability to read Sumerian and Akkadian—the latest and most widely used languages written in cuneiform script—was dependent upon the survival of scribal schools within the Babylonian temples. These scribal schools themselves survived as long as the Babylonian temples remained in use in Babylonia, and as long as priests still learned the traditional scripts. Using an extreme standard that cuneiform was not technically a dead language as long as any priest could read the ancient script, an analysis of the Graeco-Babyloniaca tablets and other surviving fragments, as well as references to cuneiform in classical sources, supports the conclusion that cuneiform could still be read in the third century A.D.[2]

The postulated conclusion represented a significant departure from the standard view among Assyriologists that cuneiform had died by the second or first century B.C. at the latest.

This work is a product of the year that I spent as a fellow at the Netherlands Institute for Advanced Studies during 1994 and 1995, and I am indebted to the institute, its staff, and the other scholars who were fellows that year for creating an environment that encouraged scholarly interests of diverse kinds. I am indebted to Mark Geller for agreeing to let an outsider critique his work and for the time he spent trying to answer the outsider's seemingly endless and often naive questions. I presented an earlier version of the work that formed the basis for this essay to a faculty seminar at the University of Miami School of Law, and I am grateful for the comments colleagues provided in that forum. I am also grateful for the comments and support provided by Carolyn Bugh Anderson, David A. Schum, and, as always, William Twining. Responsibility for any errors that survived those critiques is mine alone.

Between March 5 and April 4, 1995, Anderson attempted to apply a modified "chart method" of analysis, based upon a method first developed by John Henry Wigmore for use in legal contexts,[3] to reconstruct and depict in charted form the arguments made in the text of Geller's original lecture in an effort to determine whether, how, and with what utility a method developed in one discipline (Law) for depicting and appraising arguments might be applied in another discipline (Assyriology). Long after the fellowship year ended, Anderson undertook a second exercise. He developed a more detailed microanalysis of the arguments presented in one paragraph of Geller's lecture to test and further develop some of the tentative conclusions he had reached by the end of the first intensive exercise. This chapter presents the results of Anderson's efforts, describes the processes through which those results were developed, and gives his appraisal of the utility of and insights generated by both exercises.

The chapter proceeds in three parts. In the first part, Anderson describes the method and its application in legal contexts and in depicting and analyzing the arguments developed in Geller's lecture. In that part, Anderson also tells the story and presents the products of the month-long project that was completed at the Netherlands Institute for Advanced Studies (NIAS) in 1995, describing the obstacles that he encountered and the interactions with Geller through which those obstacles were partially overcome. In the second part, he describes and presents the product of a microanalysis of a single paragraph of Geller's argument that Anderson did long after the end of the NIAS fellowship year. For that project, Anderson did a limited amount of research in an attempt to overcome the "knowledge barriers" with respect to the arguments made in that paragraph. In the final part, Anderson develops his view, an "outsider's view," of the interactions between Anderson and Geller and Geller's text that were necessary to enable him to develop the key-list and charts into the versions presented here. In that part, he presents his appraisal of the method in a cross-disciplinary context and some insights that the cross-disciplinary applications of the method generated. In the next chapter, Geller presents his view, the "insider's view," of the interactive process and of the utility of the method as an analytic tool within the discipline of Assyriology.

This chapter includes a level of detail that would be inappropriate in other contexts. A charted analysis is ordinarily a means, not an end. The charted analysis depicts the analyst's view of how the available evidence can best be marshalled to show the strengths and weaknesses of the argument as a whole. The chart also provides a graphic depiction of the analyst's thought processes. Ordinarily, however, it is not an end product intended for publication. The end product for a lawyer may be the plan for a trial; for a scholar, it might be an elegant essay intended to communicate her arguments and conclusions effectively. Here, the charted analyses are a major part of the end product—this chapter. The chapter provides a detailed description of how the analyses were conducted and includes most of the propositions and charts that those analyses produced. If Geller's argument were viewed as the sausage, the present chapter presents Anderson's analysis of the sausage and how it was made—ordinarily, a subject about which one would not want to know in any detail. Here, the propositions and the charts produced by the analysis are not only the medium, but also a necessary part of the message.

Part 1. The Lawyer and the Assyriologist: The Method Described and Applied

Wigmore's chart method of analysis was developed as a method for analyzing a mass of evidential data to determine how the inferences based upon that data might be marshalled most effectively in support of and in opposition to a specified proposition of fact, and to depict in charted form the logical relationships among the data, the inferred propositions, and the proposition to be proved or tested. Reduced to its essentials, the method requires for its application only a proposition to be proved or tested and a body of evidential data thought to be relevant to that proposition. The method requires the analyst to specify with precision each inference necessary to demonstrate how she believes each evidential datum is logically connected to the ultimate proposition in question and how the data and inferred propositions can best be combined to demonstrate the strengths (and the weaknesses) of the argument as a whole. The resulting charted depiction of the arguments makes possible a rigorous appraisal and critique of the arguments being made.

In legal contexts, the method can be used for a variety of purposes. A detective might use it early in a criminal investigation to determine whether the available evidence justified commencement of criminal proceedings against the principal suspect and to identify other potential sources of evidence that should be investigated or explored, before or after charges had been filed. In a civil case, after all of the evidence gathering and pretrial discovery had been completed, a lawyer might use it to chart her view of the strongest logical marshalling of the evidence and inferences for each side in order to determine whether the case should be settled or tried. In other contexts, a legal analyst might adopt a historical standpoint. For example, she might seek to analyze the evidence presented at the O. J. Simpson trial to make it possible to determine whether the evidence presented left open any rational basis for the conclusion that there was a reasonable doubt that it was O. J. Simpson who murdered Nicole Brown Simpson and Ronald L. Goldman. In principle, however, the method is only a method for rigorously analyzing and depicting the logical relationships among propositions offered in support of (and in opposition to) a hypothesis. The present exercise was undertaken to test that principle—to determine and demonstrate whether and with what effect the method might be used in a context far removed from law.

Anderson and William Twining have developed a seven-step protocol for applying the chart method to a mass of evidence:[4]

1. The analyst must define her standpoint for the exercise by responding to three questions: "Who am I?" "At what stage of what process am I?" and, "What are my objectives?"
2. The analyst must specify the ultimate probandum—the ultimate proposition or hypothesis to be proved or tested.
3. The analyst must specify the penultimate probanda—the elements of the ultimate probandum or the principal propositions upon which the supporting argument is or must be based.
4. The analyst must specify, at least provisionally, the theory of the case—a concise statement of the logical theory which most strongly supports the ultimate probandum—and then should strategically reformulate the ultimate and penultimate probanda, as appropriate, to focus attention on the facts that are truly disputed or to facilitate the charting process (or both).
5. The analyst must prepare a key-list setting out each of the propositions necessary to the arguments being made or analyzed.

6. The analyst must prepare the chart or charts necessary to depict the claimed relationships among the propositions on the key list.⁵
7. The analyst must complete or refine the analysis to satisfy the identified objectives.

It was this protocol that Anderson set out to apply to Geller's arguments. The similarities and differences in applying the protocol in the two disciplines, Law and Assyriology, are illustrated below.

STANDPOINT

In the O. J. Simpson example, an analyst might specify that she was an analyst trained in Wigmorean analysis undertaking a post-trial analysis of the evidence admitted during the criminal trial of O. J. Simpson (OJS) to identify and depict in charted form the most plausible bases, if any, upon which a rational juror might have decided that there was a reasonable doubt that it was OJS who committed the murders. In undertaking an analysis of Geller's arguments, Anderson was a legal theorist adept in using Wigmore's chart method of analysis in legal contexts who had no significant knowledge of Assyriology or Babylonian history. Geller provided the text of his lecture; Anderson undertook to apply the method to the evidence and arguments presented in that lecture as evidenced by the text. Anderson's objectives were to determine whether the method could be applied to a body of Assyriological arguments and to see what, if any, useful insights the effort might generate.

THE ULTIMATE PROBANDUM

The second step requires identifying and articulating with precision the ultimate probandum—the ultimate proposition to be proved or the hypothesis to be tested. In most legal contexts involving disputed questions of fact, that proposition can be derived from the law. In theory, there is a rule of law that constitutes the major premise that governs the case, e.g., if X, then Y. The ultimate probandum is the minor premise that the prosecution (or plaintiff) must prove in order to justify result Y, e.g., this is a case of X.

In *People v. Simpson*,⁶ the source of the ultimate probandum was external. It had to be derived from the rule of law defining first-degree murder. For the murder of Nicole Brown Simpson (NBS), the ultimate probandum had to be a proposition that satisfied the conditions that the California version of that rule specified that the prosecution had to prove beyond reasonable doubt in order to obtain a conviction for first-degree murder. That proposition might be framed in the abstract as

> (a) NBS was dead; (b) NBS died as the result of an unlawful act; (c) it was OJS who committed the act that caused NBS's death; and (d) the person who committed the acts that caused NBS's death acted with premeditated intent to cause NBS (i) death or (ii) serious bodily injury.[7]

The source of the ultimate probandum in "The Last Wedge" was internal, not external. The central proposition that Geller was advancing had to be derived from his text. As Anderson framed it, the ultimate probandum was "The class of persons who could read cuneiform survived until the Sassanian conquest of Babylonia in 256 A.D."

THE PENULTIMATE PROBANDA

In a legal case, such as *Simpson*, framing the penultimate probanda in the first instance ordinarily requires only partitioning (and often subpartitioning) the ultimate probandum until it has been reduced to its elements expressed as simple, declarative sentences. In the *Simpson* example, (a), (b), (c), (d), and (d)(i)–(ii) represent the penultimate probanda. For "The Last Wedge," the penultimate probanda were not defined by the ultimate probandum. Anderson was attempting to interpret and chart the arguments that Geller was making. Given his standpoint, Anderson's task was to understand Geller's theory and to organize and reconstruct the arguments in a way that would facilitate the analysis and an understanding of the resulting product. In effect, he had to identify and articulate the propositions that would have been the major points in an outline of the argument. As an outsider from one discipline (Law) attempting to analyze arguments made by an insider from another discipline (Assyriology), he found it necessary, initially, to vary the sequence in which he normally undertook the third, fourth, and fifth steps of the analysis in legal contexts.

THEORY AND STRATEGIC PENULTIMATE PROBANDA

In *Simpson*, the only penultimate probandum in strategic dispute was (c): It was OJS who committed the act that caused NBS's death. In that case, a central problem for the prosecution was to develop a credible theory that would explain why OJS would have committed the murders—to identify a credible motive. The prosecution elected to proceed on a theory of control, a theory that might, insofar as Anderson understood it, be summarized as follows:

OJS had expressed jealous rage resulting in violence in his attempts to control NBS and prevent her from finally severing their relationship. His continuing jealous rage gave him a motive to murder her as the ultimate act of control, and the brutal manner in which she was murdered by multiple stab wounds shows that she was murdered by someone acting in a rage. OJS was the only person who had acted against NBS in a jealous rage. He had a motive to try to maintain his control and to prevent NBS from acting independently, and he went to her house to kill her as the ultimate act of control. Therefore, it was OJS who murdered NBS in a jealous rage.[8]

In light of the theory adopted, a person analyzing that case might have strategically reframed the penultimate probanda as follows:

(a) NBS was dead; (b) NBS died as the result of multiple stab wounds violently and unlawfully inflicted; (c) it was OJS who committed the violent acts that caused NBS's death; and (d) the person who committed the acts that caused NBS's death acted in a rage with premeditated intent to control NBS permanently by causing NBS's death.

In many instances, a legal analyst may use a penultimate probandum as a "magnet" to "attract" the relevant evidential propositions. Thus, in order to prove that "it was OJS who committed the violent acts that caused NBS's death," the prosecution had to prove that OJS could have caused those acts—that is, that he could have been present when those acts were committed and, thus, could have had an opportunity to commit the acts. Thus, the analyst might look for evidential propositions bearing upon the time of NBS's death and the time OJS was subsequently observed because they would be relevant to the proposition: OJS had an opportunity to commit the violent acts that caused NBS's death.

For example, a posttrial analyst might use the "opportunity magnet" to examine the database—the evidence admitted during the trial. Using that magnet, the analyst's key-list would include relevant evidential propositions derived directly from the data—e.g., witness P. F. testified: "I heard the plaintive wail of a dog at 10:15 P.M. on the evening the murder was committed"—and the inferred propositions necessary to demonstrate the logical relationship of that evidential proposition to a penultimate probandum—e.g., the plaintive wail of the dog, combined with the testimony of other witnesses that they later had found NBS's dog wailing and with blood on its paws, supported an inference that the wailing was caused by the dog's discovery that its mistress was dead, supporting the further inference that the murder occurred at or shortly before 10:15 P.M., which had to be combined with evidence establishing that a recently showered and calm and collected OJS emerged from his house at 10:55 P.M. to be driven to the airport, in order to fix the time frame within which the prosecution had to persuade the jury that OJS had an opportunity to commit the murders—i.e., that he could have been present at NBS's house at 10:15 P.M. and still have returned home, showered, disposed of his bloody garments, collected himself, and emerged from his house at 10:55 P.M.

In other instances, it is easier to start with an evidential proposition and reason "upward" to develop the inferred propositions that clarify its relevance. In the previous example, an analyst might initially ask why the testimony about a dog's wailing at 10:15 P.M. was relevant, and work upward until she saw that it was relevant to establishing the time of NBS's death and that establishing the time of NBS's death was necessary to determine whether OJS could have had an opportunity to kill NBS. Often, the need to reason upward occurs when pieces of the puzzle are "left over"—i.e., evidential data that seem relevant remain unused after the penultimate "magnets" have been applied to the entire mass of available evidential data. The process of fitting these leftover pieces into the puzzle often forces revisions of the theory and penultimate probanda. The process is reflexive.

For Anderson's analysis of "The Last Wedge," the sequence and the process were different. The evidential database was the text of Geller's lecture (later supplemented by explanatory propositions provided by Geller). Because the text of the lecture was the evidence to be analyzed, Anderson had to derive the penultimate probanda from an analysis of that text. To do that, he began by constructing a preliminary key-list of propositions that were asserted in the text.

THE KEY-LISTS

The exercise lasted one month, from March 5 until April 4, 1995. Anderson started the process by formulating a list of propositions derived by parsing Geller's lecture sentence by sentence to identify and articulate the factual and inferential assertions in the text. The result was Key-List Number 1: a list of 223 propositions with Anderson's questions and comments for Geller interspersed. Many of the questions stemmed from Anderson's lack of the background knowledge necessary to understand and interpret Geller's arguments. He had long since forgotten the small amount of Babylonian history he had been taught and knew nothing about many of the particulars, such as astronomical diaries, Elagabalus, the magi, and so on, that were central to Geller's arguments.

For example, the first line of argument in Geller's lecture was based upon the discovery of an astronomical diary written in Akkadian cuneiform script in 75 A.D. Anderson understood the words, but did not know what an astronomical diary was or whether the fact that it had been written in Akkadian had any significance. In that first key-list, Anderson extracted three propositions about the diary from eight lines of text in the lecture:

1. An astronomical diary was written in cuneiform in approximately 75 A.D.
2. The cuneiform astronomical diary written circa 75 A.D. is the latest complete cuneiform tablet that has been discovered.
3. The scribe who wrote the astronomical diary in 75 A.D. composed it in Akkadian.

Anderson's reading of those lines led him to insert the comments and queries reproduced below:

> [Mark: I assume that these propositions are not controversial. If that is correct, they seem to require the further inference that there was at least one scribe who knew and could write cuneiform in 75 A.D. The propositions might, however, also relate to and be used in other parts of your argument. For example, an argument might be made that (a) an astronomical diary is a document intended to be read and used [as opposed to a schoolboy composition]; (b) the fact that a scribe was supported to and invested the effort necessary to construct an astronomical diary in 75 A.D. [propositions 1–3] supports an inference that (c) there was a sufficient number of cuneiform readers to make the investment worthwhile. Do we have evidence showing where the diary was produced? If so, is the location at or near Uruk or one of the other locations that you argue had an active temple far later than generally believed? If so, one could combine the two arguments to provide a strengthened foundation for your overall argument. Do you intend or want to push this "evidence" further?]

The resulting first key-list, with comments and queries interspersed, occupied twenty-three single-spaced pages of text. Geller's original lecture, produced in the same format, occupied less than twelve pages.

Geller and Anderson had extended meetings during a two-day period, March 29 and 30, to review Key-List Number 1 and to discuss the interspersed comments and queries, as well as those that occurred to Anderson during the course of those meetings. Before and after each of those meetings, Anderson spent time in the NIAS library looking in encyclopedias for the answer to questions such as "Who was Elagabalus? Photius? Origen?" "When and what was the Seleucid period?" and so on. After these meetings, Anderson used his notes and extended understandings to produce a second Key-List Number 1R1.

Key-List Number 1R1 consisted of 273 propositions, with further notes and queries interspersed, and occupied thirty-one pages. For example, the original three propositions concerning the astronomical diary had become ten: refined statements of the original three; two background generalizations that, based upon their conversations, Anderson concluded would be so generally known and accepted within the community of Assyriologists that Geller thought it unnecessary to make them explicit in the text; four inferences that Geller had thought implicit and so obvious as to be unnecessary to state for his intended audience; and a fifth inference that Anderson identified and thought should be made explicit. After these, Anderson inserted further notes and queries to be discussed with Geller. The following are the resulting ten propositions.[9]

1. An astronomical diary was written in [MG(3/29)] Akkadian cuneiform in approximately 75 A.D.
2. The cuneiform astronomical diary written circa 75 A.D. is the latest complete [dateable] cuneiform tablet that has been discovered.
3. [G-MG(3/29): Astronomical diaries described events occurring on the date on which an entry was written.]
4. [I-MG(3/29): Astronomical diaries can be accurately dated by determining the dates on which the events described occurred.]
5. [G-MG(3/29): Astronomical diaries contained useful information that was recorded to be read and used by others.]
6. The scribe who wrote the astronomical diary in 75 A.D. composed it in Akkadian cuneiform.
7. [I-MG(3/29): The scribe who wrote the astronomical diary knew Akkadian cuneiform.]
8. [I-MG(3/29): The scribe who wrote the astronomical diary in 75 A.D. believed that there were and would be enough other persons who could read Akkadian cuneiform to justify the effort of maintaining an astronomical diary (from propositions 5 and 6).]

9. [I-TJA(3/30): In 75 A.D., there was an active community of priests or scholars and students who knew or were studying Akkadian cuneiform at the location where the Akkadian diary was written. (What can we say about minimum size?)]
10. [I-MG(3/29): Akkadian cuneiform was a living language in 75 A.D. and for sometime thereafter.]

[Rev. Note. 3/30. Mark: Have I interpreted the information you gave me correctly? What alternative explanations would a staunch traditionalist give to the propositions developed above? If you told me I forgot: do we have evidence showing where the diary was produced? If so, is the location at or near Uruk one of the other locations that you later argue had active temples far later than generally believed? If so, one could combine the two arguments to provide a strengthened foundation for your overall argument. Do you intend or want to push this "evidence" further?]

These interactions between Geller and Anderson enabled Anderson to revise and refine his articulation of the theory, strategic penultimate probanda, and key-lists. The processes through which these two key-lists were constructed—Key-List Number 1 from the text, followed by conversations with Geller and encyclopedia research resulting in Key-List Number 1R1—were necessary steps toward providing Anderson with some of the background knowledge necessary to understand and articulate Geller's theory, as expressed in his lecture and as stated in refined form at the outset of this chapter.[10] Based upon those processes, Anderson developed what he thought to be the best formulation of the penultimate probanda. In analyzing "The Last Wedge," given his standpoint, the penultimate probanda were propositions stating the main points developed in Geller's argument, as Anderson understood them. In that context, the primary function of the formulation and strategic reformulation of these probanda was to organize and categorize Geller's arguments in a form that facilitated the analysis and charting of the relationships between the evidential and inferential propositions to the ultimate proposition that Geller had set out to establish. If the results of the analysis were being expressed in an outline format, as opposed to a charted format, the penultimate probanda would be the main headings in the outline.[11]

Anderson and Geller had agreed to present some preliminary

results of the exercise and to describe the processes through which those results had been achieved at a meeting of the NIAS Evidence and Inference Group on April 4, 1995. Between March 30 and April 3, Anderson further revised and expanded his key-list of propositions to include an articulation of the penultimate probanda and to add additional propositions based upon conversations with Geller and upon further analysis to identify what Anderson saw as inferential propositions necessary to demonstrate the logical relationship of Geller's asserted propositions to the specified penultimate probandum. The result was the "Key-List for Evidence and Inference Presentation (April 4, 1995)" (the NIAS key-list), which is reproduced as Appendix 1 to this chapter. That list consisted of 299 propositions and spanned twenty-nine pages and, in Anderson's view, was far from complete. Although many of Anderson's initial comments and queries had been addressed, others remained or were added in the process of constructing the revised list. That list also makes it clear that Anderson still had not surmounted the interdisciplinary knowledge barriers completely.

For that presentation, Anderson also prepared an abbreviated version of the NIAS key-list that included the ultimate and the penultimate probanda (sixteen propositions) and detailed the evidential and inferential propositions and generalizations necessary to develop the arguments based upon the astronomical diary (sixteen additional propositions). That key-list and a chart depicting the propositions and their logical relationships, as Anderson saw them, are reproduced below.

In that key-list, he framed the ultimate and the principal penultimate probanda as follows:[12]

1. The class of persons who could read cuneiform survived until sometime after the Sassanian conquest of Babylonia in 256 A.D.
2. One or more active temple centers where cuneiform was read, studied, and taught survived into the third century A.D.

---

12. The Sassanian conquest in 256 A.D. was the probable cause of the termination of the class of persons who could read cuneiform.

He further subdivided the penultimate probanda into subordinate major points (subordinate penultimate probanda):

3. The Astronomical Diary produced in 75 A.D., the quantity of tablets produced in the Hellenistic period [circa 321 B.C.–256 A.D.] as evidenced by the surviving fragments, and the Greek script inscribed on the "Graeco-Babyloniaca" tablets establish that the class of persons who could read cuneiform survived until the second or third century A.D.
4. [I-MG(3/29): The Astronomical Diary establishes that Akkadian cuneiform was a living language in 75 A.D. and for some time thereafter.]
5. The quantity of tablets produced after the Hellenistic period had begun, as evidenced by surviving fragments in the Pergamon collection and elsewhere, establishes that there were a significant number of active temples with schools in operation where cuneiform was studied, read, and taught at the beginning of the Hellenistic period.
6. The Greek script of the latest of the Graeco-Babyloniaca tablets establishes that there was at least one active temple or other center where cuneiform could be read and written at the end of the second or the beginning of the third century A.D.
7. The investment in constructing new temples in the Seleucid period [312–64 B.C.] and thereafter and the evidence found at the temple at Assur establish that temples practicing Sumerian and Akkadian religions, where cuneiform was studied, taught, and could be read, survived until the second or third century A.D.
8. There is additional evidence in the documentary record left by Babylonians and non-Babylonians suggesting that the ability to read cuneiform survived until the third century A.D.
9. Throughout the Hellenistic period, Parthian regimes in Mesopotamia were characterized by syncretism and tolerance of local religions.
10. [G-TJA] A significant change in circumstances is necessary to account for the termination of an ongoing institution and its activities.]
11. The temple communities that survived until the end of the second or the beginning of the third century A.D. probably continued to operate until there was a change in circumstances.

---

13. The Sassanian state was based upon a religious ideology that did not tolerate the existence of competing religious systems.

14. Following the conquest in 256 A.D., the Sassanians pursued a policy of persecution and intolerance of non-Sassanian religions.
15. By 256 A.D., the number of temples where cuneiform was read and studied and the numbers of persons supporting them would have diminished in any event.
16. Sassanian policy and implementing actions would have represented a sufficient change in circumstances to bring about the termination of the temple school communities where the ability to read and write cuneiform had been preserved.

Anderson concluded that one "assumed" generalization and fifteen additional propositions were necessary to depict accurately the relevance of the astronomical diary to the ultimate proposition that Geller sought to support:

20. [G-TJA (assumption): All or almost all persons who could read and write classic cuneiform after 500 B.C. and who could produce texts of the kind inscribed on cuneiform tablets after 500 B.C. were persons who had been trained in schools associated with active Akkadian and Sumerian temples.]

---

22. A tablet has been discovered and exists and can be inspected that has inscribed upon it an astronomical diary (the "Astronomical Diary") that is inscribed in standard Akkadian cuneiform and that records information of the kind customarily recorded in Sumerian and Akkadian astronomical diaries.
23. [G-MG (3/29): Astronomical diaries described events occurring on the date on which an entry was written.]
24. [I-MG (3/29): Astronomical diaries can be accurately dated by determining the dates on which the events described occurred.]
25. [The events and other information described in the Astronomical Diary establish that it was inscribed in 75 A.D.]
26. The Astronomical Diary was inscribed in standard Akkadian cuneiform.
27. The Astronomical Diary was written in cuneiform in approximately 75 A.D.
28. The person who wrote the Astronomical Diary (the "scribe") in 75 A.D. had been trained in [had learned to write in] standard Akkadian cuneiform.

29. [The scribe had been trained in [had learned] the Akkadian system for constructing and recording information in an astronomical diary.]
30. [The scribe had received the kind of classical education that was commonly provided only in Akkadian and Sumerian temple schools.]
31. [The scribe had been educated in a temple school where Akkadian cuneiform was read, studied, and taught.]
32. [In the period immediately prior to 75 A.D., there was an active temple where cuneiform was read, studied, and taught.]
33. [G-MG (3/29): Astronomical diaries contained useful information that was recorded to be read and used by others.]
34. [I-MG (3/29): The scribe who wrote the Astronomical Diary in 75 A.D. believed that there were and would be enough other persons who could read Akkadian cuneiform to justify the effort of maintaining an astronomical diary.]
35. [I-TJA (5/30): In 75 A.D., there was an active community of priests or scholars and students who knew and could read or were studying Akkadian cuneiform at the location where the Astronomical Diary was written.]
36. The Astronomical Diary written in 75 A.D. establishes that there were one or more active communities of priests, scholars, and students who could read cuneiform at that time.

A chart depicting these propositions and their logical relationships was presented at the April 4 seminar and is represented below (see fig. 4.1). In the chart, a circle represents the proposition in the key-list indicated by the appended number, and the lines indicate the claimed logical relationship between one proposition and another. Unless otherwise indicated by an arrow, the "direction" of the logical support of one proposition to another is always upward, from bottom to top. The infinity symbol, ∞, under a proposition indicates that the proposition represents an evidential assertion—here an assertion drawn directly from Geller's text; in the context of a trial, a testimonial assertion that the fact finder will hear or other evidence that she will perceive with one of her other senses.

These propositions and the associated chart present a macroanalysis showing the structure of Geller's argument as a whole and developing in some detail the steps involved in the argument based

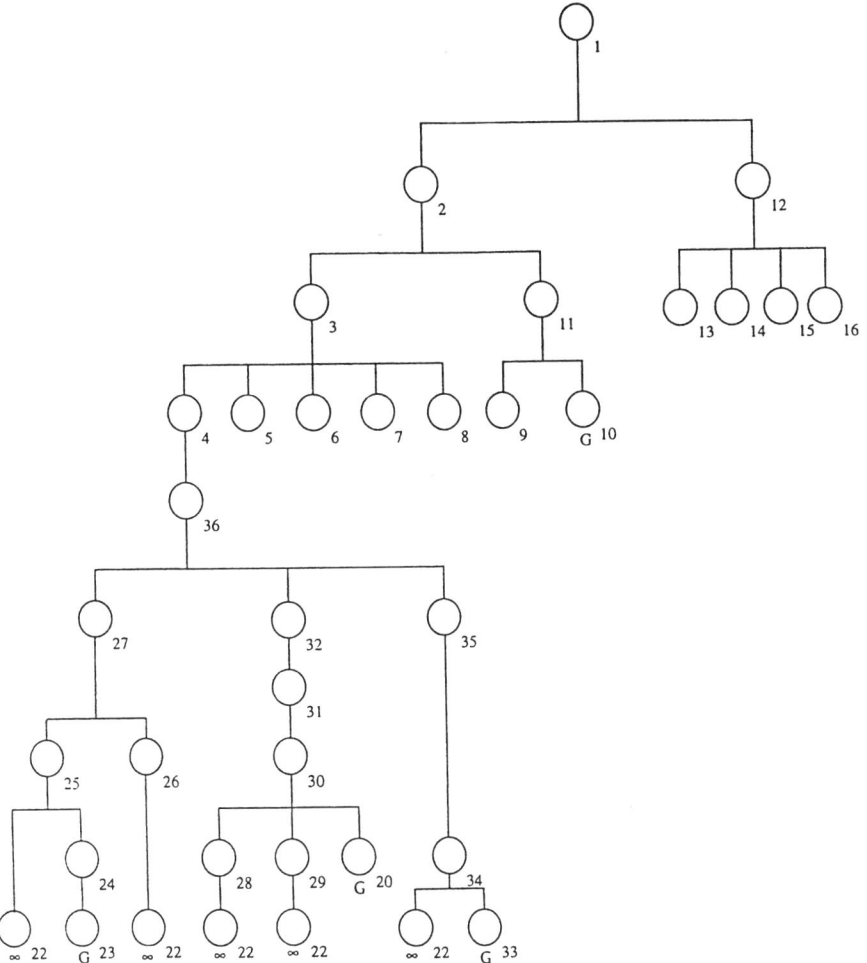

FIGURE 4.1. Last Wedge chart (April 1, 1995)

upon the astronomical diary.[13] The NIAS key-list and chart were developed for the April 4 seminar. They are presented without substantive revision here for two reasons. First, they are sufficient to demonstrate that a method for depicting the logic involved in arguments about disputed questions of fact developed in one discipline (Law) could be applied to depicting arguments about disputed hypotheses in another (Assyriology). Second, the work in progress as it then existed illustrates the nature of the barriers that hamper—and provides a foundation for illustrating the kinds of insights that were and might be generated by—such cross-disciplinary work.

The remaining propositions in Geller's argument could also be developed and depicted in charted form. The process would require revisions and deletions of many of the later propositions included on the NIAS key-list and the formulation and insertion of a number of additional propositions, because the very process of charting the propositions in an argument enables the analyst to identify omitted steps that are necessary to clarify and articulate accurately the argument she is seeking to depict in charted form. The result would be a longer, not a shorter, master key-list. Part 2 illustrates the process that would be necessary for such a revision by presenting the results of a microanalysis of the arguments made in one paragraph of Geller's text.

Part 2. The Iamblichus Argument: A Microanalysis

In his lecture, Geller argued:

> I call as my first witness one Iamblichus, a writer who appears in *The Library of Photius*. Iamblichus was a Syrian who composed erotic tales in Greek in approximately 200 A.D. He was conversant with Babylonian magic but had been educated as a Greek. The scholiast adds that Iamblichus "was a native Syrian, and not a Greek-Syrian, who knew Syriac, but also had a tutor who taught him the Babylonian language, as well as (Babylonian) customs and history." The source in Photius goes on to say that Iamblichus later continued his career as a writer in Rome, residing there in the reign of Septimus Severus, circa 200 A.D. So here we have an independent record of a Syrian who already speaks the *glossa Syriaca*, or the local dialect of Aramaic, and wishes to learn the *glossa Babyloniaca*, which in my view is most likely to be Akkadian, and during the reign of Septimus Severus. Who, though, was Iamblichus's tutor? How and where did he find a teacher for cuneiform in, say, the mid–second century A.D.? The scholiast adds this important detail: Iamblichus's teacher was a Babylonian who was taken prisoner by the Romans during Trajan's campaign there and later sold into slavery in Syria. The teacher had obviously got on well as a pedagogue or scribe in Syria, since he had been well educated. The scholiast is clear on this point: Iamblichus's teacher was skilled in "barbarian learning," having served as a royal scribe in Babylon. "Barbarian learning" never refers to Greek culture; Iamblichus's teacher was a scholar who most likely knew cuneiform. He had served as a royal scribe, being conversant in cuneiform, in Babylon in the beginning of the second century A.D. before being captured by the Romans, and he remembered cuneiform well enough to teach Iamblichus later in the century.[14]

The principal source for the arguments made in that paragraph was a cluster of notes in the margin of a copy of Photius's Biblio-

theca (what Geller refers to as "*The Library of Photius*"). The *Bibliotheca* was a book containing summaries that Photius had written in the middle of the ninth century of some 280 books written in Greek.[15] One of the books summarized, *Babyloniaca* (or *A Babylonian Story*), was written by an author identified as Iamblichus. The notes were written in the margin of Photius's summary of that story by an unknown scribe, a scholiast, who was preparing a copy of the *Bibliotheca* early in the tenth century.

The arguments made in Geller's paragraph illustrate three kinds of problems. The first is a problem of ambiguity. The paragraph could be read as an argument in support of either or both of the following propositions (from the Iamblichus key-list in appendix 2):

62. I: Iamblichus knew and could read Akkadian cuneiform until the beginning of the third century A.D.
51. I: The Tutor knew and could read Akkadian cuneiform until at least 155 A.D. (until the middle of the second century A.D.).

This may be a problem common to the public lecture format in any discipline—a sixty-minute lecture does not permit the precise and detailed analysis that is possible in a fully developed, written presentation. The second is also a problem common to many disciplines: Arguments about historical events often depend upon hearsay—here, what a translator said a scholiast said that an author said in a manuscript that no longer survives, offered as evidence of the truth of the matters asserted. The arguments made in the paragraph also illustrate a third problem—the difficulties involved in distinguishing adequately grounded arguments from inadequately grounded speculations is also a problem common to an analysis of evidential data in most disciplines.

STANDPOINT

Anderson had a different objective in analyzing the quoted paragraph. He wanted to take an argument that he had perceived as weak in his first review and use the chart method to reconstruct the arguments made to determine and illustrate exactly why he thought the overall argument weak and to provide a basis for responding to the question "So what?" For this analysis, he used three additional sources to enable him to overcome, to the extent feasible, the knowledge barriers to the analysis that the first exercise had revealed and illustrated.[16] Otherwise his standpoint was the same: He remained an analyst from one discipline (Law) attempting to apply a method of analyzing arguments developed within that discipline to arguments made by a scholar in another discipline (Assyriology).

ULTIMATE PROBANDUM, PENULTIMATE PROBANDA, AND THEORY

Either of the propositions set out above (numbers 62 and 51) could be viewed as the ultimate proposition that the arguments in the paragraph were intended to support. The ambiguity made no difference for purposes of this analysis because proposition 51 is a necessary step in the argument supporting proposition 62. As before, the penultimate probanda emerged from Anderson's "working up" from the evidential propositions in the text. The theory is clear, albeit ambiguous: The scholiast's notes support an inference that cuneiform remained a living script within Geller's definition until either the middle of the second century or the beginning of the third century A.D.

THE KEY-LIST(S) AND CHART(S)

The entire Iamblichus key-list consists of sixty-seven propositions (see appendix 2). The key-list is presented and charted in four sections in the text that follows because the book format makes it difficult to present a complex argument in a single key-list and chart—the chart may not fit on a single page, and the key-list would in any event occupy several pages, making cross-referencing back and forth between the chart and the key-list awkward. The first section presents the propositions and inferences based upon a translation of the notes a scholiast made in the margin of the summary of *A Babylonian Story* included in Photius's *Bibliotheca*. The second section incorporates the first and depicts the structure of Geller's Iamblichus argument as a whole. The support for two sections of that argument require development in more detail. The third section develops some doubts about the possibility that the tutor described could have taught Iamblichus Akkadian cuneiform. The last section develops the argument that the autobiography of Iamblichus included in *A Babylonian Story* may well have been a fictionalized account.

These key-lists and charts employ some additional terms and symbols. Every evidential proposition in the key-list is classified by it source, e.g., "The Scholia," "Generalization," "Accepted," and so on. Each inferential proposition is labeled to reflect its function—e.g., "Inference" or "Explanation." Where necessary these terms are further defined in the endnotes. One additional symbol is the open angle or "less than" symbol (<) to identify an inferential or explanatory proposition that conflicts with or otherwise diminishes the probative force of the inference to which it is appended. Propositions often appear in more than one place in a chart because they support more than one inference. In the charts that follow, the symbol "X" placed immediately below and to the left of circle representing a proposition on the chart identifies that proposition as one that has been previously charted. Each of the evidential propositions has a symbol beneath it that identifies its source, i.e., "S" for Scholia, "G" for Generalization, "A" for Accepted, and "M" for Millar (see note 16).

THE CREDIBILITY OF THE SCHOLIA

Geller's argument based upon the Scholia involves three levels of hearsay—what the translator "said" that the scholiast's notes in the margin of Photius's *Bibliotheca* "said"; what the unknown scholiast "said" that Iamblichus, identified as the author of the story that Photius summarized (*A Babylonian Story*) "said" about Iamblichus in that story; and what Iamblichus in fact said about Iamblichus. In order to determine the probative value of Iamblichus's assertion that the tutor taught Iamblichus the Babylonian language, the credibility of the declarant's assertions at each of the three levels must be measured.[17]

From the translator's "testimony," the most that we can infer is that the translator translated and interpreted and truthfully stated what the scholiast wrote in the margin of Photius's summary of *A Babylonian Story*. A translator's submission of her work to peer review should largely eliminate any veracity concerns: Did the translator believe that he or she was telling the truth? There remain objectivity and observational concerns, however: Did the translator accurately interpret the text?[18] Did the translator have access to a legible version of the scholiast's notes, or did she rely upon a copy prepared by someone else? In the analysis that follows, I have ignored credibility concerns about the translator's testimony because I thought them insignificant, given my standpoint.

If we accept the translator's "testimony" as true, the most that we can infer is that the notes that the scholiast placed in the margin of Photius's *Bibliotheca* "said" that Iamblichus "said" various things about himself in the manuscript of *A Babylonian Story*. In appraising the likelihood that those notes accurately and fairly summarized what Iamblichus said in the manuscript of *A Babylonian Story*, we must address concerns about the scholiast's veracity, objectivity, and observational sensitivity. In this analysis, Anderson ignored the veracity concerns because he had no basis for specifying or resolving those that applied to this unknown scholiast (or to scholiasts generally).[19] The remaining concerns are reflected in the key-list A and chart A (presented in fig. 4.2).

If we accept the scholiast's "testimony" as true, the most we can infer is that Iamblichus made the reported testimonial assertions about himself in the manuscript. In order to determine the probative value of those assertions, it is necessary to consider evidence that bears upon Iamblichus's credibility. Here, the primary concerns are veracity concerns: Did Iamblichus, the author, believe that the assertions he made about himself in the text of *A Babylonian Story* were true? Those concerns are substantial and are analyzed and depicted later in Key-List D and Chart D.

Key-List A

1. Accepted (A): Photius's *Bibliotheca* contains a summary ("Photius's summary") of a novel, *A Babylonian Story* (ABS), written in Greek by an author who identified himself as Iamblichus.[20]
2. A: Early in the tenth century A.D., an unidentified scribe (the "scholiast") made notes in the margin (the "Scholia") of a copy of Photius's summary indicating that the scholiast had read the manuscript of ABS.
3. Inference (I): A complete manuscript of ABS survived until the early tenth century A.D. and was read by the scholiast.
4. A: Photius's *Bibliotheca* was composed in the middle of the ninth century A.D., and only fragments of the manuscript of ABS exist today.[21]
5. Explanation (E): The manuscript for ABS may not have survived or been available to the scholiast in the early tenth century A.D.[22]
6. A: Photius's summary includes a summary of an Autobiography of Iamblichus that identifies Iamblichus as the author of ABS.
7. I: The Scholia are an amplification and correction of Photius's summary of the autobiography of Iamblichus based upon the scholiast's reading of the manuscript of ABS.

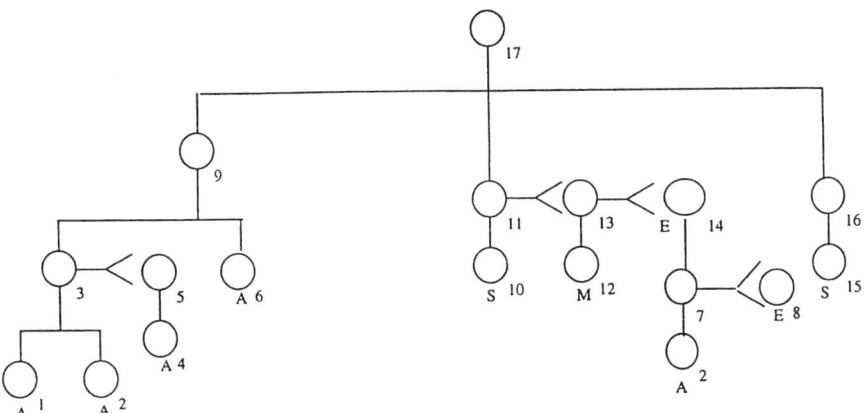

FIGURE 4.2. Chart A

8. E: The Scholia may have been based upon second- or third-hand accounts of what was in the manuscript by persons who claimed to have read the manuscript of ABS or to have known someone who had.
9. I: Iamblichus was the author of ABS.
10. S: Iamblichus was a native-born Syrian.
11. I: In ABS, Iamblichus identified himself as a native-born Syrian.
12. Millar (M; see nn. 16 and 19): Photius's summary reports that in the autobiography Iamblichus identifies himself as a Babylonian.[23]
13. I: The conflict between the report in the Scholia and Photius's summary casts doubt on the reliability of the Scholia.
14. E: The Scholia should be accepted as the more reliable account of Iamblichus's autobiography because it was intended as a correction of the summary of ABS prepared by Photius.
15. S: Iamblichus said he had been taught and had learned the Babylonian language, customs, and stories, of which ABS was one.
16. I: In ABS, Iamblichus said that he had been taught and had learned the Babylonian language, customs, and stories, of which ABS was one.
17. I: The author of ABS was Iamblichus, and Iamblichus was a Syrian who had been taught and had learned the Babylonian language, customs, and stories.

THE MACROSCOPIC IAMBLICHUS ARGUMENT

Proposition 17 was one of the two principal propositions necessary to Geller's argument. The other was proposition 57, set out below. All but two of the arguments in support of that proposition fit comfortably into a single chart that presents a macroscopic view of Geller's "Iamblichus argument" as a whole as well as a microanalysis of some of the supporting arguments. Key-List B and Chart B (fig. 4.3) depict the overview and supporting analysis.

Key-List B

18. S: Iamblichus was familiar with the Syrian language.
19. I: In the ABS, Iamblichus said he was familiar with the Syrian language.
20. I: Iamblichus was familiar with the Syrian language.
21. A: The Syrian language in the second century A.D. was Syriac.
22. I: Iamblichus knew Syriac.
23. S: Iamblichus said he had a tutor (the "Tutor") who taught him the Babylonian language.
24. I: In ABS, Iamblichus said he had a Tutor who taught him the Babylonian language.
25. I: Iamblichus had a Tutor who taught him the Babylonian language.
26. I: The Babylonian language that the Tutor taught Iamblichus was not Syriac.
27. Geller Assertion (GA) (from quoted text): The language Iamblichus wished "to learn . . . is most likely to be Akkadian."
28. I (Geller inference from proposition 27): Akkadian was the Babylonian language at the time Iamblichus sought to learn the Babylonian language.[24]

---

42. GA (in quoted text): Iamblichus continued to write in Rome until about 200 A.D., i.e. until the reign of Septimus Severus.[25]
43. G: The life span of most persons in the second century A.D. was less than sixty years.[26]
44. I: Iamblichus was not born earlier than 140 A.D.
45. S: Iamblichus knew Syriac and lived according to Syrian customs until the Tutor taught him the Babylonian language, customs, and stories.
46. I: In ABS, Iamblichus said that he knew Syriac and lived ac-

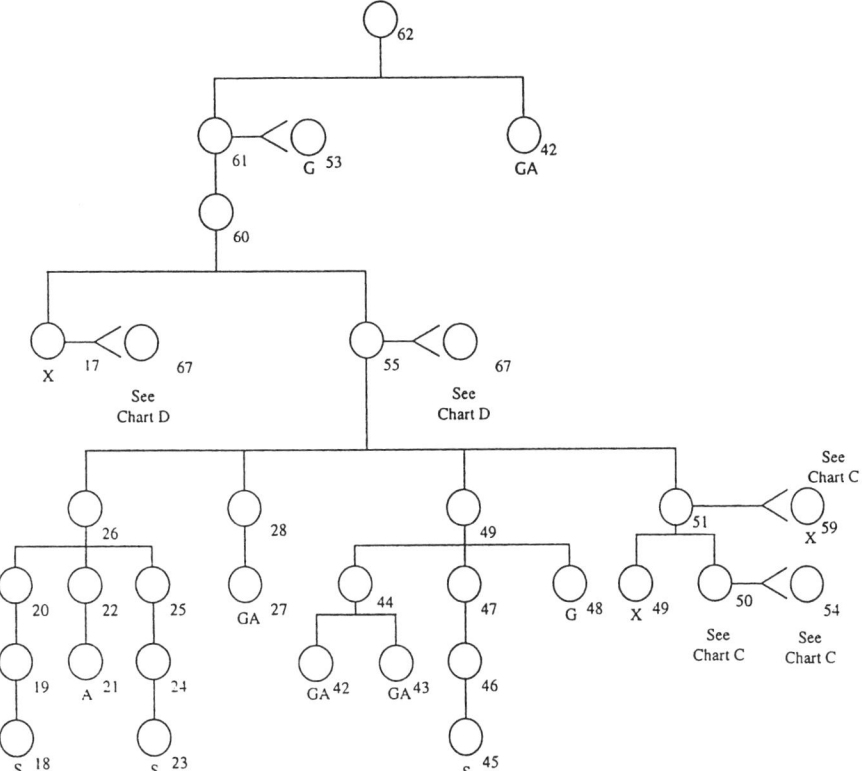

FIGURE 4.3. Chart B

cording to Syrian customs until the Tutor taught him the Babylonian language, customs, and stories.
47. I: Iamblichus knew Syriac and lived according to Syrian customs until the Tutor taught him the Babylonian language, customs, and stories.
48. G (Anderson): In the second century A.D., a Syrian would not have been mature enough to have developed a knowledge of his own language and customs sufficient to undertake or be permitted to undertake training from a tutor in a foreign language and customs until he was at least fifteen years old.
49. I: Iamblichus began to learn Babylonian language, customs, and stories from the Tutor in or after 155 A.D.
50. I (Geller): The Tutor remembered cuneiform well enough to teach it to Iamblichus.

51. I: The Tutor knew and could read Akkadian cuneiform until at least 155 A.D. (until the middle of the second century A.D.).

53. G: Few people would recall and be able to teach a language and script that they had not regularly spoken or used for forty years.
54. I: The tutor would not have recalled Akkadian or cuneiform in 155 A.D. after forty years as a slave in Syria.
55. I: The Babylonian language that Iamblichus learned from the Tutor after 155 A.D. was Akkadian cuneiform.

59. I: Iamblichus did not learn Akkadian cuneiform from the Tutor.
60. I: Iamblichus knew Akkadian cuneiform after 155 A.D.
61. I: Iamblichus remembered cuneiform for as long as he was an active writer.
62. I: Iamblichus knew and could read Akkadian cuneiform until the beginning of the third century A.D.

SOME DOUBTS ABOUT AN IMPLAUSIBLE TUTOR

The probative value of Geller's argument is wholly dependent upon the truth of the assertions Iamblichus made about himself. If those assertions were false, they are irrelevant to an argument about the survival of cuneiform. There are two types of reasons for doubting the truth of those assertions—doubts about the plausibility of the story Iamblichus tells about his education in *A Babylonian Story* and doubts of the credibility of Iamblichus stemming from how the story is told. Reasons calling into question the plausibility of the story told also provide reasons for doubting the credibility of the author of the story. Key-List C and Chart C (fig. 4.4) marshal the arguments in support of a claim that the story is too implausible to be accepted.

Key-List C

29. S: Iamblichus said the Tutor was a Babylonian royal scribe skilled in barbarian learning who was taken prisoner when Trajan invaded Babylonia [in 115–6 A.D.] and later sold as a slave to a Syrian.
30. I: In ABS, Iamblichus said the Tutor was a Babylonian royal scribe skilled in barbarian learning who was taken pris-

oner when Trajan invaded Babylonia [in 115–6 A.D.] and later sold as a slave to a Syrian.

31. I: The Tutor was a Babylonian royal scribe skilled in barbarian learning who was taken prisoner when Trajan invaded Babylonia [in 115–6 A.D.] and later sold as a slave to a Syrian.

32. G: (Anderson): A royal scribe in Babylonia would have been an adult who had received extensive training in the Babylonian language and customs of the time.

33. I: The Tutor was an adult who had received extensive training in Babylonian language and customs prior to 116 A.D.

34. G (Anderson): In order to be sufficiently educated to become a royal scribe skilled in Babylonian language and customs in the early part of the second century in Babylonia, a person would have to be at least twenty years old.[27]

35. I: The Tutor's education would have begun sometime late in the first century A.D.

36. X: In 75 A.D., there was an active community of priests or scholars and students who knew and could read or were studying Akkadian cuneiform at the location where the Astronomical Diary was written.[28]

37. I: The teachers who knew and students who learned Akkadian cuneiform in 75 A.D. would have continued to instruct students in Akkadian cuneiform until early in the second century A.D.

38. I (Geller): The Tutor had been trained in Akkadian cuneiform in Babylon prior to 116 A.D.

39. I: The Tutor knew Akkadian cuneiform when he was captured in 116 A.D.

40. G (Anderson assumption): Cuneiform was not taught to all royal scribes in Babylonia after the end of the first century A.D.[29]

41. E: The Tutor did not know cuneiform when he was captured.

---

49. I: Iamblichus began to learn the Babylonian language, customs, and stories from the Tutor in or after 155 A.D.

50. I (Geller): The Tutor remembered Akkadian cuneiform well enough to teach it to Iamblichus.

51. I: The Tutor knew and could read Akkadian cuneiform until at least 155 A.D. (until the middle of the second century A.D.).

52. I: At least forty years had elapsed between the time that the

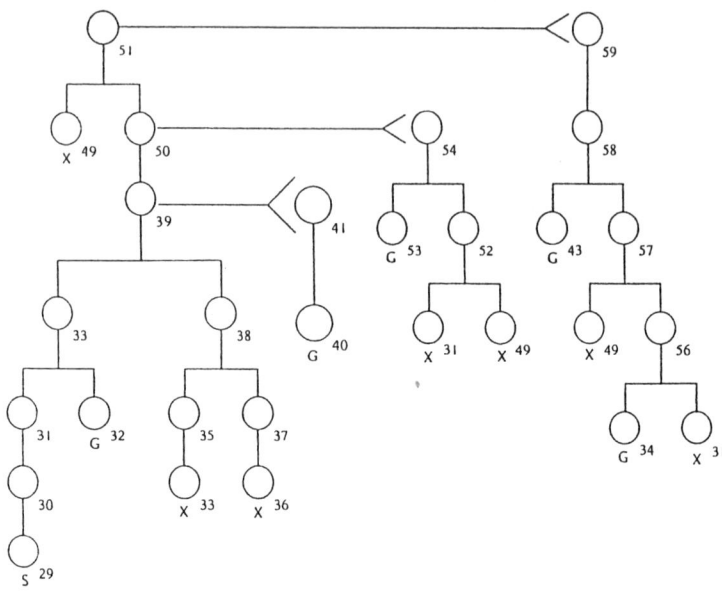

FIGURE 4.4. Chart C

    Tutor was taken prisoner and sold as a slave to a Syrian and the time that Iamblichus began studying cuneiform.

53. G: Few people would recall and be able to teach a language and script that they had not regularly spoken or used for forty years.
54. I: The Tutor would not have recalled Akkadian or cuneiform in 155 A.D. after forty years as a slave in Syria.

56. I: The Tutor was at least twenty years old in 116 A.D.
57. I: The Tutor would have been at least sixty years old when he began to instruct Iamblichus in 155 A.D. or thereafter.
58. I: The Tutor would not have lived long enough to be Iamblichus's teacher.
59. I: Iamblichus did not learn Akkadian cuneiform from the Tutor.[30]

THE AUTOBIOGRAPHY OF IAMBLICHUS IS FICTION

Arguments that a story is implausible can readily be converted to arguments that the author of that story is not credible. Such a conversion presents a risk that these arguments will be counted twice in determining the probative value of the argument as a whole, es-

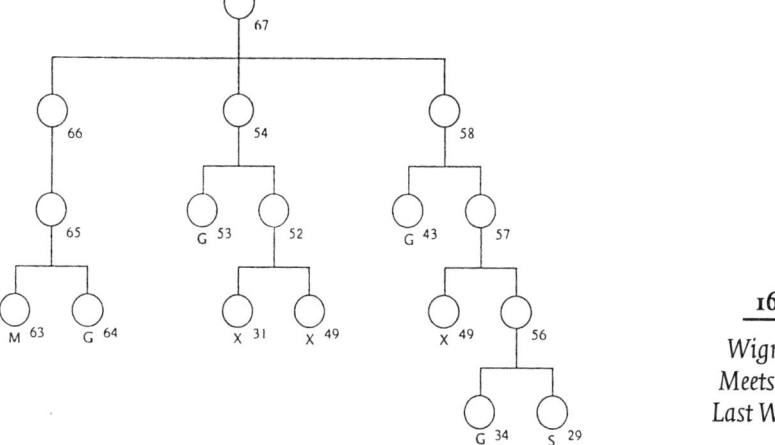

FIGURE 4.5. Chart D

pecially where there was no other evidence bearing upon the credibility of the author. Here, however, there is other evidence that supports an argument that the autobiography of Iamblichus is fiction in whole or in significant part. The additional propositions in key-list D can be combined with those in key-list C to identify the strongest argument that the autobiography was a fictional account so that the extent to which it diminishes the strength of Geller's argument can be fairly assessed. Chart D (fig. 4.5) depicts Anderson's view of the logical relationships among the propositions on key-list D.

Key-List D: Additional Propositions

63. M: Photius's summary indicates that the autobiography of Iamblichus was inserted in the middle of ABS.[31]
64. G (Anderson): It is unusual to find a reliable autobiography of an author in the middle of a novel.[32]
65. I: The author of ABS may have constructed or modified the biography of Iamblichus to lend better credence to the person identified as the author as a person having the knowledge necessary to recount the Babylonian story set out in ABS.
66. I: The facts reported in the Scholia may be based upon a fictionalized autobiography of Iamblichus.
67. I: The autobiography of Iamblichus in ABS is, to some degree, a fictionalized account.

Part 3. The Lawyer's Perspective: An Outsider's View of the Process and Product

The exercises described above yielded three insights from the outsider's standpoint that merit development. First, and not surprising, the principles of logic involved in marshalling evidence to support a hypothesis or to justify a conclusion are the same in both disciplines. A corollary also holds: Wigmore's chart method of analysis could be employed to depict the logical structures involved in demonstrating how a mass of evidential data supports an ultimate proposition to be proved or tested within a discipline such as Assyriology and, with intensive study, across disciplines. Second, the principal barriers to cross-disciplinary analysis and communication stem from the fact that the outsider does not share the stock of knowledge, the knowledge-based generalizations, that are shared by those within the discipline. Third, the application of the chart method makes it possible to examine the structure of arguments in ways that are not otherwise available.

An examination of the nature and structure of Geller's arguments illustrates these points. Moreover, those illustrations provide the foundation for some tentative suggestions by an outsider on how and to what effect the chart method might be used by insiders in any discipline concerned with evidence-based inquiries. The second and third points are developed below. That development further illustrates and strengthens the foundation for the first point and its corollary.

ON GENERALIZATIONS AND STOCKS OF KNOWLEDGE

Every inferential step in an argument can be restated in quasi-deductive form by identifying the background generalization which the analyst or the proponent believes necessary to justify the inference. Thus, Descartes's argument "I think; therefore I am" can be restated deductively as "All who think are; I think; therefore I am." The individual acquires and develops her personal set of generalizations from three sources or combinations thereof: belief-based generalizations, including prejudices and biases, that are part of the cultures shared by the groups in which the individual is born, reared, works, and lives; experience-based generalizations derived from the specific experiences of the individual; and knowledge-based generalizations acquired through study and instruction.

A charted analysis necessarily reflects the analyst's view of how the evidence and arguments can be most effectively marshalled based upon what the analyst accepts, consciously or unconsciously, as the generalizations that provide the strongest justifications for the steps in the argument. For that reason, it is almost certain that the key-lists and charts based upon independent analyses of the same evidential data for the same purpose prepared by different analysts using the same method would differ significantly in detail. The principal reasons for the differences stem from the fact that each individual brings to a problem her personal stock of knowledge and generalizations. An inferential step in an argument that seems obvious to one analyst might generate significant sources of doubt for another analyst, requiring that the argument be broken into several steps. Each would agree that the other's argument was logical, but would disagree on what steps were necessary to depict the argument accurately so that others could readily understand it and appraise its strength. Two illustrations may clarify the point.

First, assume that a driver in northern England who has been accused of driving without due care at noon on December 28 claimed that he was driving south on a road still wet from a recent rain shower and that he was blinded by the glare of the sun reflecting off the road. To a person who lived in an area in the Northern Hemisphere distant from the equator, where the winter sun is low in the southern sky at noon, the plausibility of the assertion would be immediately apparent, and the logical basis for the assertion would require no further amplification. For a person who lived in an area close to the equator, however, where the sun is almost directly overhead at noon in all seasons, the claim might require considerably more explanation and justification.[33]

Second, a rational justification for the verdict in the criminal case against OJS is, in one view, entirely dependent upon the belief one holds with respect to the following generalization:

> Police officers usually/frequently/sometimes/occasionally/rarely lie and fabricate evidence in gathering and presenting evidence that will solve a crime or will facilitate a conviction.

For those who hold the view that police "rarely" lie or fabricate evidence, the facts (a) that Detective Mark Fuhrman lied and asserted that he and other officers regularly fabricated evidence[34] and (b) that Detective Phillip Vannatter improperly carried the vial containing a sample of OJS's blood would indicate only that there was a "bad apple" working in the Los Angeles Police Department and that detectives sometimes make mistakes. Those facts would be unlikely to affect their view of the other evidence in the case significantly.

For jurors whose experience with and observations of the police led them to the view that police "usually" lie and fabricate evidence (or who were part of a group whose members held this view as a part of their culture), those facts would support a far different conclusion. Evidence showing that Detective Fuhrman had lied in the particular case and had admitted elsewhere that he and other officers regularly fabricated evidence in criminal cases would support claims that he and other officers had lied and fabricated evidence in the *Simpson* case. The fact that blood found on a gatepost in NBS's yard contained a preservative of the kind placed in vials containing blood specimens drawn from individuals would confirm that Detective Vannatter had planted OJS's blood on the gatepost and further support the view that the police had fabricated evidence in this case. That view of the evidence would fully justify a decision that all of the physical evidence gathered and testimony presented by police officers should be viewed as highly suspect and given little, if any, weight.

Although analysts trained in the same discipline will have different views on the generalizations involved in an argument, the differences are likely to be less significant and more readily explicable than the differences that arise in a cross-disciplinary analysis. The training within a discipline is designed to assure that its initiates all receive a common stock of basic knowledge. The common stock of knowledge and shared knowledge-based generalizations within a discipline are enhanced over time because those within the discipline address similar problems and must communicate the results of their analyses to others in the discipline for review and appraisal. One function of such training and experience, whether intended or incidental, is to create and maintain the barriers that in large measure define the discipline.

The present exercises brought those differences into sharp focus. Many of the comments and queries interspersed in Anderson's NIAS key-lists stemmed from his lack of background knowledge necessary to fully understand and appraise Geller's arguments. The NIAS key-list, the final product of the NIAS exercise, demonstrates that he was unable to overcome many of the barriers that divide the disciplines of Law and Assyriology in the time allotted to that exercise. For the second exercise, Anderson gathered additional information that he thought sufficient to enable him to complete the microscopic analysis presented in part 2, above. As a result, a paragraph that had generated thirty-two propositions (numbers 109–40) in the NIAS key-list generated sixty-seven propositions in the revised analysis presented in the Iamblichus key-list and charts.

Based upon his experience with these exercises, Anderson, the outsider, concluded that a full articulation of the propositions necessary to enable him to complete a comprehensive charted analysis of all of the arguments in Geller's text would require more than 500 propositions. In contrast, Geller, the insider, argues in the next chapter that only 126 propositions were necessary to restate his arguments in propositional form. Anderson was attempting to generate an analysis that developed and justified Geller's arguments in a form that he and other outsiders could understand and evaluate. Geller, on the other hand, sought only to develop an argument that could be understood and evaluated by other insiders. The analysts' standpoints differed.

TAKING ARGUMENTS SERIOUSLY

The chart method of analysis requires the analyst to depict the structure of the arguments charted in graphic form. Such a depiction makes it possible to examine the charted arguments in ways not otherwise feasible. Some observations suggested by examining Geller's arguments through Wigmorean lenses should illustrate the potential utility of the method in analyzing evidence-based arguments in other contexts.

A basic principle of proof in legal proceedings is simple. Relevant evidence should be admitted unless identifiable improper prejudicial effects substantially outweigh its legitimate probative value. The definition of relevance used in proceedings before federal courts in the United States would probably pass without serious objection in most fields: "'Relevant evidence' means evidence having any tendency to make the existence of any fact that is of consequence . . . more probable or less probable than it would be without the evidence."[35] The seeming breadth of this definition is tempered by utilitarian and policy concerns in legal and other contexts. For example, under federal rules, relevant evidence may be excluded if its improper prejudicial effects substantially outweigh its legitimate probative value.[36] Although what effects should be viewed as improper prejudicial effects may differ from discipline to discipline, the idea of identifying the improper prejudicial effects as well as the legitimate probative value of the evidence upon which an argument is based suggests a framework that might be applied in examining evidence-based arguments in any field or discipline. The analyses presented above make it possible to illustrate how that framework might be used to examine and critique some of the arguments made in "The Last Wedge."

The key-lists and charts demonstrate that all of Geller's evidence was relevant, at least tangentially, to his ultimate probandum. His arguments differed in at least two respects. First, some were more *attenuated* than others. For example, the necessary inferential steps in the argument that the astronomical diary created in 75 A.D. (proposition 22 in the NIAS key-list) makes it probable that there was at least one small community of persons who could read and write in cuneiform script in 75 A.D. (proposition 36) are relatively few and relatively direct. The support that that inference provides for the further inference that cuneiform-literate scholars survived into the second or third century is more attenuated. So, too, his argument that there were statements in *A Babylonian Story* that support the view that a tutor taught Iamblichus Akkadian cuneiform in the middle of the second century A.D. is extremely attenuated. The necessary steps in the argument are many and the inferential paths are complex and indirect.

Second, some of his arguments were far more *appraisable* than others. Once the arguments based upon the astronomical diary had been restated in a form that enabled an outsider to understand them, an outsider could appraise their apparent strength with respect to the existence of a cuneiform-literate community in 75 A.D. (proposition 36) and would infer that insiders could knowledgeably debate and probably agree upon an appraisal of the strength of that argument and of the strength of the support that that argument provided for the further inference that such communities continued to exist into the second or third century. Even with the rearticulation and analysis of the Iamblichus argument developed above, however, it is not clear to an outsider how the arguments based upon the scholiast's notes should or could be appraised. There are too many unknown and probably unknowable variables. How competent and precise an interpreter was the unknown scholiast? Was the source of his notes direct observation or secondhand reports? Did Iamblichus intend to provide an honest account in his autobiography, or was it a fictionalized account designed to lend authority to the claim that the story told was an authentic Babylonian story?[37] If these variables are unknowable in fact, it would follow that even an insider would not be able to appraise these arguments accurately.[38]

Evidence supporting attenuated but nonetheless appraisable arguments ordinarily would be admissible in legal proceedings. Evidence that is relevant but unappraisable ordinarily would be excluded in legal proceedings, because the legitimate probative value cannot fairly be determined and thus improper prejudicial effects, the risk of confusion or misvaluation, substantially outweigh any legitimate probative value. Under those principles, relevant evidence supporting arguments such as those based upon the astronomical diary would ordinarily be admissible. Relevant evidence supporting unappraisable arguments such as those based upon Iamblichus would be excluded, even if there were no specific rules regulating the admissibility and use of hearsay evidence.

No discipline has or is likely to accept rules excluding relevant evidence from consideration and debate. Nonetheless, the application of the kind of rigorous atomistic analysis that is required by the chart method of analysis used here would make it possible to classify all of Geller's arguments in terms of the extent of their attenuation and their appraisability. Presumably, an insider reviewing the argument as a whole might justifiably identify and segregate those that were unappraisable in developing a position on the likelihood that Geller's ultimate probandum is true. This suggests one way that the chart method applied here might be used to provide a different framework for reviewing and critiquing arguments in any discipline that applies the principles of logic in evidenced-based inquiries.

Anderson undertook these exercises to test his hypothesis that the chart method of analysis could usefully be applied to analyze evidence-based arguments in another discipline. The results provide strong confirmation, in his view, for the conclusion that the method can be applied across disciplines. Those results also suggest, in his view, that the method might usefully be applied within disciplines other than Law to generate insights that would contribute to an understanding of the structures of argumentation and the ways in which evidence and argumentation can be effectively analyzed and critiqued. Those, however, are suggestions that can be tested and evaluated only by scholars working in such other disciplines.

Appendix 1
Key-List for NIAS Evidence and Inference Presentation, April 4, 1995[39]

The Provisional Ultimate Probandum

1. The class of persons who could read cuneiform probably survived without interruption until sometime after the Sassanian conquest of Babylonia in 256 A.D.

The Provisional Penultimate Probanda

2. One or more active temple centers where cuneiform was read, studied, and taught survived into the third century A.D.
3. The Astronomical Diary produced in 75 A.D., the quantity of tablets produced in the Hellenistic period [circa 321 B.C.–256 A.D.] as evidenced by the surviving fragments, and the Greek script inscribed on the "Graeco-Babyloniaca" tablets establish that the class of persons who could read cuneiform survived until the second or third century A.D.
4. [I-MG(3/29): The Astronomical Diary establishes that Akkadian cuneiform was a living language in 75 A.D. and for sometime thereafter.]
5. The quantity of tablets produced after the Hellenistic period had begun, as evidenced by surviving fragments in the Pergamon collection and elsewhere, establishes that there were a significant number of active temples with schools in operation where cuneiform was studied, read, and taught at the beginning of the Hellenistic period.
6. The Greek script of the latest of the Graeco-Babyloniaca tablets establishes that there was at least one active temple or other center where cuneiform could be read and written at the end of the second or the beginning of the third century A.D.
7. The investment in constructing new temples in the Seleucid period [312–64 B.C.] and thereafter and the evidence found at the temple at Assur establish that temples practicing Sumerian and Akkadian religions, where cuneiform was studied, taught, and could be read, survived until the second or third century A.D.
8. There is additional evidence in the documentary record left

by Babylonians and non-Babylonians suggesting that the ability to read cuneiform survived until the third century A.D.
9. Throughout the Hellenistic period, Parthian regimes in Mesopotamia were characterized by syncretism and tolerance of local religions.
10. [G-TJA: A significant change in circumstances is necessary to account for the termination of an ongoing institution and its activities.]
11. The temple communities that survived until the end of the second or the beginning of the third century A.D. probably continued to operate until there was a change in circumstances.
12. The Sassanian conquest in 256 A.D. was the probable cause of the termination of the class of persons who could read cuneiform.
13. The Sassanian state was based upon a religious ideology that did not permit competing religious systems to coexist within the Sassanian state.
14. Following the conquest in 256 A.D., the Sassanians pursued a policy of persecution and intolerance of non-Sassanian religions.
15. By 256 A.D. the number of temples where cuneiform was read and studied and the number of persons supporting them would have diminished in any event.
16. Sassanian policy and implementing actions would have represented a sufficient change in circumstances to bring about the termination of the temple school communities where the ability to read and write cuneiform had been preserved.

I. The Surviving Tablets and Fragments

A. SOME BACKGROUND GENERALIZATIONS

17. [G-MG(3/30): All or almost all cuneiform tablets produced after 500 B.C. were produced by priests, scholars, or students working in a temple community.]
18. [G–Corrolary of #17 supra: A discovery of cuneiform tablets or fragments of cuneiform tablets produced after 500 B.C. at a location indicates that there was an active temple community in that vicinity at the time that the tablets were written.]
19. [G-Corrolary of #17 supra: The existence of cuneiform

tablets or fragments of cuneiform tablets produced after 500 B.C. is strong evidence that one or more active temple communities composed of priests, scholars, and students who knew or were learning cuneiform existed at the time the tablets were produced.]

20. [G-TJA (assumption): All or almost all persons who could read and write classic cuneiform after 500 B.C. and who could produce texts of the kind inscribed on cuneiform tablets after 500 B.C. were persons who had been trained in schools associated with active Akkadian and Sumerian temples.]

21. [G-TJA (common sense): An active temple that included students studying cuneiform for the future as well as priests or scholars who were receiving adequate support to maintain the temple would, absent destructive intervening causes, continue to exist for a considerable period of time, even if support declined and ultimately terminated, and the community of persons who knew cuneiform would continue for at least a generation after the temple closed.]

B. THE ASTRONOMICAL DIARY

22. A tablet has been discovered and exists and can be inspected that has inscribed upon it an astronomical diary (the "Astronomical Diary") that is inscribed in standard Akkadian cuneiform and that records information of the kind customarily recorded in Sumerian and Akkadian astronomical diaries.

23. [G-MG(3/29): Astronomical diaries described events occurring on the date on which an entry was written.]

24. [I-MG(3/29): Astronomical diaries can be accurately dated by determining the dates on which the events described occurred.]

25. [The events and other information described in the Astronomical Diary establish that it was inscribed in 75 A.D.]

26. The Astronomical Diary was inscribed in standard Akkadian cuneiform.

27. The Astronomical Diary was written in cuneiform in approximately 75 A.D.

28. The person who wrote the Astronomical Diary (the "scribe") in 75 A.D. had been trained in [had learned to write in] standard Akkadian cuneiform.

29. [The scribe had been trained in [had learned] the Akkadian system for constructing and recording information in an astronomical diary.]
30. [The scribe had received the kind of classical education that was commonly provided only in Akkadian and Sumerian temple schools.]
31. [The scribe had been educated in a temple school where Akkadian cuneiform was read, studied, and taught.]
32. [In the period immediately prior to 75 A.D., there was an active temple where cuneiform was read, studied, and taught.]
33. [G-MG(3/29): Astronomical diaries contained useful information that was recorded to be read and used by others.]
34. [I-MG(3/29): The scribe who wrote the Astronomical Diary in 75 A.D. believed that there were and would be enough other persons who could read Akkadian cuneiform to justify the effort of maintaining an astronomical diary.]
35. [I-TJA(3/30): In 75 A.D., there was an active community of priests or scholars and students who knew and could read or were studying Akkadian cuneiform at the location where the Astronomical Diary was written. (What can we say about minimum size?)]
36. The Astronomical Diary written in 75 A.D. establishes that there were one or more active communities of priests, scholars, and students who could read cuneiform at that time.
37. The tablet on which the Astronomical Diary is inscribed is the latest dateable cuneiform tablet that has been discovered.

C. OTHER LATE FRAGMENTS

1. In General

38. [Rev. 3/30]: There are many other undated fragments written in a late cuneiform script which indicates that they were written during the Hellenistic period.
39. [G-MG(3/29): The Hellenistic period began circa 321 B.C. and continued until circa 250 A.D.]
40. [Rev. #6 in original (3/30)]: These fragments are the surviving representatives that have been discovered to date of an archive of cuneiform tablets written in Babylonia [Mesopotamia?] during the Hellenistic period.
41. [Rev. #6 in original (3/30)]: The quantity of fragments that have been discovered to date indicates that the archives of

tablets produced in the Hellenistic period must have been extensive.]
42. [Rev. #5 in original (3/30)]: The size of the archive produced in the Hellenistic period indicates that cuneiform tablets were being written (and studied) well into and perhaps throughout the Hellenistic period.
43. [From ## 11–17 supra]: The existence of these fragments indicates that there were a significant number of active temple communities actively using, producing, and studying cuneiform at the beginning of the Hellenistic period.]

2. The Pergamon Collection

44. The collection of fragments in the Pergamon Museum in Berlin (the "Pergamon collection") has an impressive collection of hymns and prayers in both Sumerian and Akkadian.
45. The colophons of the texts [inscribed dates] on the tablet in the Pergamon collection that survived indicate that these texts were written or copied around 250 B.C.
46. The language of the texts from which the Pergamon collection survives is extremely conservative and archaic.
47. [I-MG(3/29): The language of the texts shows that scholars and students were actively studying and producing good classic Sumerian and Akkadian literature in cuneiform in 250 B.C.]
48. The hymns and prayers reproduced on the Pergamon collection reflect contemporary temple liturgy at the time they were written.
49. One would not expect to find evidence that scribal and literary activity in Sumerian and Akkadian were flourishing in 250 B.C.
50. The fragments from the Pergamon collection indicate that the languages of ancient Babylonian culture were still in use in the temples of Babylonia in 250 B.C.
51. [I-TJA(3/30): The quantity of fragments (and the location of their discoveries? MG?) indicates that the number of temples and the activity were such that these temples must have continued to exist for a considerable part of, and that some may have continued to exist throughout, the Hellenistic period.]

D. THE "GRAECO-BABYLONIACA" TABLETS

1. Background Information

52. There are approximately twenty tablets (the "GBTs") that have cuneiform, either Sumerian or Akkadian, on one side and a transliteration of the same text in Greek on the other.
53. [G-MG(3/30): All inscriptions on a clay tablet must be made while the clay is moist, i.e., within a finite number of hours.]
54. [I-MG(3/30): The cuneiform and the Greek inscription on the GBTs were done at the same time.]

2. Script-Dating the GBTs

55. [G-MG(3/29): Greek scholars can date surviving Greek texts accurately by the shapes of the Greek characters produced.]
56. [G-MG(3/29): The Greek script table (the "Script Table"; reproduced as fig. 3.1 above) accurately identifies the period in which the Greek characters on the various GBTs were written in conformance with script-dating principles generally accepted among scholars of ancient Greek.]
57. One of the GBTs is in the Harvard Museum (the "Harvard GBT"), and there is insufficient evidence to support an inference as to the location at which the Harvard GBT was discovered and thus where it was probably inscribed.
58. [Add. I-MG(3/30): A comparison of the Greek characters in the Script Table and the Greek characters on the Harvard GBT establish that it is probable/almost certain that that GBT was inscribed in the late second or early third century A.D.]
59. [Add. G-TJA (assumed); confirmed MG(3/30): Ranking scholars in the field of dating Greek script have examined [reproductions of] the Greek script of the Harvard GBT and concur that that GBT was inscribed in the late second or early third century A.D.]
60. [Rev. of orig. #34–3/30] The Harvard GBT was inscribed in the latter part of the second or the early part of the third century A.D.]
61. [Add. MG(3/30): A GBT that was almost certainly discovered at a site within the ancient city of Babylon is now at the Berlin Museum (the "Berlin GBT").]
62. [Add. MG(3/30): A comparison of the Greek characters in

the Script Table and the Greek characters on the Berlin GBT establish that it is probable/almost certain that that GBT was inscribed in the first century A.D.]

63. [Add. TJA assumed; confirmed MG(3/30): Ranking scholars in the field of dating Greek script have examined [reproductions of] the Greek script of the Berlin GBT and concur that that GBT was inscribed in the first century A.D.]

64. [Add. MG(3/30): There is a GBT at the museum in St. Petersburg that has yet to be sufficiently examined to enable a determination of the period in which it was inscribed.]

65. [Add. MG(3/30): The remaining seventeen GBTs are in the British Museum (the "British GBTs"), and these GBTs were almost certainly discovered at a site within the ancient city of Babylonia.]

66. [Add. MG(3/30): A comparison of the Greek characters in the Script Table and the Greek characters on the British GBTs establishes that it is probable/almost certain that the British GBTs were inscribed at various times during the second and first centuries B.C.]

67. [Add. TJA assumed; confirmed MG(3/30): Ranking scholars in the field of dating Greek script have examined [reproductions of] the Greek script on the British GBTs and concur that these GBTs were inscribed at various times in the second and the first centuries B.C.]

3. The Intrinsic Significance of the GBTs

68. The fact that these are transliterations, rather than translations, means that the Greek script was intended to show how cuneiform is to be read or would sound or be read in Greek.

69. The GBTs establish that the author [or authors?] could still read and understand classical Sumerian and Akkadian at the time the GBTs were written.

70. At the time the GBTs had been written, Sumerian had not been spoken or used conversationally for 2,000 years.]

71. At the time the GBTs were written, Akkadian was most likely not spoken or used conversationally, but could still be read and understood.

72. [Rev. orig. #22–MG(3/30):] The GBTs come from one or more temple schools that used and understood classic

Sumerian and Akkadian of the kind used and understood at temple school active in the sixth century B.C.

[Check this: Since you revised the proposition, it may not be fully supported here.]

73. The texts reproduced on the GBTs are typical samples of school curriculum texts copied by Babylonian schoolboys [3/30 add.] in temple schools prior to 500 B.C.
74. The texts include a hymn to Samas and incantations and Sumerian-Akkadian glossaries.
75. A hymn to Samas, incantations, and Sumerian-Akkadian glossaries were typical school curriculum texts for Babylonian schoolboys [3/30 add.] in temples prior to 500 B.C.
76. [Rev. (3/30):] During the sixth century B.C., students in Babylonian temple schools would regularly write their lines on the back of the tablets containing their assigned texts.
77. [(3/30) Clarifying addition:] The persons who wrote the transliterated lines of the text that appeared on the front of the GBTs wrote those lines on the back of the GBTs.]
78. The cuneiform on the GBTs looks the same as the cuneiform on school texts written as far back as the Late Babylonian period, from about 600 B.C.]
79. There are detectible differences between the features in cuneiform writing of the Seleucid, as opposed to the Persian, period.
80. The GBTs are in all respects similar to other Babylonian school texts in common use in temples circa 600 B.C.

4. The System of Transliteration

81. The system of "transcribing" [transliterating?] cuneiform into Greek is the same as the system used by Father Origen to transliterate Hebrew and Aramaic into Greek in the third century A.D.
82. [Rev. (3/31):] Origen used a column method of transliteration and translation to present the Hebrew Bible in Greek (and Aramaic) in "competing translations."
83. [Add. (3/31): In Origen's texts, the Hebrew characters of the text were presented in the first column, and a phonetic transliteration replicating the sound of each character with a Greek character was presented in the second column, and

then the translations in Greek (and sometimes Aramaic) were presented in the remaining columns.]

84. [Add. (3/31): In Origen's texts, the same Greek characters were consistently used with precision to replicate the same sounds throughout the transliterations.]

85. [Add. (3/31): The system of transliteration employed on the GBTs is strikingly similar to the system used by Origen.]

86. [Add. (3/31): The Akkadian or Sumerian text on the front of the GBTs was written in column form and the transliteration of the reverse side was presented in parallel columns the same as the parallel transliterating columns in Origen's texts.]

87. [Add. (3/31): The same Greek characters were used with apparent precision to represent the same sounds on all of the GBTs and the sounds for which each Greek character was used was the same as the sound for which Origen used that character.]

88. [Add. TJA (opponent's explanation [OE]; 3/31) from MG(3/30): The cuneiform syllabary had 600 character symbols to depict sounds in the Sumerian and Akkadian languages.]

89. [Add. TJA(OE; 3/31) from MG(3/30): The Hebrew alphabet had only 26 [?check?] character symbols to depict sounds in the Hebrew language.]

90. [Add. TJA(OE; 3/31) from MG(3/30): The Greek alphabet had only 26 [?check?] character symbols to depict sounds in the Greek language.]

91. [Add. TJA(OE; 3/31): Any claim that a system of transliterating cuneiform into Greek was the same as a system used to transliterate Hebrew into Greek is undermined by the gross disparity in the nature and number of character symbols used in cuneiform and in Hebrew.]

92. [Add. TJA(OE; 3/31): Any claim that the system used to transliterate cuneiform into Greek on the GBTs is the same as the system used by Origen to transliterate Hebrew into Greek is further undermined by the fact that there are too few GBTs to permit a firm conclusion to be drawn concerning a comprehensive description of the system of transliteration used in the GBTs.]

93. [Add. TJA(OE; 3/31): Propositions 65–69 significantly diminish the strength or degree of certainty which can prop-

erly be claimed for the conclusion presented in proposition 73 and the further inference based upon that proposition.]
94. Origen flourished [worked?] in Caesarea in the mid–third century A.D.
95. The same patterns of transliteration were used by both Origen in Caesarea and the priests in Babylon.
96. [TJA rev. based on MG(3/30)]: The similarities between the system of transcription and transliteration employed by the authors of the GBTs and the system employed by Origen suggest that Origen was familiar with and based his system upon the system used by the authors of the GBTs.
97. [Proposition 73 supports an inference: Origen was familiar with the GBTs and the system they employed.]
98. [Propositions 71 through 74 support an inference: The GBTs were in use and accessible to scholars throughout the mid-east in the early third century A.D.]
99. The transliterations by Origen in Caesarea and transliterations of the GBTs may have been done at the same time.

5. *An Unresolved Mystery*

100. [(3/30) Clarifying addition: The purpose for which the GBTs were written remains a mystery for which no plausible hypotheses have been advanced.]
101. The principal function of transliteration is to enable persons who know the language into which a foreign language is transliterated to read (typically aloud) the foreign language.
102. Jews transliterate the kaddish from Hebrew letters to the Latin alphabet to enable persons who can not read the Hebrew alphabet to say the prayer aloud.
103. The only identifiable function of transliteration from a foreign script to another script is to enable those familiar with one script to learn the foreign script and language.
104. In the ancient Babylonian schools, students did not transliterate, they translated from the language under study into the familiar language [or the reverse?].
105. If the student(s) who prepared the GBTs had been students knowledgeable in cuneiform who were studying Greek, then the Greek texts would have been translations, not transliterations of the cuneiform texts.
106. None of the GBTs has cuneiform translated into Greek.

107. "We cannot say, then, that a Greek scribe was taking rudimentary lesson in cuneiform, because the Akkadian appears to be the same as for any other Babylonian pupil."

108. "There is no obvious reason that the need for transliteration into Greek script ought to have arisen during a period of both literary and administrative scribal activity."

II. Testimonial Evidence: The Claimed Witnesses

A. THE SIGNIFICANCE OF IAMBLICHUS

[This argument is neither strong nor important to MG's thesis. If it has any utility to TJA's analysis, it is as an illustration of the problems of competence and hearsay in historical arguments. I have made revisions to the original key-list to capture the essence of MG's comments without attempting to mark the changes carefully.]

109. Iamblichus ("Iamb") was a Syrian who composed erotic tales in Greek circa 200 A.D. whose works and autobiography are in Photius's library.

[Because the dates are important, you may want to specify, to the extent possible, the dates of birth and death for this Iamblichus.]

110. [Photius was a man who collected Greek works and copied Greek manuscripts.]

[When did Photius live? Where did he or she maintain the library? What evidence do we have that Photius's transcriptions were accurate? Did the original texts of Iamb's biography survive? of any of his other works?]

111. [The scholiast was a person who made marginal notes in a French translation of Iamb's works at the end of the ninth or beginning of the tenth century.]

[How do we know who the scholiast was? Does the term *scholiast* refer to more than one person? How do we know when the marginal notes were made? Who prepared the French translations? Do the texts that were translated survive? Are the translations accurate? Where are/were the French translations?]

112. [There is no evidence to show the source or sources upon which the scholiast based her or his notes.]

113. The scholiast reported that Iamb was a native Syrian, and not a Greek-Syrian, who knew Syriac, but who also had a tutor who taught him the Babylonian language, as well as (Babylonian) customs and history.

[The foregoing proposition is the sole support for the succeeding five propositions. Is there any evidence to support any of this information in Iamb's biography? Do we have any information about other sources from which the scholiast might have based this proposition? Is there any evidence tending to establish the scholiast was a careful scholar in his or her other writings? This is a classic problem of competence and hearsay. Absent information, we have no basis for concluding that the scholiast knew or plausibly could have known the facts asserted. If there was a basis, it must have been assertions in Iamb's writings or in the writings of others; but if we do not know the writings upon which they were based, we have no basis for appraising the credibility of the sources. Given these problems, does the presentation of the argument you are making here satisfy the minimum standards of scholarly arguments in the field?]

114. Iamb was a Syrian.
115. Iamb was not a Greek-Syrian.
116. Iamb knew Syriac.
117. Iamb had a tutor who taught him the Babylonian language.
118. Iamb had a tutor who taught him Babylonian customs.
119. The [scholiast] also reported that Iamb continued his career as a writer in Rome, residing there during the reign of Septimus Severus.
120. Septimus Severus reigned circa 200 A.D.
121. Iamb spoke the *glossa Syriaca*. [An inference from propositions 91 through 93.]
122. *Glossa Syriaca* was the local dialect of Aramaic.
123. Iamb knew and spoke Aramaic.
124. Iamb wanted to learn the *glossa Babyloniaca*. [An inference from propositions 95 through 96.]
125. The *glossa Babyloniaca* that Iamb wanted to learn was "in my view most likely to be Akkadian."

[What is the basis for your view? This appears to be the crucial step in this line of argument. Unless it is generally accepted among Assyriologists that (a) most royal scribes in Babylonia at the time that Iamb's tutor had that position would have been able to read and write cuneiform and that (b) cuneiform was "the glossa Babyloniaca" at the time when Iamb wanted to learn "the Babylon language," the support for this step needs to specified with care. I assume that propositions from the scholiast's further notes reported below are the source of your speculation, but the relationship is not clearly enough specified and the further conclusion that "Iamb's teacher 'most likely knew cuneiform'" involves a further crucial step for which you do not specify the support, if any. Based upon our conversations, I gather that in reality this line of argument is offered as an interesting set of speculations that could conceivably be true, but that you are not claiming that it is a well-supported argument favoring your conclusion. I think that the propositions supporting your view should be carefully specified and presented in a way that makes the speculative nature of the argument clear. Otherwise, I think that this "in-my-view" argument will draw serious criticisms that may undermine and obscure the arguments developed in other parts of the analysis.]

126. Iamb had the desire and the tutor in Syria in the mid–second century A.D.
127. The scholiast adds: Iamb's teacher was a Babylonian who was taken prisoner by the Romans during Trajan's campaign there, and later sold into slavery in Syria.
128. The scholiast reports: Iamb's teacher was skilled in "barbarian learning," having served as a royal scribe in Babylon.

[Same queries concerning the actual or possible sources of the scholiast's knowledge.]

129. Iamb's teacher was skilled in "barbarian learning."
130. Iamb's teacher was a royal scribe in Babylon.
131. Iamb's teacher was a scholar. [An inference from propositions 106 and 107]
132. "Barbarian learning" never refers to Greek culture.
133. [Iamb's teacher was a scholar in Babylonian learning.]

[TJA formulation of the next intended step in MG's inferential structure. Did I get it right?]

134. Iamb's teacher "most likely knew cuneiform."

   [The problems with this conclusion are similar to the ones identified under proposition 102 above. This proposition appears to assume the position you are arguing. Did all Babylonian scholars circa 115 A.D. know cuneiform? Would this proposition be generally accepted among your scholarly peers? If not, is there evidence to support it? What am I missing?]

135. Trajan conquered Babylonia circa 115 A.D.
136. The tutor was a royal scribe in Babylonia by 115 A.D.
137. The tutor must have been a fully educated adult in 115 A.D.
138. Iamb was actively writing in Rome in 200 A.D.
139. Iamb cannot have been too old a man to be recognized as an active writer in 200 A.D.

   [What do we know about life expectancies in this period and about Iamb's date of birth? The propositions advanced by the scholiast seem inconsistent with the generally accepted historical facts. For example, if Iamb were born as early as 140 A.D., he probably could not have been an educated Syrian adult in a position to seek a Babylonian tutor earlier than 160 A.D. But if the tutor had been only twenty-five when he was captured in 115 A.D., then he would have been sixty when Iamb was old enough to acquire his services. The ages can be made to work, but the time differential makes the scenario described seem sufficiently implausible to require some amplification and explanation.]

140. Iamb's teacher knew cuneiform so well that he was able to recall and teach it to Iamb later in the century.

B. THE SIGNIFICANCE OF ELAGABALUS

141. The Roman emperor known as Elagabalus [circa 218–22 A.D.] insisted on wearing Syrian dress.
142. Elagabalus lived with or married a vestal virgin.
143. At the time of Elagabalus, it was generally viewed by Romans as inappropriate to wear Syrian dress or to live with a vestal virgin.
144. In Babylonian culture, it was traditional for the king to marry a priestess to insure fertility in the land.

145. According to Dio, Elagabalus said "I did it [married a vestal virgin] in order that godlike children might spring from me, the high priest, and from her, the high priestess."
146. [The quote supports the view that] a Roman emperor in the third century A.D. introduced Near Eastern practices to the office of the Roman emperor in the face of critical commentary from his contemporaries.
147. Elagabalus's [apparent knowledge and] behavior suggests that Babylonian cults may still have been functioning in temples in Mesopotamia in the third century A.D.

III. Evidence Concerning the Survival of Babylonian Temples

A. THE SYRIAN CULTS

148. The cults and shrines of Mesopotamian gods proliferated in neighboring Syria to a surprising extent.

    [When? Surprising to whom? Why surprising?]

149. Paganism survived side by side with Christianity in the Christian city of Edessa until the sixth century A.D.
150. The cults of the Babylonian gods Bel, Belti, Nabu, Nergal, Shamash, Tammuz, Nanai, and Adad were all represented [in Syria until when?].
151. The [A?] Temple of Bel was constructed in Palmyra in 32 A.D.
152. A Nabu temple was also built in Palmyra in the first century A.D.
153. The cult of the moon god Sin was still prominent in Parthian Harran.

    [When and where is that and in what sense "prominent"?]

154. "Hatra also demonstrates Babylonian influence in the cult. . . ."

    [What is the meaning and significance of that assertion?]

155. Many of these same Babylonian gods occur in theophoric personal names in inscriptions and records from Syria in the second and third centuries A.D.

    [What is the significance of the qualifier "theophoric"]

156. Many such persons with good Babylonian names are known from Palmyra, Dura-Europus, Edessa, and elsewhere [in Syria? when?].
157. [Propositions 72 through 80 provide some evidence that Babylonian cults may have flourished in Syria until the third century.]

[Mark: This seemed to me to be the inference to be drawn. Is it the one that you intend be drawn? If so, is the significance of this inference that it would support further inferences along the line that the survival of these cults would require the training and survival of priests and that these cults and their rituals were only inscribed in cuneiform, and thus that the survival of the cult implies the survival of the language of training and practice—i.e., cuneiform? If that is a supportable line of argument, I think it should be developed and made explicit.]

158. The use of proper names associated with a civilization may continue in use well after the civilization itself has disappeared.

B. THE MESOPOTAMIAN TEMPLES

1. Some Proponent's Assertions

159. The older temples of the major cities of Babylon [Babylon cities of?], Borsippa, Uruk, Kish, and Nippur, were still in use during the Seleucid period.

[Mark, a general comment: Although it is probably not necessary for the specialist audience that you are addressing, a chronology fixing the periods, rulers, campaigns, and major historical figures you cite would help me and will be necessary for the audience to whom my analysis will be addressed. Is there a simple source from which this can be compiled?]

160. Two new, enormous temples were built along traditional lines in Uruk during the Seleucid period.
161. The construction of new and large temples indicates substantial investments were being made for the support of Babylonian religion during the Hellenistic period [when?].
162. Investment in Babylonian religion in the Hellenistic period

is evidence that is inconsistent with the view that Babylonian religions were [everywhere?] on the wane after the third century B.C.

2. Some Rival Evidence Identified

163. Trajan reported that he found the city of Babylon in ruins during his Parthian campaign of 115 A.D.
164. Septimus Severus reported that Babylon looked deserted in 199 A.D.
165. [Propositions 87 and 88 support an inference that Babylon was dead or dying by the first century A.D.]

3. The Rival Evidence Explained

166. The residents of Babylonia may have fled the city in the face of Trajan's and later Severus's advances.
167. Trajan and Severus may have mischaracterized the state of the mud-brick city of Babylonia as a "ruin" because they were comparing it with Hellenistic cities built in durable stone with ornate architecture.
168. The fact that Dioskurides left a neatly engraved dedicatory Greek inscription on the amphitheater at Babylonia in the late second century indicated that he did not view Babylonia as a dead city or a ruins at that time.

[Mark: This reference is likely to be obscure (and the inference it supports opaque) to all but the most sophisticated of your specialist readers. It is probably a good "in-joke" if that is its intent, but if it constitutes a significant step in your argument, it should be developed.]

C. THE TEMPLE AT ASSUR

1. Additional Supporting Evidence

169. The temple cults were still functioning in the third century A.D.

[A note to myself: This is clearly a penultimate probandum in the overall argument. It appears on the key-list in this position only because this is the point in the current draft where it is first made explicit. Mark: At a later stage, we should discuss whether and when you wish to make other "penultimate probanda" explicit.]

170. There exists an important group of inscriptions written on stone that were discovered at Assur.
171. These inscriptions are dedicatory inscriptions to the local gods of Assur, including the chief god Assur, his spouse Sherua, and gods known from Syria in this period [which period, the "third century"?], such as Nannai, Nabu, and Nergal.
172. Many of these votive plaques were offered during the first half of Nisan.
173. [The offering of votive plaques dedicated to gods such as those identified in proposition 95 during the first half of Nisan was an established part of the akītu ceremony of the Babylonian new year festival.]

[Proposition 97 seems to be the implicit proposition necessary to give logical coherence to the argument that propositions 95 and 96 support proposition 98. Is proposition 97 generally accepted among Assyriologists?]

174. Propositions 95 through 97 imply/support the inference that the akītu ceremony was still being conducted at Assur at the time these dedicatory inscriptions were made, a hypothesis that has been advanced by other scholars as plausible.
175. Proposition 98 supports the further inference that "the cult" continued to be active through "this period."

[This is how I would interpret the argument you are making—but what are "the cult" and the "period" to which you refer here?]

176. The [this?] archeological information supports the hypothesis that the Assur temple was still in use throughout the Parthian period, at least until the Sassanian conquest.
177. The hypothesis specified in proposition 100 was first advanced as possible/plausible/probable by Andrae.

[Mark: The specification of the foregoing propositions illustrates two points that we should discuss. First, here and elsewhere you routinely combine two forms of argument—an argument from the historical record and an argument from parallel scholarly authority. The combination is fine, unless you want to signal additional strength—

e.g., not only do I so read the evidence, but others in our or related fields have so read the same or other available evidence. Second, at various points you do give some indication of the degree of certainty that the available evidence warrants for a particular conclusion—e.g., the evidence "suggests"; it is likely that; etc. I think you probably need to review and make clear your position on the strength of each of your arguments and on their combined strength as is bears upon the degree of certainty we should assign to your ultimate probandum—that cuneiform remained a "living language" (as you define the term) until at least the third century A.D.]

2. *Opposing Explanations or Rival Hypotheses*
    178. [Cuneiform was not a known or used language at the temple at Assur in the Parthian period.]

    [TJA interpretation of the rival hypothesis you are addressing here.]

    179. No cuneiform tablets have been discovered at the temple site.
    180. All the votive inscriptions that have been discovered are in Aramaic.
    181. Irrespective of the religions that may have been practiced at the temple in this later period, Aramaic had fully replaced Akkadian as the language of the Assur temple by the third century A.D.

3. *Proponent's Counterexplanations*
    182. Most of the Aramaic inscriptions are written in stone, not on clay tablets.
    183. Only one group of images [Aramaic inscriptions?] decorates a pithos or vase.
    184. Inscriptions are given by devotees of the cult—by parishioners, not priests.
    185. Devotees of the cult would doubtless have spoken [and known] only Aramaic by the third century A.D.
    186. [Priests and students in all temples throughout the relevant period would have written on clay tablets.]
    187. [No conclusion as to the language of the temple can be

drawn unless and until tablets produced at that temple are discovered.]
188. The failure to discover clay tablets is not surprising [significant?].
189. Archeology is a science guided by accident and coincidence.
190. [The fact that new archeological discoveries requiring substantial revisions of existing scholarly views continue to be made strongly supports proposition 113.]
191. [Tablets of clay are less likely to survive than stone.]
192. There is a remnant of a cuneiform inscription on the edge of a stele at the Assur temple.
193. The statue on which the remnant inscription was found is from 12 or 13 A.D.
194. [The fact that cuneiform was used on a stone inscription in 12 or 13 A.D. suggests that cuneiform continued to be used for some period thereafter.]

[Mark: I have interspersed some of the propositions that seem to be necessary, but unstated, steps in the argument you are making here. Are these correct? Why is the presence of a cuneiform inscription dating from 13 or 14 A.D. "striking"? If this is a significant part of the argument, more than a rhetorical device, the significance should probably be made explicit.]

IV. Further Testimony: The Literary Evidence

A. THE WRITING OF LUCIAN

195. Lucian was a Babylonian who lived in the second century A.D. and wrote about Babylonia in Greek.
196. Lucian wrote a story about a man named Menippos (a) who wished to travel to the Netherworld and (b) who went to Babylon to get charms and rites from a magus (c) in order to open the gates of Hades and (d) who found a Magian named "Chaldean Mithrobazarnes" (e) who prescribed and administered a complex ritual for Menippos to follow in order to get to the Netherworld and back, which ritual (f) required Menippos to bathe in the Euphrates for each of twenty-nine days beginning with the new moon and (g) for which ritual Chaldean Mithrobazarnes (1) invoked

demons (2) in a language that Menippos could not understand (3) at the time of each bathing, and (h) as part of which ritual (1) Chaldean Mithrobazarnes would spit in Menippos's face three times (2) after which they would eat a simple vegetarian meal and sleep outside, and (i) in which the final ritual consisted of (1) Menippos's being bathed a final time, (2) this final time being in the River Tigris, and (3) his being purified from head to foot "with torches, and incompanying[?] incantations, (j) after which Menippos was dressed in a special costume consisting of a lion's skin, with lyre and cap and (k) required to walk home backward and (l) not look at anyone he met.

[Mark: I have partitioned the detail because I think you need to work on this argument. It is either extremely significant or highly vulnerable. I cannot tell which from the way it is made in the present text. I take it the argument is (a) Lucian's story could only have been written by someone familiar with Akkadian ritual practice; (b) at the time Lucian wrote, Akkadian ritual practice was recorded only in cuneiform texts; thus (c) either Lucian or a contemporary teacher must have been able to read cuneiform text. If I am correct, these propositions need to be made explicit, and the details described need to be the details that have counterparts in your later description of Akkadian ritual practice.]

197. Lucian interpreted CM's [Chaldean Mithrobazarnes's] invocations to the demons as foreign-sounding meaningless words.

[This seems to cut against your argument: If Lucian was familiar with Akkadian ritual practice, he would have known the significance and understood the meaning of the incantations. Is that what you mean to suggest?]

198. Lucian is describing what appears to be an Akkadian purification ritual, "known also [why "also"?] from very late Seleucid-period texts."
199. The *process of* bathing in the Tigris during the lunar month is *reminiscent* of Akkadian ritual practice.

[I have marked with italics the weasel words that undermine your argument here and in the propositions that follow. You need, I think, to specify the strength you claim for this argument more clearly. Are these details that are merely "reminiscent" of Akkadian ritual practice—i.e., their presence could well be accidental—or are the details that Lucian included so clearly elements of Akkadian ritual practice that the possibility of coincidence can almost certainly be ruled out, or does the degree of certainty fall somewhere between these two positions?]

200. Being dressed in a lion's skin with a musical instrument is *reminiscent* of Akkadian ritual practice.
201. Akkadian ritual practice was normally accompanied by incantations and invocations to gods or demons.
202. Other details of Lucian's account are *indicative of special* rituals *associated with* the Netherworld [in Akkadian ritual practice?].
203. [The ritual described by Lucian has elements virtually identical to elements in ritual Enkidu underwent under Gilgamesh in preparing to go down to the Netherworld.]
204. [The ritual by which Gilgamesh prepared the Mesopotamian hero Enkidu to go the Netherworld is an Akkadian ritual found in written form only in cuneiform.]

[Mark: The relevance of this line of argument assumes an unstated premise such as proposition 128. Is that proposition correct? If not, what is the relevance-giving proposition?]

205. When Enkidu was preparing to go down to the Netherworld, Gilgamesh warned him not to indulge in such normal human behavior as (a) wearing a clean garment, (b) wearing shoes, (c) carrying a staff, (d) being anointed, or (e) kissing his wife or son.

[Mark: How does this advance the argument? Your report of Lucian's account does not have Menippos receiving identical or even similar warnings.]

206. The Netherworld was known in Mesopotamia [at the time Akkadian cuneiform was the language] as "the Place of No Return."
207. [If Lucian was aware of the details of Mesopotamian ritual practice, he probably knew that the Netherworld was known as "the Place of No Return."]

[This seems to be a necessary step in your argument, as I understand it. Is it?].

208. Lucian's awareness that the Netherworld was known as "the Place of No Return" may have inspired him to report that the Magian, CM, instructed Menippos to return home walking backward and to avoid greeting anyone on the way.
209. Returning home by walking backward without greeting anyone is a symbolic metaphor for not returning at all.

[Parsed into its components in this way this argument seems too weak to include in text. Have I missed something?]

210. The ritual details that Lucian included in his text were recorded at the time he wrote in Mesopotamian ritual texts [written in cuneiform?].
211. None of the ritual details included in Lucian's story could have been found in Homer or Virgil.

[This strikes me as potentially powerful if I am reading it correctly. Am I?]

B. THE EVIDENCE CONCERNING THE MAGI

[The transition is cute, but confusing, as is the significance of the arguments in the opening paragraph. I think the argument may be logically compelling, but its force is not clear as the ideas are presently organized and expressed.]

212. Tacitus associated the term *Magian* with the Chaldeans.
213. [I: Scholars in the xxxx century A.D. confused the Chaldeans and the Magians.]
214. According to Nock, there is "nothing to suggest that the any of them [the magi] were familiar with the Persian language."
215. [I: No evidence has been found that the magi knew Persian.]
216. [Assumption: Nock (and others) have examined the evidence concerning the magi's possible knowledge of Persian carefully.]
217. [I: The magi did not know Persian.]
218. [G: Persons who are part of a society know its language.]
219. [I: The magi were not Persian.]
220. The evidence concerning the magi is scarce.

221. The evidence concerning the magi is ambiguous.
222. The name *Magian* or *magi* can mean *magician*.
223. Apollonius of Tyana was a wonder-worker in the first century who interviewed magi in Babylon during a trip that he made to India to visit the philosophers there.

   [Did Apollonius know in advance that the magi were in Babylonia? In light of propositions 145 and 146, how do we know that he interviewed the magi, as opposed to some local wise men?]

224. According to Apollonius, the reason for his wanting to interview magi was to learn about "the wisdom which is indigenous among you and is cultivated by the magi, and of finding out whether they are such wise theologians as they are reported to be."

   [The assertion is ambiguous in ways that you may want to address. First, it implies that Apollonius had a preformed view that a group of wise men known as magi existed and resided in Babylon. If so, do we know the source of his pretrip knowledge? Second, how is the shift from the second person *you* to the third person *magi* and *they* explained? By whom and when was the quoted passage written—by Apollonius or someone else; before, during, or after Apollonius's trip? For what purpose was it written, if we know? The significance that you attach to this statement may be affected by the answers to those questions—e.g., see bracketed portion of proposition 149.]

225. [If Apollonius knew that the magi lived in Babylonia and he stopped there because he knew that a form of wisdom to which he desired access was indigenous among them, then] Apollonius's statement implies that the magi had inherited the ancient wisdom of Babylonia.

226. Apollonius also reports that the [Babylonian] king was sacrificing in the company of the magi, since "religious rites are performed under their supervision."

   [Is not the key passage that "religious rites were performed under their supervision"? Do you intend the "since" to connote that this is an inference on Apollonius's part drawn from the fact that he observed the king making sacrifices in the company of the magi?]

227. There is no evidence here of separate Magian or Persian temples in Babylonia [in the first century A.D.].
228. [Inference: The king made his sacrifices and the magi supervised religious rites in the ancient temples.]
229. [Inference: The ancient temples were still active in the first century A.D.]
230. Greek and Latin writers in the second and third centuries A.D. were not able to distinguish clearly between the magi and the Chaldeans.

[Two comments here: First, I assume that the significance of the continual references to the Chaldeans will be apparent to your intended audience. It is not clear to me. I would understand it, for example, if you were arguing that some references to Chaldeans must be interpreted as references to magi, but this does not seem to a part of your argument. Second, for illiterates like me and other nonspecialists, it would be extremely useful if you specified time spans for various individuals and periods in parentheses when you first mentioned them.]

231. The Chaldeans and the magi were both priests known for their interest in astrology and magic.
232. Julian referred to the Chaldeans as a "sacred race, skilled in theurgy" (magic).
233. The third-century writer Diogenes Laertus ["DL"] wrote "that the Chaldaeans 'apply themselves to astronomy and forecasting the future,' while the magi spend their time in worshiping the gods, in sacrifices and prayers, but also practice divination and forecasting the future."

[You attribute the whole proposition to DL, but you indicate that only the part concerning the Chaldeans, the less important part for your thesis, is quoted from DL. Why the partial quote?]

234. Ammianus Marcellinus ["AM"] referred to the occult arts and divination among the Chaldeans, "to which Zoroaster added his own ideas which were kept by the magi."
235. I: The magi and the Chaldeans were often considered to be one and the same, "at least perhaps" [why "at least perhaps"?] during the Parthian rule of Mesopotamia in the second and third centuries.

[Does AM tell us what Zoroaster did or is Zoroaster a separate source for a separate proposition in your argument? If this were a trial, I would object to propositions 154 to 159 on the grounds that either they were irrelevant or, in the alternative, they were presented in such a way that any attenuated relevance to a fact of consequence they might have was substantially outweighed by the risk that they would improperly confuse the issues and distract the jury from its main task. I would win on the latter ground. I understand why you need to argue that the magi remained active religious personages until the third century. The significance of the Chaldeans and of the confusion between the two groups is not clear. The point you want to make needs to be clarified.]

236. It is the magi who may have kept the ancient Babylonian temples in use and maintained the traditional forms of sacrifice.
237. The magi may have gained their reputation for esoteric wisdom and knowledge of magic and divination by carrying on the traditional learning of the Babylonian temples, "the so-called Chaldeans."

[Who was "so-called" by whom?]

238. The magi could [only] have acquired the knowledge necessary to carry on the traditional learning and forms of sacrifice from the tablets.
239. The magi may have been reading cuneiform and using the ancient script.

[You need to refine and express your conclusion here precisely. Are you making probability assertions in propositions 160 to 163 or merely suggesting possibilities that cannot be fully discounted or ignored on the available evidence?]

C. SOME CONCLUSIONS ARTICULATED

240. [We know that] cuneiform script was used primarily by professional scribes.
241. [We know that] professional scribes in Babylonian usually operated out of temples.
242. [We know that] in ancient Babylonia priests were often also scribes.

243. [We know that] in ancient Babylonia scribal schools [always?] belonged to the temples.
244. I: As long as the ancient temples were in use in Mesopotamia, it is likely that cuneiform script survived [remained in use?] as well.

[This is the heart of an essential part of your argument. It sounds right, but the source of your knowledge should be specified.]

D. THE EVIDENCE OF RABBI MAR SAMUEL

245. There is further evidence that the priests in Babylonian temples were consulted [as late as xxxx to obtain information that could have been obtained only from the ancient tablets.]

[This is a more specific and stronger form of the assertion you make in the first sentence of the last paragraph on page 10. I think that you need to clarify the meaning. I also think, in text or notes, you need to indicate the nature and extent of the examples in addition to Rabbis Samuel and Rab and where they may be found. Is the Talmud the only source for such late examples?]

246. Mar Samuel is a third-century rabbi identified in the Talmud.
247. The Talmud states that Mar Samuel went to a Babylonian temple to consult with a priest regarding a question of astronomy.
248. In my view, the priest looked up the information on a tablet and translated it for Mar Samuel.

[The "in-my-view" problem again: I think that you have to articulate the basis for your view. For example, do the tablets indicate that Babylonian astronomical knowledge was inscribed originally in cuneiform on tablets? Had any Babylonian astronomical knowledge been written down in any other medium by the third century A.D.? The Talmud reference provides evidence that the Babylonian temples were viewed as centers of learning in the third century; it does not provide an independent foundation for speculating how that learning was recorded.]

249. Mar Samuel's great academic rival was another rabbi known as "Rab." [Source?]

250. Many arguments are recorded between these two Talmud scholars. [Where?]
251. Rab is reported to have said, "He who learns a single word from a Magian is worthy of death." [Where?]
252. [I: Rab was aware that some persons were learning from the Magians.]
253. [I: Rab would have been aware that Samuel had gone to a Babylonian temple to consult with a priest.]
254. [I (from propositions 160, 173, 174, 175, and 177): It was the fact that his great rival had consulted with magi priests in the temple that provoked Rab to make the assertion recorded in proposition 175.]
255. [I: (from propositions 160, 175, and 176): Rab was aware that the Magians were the priests running the Babylonian temples in the third century.]
256. The case of Mar Samuel, and the objections of his colleague Rab point in the same direction, namely that cuneiform was in use so long as the temples were in use.

> [Mark: Proposition 180 omits too many steps in the logical argument you are making. I think that you have identified the main inferences that are possible here in propositions 176 to 179. Your series of propositions and those inferences can be ordered and marshalled as an argument that the temples were still active and being operated by the magi. A separate line of argument is necessary to bring in the cuneiform. You have developed the necessary propositions, but you need to identify them as necessary components to the conclusion asserted here, and the strength of the conclusion asserted here can be no stronger than the strength you are willing to attribute to the supports.]

257. Inference: Cuneiform was still in use in the third century A.D.

V. A Summary of the Evidence

> [Mark: I have recorded my interpretation of the propositions you intend as implicit in rhetorical summary at the top of page 11 here in order to make sure that they are available for analysis when I go back through the detailed arguments in order to understand and specify the logical structures involved in your arguments. I have not done

that part of the analysis yet. Please check my interpretations carefully to be sure I have accurately articulated the conclusions that you argue the several phases of the evidence support.]

258. The testimony of the witnesses indicates that cuneiform survived until the third century A.D.
259. Iamb was seeking and found a teacher who could teach him cuneiform circa 200 A.D.
260. Elagabalus's knowledge and behavior suggest that ancient Babylonian religious practices were still being practiced in the early third century A.D.
261. Luician's writing suggests that Latin scholars in the second century A.D. had access to knowledge of the ancient Babylonian rituals, knowledge that was then recorded only on cuneiform tablets.
262. Apollonius sought knowledge of Babylonian wisdom from magi in Babylonia in the first century A.D., suggesting that the temples were still in active use and centers of knowledge of a kind recorded only on cuneiform tablets.
263. Babylonian cults and other indicia of Akkadian culture survived in Assur and other Syrian cities into the third century A.D.
264. The GBTs from Babylon show that there were people capable of reading cuneiform after the introduction of "very late Greek writing" into the area.

[Mark: You have not indicated how late this very late Greek writing would have first arrived in Babylonia. Given the centrality of the GBTs to your argument, I think you should do this with as much precision as the record permits.]

VI. The Retrospectant Evidence

A. THE CAUSE OF DEATH

265. The names on Aramaic magic bowls [made and inscribed when?] found at many archeological sites in Babylonia do not include any Babylonian names, only good Persian names born by Jews, Pagans, and perhaps Christians.
266. There is little evidence of the survival of the Babylonian temples into the Sassanian period after the mid–third century.

267. The critical blow that constituted the immediate cause of the death of cuneiform was probably the destruction in 256 A.D. during the Sassanian conquest of Babylonia.
268. The Sassanian rulers pursued a policy of intolerance and persecution.
269. The Sassanian policy was evidenced, in part, by the execution of Mani, the so-called Apostle of Babylon.

[Does this proposition have any particular significance in your argument? Is the Sassanian policy a subject of historical dispute? Was Mani a magus or someone associated with a temple that figures in your argument? Or is this a proposition offered simply to illustrate a noncontroversial point?]

270. The Sassanian policy was necessary because the Sassanian state was based upon a religious ideology which did not allow for competing religious systems in the new Iran.
271. The former Parthian regimes were characterized by syncretism and tolerance of local religions.

[Note for later analysis: This proposition also bears upon the likelihood that the ancient temples and rituals survived into the Parthian period.]

272. [Rival assertion:] Judaism and Christianity survived under Sassanian rule.
273. [Rival assertion:] According to Christian Syriac writers, paganism survived under Sassanian rule.
274. [Rival assertions explained:] Babylonian temple cults "with Mesopotamia" [why "with Mesopotamia"?] that survived into this period would have been fragile at best, and not much provocation would have been needed to shut them down.
275. [Further explanation suggested:] Unlike Christianity and Judaism, Babylonian cults and cuneiform learning were temple based, and the closure and destruction of the temples would have terminated the centers necessary to survival.

[Mark: Proposition 275 is simply a fairly obvious and seemingly strong explanation that occurred to me. It is offered from the for-what-it's-worth department.]

276. Cuneiform did not long survive the advent of the Sassanian empire.

B. EVIDENCE FROM INHERITANCE

[There is an interesting logical structure embedded at this point in the argument that merits further study. You are concluding with an argument that sets the significance of your arguments and conclusion in context and looks to the future. In point of fact, the same evidence provides retrospectant evidence, perhaps strong evidence, for your central thesis that cuneiform survived into the third century A.D. I note the point here so that we do not lose it.]

1. *The Tablets That Survived*

277. The cuneiform tablets that survived into the first century A.D. and onward "tend to be directly related" [do these words express the concept you want to express?] to temple affairs such as the astronomical diaries written by the priests, and the incantations and prayers.
278. The cuneiform tablets that survived into the first century A.D. and onward did not include tablets using cuneiform for everyday transactions such as legal transactions.
279. By the first century A.D. Aramaic and Syriac were the primary languages of the population and of commerce.
280. There are legal documents in Aramaic and Syriac that survived into late periods in Mesopotamia.
281. The Roman perception that Babylonian priests were interested in forecasting the future and countering demons can only/was probably/may have been based upon information derived from information recorded on tablets that survived until the Roman invasions and conquest of Mesopotamia. [A reformulation of the Geller proposition]
282. [TJA Inference: Cuneiform tablets must have been created for everyday-life transactions during the time when cuneiform was the dominant or only script in Mesopotamia.]
283. [TJA Inference: The later survival of cuneiform tablets with temple-related texts provides further evidence that the temple cults continued long after Akkadian had ceased to be the dominant spoken language.]

2. *The Uses of the Surviving Texts*

a. Recent textual discoveries

284. Jewish texts [written in the xxxx century] [this should be specified] contain significant amounts of material that appear [degree of certainty: must have been/almost certainly/was probably?] to have been based upon [the kind of] Babylonian science [preserved only in cuneiform tablets.]

285. A recently published Aramaic text from the Dead Sea Scrolls is an astronomical charting of the course of the moon through the heavens, "reflecting" the Akkadian text known as MUL.APIN, which partly charts the same heavenly phenomena.

> [MG: Can you be stronger here? Could the Dead Sea Scroll text have come from or been based upon any other source? Could it have been written by persons who had not been informed of the existence and essential content of MUL.APIN?]

286. A second [recently published Aramaic?] text from the Dead Sea Scrolls consists of "omens taken from the physical appearance of a man, which is based upon a well-known genre of physiognomic phenomena from Babylonia."

> [The meaning of the quoted language is too abstruse. What are you trying to say, and how strongly can you make the assertion based upon the parallels?]

287. Other "astronomical omen texts" have appeared in the recently discovered Cairo Genizah.
288. There are no comparable parallels between these two texts and Greek texts.
289. Robert Sharples confirms that Theophrastus knew nothing similar. [Is this assertion significant beyond its rhetorical value?]

b. Earlier texts

290. The attempts of nineteenth-century Jewish scholarship in Talmud and rabbinic literature to prove that Greece and Rome were the primary contributors to ancient Jewish culture have failed in significant respects.

[Unless this point will be obvious and immediately accepted, a few more illustrations or other further development may be warranted.]

291. The rabbis mentioned in the Babylonian Talmud knew no Greek.
292. In Parthian and Sassanian Babylonia, Greek was a foreign language.
293. The few Greek words that filtered through [Do you mean that were known in Babylonia?] came through the early literary strata of the Mishnah, which was edited in Roman Palestine.

[The significance of this sentence in your argument is not clear to me.]

294. The rabbis [mentioned in the Babylonian Talmud?] developed systems of science such as medicine, divination, and magic based primarily upon age-old and respectable traditions of Babylonia.

[This argument supports your thesis only if the systems were based upon information that would have been recorded only in and available only from cuneiform texts. The issue is not the source of Talmudic culture, but the extent to which the knowledge of early Talmudic scholars evidences a kind of knowledge that could have been obtained only if there existed scholars who could read and interpret cuneiform for them.]

295. The [which?] Talmud scholars continued to use a value of 3 for pi long after the true value was discovered in Greece.
296. Three was the value assigned to pi in traditional Babylonian mathematics.

[Was 3 the value assigned to pi in cuneiform texts?]

297. The similarities between the knowledge of symptom recording and diagnosis as contained in Babylonian cuneiform texts and the knowledge developed both by Hippocrates and his school and by the rabbis in the Talmud suggest that the knowledge contained in the cuneiform texts was the source of the knowledge developed by both later groups.
298. The transmission of this knowledge would not have been

possible unless there had been Babylonian priests who were capable of reading and did read cuneiform tablets to transmit this information to those responsible for the later documents that reflect the content of that knowledge.

299. There is sufficient evidence that knowledge based upon cuneiform text influenced later literatures in Greek, Aramaic, Syriac, and Arabic to merit further study.

[End of revisions to key-list no. 1, which was based solely upon Geller's March 5, 1995 draft, based upon discussions with MG on 3/29/95 and 3/30/95 and further analysis of propositions in light of those discussions.]

Appendix 2
Iamblichus Key-List

1. Accepted (A): Photius's *Bibliotheca* contains a summary ("Photius's summary") of a novel, *A Babylonian Story* ("ABS"), written in Greek by an author who identified himself as Iamblichus.
2. A: Early in the tenth century A.D., an unidentified scribe (the "scholiast") made notes in the margin (the "Scholia") of a copy of Photius's summary indicating that the scholiast had read the manuscript of ABS.
3. Inference (I): A complete manuscript of ABS survived until the early tenth century A.D. and was read by the scholiast.
4. A: Photius's *Bibliotheca* was composed in the middle of the ninth century A.D., and only fragments of the manuscript of ABS exist today.
5. Explanation (E): The manuscript for ABS may not have survived or been available to the scholiast in the early tenth century A.D.
6. A: Photius's summary includes a summary of an autobiography of Iamblichus that identifies Iamblichus as the author of ABS.
7. I: The Scholia are an amplification and correction of Photius's summary of the autobiography of Iamblichus based upon the scholiast's reading of the manuscript of ABS.
8. E: The Scholia may have been based upon second- or third-hand accounts of what was in the manuscript by persons

who claimed to have read the manuscript of *ABS* or to have known someone who had.
9. I: Iamblichus was the author of *ABS*.
10. The Scholia ("S"): Iamblichus was a native-born Syrian.
11. I: In *ABS*, Iamblichus identified himself as a native-born Syrian.
12. Millar ("M"): Photius's summary reports that in the autobiography Iamblichus identifies himself as a Babylonian.
13. I: The conflict between the report in the Scholia and Photius's summary casts doubt on the reliability of the Scholia.
14. E: The Scholia should be accepted as the more reliable account of Iamblichus's autobiography because it was intended as a correction of the summary prepared by Photius.
15. S: Iamblichus said he had been taught and had learned the Babylonian language, customs, and stories, of which *ABS* was one.
16. I: In *ABS*, Iamblichus said that he had been taught and had learned the Babylonian language, customs, and stories, of which *ABS* was one.
17. I: The author of *ABS* was Iamblichus, and Iamblichus was a Syrian who had been taught and had learned the Babylonian language, customs, and stories.
18. S: Iamblichus was familiar with the Syrian language.
19. I: In the *ABS*, Iamblichus said he was familiar with the Syrian language.
20. I: Iamblichus was familiar with the Syrian language.
21. A: The Syrian language in the second century A.D. was Syriac.
22. I: Iamblichus knew Syriac.
23. S: Iamblichus said he had a tutor (the "Tutor") who taught him the Babylonian language.
24. I: In *ABS*, Iamblichus said he had a Tutor who taught him the Babylonian language.
25. I: Iamblichus had a Tutor who taught him the Babylonian language.
26. I: The Babylonian language that the Tutor taught Iamblichus was not Syriac.
27. Geller Assertion (from quoted text): The language Iamblichus wished "to learn . . . is most likely to be Akkadian."
28. I: (Geller inference from proposition 27): Akkadian was the Babylonian language at the time Iamblichus sought to learn the Babylonian language.

29. S: Iamblichus said the Tutor was a Babylonian royal scribe skilled in barbarian learning who was taken prisoner when Trajan invaded Babylonia [in 115–6 A.D.] and later sold as a slave to a Syrian.
30. I: In ABS, Iamblichus said the Tutor was a Babylonian royal scribe skilled in barbarian learning who was taken prisoner when Trajan invaded Babylonia [in 115–6 A.D.] and later sold as a slave to a Syrian.
31. I: The Tutor was a Babylonian royal scribe skilled in barbarian learning who was taken prisoner when Trajan invaded Babylonia [in 115–6 A.D.] and later sold as a slave to a Syrian.
32. Generalization ("G") (Anderson): A royal scribe in Babylonia would have been an adult who had received extensive training in the Babylonian language and customs of the time.
33. I: The Tutor was an adult who had received extensive training in Babylonian language and customs prior to 116 A.D.
34. G (Anderson): In order to be sufficiently educated to become a royal scribe skilled in Babylonian language and customs in the early part of the second century in Babylonia, a person would have to be at least twenty years old.
35. I: The Tutor's education would have begun sometime late in the first century A.D.
36. X: In 75 A.D., there was an active community of priests or scholars and students who knew and could read or were studying Akkadian cuneiform at the location where the Astronomical Diary was written. (See note 28)
37. I: The teachers who knew and students who learned Akkadian cuneiform in 75 A.D. would have continued to instruct students in Akkadian cuneiform until early in the second century A.D.
38. I (Geller): The Tutor had been trained in Akkadian cuneiform in Babylon prior to 116 A.D.
39. I: The Tutor knew Akkadian cuneiform when he was captured in 116 A.D.
40. G (Anderson assumption): Cuneiform was not taught to all royal scribes in Babylonia after the end of the first century A.D.
41. E: The Tutor did not know cuneiform when he was captured.
42. GA (in quoted text): Iamblichus continued to write in Rome until about 200 A.D., i.e., until the reign of Septimus Servus.

43. G: The life span of most persons in the second century A.D. was less than sixty years.
44. I: Iamblichus was not born earlier than 140 A.D.
45. S: Iamblichus knew Syriac and lived according to Syrian customs until the Tutor taught him the Babylonian language, customs, and stories.
46. I: In ABS, Iamblichus said that he knew Syriac and lived according to Syrian customs until the Tutor taught him the Babylonian language, customs, and stories.
47. I: Iamblichus knew Syriac and lived according to Syrian customs until the Tutor taught him the Babylonian language, customs, and stories.
48. G (Anderson): In the second century A.D., a Syrian would not have been mature enough to have developed a knowledge of his own language and customs sufficient to undertake or be permitted to undertake training from a tutor in a foreign language and customs until he was at least fifteen years old.
49. I: Iamblichus began to learn the Babylonian language, customs, and stories from the Tutor in or after 155 A.D.
50. I (Geller): The Tutor remembered Akkadian cuneiform well enough to teach it to Iamblichus.
51. I: The Tutor knew and could read Akkadian cuneiform until at least 155 A.D. (until the middle of the second century A.D.).
52. I: At least forty years had elapsed between the time that the Tutor was taken prisoner and sold as a slave to a Syrian and the time that Iamblichus began studying cuneiform.
53. G: Few people would recall and be able to teach a language and script that they had not regularly spoken or used for forty years.
54. I: The Tutor would not have recalled Akkadian or cuneiform in 155 A.D. after forty years as a slave in Syria.
55. I: The Babylonian language that Iamblichus learned from the Tutor after 155 A.D. was Akkadian cuneiform.
56. I: The Tutor was at least twenty years old in 116 A.D.
57. I: The Tutor would have been at least sixty years old when he began to instruct Iamblichus in 155 A.D. or thereafter.
58. I: The Tutor would not have lived long enough to be Iamblichus's teacher.
59. I: Iamblichus did not learn Akkadian cuneiform from the Tutor.

60. I: Iamblichus knew Akkadian cuneiform after 155 A.D.
61. I: Iamblichus remembered cuneiform for as long as he was an active writer.
62. I: Iamblichus knew and could read Akkadian cuneiform until the beginning of the third century A.D.
63. M: Photius's "Summary" indicates that the autobiography of Iamblichus was inserted in the middle of ABS.
64. G (Anderson): It is unusual to find a reliable autobiography of an author in the middle of a novel.
65. I: The author of ABS may have constructed or modified the biography of Iamblichus to lend better credence to the person identified as the author as a person having the knowledge necessary to recount the Babylonian story set out in ABS.
66. I: The facts reported in the Scholia may be a based upon a fictionalized autobiography of Iamblichus.
67. I: The autobiography of Iamblichus in ABS is, to some degree, a fictionalized account.

Notes

1. The text of the lecture as delivered is reproduced in the preceding chapter. The arguments were developed, annotated, and published in expanded form in M. J. Geller, "The Last Wedge," in *Zeitschrift für Assyriologie und Vorderasiatische Archäologie* 87 (1997); 43–95 ("Geller [1997]").

2. Ibid., 43.

3. The method was developed by John Henry Wigmore and first published in 1913. See "The Problem of Proof," *Illinois Law Review* 8, no. 2 (1913): 77–103, and *The Principles of Judicial Proof* (Boston: Little, Brown, 1913). The final version of Wigmore's views and methods was presented in *The Science of Judicial Proof* (Boston: Little, Brown, 1937). Anderson and William Twining further developed and refined the method in *Analysis of Evidence* (Evanston, Ill.: Northwestern University Press; London: Butterworths, 1997).

4. The seven-step protocol and procedures to be followed in doing a charted analysis are described and discussed more fully in Anderson and Twining, *Analysis*, 117–48. A parallel protocol for doing an analysis in a narrative or outline form is discussed there at 158–65.

5. Steps two through six are not necessarily sequential; ordinarily, they are reflexive—theories change as the analysis develops and new possibilities are discovered and others are discarded.

6. *People v. Simpson*, No. BA098721I, Cal. Sup. Ct. (L.A. 1995). Transcript and other documentary evidence from the trial are available on-line at the Westlaw database [http://www.westlaw.com] as OJ-TRANS.

7. The ultimate probandum for the murder of Ronald L. Goldman (RLG) could be framed by substituting RLG for NBS.

8. There were alternate theories that the prosecution might have chosen. For example, the prosecution team reportedly considered, but rejected, an "exploding bomb" theory: OJS went to NBS's house that evening intending to vent his anger by committing an act of vandalism, such as slashing the tires on her car. His anger "exploded" when he found NBS with another man, RLG, in the yard in front of her house.

9. "MG(3/29)" means that the proposition was revised based upon conversations with Mark Geller on March 29, 1995. In the propositions in this key-list and in the key-list in appendix 1, "MG" refers to Geller; "TJA" refers to Anderson; "G" identifies a generalization, ordinarily a background generalization known and shared among Assyriologists that only needed to be articulated to make the argument clear to outsiders such as Anderson and to articulate the argument more completely and precisely for purposes of analysis. "I-MG" means an inference that Geller confirmed was intended and that Anderson thought should be made explicit for purposes of the analysis. "I-TJA" means an inference that Anderson thought was implicit and should be made explicit. Brackets, [ ], were used to set off explanatory, inferred, or general propositions in the key-list that were not articulated in Geller's text. Bracketed material between propositions contains comments and questions that Anderson wanted to discuss with Geller.

10. The resulting argument was significantly revised and expanded for publication, and the more detailed account that Geller developed placed more emphasis on an analysis of the Graeco-Babyloniaca tablets. See the published version of Geller, "The Last Wedge," 47–9, 64–95.

11. The protocols for an outline method of analyzing evidence and their relationship to those used in the chart method of analysis are discussed in Anderson and Twining, *Analysis*, 158–61.

12. Appendix 1 is the original version of the NIAS key-list with typographical errors corrected and minor changes to maintain consistency across chapters and to conform to the publisher's style. The propositions in text have been edited to clarify the meaning where necessary. Copies of the NIAS key-list with references to page and line numbers to the text of Geller's lecture and copies of Key-Lists Nos. 1 and 1R1 are available from the author.

13. If I were redoing NIAS key-list and chart today, I would, among other things, further subdivide the ultimate and penultimate probanda and insert an additional penultimate probandum to separate arguments based upon the astronomical diary and other tablets and fragments (proposition 3) from those based upon other kinds of evidence (propositions 7–8) because the nature and structure of the arguments supporting the former proposition are different in kind than those supporting the latter ones, a point illustrated below.

14. Chapter 3 in this volume, pp. 129–30.

15. *Encyclopedia Britannica*, 11th ed., Macropedia 8:950.

16. The translation of the scholiast's notes set out in a footnote in the published version of "The Last Wedge," 50 n. 28; Fergus Millar, *The Roman Near East: 31 B.C.–A.D. 337* (Cambridge: Harvard University Press, 1993), 489–91, an authority cited by Geller; and *Encyclopedia Britannica*, 11th ed.

17. David Schum has suggested that assessing credibility of an assertion requires that the analyst consider three questions. First, from the fact that the assertion was made, the analyst must first ask, "Did the person making the assertion believe it was true at the time it was made?" This question requires analysis of any veracity concerns arising from attributes of the person making the asser-

tion or the circumstance in which it was made. Second, "did the person accurately interpret and recall the event asserted?" This question requires analysis of objectivity concerns, such as expectations, biases, or memory concerns that may have influenced the person's interpretation or ability to recall the event reported. Finally, was the person situated to accurately perceive the event? This question requires analysis of observational sensitivity concerns: concerns arising from the conditions under which the observations were made, such as lighting, eyesight, hearing, and so on. The analysis that follows identifies only the specific concerns that appear to apply to each of the declarants involved in this argument. See David Schum, *Foundations of Probabilistic Reasoning* (New York: John Wiley and Sons, 1994), 100–9.

18. For example, the Cockle translation that Geller quotes in the published version of his lecture differs in meaning from the translation that Millar uses in his book; see n. 16. Anderson has ignored the difference because the version quoted by Millar can be read to provide stronger support for Geller's argument than does the version on which Geller relied.

19. One reviewer of a draft of this chapter suggested that a future historian trying to read and interpret the marginal notes she had made in her academic texts would be well advised to exercise extreme caution before using them as a basis for any reliable inferences.

20. "Accepted" is used to identify an assertion that, based upon Geller's text and other available information, Anderson concluded would be generally accepted among Assyriologists as true without further citation or documentation.

21. The date is taken from the *Encyclopedia Britannica*, 11th ed., Macropedia 8:950.

22. Wigmore used the term "Explanation" to indicate an opposing explanation of other facts taking away from the (probative) value of the proposed inference based upon those facts. Here, it denotes an explanatory proposition based upon generalizations that the analyst believes will be understood and accepted without evidential support. See Anderson and Twining, *Analysis*, 72–6.

23. Millar, *Roman Near East*, 489 (quoting from a translation of a passage in Photius's summary).

24. Geller's assertion presented two further ambiguities to an outsider. The assertion could be charted as an inference based upon three other propositions: (a) that the language Iamblichus wanted to learn was not Syriac (proposition 26 in the Iamblichus key-list); and (b) that (i) there were active communities in which Akkadian cuneiform could be read in 75 A.D. (propositions 35 and 36 in the NIAS key-list, and (ii) Akkadian cuneiform was still being used in the latter part of the second century A.D. (proposition 60 in the NIAS key-list). The assertion might also reflect background knowledge obvious to insiders—either that Akkadian was the only plausible alternative to Syriac in the Babylonian region or that Akkadian in fact remained a spoken language throughout the first and early second centuries A.D. among the elite in that region. See, e.g., Millar, *Roman Near East*, 497. Second, Geller's main argument concerns the survival of cuneiform, not the survival of Akkadian. The survival of Akkadian was presumably a necessary condition to the survival of cuneiform, but it also seems plausible, perhaps probable, that Akkadian would have survived as a spoken language for a considerable period after cuneiform ceased to be used as a script. The treatment of the assertion that is supported by an assumption recognizes the argument without resolving the ambiguity (see n. 31).

25. This fact is not contained in the translation of the Scholia quoted in the published version of "The Last Wedge" or in Millar *Roman Near East* (see n. 17).

26. See "Roman Life Expectancy" [http://web3.cc.utexas.edu/depts/classics/documents/Life.html.] for the source of this generalization.

27. This generalization seemed intuitively sound to Anderson, the outsider. Although insiders with knowledge about the role and training of royal scribes in this period might well be able to formulate a more precise, context-specific, knowledge-based generalization, Anderson has included this and a few other conservatively formulated generalizations (propositions 34, 48, 53, 64) that he thought intuitively sound. The distinction between *"synthetic-intuitive"* and *"context-specific"* generalizations and the roles generalizations play in justification and analysis are discussed and developed in greater detail in Terence J. Anderson, "On Generalizations: 1. A Preliminary Exploration," *South Texas Law Review* 40 (1999): 455. See also Anderson and Twining, *Analysis*, 367–84.

28. Proposition 36 is a restatement of proposition 35 in the NIAS key-list (based upon the astronomical diary) and chart. The symbol "X" is used to identify a proposition for which the supporting arguments have been stated and charted in either the same or a prior chart. See Chart A.

29. Geller's argument that cuneiform survived into the first or second century A.D. was a radical departure from the orthodox view. This generalization is based upon the assumption that substantial evidence exists for the orthodox view he was challenging.

30. The only question relevant to Geller's argument is whether the Tutor taught Iamblichus cuneiform (see n. 25).

31. Millar, *Roman Near East*, 489.

32. The inclusion of statements about the narrator is a literary device; placing the statements in the middle of the story makes them part of the story and raises significant questions about their accuracy in fact.

33. The example is drawn from and developed in greater detail in Anderson, *Analysis*, 271–3.

34. The evidence that Fuhrman lied in the OJS trial and admitted in prior tape-recorded conversations that he and other officers routinely planted and fabricated evidence is presented and discussed in detail in Gerald F. Uelmen, *The O. J. Files: Evidentiary Issues in a Tactical Context* (St. Paul: West Group, 1998).

35. Federal Rules of Evidence, rule 401.

36. Federal Rules of Evidence, rule 403.

37. There is a further question for which Anderson, the outsider, did not find an answer. Was there a language other than Syriac or Akkadian spoken in Babylon at the beginning of the second century A.D.? This, however, is a question that insiders presumably could answer and thus be able to appraise Geller's "view" that the language Iamblichus learned was "probably" Akkadian. See propositions 27–8 in key-list B and accompanying note. See, also, Millar, *Roman Near East*, 497 (expressing a similar view).

38. The basis for this distinction is related to the discussion of generalizations, above. The presence of significant unknowable variables makes it impossible to appraise an argument accurately because it makes it impossible to identify knowledge-based generalizations that justify each of the necessary inferential steps in the argument. Attenuated inferences that are not dependent upon unknowable variables can be appraised because knowledge-based generalizations justifying the several inferential steps can be identified, and the effects of the at-

tenuation on the argument can be reflected in the formulation of those generalizations. For example, it should be possible to obtain some data tending to show how long temples in the third, second, and first centuries B.C. continued to exist under various types of circumstances. From that information, it would be possible to extrapolate generalizations about the life expectancy of isolated temples. Those generalizations would make it possible to appraise an argument that the presence of a temple community in 75 A.D. supports an inference that temple communities continued to exist for another century or more alone and in combination with Geller's other arguments supporting the survival of temples into the second and third centuries. The nature of generalizations and method of generalization analysis are developed in Anderson, "On Generalizations."

39. Some of the propositions on this key-list refer back to prior propositions, e.g., proposition 93. As the key-list went through successive drafts, propositions were inserted that made the cross-references inaccurate. Time did not permits revision before the seminar on April 4, 1995. None of these propositions appear in the chapter's text and, thus, do not affect the analysis developed there. The April 4, 1995 Key-List, as presented, has been reproduced here, warts included; the cross-references remain inaccurate.

5 Wigmorean Analysis and the Survival of Cuneiform

M. J. Geller

THE CONCLUSIONS reached by a Wigmorean analysis of my article "The Last Wedge"—namely, that the argumentation did not entirely support the conclusions posed—were somewhat disappointing from my point of view. The question is whether Wigmorean analysis has found a flaw in the argumentation, or whether other kinds of logic were used in the original article which could not be fully appreciated or comprehended by Wigmorean methods of analysis.

The thesis of the article is complicated, and was originally broken down into some 250 Wigmorean propositions. As far as the arguments themselves, many fewer were presented, along the following lines:

> The ability to read Sumerian and Akkadian—the latest and most widely used languages written in cuneiform script—was dependent upon the survival of scribal schools within the temples. These scribal schools themselves survived as long as Babylonian temples survived in Babylonia, and as long as priests still learned the traditional scripts. The criterion utilized is an extreme one, namely, that as long as any priest could read the ancient script, cuneiform was not yet a dead language. The question is when this was likely to have taken place.

Evidence is deduced from a small group of cuneiform tablets, probably all coming from the city of Babylon, which were written in cuneiform script—either Akkadian or Sumerian—on one side and in Greek transliteration on the other side. Because these tablets were inscribed in clay, the assumption is that both scripts were written on the same day, perhaps even by the same scribe. The subject matter is typical school exercises, probably reflecting the temple school curriculum, and the tablets can be dated by the

Greek script between approximately the first century B.C. and the second century A.D., much later than cuneiform had been thought to survive.

Two questions are raised by these tablets: (a) Did the system of transliteration accurately reflect the phonology of the languages written in cuneiform? and (b) why were these tablets written? In answer to the first question, comparisons are drawn with Origen of Caesarea, the third-century A.D. church father who not only collected translations of the Hebrew into Greek, but also incorporated into his work transliterations of Hebrew into Greek. The system of transliterations used both in the Graeco-Babyloniaca corpus and by Origen are remarkably similar. It seems likely, then, that the Graeco-Babyloniaca tablets reflect accurate readings of the cuneiform. The second question is more speculative—namely, the reason for transliterating into Greek script, for which the comparisons with Origen are not helpful. In this case, the pattern has been noted in late astronomical diaries that many public documents were recorded as having been written on parchment, and read out in public. This change, which becomes apparent circa 150 B.C., might provide the clue to the reason for writing these tablets, namely that scribes were being trained to write in Greek script on parchment. Greek script was traditionally associated with writing on leather, and it had the additional advantage of recording the vowel and consonant sounds, as opposed to Aramaic script, which omitted most vowels. This seems, then, to offer a plausible explanation for writing both cuneiform and Greek scripts on clay tablets in the context of Babylonian scribal schools.

The question remains as to how long this practice would have remained in use. Here we can turn to classical sources for certain clues. It appears that Strabo, writing in 18 or 19 A.D., refers to famous Babylonian astronomers by name, and these same names appear on the colophons of cuneiform astronomical texts dating from the mid–first century B.C. Second, the strongest evidence we have for the continuation of cuneiform is the discovery of the latest dated cuneiform tablet, an astronomical diary from 75 A.D. Most scholars regard this tablet as an unusual oddity, rather than any serious reflection on the survival of cuneiform.

Evidence can also be adduced from a certain Iamblichus, writing in circa 200 A.D., who found a teacher for Babylonian (i.e., Akkadian) in the second century A.D. This data is further supported by another literary source, Lucian's tale about Menippos, a Babylonian who attempted to visit the Netherworld and return. Not only is Menippos's name an Akkadian name (and not Persian or Aramaic), the priest whom he hires to help him get to the Netherworld prescribes certain rituals which are best attested in Akkadian ritual texts. The priest is a Magian, which raises the question as to the identity of the magi in Parthian Mesopotamia (see below).

This brings us back to the question of the role of the Babylonian temples in Parthian Mesopotamia, and for how long they were in use. Here the supposition is that as long as the Babylonian temples were in use, the scribal schools were probably still functioning with students learning the traditional scribal arts, that is, in cuneiform script. The archaeological reports are deduced here which suggest that cities like Assur show continual use of the temples until the mid–third century A.D., although the inscribed evidence is in Aramaic carved into stone, rather than cuneiform. Other evidence is more indirect. The Roman emperor Elagabalus, for instance, was a Syrian priest who married a vestal virgin, which shocked his Roman contemporaries, and he may have introduced certain rites into Rome which reflected the new year festival known from Syria, which ultimately derives from Mesopotamia. The practice of the new year (akītu) festival in Syria is attested by a bas-relief from Palmyra showing the primordial battle between the gods Bel (earlier Marduk) and Tiamat, which is the central theme of the creation epic recited at the akītu festival. This evidence conforms with Aramaic inscriptions from as late as the third century A.D. from Assur in Mesopotamia, which are votive inscriptions from the temple addressed to Mesopotamian gods dated to the month of Nisan, the traditional month of observance of the akītu festival.

The Babylonian Talmud offers further hints of the continuous occupation of Babylonian temples into the third century A.D. One third-century Babylonian sage, Mar Samuel, considered to be an expert in both astronomy and healing, was also distinguished by his conversations with a pagan colleague with whom discussions were held in a type of temple or sacred building, one Bei Avidan. The pagan expert bears an Akkadian name, Ea-uballiṭ, indicating that he is neither a Persian nor a magi, but likely to be a priest who was capable of quoting from cuneiform sources.

The identification of the magi is itself problematical. The magi do not appear to have had their own temples, but the name was probably a contemporary term for a pagan priest (i.e., a magus or magician) who preserved the ancient wisdom of Babylonia, most notably in the areas of astronomy and healing arts. The Romans frequently confused Magians and Chaldeans, since both were known to be experts in the fields of astronomy and therapy (magic and medicine). The supposition here is that since the magi had no temples of their own, they used the Babylonian temples and even perhaps derived their knowledge of astronomy and healing from cuneiform tablets. The role of the magi also appears to have changed dramatically in the aftermath of the Sassanian conquest (227 A.D.), which ushered in a period of religious intolerance which might have ultimately caused the abandonment of the Babylonian temples and the loss of the ability to read cuneiform tablets.

The evidence thus presented attempts to include indirect evidence drawn from as wide a field of sources as possible, from Akkadian, classical, and Jewish sources, allowing for the possibility that more material may come to light which fills in the many gaps in evidence left by the available sources.

Wigmorean Analysis

Terence J. Anderson attempted the first Wigmorean analysis of the arguments described above in March and April, 1995, although since that time some of the arguments have been altered and some new propositions have been added. The following arguments will try to follow the scheme outlined at that time by Anderson, while adding some additional propositions reflecting the changes and deleting others.

I. The Ultimate Probandum

1. The class of persons who could read cuneiform probably survived without interruption until sometime after the Sassanian conquest of Babylonia in 256 A.D.

II. The Penultimate Probanda

2. One or more active temple centers survived into the third century A.D.
3. Temples housed temple schools, where languages written in cuneiform script were read, studied, and taught.
4. Students learned to read tablets in the traditional cuneiform script.

5. Generalization ("G"): A dead language is one written in a script which no one can read.
6. G: A single priest or student reading the script means that the language is not yet dead.
7. The astronomical diary dated to 75 A.D. (the latest *dated* cuneiform tablet) was composed by the scribe himself, because it records observations of the stars on a specific day in that year, and was not simply copied.
8. The astronomical diary establishes that Akkadian, written in cuneiform, was a living language in 75 A.D. and for sometime thereafter.
9. The above statement (proposition 8) is based on the inference that the last dated tablet is not the same as the last tablet written in cuneiform, because other tablets written later than 75 A.D. could have been undated.
    a. Astronomical diaries can be accurately dated by determining the dates (astronomically) on which the events described occurred.
    b. Astronomical diaries contained useful information that was recorded to be read and used by others.
10. The quantity of tablets produced after the Hellenistic period had begun, as evidenced by the surviving fragments which can be dated to the second and first centuries B.C., establishes that a significant number of active temples with schools where languages written in cuneiform were studied, read, and taught were in operation at the beginning of the Hellenistic period.
11. The flourishing scribal activity of the earlier Hellenistic period (second through first centuries B.C.) probably indicates that the momentum was sufficient to keep the language in use for the next several centuries. The existence of such an extensive number of tablets indicates that there were a significant number of active temple communities using, producing, and studying languages written in cuneiform in the Hellenistic period.
    a. The hymns and prayers reproduced on the tablets (mostly now housed in the Pergamon Museum in Berlin) reflect contemporary liturgy at the time when they were written.
12. As long as temples were in use, cuneiform was being studied and read.

13. Throughout the Hellenistic and Parthian periods (321 B.C.–256 A.D.) Mesopotamia was characterized by syncretism and tolerance of local religions.
14. G: A significant change in circumstances is necessary to account for the termination of an ongoing institution and its activities.
15. The temple communities that survived until the end of the second or beginning of the third century A.D. probably continued to operate until there was a change of circumstances.
16. The Assur temple was in use until the mid–third century A.D., and temples in Babylon and Borsippa were probably in use until this date (although the evidence is less easy to find in the archaeological record).
17. The Sassanian conquest in 256 A.D. was the probable cause of the termination of the class of persons (i.e., priests) who could read cuneiform.
18. The Sassanian state was based upon a religious ideology that did not permit competing religious systems to coexist within the Sassanian state.
19. Following the conquest in 256 A.D., the Sassanians pursued a policy of persecution and intolerance of non-Sassanian religions.
20. Sassanian policy and implementing actions would have represented a sufficient change in circumstances to bring about the termination of the temple school where the ability to read and write cuneiform had been preserved.

III. The Graeco-Babyloniaca Tablets

A. BACKGROUND INFORMATION

21. There are approximately twenty tablets (the "GBTs") which have cuneiform, either Sumerian or Akkadian, on one side and a transliteration of the same text in Greek on the other side.
22. G: All inscriptions on a clay tablet must be made while the clay is moist (i.e., within a finite number of hours).
23. The cuneiform and the Greek inscriptions on the GBTs were done at the same time.
24. Both the cuneiform and the Greek scripts may have been written by the same person.

B. DATING THE GBTS

25. Epigraphists can date surviving Greek texts fairly accurately by the shapes of the Greek letters.
26. At least one GBT, from the Harvard Semitic Museum, is judged by Greek epigraphists to have been written in the second century A.D., or maybe even later.
27. The GBTs appear not to have been written before the first century B.C., and the majority of GBTs appear to have been written sometime in the first century B.C. and first century A.D.

C. INTRINSIC SIGNIFICANCE OF THE GBTS

28. Most, if not all, of the GBTs came from Babylon.
29. The GBTs may have come from the same temple school or archive.
30. The GBTs represent examples of the typical school curriculum known on school texts since the sixth century B.C., or even earlier.
31. At the time the GBTs were written, Akkadian was most likely not spoken or used conversationally, but could still be read and understood.
32. The texts include a hymn to the sun god (Shamash), incantations, and Sumerian-Akkadian glossaries, which were typical school texts.
33. Since the GBTs only *transliterate* the cuneiform into Greek but do not *translate* it into Greek, the GBT tablets were not used to teach Akkadian speakers Greek.
34. Since anyone who could write Greek would be unlikely to need to learn cuneiform (for administrative or other purposes), it is unlikely that the tablets are being used to teach a Greek speaker how to write cuneiform.
35. The GBTs may have been used to train scribes to write in both cuneiform and Greek script.
36. One late (undated) tablet of omens preserves a colophon stating that the text was copied from a parchment original in Borsippa.
37. From circa 150 B.C. onward, the astronomical diaries begin repeatedly to record public pronouncements which were written on parchment (i.e., leather) and read out in the temple.

38. The language of these public pronouncements was probably Akkadian.
39. Scribes needed to learn how to write on parchment.
40. Cuneiform was rarely written in ink (only a few examples exist).
41. One used ink to write on parchment (i.e., a brush rather than a stylus).
42. One would have probably transliterated Akkadian into an alphabetic script (i.e., Aramaic or Greek) to write on parchment in ink.
43. Aramaic script was unsuitable for transliteration since it did not preserve most vowel sounds.
44. Greek was suitable for transliteration since it did preserve most vowel sounds.
45. The tradition of transliterating a Near Eastern language into Greek may have served as a model for Origen, the church father who transliterated the Bible into Greek in the third century A.D.

D. THE SYSTEM OF TRANSLITERATION IN THE GBTS

46. The system of transliteration of Akkadian and Sumerian into Greek was virtually identical to that used by Origen in the third century to transliterate the Bible into Greek.
47. Origen did not invent his system of transliteration. The same system of transliteration was used by both Origen in Caesarea and priests in Babylon.
48. Hebrew words (proper names, etc.) were being transliterated into Greek already in 250 B.C. in the Septuagint (the Greek Bible translation written in Egypt).
49. The system of the GBTs is probably closer to that used by Origen than to that found in the Septuagint.
50. The third century A.D. was a period when Semitic languages were being transliterated into Greek, in both Palestine and Mesopotamia.
51. The system of transliteration also resembles the way in which Greek words were being transliterated into Latin, during the same period of the GBTs.

IV. Testimonial Evidence

A. IAMBLICHUS

52. Iamblichus was a Syrian who composed erotic tales in Greek circa 200 A.D.
53. Iamblichus's dates of birth and death are unknown.
54. The scholiast reports that Iamblichus ("Iamb") was a native Syrian (not a Greek-Syrian) who knew Syriac but sought a tutor to teach him the Babylonian language, customs, and history.
55. Iamb continued his career as a writer in Rome during the reign of Septimus Severus (circa 200 A.D.).
56. Iamb's teacher was a Babylonian who had been taken prisoner by the Romans during Trajan's campaigns in 116 A.D. and was later sold into slavery in Syria.
57. Iamb's teacher was skilled in "barbarian learning," having served as a royal scribe in Babylon.
    a. A royal scribe in Babylon would have had to know how to read cuneiform.
    b. Iamb's teacher had been trained in cuneiform before Trajan's campaign.
    c. Iamb's teacher studied to be a scribe in the late first century A.D., which is not long after the latest *dated* cuneiform tablet from Babylon has come to light.
58. "Barbarian learning" never refers to Greek culture.
59. Iamb already spoke the *glossa Syriaca* (i.e., Syriac), the Aramaic dialect of Syria.
60. Iamb wanted to learn from his teacher (the expert in "barbarian learning") the *glossa Babyloniaca* (i.e., Babylonian language), which must be considered to be Akkadian.
61. Iamb wished to learn cuneiform.

B. FAMOUS SCRIBES

62. Strabo, writing in 18 to 19 A.D., mentions by name three famous Babylonian scholars known to the Greeks, namely, Kidinnu, Naburianos, and Sudinos.
63. Kidinnu is mentioned by name in the colophon of a Babylonian (cuneiform) astronomical text dating from 103 B.C.
64. Naburianos is mentioned in a colophon of an astronomical text from 49 B.C.
65. Sudinos—the third scholar mentioned by Strabo—is an-

other Babylonian proper name, although not found in a colophon.
66. Few Babylonian scholars would have been known to the Greeks.
67. Babylonian astronomy and mathematics had made an important impact on Greek science.
68. Kidinnu and Naburianos of both the cuneiform tradition and Strabo are the same persons.
69. Naburianos also appears on one of the GBTs as an authority appearing in a colophon practice-tablet.
70. This Naburianos appearing in a GBT colophon is the same scholar mentioned in Strabo and in the astronomical tablet from 49 B.C.

C. ELAGABALUS AND THE AKĪTU FESTIVAL

71. Elagabalus ("Elag"), a Roman emperor, was a Syrian and originally a priest of the sun god.
72. Elagabalus is a Semitic name, but he was also known as "the Assyrian."
73. Elag also had a Roman name, but was known by his Semitic name.
74. Elag married a vestal virgin.
75. Elag's contemporaries in Rome were shocked.
76. Having sex with a vestal virgin was taboo.
    a. Having sex with a priestess was a known practice in Mesopotamia.
77. Elag saw nothing wrong in his behavior.
    a. Elag's marrying a vestal virgin was consistent with his background from Syria.
78. Elag introduced foreign new-year celebrations, known from Syria, into Rome.
79. The new year festival (akītu) originates in Mesopotamia.
80. The new year festival was known to Elag from Syria.
81. The new year festival may still have been celebrated in both Syria and Mesopotamia in Elag's time.
82. The celebration of the new year festival was attested in Palmyra (Syria) in 32 A.D. in the month of Nisan.
83. Third-century A.D. votive inscriptions from Assur in Aramaic were probably written during the Nisan new year festival.
84. The akītu festival was still being celebrated in Mesopotamia as long as temples were in use, until the third century A.D.

D. BABYLONIAN TALMUD

85. Mar Samuel was a third-century A.D. Babylonian rabbi.
86. Mar Samuel was an astronomer and physician (or healer).
87. Mar Samuel consulted with a scholar named Ea-uballiṭ (or Anuballiṭ), an expert on astronomy and healing.
88. Ea-uballiṭ has an Akkadian name, not a Persian name.
89. Mar Samuel was criticized for consulting a Magian.
90. Ea-uballiṭ was a Magian.
91. Could Ea-uballiṭ read cuneiform?

E. LUCIAN

92. Lucian writes about Menippos, who wishes to visit the Netherworld and return.
93. Menippos is an Akkadian name.
94. Menippos lives in Babylon.
95. Menippos finds a Persian priest (a Magian) to administer the correct spells and ritual which would allow Menippos to visit the Netherworld.
96. The rites include bathing in the Euphrates everyday for a month, while the magi invoked spells in a language which Menippos could not understand.
97. The language could be (a) Akkadian or (b) Persian.
98. The rites included eating vegetarian meals and sleeping on the grass.
99. The rites included walking home backward without greeting anyone.
100. The rites included dressing in a lion's skin and cap and carrying a lyre.
101. Such rites are not known from classical literature.
102. The eating of vegetarian meals and sleeping on grass is reminiscent of warnings in the *Epic of Gilgamesh* to Enkidu to avoid normal human behavior when visiting the Netherworld.
103. Akkadian rituals prescribe priests to wear a lion's skin and a cap and carry a musical instrument.
104. Akkadian rituals for ghosts prescribe that one not look behind or speak with anyone.
105. Walking home backward is reminiscent of the Mesopota-

mian description of the Netherworld as "the Place of No Return."
106. Menippos's Magian helper was citing Akkadian ritual instructions.
107. Menippos's Magian priest from Babylon could read cuneiform.

F. MAGI

108. Roman writers often confused magi with Chaldeans, because both were known from expertise in astronomy and healing arts.
109. Apollonius of Tyana visited Babylon in the second century A.D.
110. According to Apollonius of Tyana, the magi were experts, familiar with ancient local wisdom of Babylon.
111. Apollonius notes that the magi were sacrificing in the local temples.
112. The magi had no temples of their own.
113. The magi used the Babylonian temples.
114. The magi were the same priests who taught cuneiform in the temple schools.

V. Death of Cuneiform

115. Akkadian proper names are attested in Syria and in Mesopotamia in the second and third century A.D.
116. No Akkadian proper names are found in Mesopotamia (or Syria) by the fourth century A.D.
117. Akkadian was no longer a spoken or readable language by the fourth century A.D.
118. Sassanian intolerant rule forced Mani (the founder of Manichaeism) out of Babylon.
119. Widespread destruction in the third century A.D. accompanied the Sassanian conquest of Mesopotamia.
120. Sassanian rulers supplanted local religions with Mazdaean religion.
121. Without temples, no priests taught cuneiform in schools.
122. Cuneiform was no longer needed for liturgy.
123. Aramaic had completely replaced Akkadian as a written language as well as spoken vernacular.

124. Early examples of Aramaic's being written on clay (seventh–sixth century B.C.) in Syria can no longer be found.
125. One example exists from the third century B.C. of Aramaic's being written in cuneiform script, but no other example is ever found in later periods.
126. By the end of the third century A.D., no language written in cuneiform could be read, and thus any language written in cuneiform qualifies as a dead language.

Conclusion

The use of Wigmorean analysis for a nonlegal argument has been instructive in pointing out certain areas of weakness in the argumentation. The propositions (e.g., those referring to Elagabalus) are weak, as is the entire sequence of argumentation which infers that new year rituals and practices which existed in Syria in the late period (second century A.D.) probably existed in Mesopotamia as well. The inferences here are that (a) these rituals all originated in Mesopotamia, and (b) documentation is unevenly distributed in this period between Syria and Mesopotamia, with more surviving from Syria than from Mesopotamia on parchment, papyrus, or ostraca. The suggestion is that Syria was witness to the survival of Mesopotamian culture, although we have little evidence from Mesopotamia itself.

The propositions regarding literary references to the use of cuneiform, such as Lucian's account of Menippos's attempt to visit the Netherworld, or a rabbi in the Talmud consulting a Babylonian colleague, are also tendentious arguments. In both cases priests or experts are consulted on technical subjects (rituals to get to the Netherworld, or for astronomy and healing), which might indicate that the Babylonian experts have derived the required information from reading cuneiform tablets. Nevertheless, there are other possibilities, such as earlier technical translations of cuneiform texts into Aramaic which became manuals for use in Babylon in the second and third centuries A.D., rather than the information's having been read directly from tablets. Such Aramaic manuals, if they had existed, would not have survived if written on parchment or papyrus.

Other inferences from the Graeco-Babyloniaca tablets can be made, and here as well some of the argumentation is weak, as can be seen from the Wigmorean propositions. The fact that the tablets only *transliterate* into Greek script rather than translate into Greek language is an important distinction because it does not imply bilingual education in the Babylonian schools. Nevertheless, if one uses Origen of Caesarea as an analogy, as is argued in the article, then other inferences must be considered: (a) Origen also transliterated Semitic languages (Hebrew and Aramaic) into Greek script in the third century A.D., using a system of transliteration similar to that found in the Graeco-Babyloniaca tablets; (b) Origen himself was a Greek speaker; (c) Greek was much more widely spoken in Palestine (under Graeco-Roman domination) than under Parthian-ruled Mesopotamia; and (d) the inference drawn in the article is that Greek script was used to transliterate Akkadian into Greek for the specific purpose of writing on parchment in an alphabetic script, because writing materials determined whether scripts used were syllabic (i.e., as cuneiform, used on clay) or alphabetic (Greek or Aramaic, used on parchment). Greek was the preferred alphabetic script because it preserved the vowels more fully than does Aramaic script. However, no inferences can be drawn as to why alphabetic scripts on parchment were being introduced into Mesopotamia, or about the use of Greek language in Mesopotamia. Similarly, it is not clear why Origen himself transliterated Hebrew in Palestine into Greek script. The weakness in the argumentation above is that one can only point to the similar phenomenon of transliterating into Greek script in both Parthian Mesopotamia and Roman Palestine, which does not explain very much. Nevertheless, the implications for the survival of cuneiform are clear, namely that cuneiform script was still being read during the period when transliterating into Greek script appeared to be the fashion. This supports the general argument that a language is to be defined as dead only when all ability to speak, read, and write the language is lost, and when the only chance to recover facility in the language that remains is decipherment.

If Wigmorean propositions point to so many potential weaknesses in the argumentation and inferences drawn from it, why should the article be acceptable in its present form, rather than scrapped altogether? After listing the propositions, I would still submit the article in its original form because there is more to a nonlegal argument than the argumentation itself. In a field like Assyriology it is desirable to point out what may be possible, if not provable, and to try to identify from where future evidence might be forthcoming. It is not possible to prove, or even to argue terribly convincingly, that Iamblichus was able to find a teacher for cuneiform (*glossa Babyloniaca*) in second-century Syria because the source of the information is obscure, the man himself is also virtually unknown, and the linguistic situation in second-century Syria is far from clear. The presentation of such evidence is to draw attention to a possibility that Iamblichus might have found a cuneiformist, and if he *had* done so, the very fact that cuneiform was still familiar to an individual in the second century A.D. could itself be significant. What is possible or at best even plausible is most often not provable, nor can such propositions stand up to the scrutiny of Wigmorean analysis. Nevertheless, there is value in gathering diverse strands of evidence which have little validity as proof in themselves, but may encourage others to participate in the search for proof. I would therefore argue that strict logic and a sequence of propositions do not always offer what is required in the field of Assyriology, but rather that we start from trying to ask the unprovable and unarguable—as, for example, "Why does a language cease to be spoken?" "Why is its script no longer used?" "What are the factors that bring about the phenomenon which we call a *dead language?*"

Legal argumentation is not the same as other kinds of argumentation in the humanities, because in the latter case one is not trying to establish anything as specific as innocence or guilt. Although in law one deals with reasonable doubt as a potential goal with which to counter an argument, when dealing with antiquity the same type of argumentation cannot apply, because overcoming reasonable doubt is a luxury which the sources of evidence cannot commonly afford. Antiquity offers such scanty data on so many issues that one is usually dealing only with reasonable doubt. Often one has at one's disposal scraps of evidence from disparate locations and times—sometimes separated by entire regions and centuries—which the historian must try to formulate into a coherent picture. The tendency, therefore, must be to include as much information as might seem relevant, or even vaguely relevant, in the hope that future discoveries in archives or archaeological excavations might substantiate the hypotheses. In one sense, then, even weak circumstantial evidence could be useful in a general way, simply by drawing attention to data which might someday clarify a problem, although at the moment the relevance is unclear and the argumentation is necessarily weak.

6 The Mountebank
A Case Study in Early Modern Theater Iconography

M. A. Katritzky

IN THE SIXTEENTH and seventeenth centuries, only the most successful professional theatrical performers were employed by troupes whose reputations ensured that their tours were financially underwritten in advance by wealthy patrons. The rest toured on a speculative basis, either independently or under the sponsorship of early modern travelling salesmen known as mountebanks, charlatans, or quacksalvers.[1] Despite the vigorous protestations of many professional actors against such classification,[2] they were commonly grouped together with mountebanks (even the official license-granting offices were known as *Soprintendenza sui comici e ciarlatani*),[3] who are recognized as an influence on the rise of professional acting, through their use of entertainment to attract customers for their wares.

Gentilcore identifies charlatans as "an important test case for historians, since attitudes to them reveal a great deal about shifts in mental categories over time."[4] They have attracted increasing scholarly attention on several disciplinary fronts, which has

---

My thanks to The Netherlands Institute for Advanced Study (1994–5), Wimbledon School of Art (1995–9), the Harold Hyam Wingate Foundation (1996–7, 1998–9), Herzog August Bibliothek Wolfenbüttel (summers, 1996, 1997, 1998, 1999) and Alexander von Humboldt-Stiftung (1997–98, Professor Dr. Christopher Balme and Professor Dr. Hans-Peter Bayerdörffer, Institut für Theaterwissenschaft, University of Munich) for supporting this research with fellowships. Thanks also to Jill Bepler, Carol Clark, Mariacarla Gadebusch, David Gentilcore, Natsu Hattori, Robert Henke, Colin Jones, Ingeborg Krekler, Jonathan Marks, Vivian Nutton, Margaret Pelling, and Roy Porter; my friends and colleagues at NIAS (1994–5); the Gladys Krieble Delmas Foundation (Travelling Fellowship to Venice, 1996); British Academy (travel and research grants, 1995, 1996, 1997); Society for Theatre Research (Kathleen Barker Award, 1999); European Science

generated publications based on a varied range of historical documentation.⁵ The textual documents offer an abundance of direct and oblique contemporary evidence in fiction (including prose,⁶ poems,⁷ monologues,⁸ commedia dell'arte scenarios,⁹ farces, and plays),¹⁰ in nonfictional sources (such as travel accounts written for publication;¹¹ private travel accounts, memoranda, and diaries;¹² letters¹³ and legal or official documents;¹⁴ tracts written by theatrical¹⁵ or medical practitioners;¹⁶ economic, historical, religious, political, or polemical texts¹⁷), and in the surviving handbills, posters, and other publicity material of the mountebanks themselves.¹⁸ The iconographic sources, although equally rich and varied, typically play a subordinate or purely decorative role in mountebank studies, with the same few illustrations being reproduced again and again, and major sources of visual evidence receiving little or no recognition. Most studies of mountebanks are based on a limited selection of documents, relatively few of which yield detailed, unambiguous information concerning the aspects of most interest to theater historians—namely the exact nature of the drama and spectacle they offered their potential customers and the entertainers who performed it, and their relationship to the performers and performances of professional acting troupes. The theatrical costumes in which mountebanks' assistants are often depicted have sometimes been interpreted as being merely borrowed from stage or carnival. Even when they are taken to indicate genuine

---

Foundation (Theatre Iconography Network, 1997–2000); and Leverhulme Trust (Research Grant 1999–2001). Otherwise unattributed translations are mine. Photos courtesy of Staatliche Museen zu Berlin, Preusssischer Kulturbesitz (plates 3, 4, 11); Christie's, London (plates 7, 9); the Trustees of the Ashmolean Museum, Oxford (plate 8); The Bodleian Library, University of Oxford (plates 12 [Mason C. 16(2) T/page], 15, 16); Windsor Castle, Royal Library, © Her Majesty The Queen (plates 2, 6); Wolfenbüttel, Herzog August Bibliothek (=WoBüHAB, plate 14 [Gh 255]).

Relevant to issues examined in this chapter are three publications to which the author has contributed since submitting the final version of the present article. (Ludica: Annali di Storia e Civiltà del Gioco 5–6, 2000 (2001) ("The Doctor on the Stage," Robert Jütte [ed.], "Gendering Tooth-Drawers on the Stage," 144–81, 298–9; Renaissance Studies 15, 2001, "Medicine in the Renaissance City," Vivian Nutton [ed.], "Marketing Medicine: The Image of the Early Modern Mountebank," 121–53; Maske und Kothurn 48, 2002, "Theater am Hof und für das Volk. Beiträge zur vergleichenden Theater- und Kulturgeschichte: Festschrift für Otto G. Schindler," Brigitte Marschall [ed.], "'Unser sind drey': The Quacks of Beer, Printz, and Weise 217–42.

theatrical activity, there is no agreement on whether this was of a strictly limited nature, or could also include the performance of full-length stage plays.

My approach to these issues has not been to turn to complex decompositional techniques in order to reanalyze in minute detail the known evidence, which is rightly regarded as being inconclusive and ambiguous, but rather to augment this evidence with documentation previously disregarded in this respect. Elsewhere, I have published detailed studies of two substantial sources of such documentation, namely twenty-three *album amicorum* illustrations (many previously unpublished in this context) of mountebanks on trestle stages, and an account of a mountebank troupe seen in 1598 by the Swiss physician Thomas Platter the younger of Basle (1574–1628), whose voluminous travel diary suggests that he was an unusually credible, informed, and conscientious witness.[19] Platter represents a source which is detailed, reliable, and conclusive enough to indicate a clear and unequivocal solution to the much-debated question of whether the repertoire of mountebank troupes could include full-length plays. Here, a wide range of written and visual documentation is examined in order to gain a broader perspective on these issues, in the context of five specifically visual aspects of early modern mountebank activity. These are, first, commercial aspects, such as the wares they sold; second, their venues, stages, and audiences; third, the personal appearance and routines of the chief mountebank; fourth, his companions; and fifth, the types of entertainment offered by mountebank troupes as a whole. A preliminary comparative analysis of the previously known and newly identified images and texts offers evidence which places the theatrical activity of early modern mountebanks in considerably sharper focus.

Theater Iconography

The legitimacy of theater iconography as a valid research procedure for theater scholars is no longer in question.[20] It is, in its broadest sense, an interdisciplinary field of academic inquiry which draws heavily on art-historical methodology to focus on effective ways in which information of theater-historical significance can be gained from visual material, in order to facilitate investigation of the performing arts from a visual perspective.[21] The last decade has seen an upsurge in interest in the critical use of visual sources for historiographical purposes. New technologies are being developed, and many areas of the humanities now routinely draw on art-historical methodologies to develop their own iconographical subdisciplines. The performing arts—whether manifested as drama, music, court festival, or some other form of performance (unlike the literary and fine arts, which produce lasting monuments such as novels and paintings)—are characterized by their ephemeral nature. In retrospect, they can no longer be studied directly, but only through secondary documentation. Prephotographic visual evidence relating to the theater can be broadly divided into several categories. These include general archaeological and architectural evidence, as well as items of costume, artifacts, and pictorial material (such as designs for settings or costumes) which predate an actual specific performance or intended performance itself because they were created directly in the course of its preparation; those which postdate a specific identifiable performance; and those which cannot be related to a specific performance (such as portraits of actors in nontheatrical contexts, theatrical book illustrations of a general nature, and views of performing spaces).

The value of a picture as documentary material for the theater historian is not related purely to its pictorial content, but also to how far it is physically accessible and art-historically documented. We need to know the extent to which its historical evidence can be interpreted and corroborated, for example, through external sources concerning its place and date of production, its artist and patron or commissioner, and the performers and performance it depicts. If visual documents do not bear precise dates or are not classifiable according to their function, the information that may be inferred from them will generally be rather arbitrary. Anonymous or undated pictures can be of only limited documentary value. If the artist or date of such a picture has been wrongly identified, it may, despite containing a wealth of information relevant to the theater, dance, or music historian, be even more misleading. Even after such identification has been shown to be faulty, its acceptance may well persist in the popular literature unless a plausible alternative is offered.

Despite a spirited postmodernist challenge which seeks to depose the supremacy of the aesthetic in favor of a pragmatic eclecticism, it remains a central tenet of art history that the images which form the subject of its study are monuments which "earn" the right to be studied through their inherent cultural or aesthetic worth, and that this is a hierarchical system, with the greatest masterpieces deserving the most attention. Taken for granted by the majority, this tenet is stoutly defended by our most sophisticated art historians, scholars who have themselves made major contributions to the study of visual images as both documents and monuments. For Ernst Gombrich, for example, "the history of art . . . is rightly considered to be the history of masterpieces and of the 'old masters,'" and Francis Haskell takes the position that "aesthetic discrimination must always lie at the heart of any serious discussion involving the arts, even in an inquiry . . . that is not intended to make a contribution to art history".[22] It is clear that the basic techniques of the discipline are most effectively learned with respect to the great masters and their masterpieces. These are embedded in a cultural continuum, and successful theoretical interpretations are grounded in a firm grasp of the subject's historiography, genres, and techniques. However, it is also clear that despite being an area of inquiry of considerable academic potential, and one which is as dependent on the application of art-historical techniques to the study of visual images as traditional art history, the study of images as historical documents continues to be marginalized by many art historians. Images are not exclusively the monuments of art history. They can also be the documents of other academic disciplines, to be studied not for their own sake, but in order to illuminate, for example, other cultural monuments. Viewed from this perspective, there is little correlation between the aesthetic value of a visual source (man-made work of art or artifact) as art-historical monument, and its historical significance as cultural, economic, or political document.[23]

A comparative approach to the study of theatrical events, utilizing visual as well as textual documentation, was pioneered by Aby Warburg. He brought a breadth of vision and originality to his study of theatrical events which was based on a thorough understanding of the standard techniques and skills of his own discipline, art history. He accepted visual as well as textual material as historical documents worthy of study in their own right, independent of any aesthetic merits, and recognized the value of art-historical techniques for gaining the maximum theater-historical information from them. The sentence in which he outlines his approach is a succinct manifesto of theater iconography:

> At first glance, [festival] accounts now strike us as dry or curious reports, and there exists only one way to transform them into genuinely vital evocations of the past. That is by attempting to examine them in conjunction with contemporary works of art which depict such festi-

vals. To date, such an attempt has been made neither with respect to a specific area of research nor on a more general scale. . . . I gladly grasped the prestigious opportunity [which these newly discovered documents] offered me to attempt an art-historical investigation into the historical significance of the *intermedi* of 1589 for the development of theatrical taste.[24]

Unlike art historians, theater historians study pictures not as the primary object of their research, but as evidence that points to it. This approach requires effective decoding in order for the significance of any particular portrayal of a performance to become clear. The visual appearance of prephotographic depictions of performers, their gestures, costumes, props, postures, facial characteristics, expressions, and body types, and even the settings in which they are depicted, have as much to do with the identity of the artists who depicted them, and the pictorial heritage those artists drew on, as with the actual appearance, performances, and settings of the entertainers they depict. Theater historians are becoming increasingly aware of the importance of taking into consideration iconographic precedents when interpreting pictures (of whatever level of artistic competence) whose theater-historical significance is inextricably connected with their art-historical interpretation. The evolution of some iconographic motifs demonstrates that, in general, depictions of certain early modern performers borrowed from previous art, becoming progressively stereotyped as artistic conventions increasingly overrode considerations of realism.[25] An understanding of this process, essential to an interpretation of the iconography and its significance, requires the consideration of as wide a range as possible of compositionally and stylistically related pictures, not all of which are directly related to the performing arts.

Works of art are not created in a vacuum, and it would be naive to accept performance-relevant pictures, of whatever period or medium, as factually accurate "snap-shots," or even syntheses or compendia, of exactly what a particular artist saw on a specific occasion. Every pictorial record is—to a greater or lesser extent—affected by artistic imagination, precedents, and traditions as well as by commissioning pressures. Some depictions of performers reflect specific performances by identifiable entertainers; others are more general evocations of contemporary stage practice or folk customs; and a third category is based solely on iconographic precedents. This point is of central importance to the study of all "applied" iconography, and such factors have to be given no less consideration than their actual visual content when the theater-historical significance of particular pictures is assessed.

Sources of Visual Evidence

Itinerant theriac sellers, or *Pauliani* (vendors of snake-bite antidotes), have been identified on images dating back to the early fifteenth century.[26] One of the earliest indisputable images of a travelling medical salesman who is not simply using his bench or table to display goods or seat customers, but is a mountebank in the literal sense of having "mounted a bank" for the purpose of entertaining a crowd, is in a painted roundel which forms part of Giulio Romano's decorative scheme of the 1520s for the Palazzo del Te in Mantua.[27] This roundel, which Aby Warburg identifies as representing a snake-charming theriac seller, is within an iconographic tradition spread by a wealth of renaissance prints.[28] By the late sixteenth century, the association of selling and performance in mountebank depictions was routine. Most images of early modern mountebanks may be categorized within a limited range of artistic genres. Mountebanks' trestle stages are often depicted in the context of representations of the month of February or of the pre-Lenten carnival; produced for series of the months (plate 10), as grand-tour souvenirs of the Italian carnival (plates 7, 11), or as genre scenes in series of plates depicting Italian or Venetian costume in *alba amicorum* or costume books (plates 3–5, 8, 11). They also feature in emblematic and allegorical representations (e.g., of *Discors concordia* [plate 1], the planet Mercury, the moon, *Peace*, *Vanitas*, and *Melancholia*), and in depictions of town squares and village greens, typically on market day or during the annual fair. Prints were sometimes intended as title page illustrations (plate 12) or popular prints (plates 2, 6, 15), and could have commercial (plate 16), topographical (plate 14), or religious (plate 15) significance. Some mountebank images are elements within the context of a complicated decorative schema; others are pastiches or copies of earlier works (plate 13).

Alba amicorum (friendship albums) are pocket-sized albums in which friends and patrons could be requested to enter their names and titles accompanied by short texts, and sometimes by suitable illustrations. Although specific aspects of album iconography have been addressed,[29] these pictures are a substantial theater-iconographical source which, until recently, had received little or

Discors concordia.

QVAMVIS *sit rerum dispar natura, minusque*
  Conueniant, subigit, iungit & arte modus.
Quæ mage diuersa inter se virtute resistunt
  Antidotus quàm quæ theriacalis habet?
Hæc tamen ars miscet, tandem & rediguntur in vnum,
  Vnius vt nomen post medicina gerat.
Pestiferam illa arcet tabem, infectosque tuetur:
  Excitat optato frigida membra tono.

Pro

PLATE 1. *Discors concordia* (violin-playing mountebank with snake), Ioannis Sambucus, *Emblemata . . .* , (Antwerp: 1564), 188. Bayerische Staatsbibliothek, München (in one of three copies of this edition in this collection which were interfoliated for use as *alba amicorum*).

PLATE 2. *Two mountebanks on a trestle stage* (detail: *L'Arboro della pazzia*), 1568, engraving. Windsor, Royal Library.

PLATE 3. *Three mountebanks on a trestle stage*, album amicorum (1587–94) of M. A. Pribil. 10 × 15 cm. Berlin, Kupferstichkabinett, 79.A.3, fol. 403v.

PLATE 4. *Ceretani, o cantimbanchi*, one of a series of dismembered *album amicorum* sheets, of which two are dated 1594 and 1595. 15 × 9.5 cm. Berlin, Kupferstichkabinett, 79.C.28, fol. 21r.

PLATE 5. *Three mountebanks on a trestle stage*, dismembered album leaf remounted into a scrapbook compiled by Frommann (the verso of this leaf bears the date 1603). Württembergische Landesbibliothek, Stuttgart, 2'888, vol. 34, fol. 71v.

PLATE 6. Girolamo Porro (active circa 1574–1604), *Three mountebanks on a trestle stage* (details from two impressions of *Le bararie del mondo*), engraving 39 × 50 cm. Upper image: Windsor, Royal Library. Whole picture reproduced in Katritzky 1987b, fig. 166.

PLATE 7. Sebastian de Vrancx, *Three mountebanks on a trestle stage* (detail: *Carnival in the Piazza San Marco, Venice*), circa 1600, oil on canvas, 48 × 73.5 cm. London art market, 1979 (as Louis de Caulery). Whole picture reproduced in Katritzky 1997, fig. 9.

PLATE 8. Pieter de Jode after Sebastian Vrancx, *Two mountebanks on a trestle stage* (detail: *Romanorum viri et feminæ habitus*, plate 3 from *Variarum gentium ornatus*), circa 1600, engraving. Oxford, Ashmolean Museum. Whole picture reproduced in Katritzky 1996, fig. 24.

PLATE 9. Sebastian Vrancx, *Three mountebanks on an outdoor trestle stage* (detail: *Busy market scene*), ink, 27.5 × 38 cm. London art market, 1977. Whole picture reproduced in Katritzky 1996, fig. 23.

PLATE 10. Aegidius Sadeler after Pieter Stevens, "Mountebanks on outdoor trestle stages" (detail: *Februarius*), 1607, engraving. Rijksmuseum, Amsterdam. The drawing for this print is in the Crocker Art Museum, Sacramento, Calif. (For a painted version of the composition, see Katritzky 1996, fig. 22.)

PLATE 11. *Three mountebanks in the Piazzetta, Venice*, detail, album amicorum, 8 × 12 cm. Berlin, Kupferstichkabinett, 79.A.10, folios unnumbered.

RECVEIL
GENERAL
DES RENCONTRES,
QVESTIONS, DEMANDES,
& autres œuures Tabariniques,
auec leurs responses.

*ENSEMBLE L'EXTRACTION DE
sa race, & l'antiquité de son chapeau.*

OEVVRE AVTANT FERTIL EN
gaillardises, que remply de subtilitez, composé
en forme de Dialogue, entre Tabarin &
son maistre.

Troisiesme edition augmentee de plusieurs questions.

A PARIS,
Chez ANTHOINE DE SOMMAVILLE, 1.
Palais, en la gallerie des Libraires.

.M.DC. XXII.
Auec Priuilege du Roy.

PLATE 12. The mountebank Mondor with Tabarin and a boy assistant, title-page engraving to Recueil General des Rencontres, Questions, Demandes, & autres œuvres Tabariniques, avec leurs responses (Paris: 1622).

PLATE 13. After Callot, *Three mountebanks on a trestle stage*, ink. Düsseldorf, Kunstmuseum.

PLATE 14. A mountebank in Harlequin costume on a trestle stage, detail: engraving, in Francesco Scoto, *Itinerario, overo nova descrittione de' viaggi principali d'Italia* (Padua: 1670).

PLATE 15. Stefano della Bella, *Four mountebanks on an outdoor stage* (detail: *The Kingdoms of Heaven, Earth, and Hell*), engraving. Oxford, Bodleian Library, Douce Prints W.2.3a, 68.

PLATE 16. *Teatre de Gille le Niais*, engraving. Oxford, Bodleian Library, Douce Prints E.1.4, 76.

no explicit recognition in this context.[30] An aspect of album pictures which has significant interpretational implications for their theatrical images is that many are paired with inscriptions, either on the same pages or facing them, which may indicate their dates and cities of origin and sometimes other details of documentary significance, such as whether they were commissioned from professional artists or painted by the contributors themselves, symbolic nuances associated with their subject matter and artistic borrowings, and the extent to which they carry any deeper moralistic messages. If these inscriptions are interpreted in conjunction with knowledge of any iconographic precedents and parallels, they can be a valuable analytical tool. However, dated inscriptions can generally be used as only approximate indications of the possible dating of the actual pictures which accompany them, because some albums have had additional pictures mounted into them at a later date than those of their inscriptions, or have been provided with pictures before any inscriptions are made.

Virtually identical costume plates appear in albums and in some manuscript costume books of the period. Albums such as that published by Georg Straub in 1600 emphasize that the demarcation between the two genres is far from clear-cut even among printed examples, and that differences between their related illustrations are primarily contextual, rather than iconographic.[31] Some scholars seek to minimize this problem by regarding all album pictures as purely decorative images, subordinate to individual textual entries.[32] In the 1970s, however, Nickson had already noted the significant insight that not all album pictures are specifically attached to signed inscriptions, and suggested that some may have been collected as travel mementos, and that the most frequent examples of this category are genre pictures showing local costumes and customs; and Nevinson suggests the possibility that such costume pictures might have been sold unbound, as series or single leaves, so that they could be used for a variety of purposes.[33] Such series were popular in the half-century from around 1570 to 1620, when they focused on places visited by their (generally male) owners, often during their academic travels, and served as fashionable and effective ways of demonstrating that those owners were well-educated and widely traveled men of the world. One recurring motif is that of mountebanks on a trestle stage. The numerous variations of this popular composition in album illustrations, and the complex iconographic links with pictures from other sources, confirm that early illustrators looked to many sources, both in art and on the stage itself, to build up their own increasingly strong iconographic traditions and conventions.

Early studies of mountebanks tended toward literal interpretations of the iconography, and toward broad generalizations drawn from a limited range of visual and textual documentation of very varied dates, provenances, and media.[34] The care which must be exercised in any attempt to use pictures as historical evidence has received much recent emphasis.[35] It is not always possible to establish whether outdoor performers in a particular picture are actually intended to represent mountebanks, in whatever context, or simply an independent travelling troupe, amateur actors, or even costumed carnival revellers. Not all images intended as representations of mountebanks actually depict them. As with the written documentation, some are representations of representations: records of performers playing mountebanks in a stage or carnival context.[36]

Visual Aspects of Early Modern Mountebank Activity

MOUNTEBANKS' CONTAINERS AND WARES

Underlying any discussion of the iconography is the question of how to identify mountebank images. Pictures which carry, or are linked with, written confirmations of their subjects (e.g., plates 1, 2, 4, 6, 12, 16) suggest a characteristic feature of mountebank iconography, namely the depiction of a container of the type used for the transport of commercial wares. The presence of such a container on or near the stage may be taken as a reliable visual cue to mountebank activity. However, because mountebanks tended to clear the stage of wares before they started acting, pictures of entertainers without such containers—regardless of whether they are on trestle stages—do not always show independent performers of the type who generated their income through a direct entrance fee rather than by the sale of wares.[37]

Sometimes, especially before around 1580, troupes are depicted presenting their wares in nondescript baskets (plate 2), boxes (plates 1, 6), sacks (plate 10), or chests (plate 16). However, the container typically depicted is a capacious domed trunk (plates 3–5, 7–9, 11–15), described as "deux petis caques . . . ce coffre";[38] "Reagal, boittes et couleuvres";[39] a large locked chest[40] or "coffer";[41] "rich Cabinets";[42] a "trunke";[43] a fine case;[44] or "gran valigione."[45] In the iconography, its visual impact is almost invariably enhanced by a wooden stand, generally ornately carved; some trunks are covered with rich crimson leather, and most have metal studs, a lock, and handles. The wares themselves were thrown to the crowd (sometimes together with notes from the actresses soliciting further attentions from specific members of the audience) in the handkerchiefs or gloves in which purchasers passed their money up to the stage.[46] Their packaging included "glasses, made for the purpose" for liquids and "several papers" for powders;[47] bottles and flasks;[48] small tins for ointments, and perfumed paper envelopes for powders (of either of which the mountebank would commonly expect to sell a couple of hundred in an afternoon, and have more in stock in case demand called for them);[49] an "*ampulla*, or vial";[50] and sealed tins.[51] In many such pictures, the packaging, where visible, is small, round tins, boxes, or bags (plates 2–4, 12), but sometimes glass vials or jars (plate 16) or small sacks are on offer. Occasionally, a picture affords an unusually detailed look into the contents of a chest containing an impressive selection of ephemeral printed material and differently packaged wares.[52] In some regions it was obligatory to display any medical wares with the appropriate license or handbill giving information on how and when to take them.[53] The northern and later iconography is replete with depictions of the gaudy, outsize certificates and charters which German and Dutch quacksalvers, in particular, delighted in displaying, proclaiming their alleged qualifications and cures.

Written records offer abundant indications concerning the typical nature of mountebanks' wares and containers. Closely guarding the secrets of their "filthy receites"[54] and "useless and sometimes harmful remedies,"[55] early modern mountebanks increasingly peddled not only the patent medicines and cosmetics, herbs, and spices with whose sale they were primarily identified, but also printed material and miscellaneous trinkets, by no means all of a medical or cosmetic nature. Philipp Begardi's *Index Sanitatis* of 1539 lists "various wares: confectionery, powders, waters, oils, unguents, plasters . . . composites with all sorts of simples, chest pills, worm tablets, plague powders and all manner of roots." In an early example of what Roy Porter calls the "hidden agenda of [quack] mythologies," Begardi also reveals some of the high-sounding names under which they were marketed:

> Electuarium vite . . . aqua vite . . . pearl tablets . . . rhubarb tablets, although not one of them has ever even touched a genuine pearl or rhubarb . . . oleum virtutum, oleum benedictum, oleum sanctum &

etc. . . . Spanish plaster . . . Venetian ointment . . . heathen balsam . . . Alexandrian tyriack . . . Greek and Barbarian mithradate . . . Calcuttan beans . . . and Indian fruits & etc. . . . ,

commenting dryly that

> they give their wares important names, and high-sounding titles from far-off countries, even though for the most part their only adventure has been to grow and gather the simples, from which they have cooked and manufactured them, on the alpine meadows; and they have added nothing better than gum and wax, turpentine and olive oil, or honey and refined sugar.[56]

Heywood's traveling "pothecary" was one who knew how to puff his wares with beguiling names:

> Here lieth much riches in little space—
> I have a box of rhubarb here,
> . . . .
> Here have I diapompholicus—
> A special ointment, as doctors discuss;
> . . . .
> Here is syrapus de Byzansis—
> A little thing is enough of this,
> . . . .
> Here be other: as, diosfialios,
> Diagalanga, and sticados,
> Blanka manna, diospoliticon,
> Mercury sublime, and metridaticon,
> Pelitory, and arsefetida,
> Cassy, and colloquintita.
> These be the things that break all strife
> Between man's sickness and his life.[57]

Jonson's list of the applications of mountebank remedies subverts their use of technical jargon to his own dramatic purposes,[58] but numerous contemporary documents suggest that such rhetoric is based on actual mountebank practice, and that it was customary for them to stress the exotic, often Eastern, origins of their wares. According to a Roman edict of 1612, Italian charlatans,

> in order to deceive, make many, indeed nearly all of the titles of their remedies hyperbolic, very misleading, specious, . . . [calling them] inestimable gems, treasures of infinite value, incomparable secrets, which astound the world. . . . better still if they are Persian, Arab, Chaldean or from other remote regions (which they have not even seen).[59]

Himantomus observes that German mountebanks, even those who have never set a foot outside their own country, invariably claim to have imported their wares from "India, Turkey, or suchlike remote countries."⁶⁰

Written documentation which comments on mountebanks' wares sometimes gives only the vaguest indications (unguent;⁶¹ bars of soap and suchlike;⁶² things for the charlatan to sell⁶³); or notes an exclusively medical stock (drugs;⁶⁴ "Angelicall & divine Elixir Fioravantyne"⁶⁵). Generally, a range of medical, cosmetic, and herbal wares are noted: "poivre et coumin et autres espices . . . herbes . . . oignemens";⁶⁶ miraculous roots and herbs;⁶⁷ a huge range of medicinal and cosmetic remedies and aids, including metal supports for injured legs, mirrors, and eyeglasses;⁶⁸ "spetiall receipts, salues, Oyles . . . distilled waters, and divers oyntments for burning Aches and stitches, and the like, but espetially for the Itch and scabbs . . . Angelica of Misnia";⁶⁹ oil, unguent, herbs, and preserves;⁷⁰ "oils and drugs . . . vile medicines . . . unprepared antimony . . . precious liquor . . . this blessed *unguento*, this rare extraction . . . *oglio del Scoto* . . . experimented receipts . . . the powder that made Venus a goddess";⁷¹ "unguens, baumes, huiles, extractions, quintessences, distillations, calcinations, & autres fantastiques confections . . . fards, cataplasmes, compositions, embrocations, baings & fomentations";⁷² "waters Oyles and Oyntments of great Raritie";⁷³ "alcuni secreti medicinali e . . . cosette e galanterie vendibili . . . sue galante mercanzie, o di profumeria o di saponetti, o di moscardini, o di simili coserelle, che hanno qualche grazia et allettamento";⁷⁴ "pure, precious, balsamic Indian heart-strengthener . . . the best Venetian theriac . . . precious Indian balsam . . . a reliable precious cream for burns . . . a precious eye and tooth water . . . mish-mash and smeared together stuff. . .a reliable precious *medicament* . . . *aquam Saphiricam* . . . purgative powder";⁷⁵ "poudres aromatiques, des remedes, des secrets & des curiositez . . . boules ou boulettes, poudres et muscadins."⁷⁶

No firm lines can be drawn between the medical and cosmetic products peddled by mountebanks and those prescribed by qualified physicians. In the play *Sejanus*, Ben Jonson has the physician Eudemus offer the following advice to Sejanus's wife Livia:

('Tis now well, ladie, you should
Use of the *dentifrice*, I prescrib'd you, too
to cleere your teeth, and the prepar'd *pomatum*
to smoothe the skin)
. . . .

> When will you take some physick, lady?
> . . . .
> to morrow-morning,
> I'le send you a perfume
> . . . .
> I'le have an excellent new *fucus* made,
> Resistive 'gainst the sunne, the raine, or wind,
> Which you shall lay on with a breath, or oyle,
> As you best like . . .[77]

These were all products typically available from mountebanks as well as from sedentary apothecaries, either directly or via regular physicians. To this common stock of medicines, herbs, spices, cosmetics, and other medically oriented products, mountebanks might add all sorts of other wares. The French (or possibly Venetian) theriac seller or "Triacleur" of an early sixteenth-century farce offered, in addition to "des oingnemens plusieurs . . . des drogues beaucoups," a bizarre and comical selection of curiosities which may be regarded as pagan pendants to the no less improbable Christian relics purveyed by the pardoner who was his economic rival and travelling companion.[78] Some documentation records printed material (including newsletters, ballad sheets, and fables) or other miscellaneous goods ("N*ewes out of India, or The Original of the Turkishe Empire, or Mery Tales, or Songes and Ballets or A Pouder to kil wormes, or A Preservative againste the Plague, or A water to make the skynne faire and white, or Pinnes, Pointes, Laces and whistles*";[79] "pomade . . . precious medicines, dental powders; . . . Venetian soap . . . fragrant powder or water or suchlike . . . a selection of printed material";[80] "ogli, balotte, saponeti, historie et cose simili";[81] "saponetti odorati, pomate, polvere da far bianchi i denti, da far morire i topi, saper far profumi, vender crocette, ò imagini, o simili";[82] "a world of new-fangled trumperies . . . drugs and confections . . . many of them . . . very counterfeit and false. . . . oyles, soveraigne waters, amorous songs printed, Apothecary drugs, and a Commonweale of other trifles . . . trinkets";[83] "oglii, unguenti, pomata, lituari contra veleno, balle moscardini, acquemuschiate, zibetto, muschio, instorie et altre carte stampate";[84] "onguent . . . contre la peste . . . savonnettes . . . emplastres . . . sornettes . . . pomades . . . chansons"[85]).

MOUNTEBANKS' VENUES, STAGES, AND AUDIENCES

Garzoni's comment of 1586, that "per ogni città, per ogni terra, per ogni piazza, non si vede altro che ceretani, o cantinbanchi,"[86] is echoed by Moryson. He visited Italy in the 1590s, and reports that "not only in Carnavall but all the yeare long, all the markett places of great Cittyes are full of Montebankes, or Ciarlatanes."⁸⁷ Guarinonius confirms that "*Ziarlatani*" were to be found "in almost all Italian cities, but especially Venice, every evening in the squares,"⁸⁸ and a French physician maintains that "les Theriacleurs, Charlatans . . . vagabondent de ville en ville, de bourgade en bourgade, par les marchez plus signalez & foyres plus celebres. . . . Toute la France en est plaine, toute l'Italie en fourmille, toute l'Alemaige en regorge," and describes how whole troupes parade in their finery, "recherchent . . . les carrefours & places publiques des villes & bourgades où ilz font eriger des eschafaux & theatres," of a sufficiently elaborate structure to allow the charlatan to affix "au frontispice de son theatre, de tres-amples lettres patentes."⁸⁹ The English traveller Thomas Coryat notes that they are

> also in other Cities of Italy; yet . . . there is a greater concurse of them in Venice then else where, and that of the better sort and the most eloquent fellowes; and . . . there is a larger tolleration of them here then in other Cities. . . . The principall place where they act, is the first part of Saint Marks street that reacheth betwixt the West front of S. Marks Church, and the opposite front of Saint Geminians Church. . . . twice a day, that is, in the morning and in the afternoone, you may see five or six severall stages erected for them.⁹⁰

A letter of 1613 from the great Harlequin Tristano Martinelli to Alessandro Striggi notes that "always in the whole world, and especially in Mantua, . . . charlatans have always placed their benches in the town squares in order to mount them as mountebanks."⁹¹

Mountebanks were drawn to the city, where big crowds maximized the potential for profits, and set up their trestles, benches, tables, stages, or scaffolds in busy marketplaces and town squares all over Europe, especially at the time of carnival and annual fairs. Although it is very rare for pictures to show trestle stages in clearly indoor settings,⁹² indoor as well as outdoor venues are indicated by the written documentation that "they take up their standing in Market places, or void roomes meete for the concourse of people,"⁹³ and perform in a "most noble Italian Gentlemans Pallace . . . uppon a Scaffolde made for the nonce."⁹⁴ In the final months of 1598, Thomas Platter made frequent visits to performances by an Italian troupe staging comedies in Avignon

> for several weeks on a raised platform in a covered tennis court . . . and when they noticed that not many people were coming to their

comedies any more, even though they still had to pay a high rent for the tennis court, they set up a long table in the market place, called the (Place de) Change, and after the midday meal they all stood together on this same table, one next to the other . . . and played an amusing comedy on that same table for a couple of hours or so . . . and when they see that their skills start to count for nothing anymore, they pack up and move to another city.[95]

A letter of March 1602 records that, in Florence during that Easter season, mountebanks were to be prohibited from attempting "to mount a bench, perform, or get others to perform comedies in the piazzas, the streets, and public places in the city, nor in inns, taverns, or other places."[96] The most primitive form of stage was created by "the rabble of these ground *ciarlatani*, that spread their cloaks on the pavement,"[97] or simply "stand upon the ground."[98] Most, however, used a simple raised structure. They "set a stoole to stand upone, or make a little scaffold for the purpose, from which they play their part";[99] are mounted on "a scaffold," "stalls," "banckes or litle scaffolds," or "stand upon tables like stages";[100] "assemble a stage with a banner at the front" or a bank;[101] or perform on a scaffold,[102] "a stage which is compacted of benches or fourmes,"[103] a long charlatan's bench;[104] or "sur des bancs & sur de petits theatres."[105]

They are often depicted in recognizable city settings, such as Padua (plate 14), Rome (plates 8, 10) or Antwerp, of which the most popular are the Piazza San Marco and Piazetta, Venice (plates 7, 11). Sometimes, the iconography places mountebank stages in unidentified Italianate piazzas and settings (plate 9), in a pastiche, capriccio, or allegorical setting (plates 6, 15), on stony outdoor ground (plates 3, 4, 13), or in indeterminate indoor or outdoor settings. The mountebank of plate 1 appears to be standing (or balanced on a high stool or support) at ground level, behind a simple table constructed from two planks raised on a barrel and a box. Generally, mountebanks are depicted on trestle stages. Where their structure can be made out, they are supported on four (plates 5, 6), six (plates 3, 14), or eight legs (plates 2, 4, 5[?], 13)—in plate 13, an extra back support is also indicated. These trestles range in height from around one meter (plates 2–4, 6, 15, 16), to just under two (plates 7–10, 13, 14), or even an implausible three or so (plate 11); and the size of their platforms varies from very cramped (plates 2–4, 6, 14) through slightly larger (plates 5, 7, 8, 10, 13) to a quite substantial area (plates 9–11, 15, 16). Mountebanks' stages with backdrops are no rarity in the iconography (plates 7–9, 12, 15, 16).

How closely do these pictorial indications match probable performance practice? Hummelen has used iconographic evidence to generate detailed estimates of the construction and dimensions of outdoor *rederijker* stages, but Rudlin questions the stability of the stages in mountebank pictures, and regards their depiction as "a token suggestion of the trestle structure necessary to raise a platform to such a [=head] height."[106] Although iconographic conventions may well have contributed to a certain conformity and simplification, these pictures do appear to indicate that not all mountebank trestle stages were elaborate, custom-built, head-height stages which had to be reconstructed at each venue. At least around 1600, some mountebank troupes appear to have relied on sturdy, ready-made portable benches or tables of modest height and dimensions. The audiences in plates 7 through 11 and 14 through 15 give some indication of the popularity of mountebank shows, although none of them come near to matching contemporary assertions such as Platter's, that in the Place de Change, Avignon, Zany Bragetta's troupe drew "a large crowd of folk . . . 100 to 500 or even 1000 people,"[107] or Coryat's, that Venetian mountebank audiences "perhaps may consist of a thousand people that flocke together about one of their stages."[108]

THE CHIEF MOUNTEBANK'S PERSONAL APPEARANCE AND ROUTINES

Iconographic precedents exert a stronger influence than genuine appearance on many depictions of costume. The precise nature of the costume in which the Dutch mountebank Hans Buling, described as "extremely fantastical in his dress" by the historian John Granger, is depicted on his late-seventeenth-century handbill, requires evaluation in the light of its artist's reliance on an engraving of a mountebank by Marcellus Laroon.[109] The evidence appears to suggest that mountebank troupe leaders drew on three main types of visual model in their choice of personal appearance. These were stock costumes of the commedia dell'arte; costumes which evoked exotic oriental itinerants such as Gypsies, Hebrews, or Turks; and the typical outfit of conventionally qualified sedentary physicians. This latter was by far the most popular model, and inspired a wide spectrum of imitations, from flashy parody through authentic mimicry, right down to the feeblest attempts to ape and fake the trappings of medical authority and success.

From earliest times, the mountebank is concerned to emphasize his credibility. Audiences are assured that "je ne sui pas de ces povres prescheurs ne de ces povres herbiers qui vont par devant ces mostiers a ces povres chapes mau cozues."[110] The mountebank "seeketh not after gaines, as the covetous and beggarly knaves doe, but as it becommeth a good Gentleman he travaileth farre and wide upon his owne Charges," and kept up appearances accordingly: "standing first up like a worshipful man, Arayed in his silkes and velvettes, And al to be rayed with braslettes & bowed peeces of golde, And chained about the neck with a great thing (of copper and gylt, as many iudge, but) of pure and fine gold, as farre as the eye seeth."[111] Gold chains, rich furs and fabrics, and expensive clothes and accessories, integral to the image of the early modern physician,[112] were popular components of the mountebank's outfit in Italy, Germany, and France. The economic threat represented by charlatans who, despite stringent sumptuary laws, successfully mimicked their image, inspired regular physicians to numerous warnings to the common man against the dangers of judging medical practitioners by their outward appearance and apparel alone, in anti-mountebank diatribes which highlight the deep impression evidently made by velvet and gold.[113]

The mid-sixteenth-century humanist physician Dr. Pierre Tolet criticized the foreign origins, brightly colored clothing, and loquacity of itinerant healers; Peter van Foreest warns against "incompetents whose only claim to medical knowledge lies in the length of their beard and the gravity of their expression"; and another physician, William Clowes, dismissed a mountebank he met in a patient's house as "a gaudy fellow . . . floriously glittering, like the man in the moon, with his bracelets about his arms, therein many precious jewels and stones of St. Vincent his Rocks, his fingers full of rings, a silver case with Instruments hanging at his girdle and a gilt spatula sticking in his hat."[114]

In a medical treatise of 1610, the French physician Sonnet de Courval is similarly scathing of the superb and magnificently sumptuous clothes and gold chains of a charlatan in Paris: "ordinairement fait plus d'estime, & donne plus de creance à l'apparence exterieure d'une façon galante & d'un maintien bravache, accompagné d'une vaine pompe de somptueux habits . . . vestus de superbes & magnifiques vestements, portans au col des chaines d'or."[115] Himantomus describes the typical German quacksalver as being expensively dressed, in a black velvet–lined fur coat, carrying a gold chain around his neck, and displaying a clutch of showy certificates and testimonials written in gold and silver letters on large parchment skins authenticated with great seals; and Plathner was one of many writers confirming this image well into the eighteenth century.[116] Moryson distinguishes between Italian "Emperiks" and those of Germany, who are "never with any foole to make sporte, rather carrying the gravity of great Doctors. For they ride in Coaches, and cary about them Testimonialls under great Seales."[117] According to an English account of 1678, quacks generally wore "a decent black suit, and if credit will stretch so far in Long Lane, a plush jacket"; and Italian legal documents of 1692 describe the Florentine charlatan Lazzaro Tambi, known as "il Dottore," as "dressed in black with a cassock down to his knees."[118] Stolberg castigates the common man for being swayed by would-be physicians who wear

> a beaver hat, a velvet coat and velvet cloak, or one which is at the least lined with velvet, and silk stockings, together with other expensive accessories. . . . you let yourselves be persuaded that all learning, knowledge and art are solely vested in such apparel. . . . So that you may now learn to avoid such mistakes, let quacksalvers be quacksalvers.[119]

Corvino's jealous interrogation of his wife Celia vividly recreates the bizarre appearance of Jonson's Volpone: an actor playing the part of an elderly suitor taking on the visual and verbal disguise of a stage mountebank based on the spectacularly successful mountebank Dionisio Scoto of Mantua, but (*pace* Henke) not necessarily accurately reflecting typical mountebank costume:[120]

> . . . were you enamoured on his copper rings?
> His saffron jewel, with the toadstone in't?
> Or his embroidered suit, with the cope-stitch,
> Made of a hearse-cloth? Or his old tilt-feather?
> Or his starched beard?[121]

A possibly more soberly dressed stage mountebank is one described as a "black gowned Mountebanke . . . borne blind."[122]

A second type of costume worn by chief mountebanks was one or another of the stock costumes of the commedia dell'arte, such as the masked servants Harlequin or Zanni, or the military captain. The leader of the Italian mountebank troupe described by Platter wore the suit of the servant Zanni, as do the chief mountebanks in several pictures of the 1570s.[123] The pathetically small trunk of the solitary mountebank in plate 14 hints at his low turnover, and his harlequin costume and musical instrument indicate that he is entertaining the crowd himself. The charlatan Christophe Contugi, one of several who sold his drugs under the name of Orviétan, appeared in the farces staged by his troupe in the 1640s as Capitan Spacamond.¹²⁴ Inigo Jones has left sketches of two mountebank-related types who featured in his masques. The costume of Wolfgangus Vandergoose appears to be a cross between that of a German alchemist and the *tedesco* (teutonic mercenary soldier of the commedia dell'arte stage). Jones's sketches show the other, described as a mountebank wearing "the habit of a grave doctor," as a bearded man in extravagantly theatrical garb, with knee-high soft boots, hose with decorative trim at mid-thigh, a short cloak and outsized academic cap, holding up a urine bottle in his left hand while his right hand holds on to the bulging purse at his belt.¹²⁵

The third important category of chief mountebank costume suggested by the documentary records is the exotic, often with a strong oriental flavor. One of Balde's medical satires contrasts a charlatan with ten gold rings on each finger, an impressive gold-embroidered crimson coat, the finest imaginable silk hat, and shoes with raised cork platforms, who smells of pomade and travels in a stately coach, with a Gypsy woman in a tattered bearskin, reading people's health out of their palms.¹²⁶ In the first of a cycle of six substantial novels concerned with "unqualified" healers, the physician Ettner von Eiteritz has a soldier pretend to be a quacksalver by acquiring a long-tailed monkey and Gypsy costume.¹²⁷ For the amusement of Lady Anne Baynton (eldest child of his late master John Wilmot, the third Earl of Rochester), Thomas Alcock wrote an account of a notorious episode in which he himself had participated. This was during a period of several weeks, almost certainly in the year 1676, when Rochester duped London society as a fake Italian mountebank. Alcock vividly describes Rochester's exotic costume as "the noble Doctor Alexandr Bendo." He wore

> an old overgrown Green Gown . . . lyned through with exotick furrs of diverse colours, an Antique Cap, a Great Reverend Beard, and a Magnificent false Medal sett round with glittering Pearl, rubies, and Diamonds of the same Cognation, hung abt his Neck in a Massy Gold like Chaine of Princes mettle.¹²⁸

Dr. Bendo's eccentric appearance was complemented by the costumes of his laboratory assistants, who were "dress't like the old Witches in Mackbeth." This theatrical garb appears to have contrasted strongly with the sober costume of Mrs. Bendo, the fictional wife with whom Alexander Bendo offered private consultations and home visits to female clients too modest to unveil themselves in front of a male mountebank. Her "habit of a grave matron" also concealed none other than the heavily disguised Lord Rochester himself. It is extremely difficult to establish reliable criteria for differentiating between depictions of carnival masks, troupes of independent actors, and mountebank troupes in the numerous early modern depictions of characters in exotic costume of an oriental or orientally inspired nature, parading through urban settings.[129]

Although the mountebank's success depended primarily on his oratorical skills, given countless contemporary testimonies (both positive and negative),[130] his own personal routine often included a spectacular element. The mountebank's supernatural powers—and by extension, those of his patent medicines—might be demonstrated in collaboration with "Quelque serpent ou autre beste/ A manger pour montrer mes euvres."[131] As early as 1483, a charlatan in *Epirota* is reported as drinking poison and "putting a snake around his neck with greatest confidence. He has an alliance with the monster. He and the snake are friends."[132] A century later, Moryson notes that "some carry Serpents about them,"[133] and Whetstone witnessed a dramatically encumbered "mountebanke, his necke bechayned with live Adders, Snakes Eau'ts, and twentie sundrie kinde of venemous vermines, whose mortall stinges were taken away by Arte . . . Viperous Beastes, by cunninge usage . . . made so Domesticke and affable."[134] Garzoni dwells on mountebank tricks at length, explaining how they lined their stomachs to protect them from the effects of demonstrating their antidotes by the public taking of arsenic, and their use of serpents, as for example by Mastro Paolo of Arezzo, who encouraged the purchase of his antidotes by producing from his trunk exotic snakes, giant lizards, and even an Egyptian crocodile.[135] More homely demonstrations include ones which involved displaying to the audience a live worm, apparently expelled by a stage mountebank from his assistant,[136] or "une anguille au lieu d'une couleuvre."[137] German quacksalvers customarily exhibited animals of a humbler order, typically, live poisonous spiders, toads, and lizards, but often heightened the spectacular effect by making a show of ingesting one or another of them, in addition to poisons such as arsenic or mercury, before "curing" themselves with their patent antidotes.[138] Charlatans in France "font parade sur leurs theatres de certains animaux incognus venus d'estrange pays," and others proved the efficacy of their miraculous patent cures by publicly poisoning themselves, piercing their limbs with daggers or, in the case of Signor Hyeronimo, burning his hands in a naked flame to the point of completely blistering the skin.¹³⁹ Under the marginal gloss *Strange Matters*, Coryat tops even this:

> I saw one of them holde a viper in his hand, and play with his sting a quarter of an houre together, and yet receive no hurt; though another man should have beene presently stung to death with it. . . . Also I have seene a Mountebanke hackle and gash his naked arme with a knife most pittifully to beholde, so that the blood hath streamed out in great abundance, and by and by after he hath applied a certaine oyle unto it, wherewith he hath incontinent both stanched the blood, and so throughly healed the woundes and gashes, that when he hath afterward shewed us his arme againe, we could not possibly perceive the least token of a gash.¹⁴⁰

In 1616, an Italian received payment from the mayor of Coventry for "thrusting himself through the side to make experiment of his oyle."¹⁴¹ The renowned commedia dell'arte actor Nicolò Barbieri recalls a Savoyan licensing official ("a theologian, but not well-versed in worldly deceptions"), who in 1596 had asked the mountebank Monferino, by whom the then twenty-year-old performer was employed, if he were a necromancer, claiming that in Italy, he himself had seen charlatans who had performed various types of sorcery, such as using a small pellet to remove stones from people's eyes, or taking fire deep into their throats and spewing it out again in a multitude of sparks, or cutting their arms with large knives and using magic to heal them.¹⁴² The diarist John Evelyn, who in 1645 had visited "*Piazza Navona* . . . to heare the Mountebankes prate, & debite their Medicines," decades later recalled (with considerable regret that he had not obtained his secret), "a certaine *Mountebank* at Rome in the *Piazza Navona*" whom he had seen giving a very spirited demonstration of an apparently self-igniting ring.¹⁴³ The diary of Johannes Wrage, a young apothecary engaged to accompany Ferdinand Albrecht, Duke of Braunschweig-Lüneburg, on his travels, notes a charlatan of 1658 in the Place des Terraux, Lyon, who fixed fireworks to his person, which he set off before "flying" down nonstop from the top of a tower, on a rope, like a kite, "which was exceedingly strange to watch."¹⁴⁴ Jonson's Kitely rhetorically asks: "should I, like one of these penurious quacksalvers, but set the bills up to mine own disgrace, and try experiments upon myself?"¹⁴⁵ Descriptions of public physical examinations, tooth-drawing, and even open-wound operations proliferate. By 1672 such demonstrations were so commonplace that a Roman edict forbade mountebanks "to swallow poisons of any sort, nor have themselves bitten by snakes or other poisonous animals, nor to cut or burn their own flesh . . . without our permission . . . so that people are not deceived."[146] Despite their heightened sense of the theatrical, and the contrasting ways in which they presented their personae and natural or supernatural medical skills, Gentilcore concludes that, concerning their remedies and language, "charlatans were not so different from the regular physicians and apothecaries. Indeed, many charlatans were educated, to judge from their detailed handwritten petitions to the medical authorities for licenses."[147]

Some pictures show the chief mountebank concerned to project a dignified and trustworthy image: well groomed and richly attired, in a fashionable outfit with starched white ruffs and cuffs, elaborately trimmed headgear, and even the occasional display of gold neckchains or expensive weaponry. In others, his evident lack of style and cash has resulted in a rather more rough-and-ready image, or he wears theatrical costume (plate 14). Depictions of crowd-pulling stunts involving mountebanks with reptiles, fire, or dangerous chemicals or weapons of the type described in the written documentation include Giacomo Franco's much-reproduced print of 1609 and certain popular prints in which violin-playing quacks display venomous snakes (e.g., plates 1, 2). In plate 2, the quack has a hissing snake coiled tightly around his neck, a masked zanni holds a large bowl of wares (perhaps snake antidote), and security is provided by the fierce-looking dog under their trestle stage. Much of the iconography, however, presents an unrelentingly pedestrian image of the mountebank. He may, particularly if solo, play a stringed instrument in order to gain the attention of the crowd (plates 1, 2, 14). Typically, however, whether successful or struggling, he addresses the audience verbally, often holding a sample of his wares up for their inspection.

MOUNTEBANK'S COMPANIONS

Where it offers specific information, the written documentation records a vast range of size and personnel in mountebank troupes. Only rarely is the mountebank, like a blind man noted by Coryat, unaccompanied,[148] or with just one companion. Most often, the mountebank has two or three companions, among whom a zanni and a woman are favored. The presence of women on the stage was stringently discouraged by the authorities, and Ottonelli is as concerned to rid mountebanks' benches as comedians' stages of the diabolical and infernal scourge of "women frivolously and suggestively adorned for the purpose of enticement,"[149] although it was generally understood that they were a central component of the commercial success of mountebanks, who "by Musicke *woomen* and good words promising wonders: doo persuade manie to buie of them."[150] Smaller genuine and stage troupes include those of the mountebanks observed by Moryson in the 1590s, aided by "a Zani or Foole with a Visard on his face, and sometymes a woman";[151] of the *Primo Sautabanco* Ramundo, who has two "descipuli," Patrasso and Gorgillo;[152] and of Jonson's Volpone, in the guise of Scoto of Mantua, accompanied by his servants Nano, in the guise of Zan Frittata, and Mosca.[153] The stage charlatan Gratiano is accompanied by an Arlecchino and his slave-boy, the Turk Turchetto, who wears dress appropriate to his calling but is actually a young woman called Alissa;[154] stage mountebanks in an English masque and play are assisted, respectively, by their men "zany" and "herlekin" (a third assistant, John Farino [also sketched], did not appear in the masque itself)[155] and by a harlequin and scaramouche.[156] Other small troupes could consist of "two, three or more people, including a *Magnificus*, or Venetian citizen, otherwise known as Master Pantalone, who is the master, and *Zane* his servant";[157] or mountebanks assisted by zanies, Gratians, puppets, women who play the lyre, lute, or harp, and other types of buffoons and comedians;[158] "Zanyes *and* Jack-Puddings";[159] "Monkies, Jack-puddings";[160] "4 zanyes";[161] a "Zani," Gratian, and Florinde;[162] or courtesans and masked and costumed actors.[163]

Among the few troupes larger than the troupe of seven (including two women) described by Platter as being led by Zany Bragetta in 1598[164] are the company of ten led by the Frenchman John Puncteus, licensed in London in 1630 "to exercise the quality of playing, for a year, and to sell his drugs";[165] a company of eight men and women led in 1616 by Girolamo di Ferrante (one of many mountebanks to assume the stage name Orvietano);[166] and "une grande suitte & Caravane d'Escornifleurs, batteurs de pavé, Basteleurs, Comediens, Farceurs & Harlequins . . . bouffons & maistres Gonins" recorded in 1610.[167] A significant number of written records appear to imply troupes of around five or so, with zannis and women again featuring prominently in these medium-sized troupes. At Christmas 1580, Whetstone saw "a Mountebanke . . . & with him a Zanni, and other Actors of pleasure: who presented themselves onelie with a single desire, to recreate . . . [Whetstone's host's] worthie companie: and not with the intent of common Mountebanckers to deceyve the people with some unprofitable Marchandize," a desire in which they were singularly unsuccessful, since "the Mountibanck, with discribing the quallities of his Vermin, and the Zanni in showing the knavish conditions of his Maister, . . . wasted a good part of the night, and wearyed the moste part of the company."[168] A letter of 1602 details the mountebank's favored companions as "*Zanni*, infamous actors . . . dishonest and lascivious women";[169] while Coryat notes a "whole rabble. . . . some weare visards being disguised like fooles in a play, some that are women (for there are divers women also amongst them) are attyred with habits according to that person that they sustaine."[170] The assistants of another Orvietan, whose own stage role was Captain Spacamond, are listed as "La Signore Clarice, cette brave & superbe Actrice," Docteur, Brigantin, Polichinelle, and Roquentin.[171]

In the iconography, mountebank stages are only rarely occupied by one (plates 1, 14), or by more than three (plates 10, 16), figures. Typically, the chief mountebank is accompanied by just an assistant in zanni costume (plate 2), or by a zanni and a woman (plates 3, 4, 8, 13, 15); or by a zanni and boy (plate 12) or man, in theatrical (plate 6) or everyday costume (plates 5, 9); or by a couple (plate 7). Some pictures give insufficient detail to identify individual figures by costume (plate 11). Stages where no zanni costume is worn (plates 7, 14, 16) often feature figures in the costumes of other commedia dell'arte servants, such as Harlequin, worn by the sole figure on the stage of plate 14. Despite his monochrome costume, an inscription identifies as a harlequin the far-left figure in plate 16,[172] which also features characters identified as Gazette, Padelle, and Gille le Niais, the latter identified by the accompanying text as the chief mountebank, even though he wears stage costume, and another onstage figure, clad as a physician, is holding out a vial to the crowd. Sometimes the character in zanni costume appears to be the chief mountebank himself, often accompanied only by a woman; or it is impossible to identify the chief mountebank, if he is indeed on stage, as in plate 10, where four performers in commedia dell'arte costume (a dancing pair of zannis, one playing a lute, and a pantalone with a woman) occupy the foreground stage. Rarely, one or more backstage figures are indicated (plate 15). The women wear floor-length gowns and covered arms, but while their necklines are more likely to be chastely high than seductively low, many of them flirt openly with their companions. Typically, the zannis are depicted with hat, mask, beard, and purse or weapon (or both) at their belts. Many carry a musical instrument. Examples of variations to standard zanni costume which are of particular theatrical significance are those of plates 5 and 12. Plate 12 depicts Tabarin, the mountebank Mondor's more famous assistant, who modified traditional zanni costume by substituting his own hat, which became a significant feature of his act. In plate 5, the zanni's loose white suit, decorated with pale gold horizontal stripes, is further modified by a very makeshift secondary disguise as Cupid. He has a white cloth blindfold around his eyes, red hat and stockings, and straw or bristle "wings." His quiver, made from an old leather boot, is filled with "arrows" (actually wooden cooking spoons), one of which he aims in the red bow he wields, perhaps in some satirical reference to alleged aphrodisiac properties of the wares being hawked by the mountebank. The nonstandard hat of the zanni in plate 15 is perhaps iconographically inspired, by the engravings of Jacques Callot, rather than a firsthand reflection of genuine stage practice.

TYPES OF ENTERTAINMENT

Medieval dramatic monologues thought to be based on the sales patter of thirteenth-century charlatans entreat audiences to sit down and be quiet in terms which unequivocally raise their expectations of being entertained: "Seigneur qui ci este venu, . . . Aseeiz vos, ne faites noise; si escouteiz, c'il ne vos poize" and "Escoutez tuit et entendez."[173] Expectations of entertainment are also confirmed, for example, by two sisters who testified at the trial of the mid-sixteenth-century charlatan Jacques Humeaul that they had not believed a word of his sales patter, but had "simply gone along for a laugh,"[174] and by commentators such as Rastel, who notes of mountebanks that "the Lordes and Signiours of the Townes . . . contemne them undoubtedly in their Judgement. . . . Yet they laugh at them, and say that so good and eloquent an Oration, as they make to the people, doth them a farthingworth of good, at ye least, in relieving their spirits."[175] Surviving mountebank speeches indicate that, by the early eighteenth century, their wares were routinely bought as mementos, and the entertainment element of their act had become generally acknowledged as its main raison d'etre.[176]

Although early modern mountebank performance practice cannot fruitfully be examined independently of the commercial business (the marketing of medicine and medical services by itinerants) in which it was inextricably embedded, it is possible to identify several consistently recorded elements, including short routines, plays, and, perhaps most notably, music.[177] Singing ends the lengthy tooth-pulling session of a short comic dialogue of 1546;[178] Rastel notes that "some of the Mountebankes, do either by Singing, or plaieing upon Instrumentes, so hold the people . . . that for theyr fitte of mirthe onely, they are worthy of somewhat";[179] Braca's stage mountebanks fool around and play their instruments;[180] an English traveler finds noteworthy the persuasiveness of their "Musicke";[181] and the Turkish slave-boy of Scala's charlatan sings and plays the lute.[182] Short spectacular and comic routines, acrobatics, and tricks also played an important part in the repertoire of the typical troupe. Moryson writes of mountebanks' wares that "some buy for use, others only to have more sporte from the foole";[183] Coryat got "infinite pleasure," not from the mountebanks' doubtful goods, but from the "passing variety of sport" with which they leavened their sales patter;[184] an early translator of Garzoni into English equates quacksalvers with "countrey iugglers";[185] *Volpone*'s stage mountebanks offer their audience "pleasure and delight" by accompanying their singing with musical instruments, and Jonson suggests that mountebanks also routinely offered juggling, tumbling, and forced tricks.[186] In 1630 an Italian mountebank troupe led by Francis Nicolini was licensed in London "to dance on the ropes, to use Interludes, and masques, and to sell his powders and balsams."[187] Bolognese licenses of 1651 authorize mountebanks to attract crowds by means of sleight of hand and card tricks, puppet booths, onstage displays of horsemanship, and clowning;[188] and Bernier dismisses them as "les fleaux de la Medecine," their sales pitch as "mille jongleries" and "n'est que mommerie," and lists three of the six most important elements of charlatanry as "la mascarade, . . . la raillerie, . . . et mêmes les tours de passe-passe, de cartes & de goubelets."[189]

Often, a combination of performance techniques featuring music as well as comic or acrobatic routines is recorded. Sonnet de Courval notes the "mille singeries, tours de souplesse & bouffonneries" of Galinette de Galina, the performer from the Hôtel de Bourgogne engaged by Signor Hyeronimo for his Paris season of circa 1602, and the "douce harmonie & harmonieuse douceur des instrumens" of the four accompanying violinists.¹⁹⁰ Coryat indicates that mountebank performance practice includes

> musicke . . . Sometimes vocall, sometimes instrumentall, and sometimes both together . . . [a] singular variety of elegant jests and witty conceits, . . . the jester . . . playing his part, and the musitians singing and playing upon their instruments . . . such savory jests (but spiced now and then with singular scurrility) that they minister passing mirth and laughter to the whole company . . . , extemporall songes, and . . . a pretty kinde of musicke . . . made with two bones betwixt . . . [the] fingers . . . such strange jugling trickes as would be almost incredible to be reported.¹⁹¹

The churchman Ottonelli recalls, from the 1630s, a charlatan in Palermo who "performed a very obscene act with gestures of the greatest impurity," and comic troupes in Sicily who "in the manner of charlatans" wanted to sell wares "and after the sale play a comedy in a public square." He notes that the mountebank's medley of entertaining attractions typically includes clowning, the singing and playing of instruments, female performers with alluring skills, and comic plays lasting up to two hours.¹⁹² In 1616, the citizens of Florence were fascinated by "the shapely Vettoria [who] . . . packs in large crowds with her dangerous leaps, her divine dancing, her sweet singing and her beautiful gaze," one of Girolamo di Ferrante's mixed troupe of eight, who "in the piazza every evening . . . perform comedies which last until half an hour after sunset."¹⁹³

It is clear from such accounts that it was quite usual for mountebank troupes to act, although the status of their performances is generally left open and has been much disputed. Garzoni describes several mountebank routines, including the antics of a Milanese mountebank and his assistant Gradella, who pad out a sketch involving the parts of a foppish lover and his mocking servant with a largely profitless two-hour display of singing, playing, and dancing.¹⁹⁴ The success of Tabarin (Paris, 1584–1633), who, as depicted in plate 12, wore a zanni suit for his stage act, was such that Mondor's patent medicines became nothing more or less than entrance tickets to the performances of his assistant Tabarin. Publications suggest that their routines used short farces of the commedia dell'arte type (some, according to Marks, almost identical to those staged by the actors of the Hôtel de Bourgogne), to vary a set formula of posing an apparently serious medical question. This is addressed in unrelentingly pompous manner by the humorless Mondor, only to be triumphantly deflated and capped by Tabarin with some earthy insight which relied for its comic content on devices such as misogynous remarks, puns, and double entendres of a crude or farcical nature.[195] Plate 16 depicts the troupe of Gille le Niais using "ces farces et ces dialogue" to persuade the common public to buy their "huile, Baume, et Pomade." A letter of March 1602, commenting on a Medici decree which prohibits the three mountebank companies then in Florence (led by Scoto of Mantua, Marsilio Savino of Venice, and Decio Albani of Siena) from continuing to perform or commission comedies during the Easter period, notes that "without this decree, the people would have abandoned the holy services in order to run after these spectacles and comedies."[196] Looking back on his visit of 1645 to Rome, Evelyn recalled that the charlatans of the Piazza Navona customarily "invited people to their stages, by . . . *Pantomimes*."[197]

The suggestion of some written records that mountebank troupes could include full-length plays in their repertoires has received an exceedingly cautious reception. Eyewitness reports such as Moryson's, who had

> often seene ciarlatans or mountebanchs (mounted on a scaffold) make sporte like a play, in the markett place. . . . they have a zani or foole, to drawe Company by mirth, that they may better vent theire wares . . . make Comicall sporte . . . drawe the people about them by musicke and pleasant discourse like Comedies, having a woman and a masked foole to acte these partes with them. . . ,

and Isabella Andreini's complaint, in a letter to the governor of Milan, that "those who mount benches in the public piazza perform comedies and thus ruin them, and so I beseech you to write to the Duke asking him not to allow [the mountebanks] to perform comedies," are widely rejected as conclusive evidence that mountebanks could stage genuine drama.[198] Regarded en masse, however, the evidence becomes too persuasive to dismiss. Mercurio repeatedly implies that mountebanks staged proper plays.[199] Ferdinand Albrecht, Duke of Braunschweig-Lüneburg, who notes in a diary entry for 1658 some "Charletans" who staged "Comoedien" (or comedies), emphasizes the dramatic nature of their performance by giving the High German translation in his printed travelogue as "Lustspielen" (comic plays).[200] Detailed analysis indicates that the numerous short comic scenes described in Guarinonius's medical treatise of 1610 are dramatic episodes from full-length commedia dell'arte plays.[201] Most tellingly, the Swiss physician Thomas Platter reports, in reliable and repeated detail, visits of 1598 to watch the mountebank Zany Bragetta and his six companions draw the crowds. Their repertoire included musical interludes; lengthy pseudo-scientific monologues and dialogues; comical disputes concerning their wares; musical interludes in which the troupe accompanied their own singing on the lute, harp, and viola; and routines involving imitative whistling, fake decapitation, jumping, and dancing—but also full-length pastoral and commedia dell'arte plays.[202]

The visual evidence affords only restricted insights into the spectacular and dramatic elements of mountebank shows. Here the emphasis is on the roles of music, of beautiful, impressively costumed women assistants, and of the oratorical skills on which the mountebank's success was primarily dependent, in attracting and entertaining the crowd. Where present, the zanni and female assistant very often play or hold instruments. More rarely, the quack himself plays a stringed instrument. There are no spectacular acrobatic or juggling displays in these pictures, but singing and dancing are sometimes depicted; many of the assistants wear theatrical costume, and several pictures indicate comic dialogue or dramatic episodes. The contextualization of visual images is never entirely straightforward, even for those which carry, or are associated with, explanatory text (e.g., plate 16). Plate 12 shows Tabarin and Mondor engaged in a comic dialogue which, from the knowledge of their question-and-answer routines and printed farces offered by the book to which this forms the title-page illustration, may be assumed to be based on a stage act of this type. The inscription to plate 5 confirms that its depicted zanni is disguised as Cupid, but the image offers insufficient evidence to establish whether he is engaged in a short solo comic routine or a more extensive dramatic offering, or even whether his routine involves some reference, verbal or nonverbal, to the aphrodisiac properties of the wares being sold by the chief mountebank. Plate 6 depicts a comic routine involving Zanni and Pantalone. Here, too, however, it is unclear whether the comic masked servant-master pair of the commedia dell'arte are taking part in an isolated dialogue or in a more substantial dramatic episode. The foreground stage of plate 10 appears to depict comic business featuring two dancing zannis and a pantalone with a woman, and the stage of plate 15 a chief mountebank accompanied by a dancing masked comedian and woman. This latter is one of many such pictures which borrow heavily from earlier images (here, the influential prints of Jacques Callot), and depend on artistic influences which must be taken into account in any assessment of their exact significance for the theatrical activity of mountebanks.

Conclusions

Visual images can be investigated not only as aesthetic works of art in their own right, or as illustrations, but also as historical documents which encode valuable evidence concerning past events. The development of successful techniques for the decoding of visual evidence is impeded by the attitudes that are commonly accepted as underpinning the formal art-historical study of images, which has traditionally focused on the study of art primarily for the sake of its inherent aesthetic or cultural worth, and not as historical evidence. The systematic study of images as theater-historical documents is attracting increasing attention among theater historians, who are using interdisciplinary collaboration to refine this approach as a technique in the service of theater research.[203]

Mountebank pictures form a major pool of evidence relevant to the study of these performing traveling salesmen. The many iconographic connections among illustrations featuring mountebanks preclude the possibility that all are depicted solely from life, indicating that artistic influences and traditions played an important role in the depiction of this subject and that, as with theater iconography in general, successful interpretation of these pictures is dependent on art-historical methods. Comparative analysis of the visual and verbal documentation yields much valuable evidence concerning early modern mountebank activity. It suggests that a whole range of indoor and outdoor venues were host to the mountebank's trestle; that his trunk might routinely contain cosmetics, trinkets, and even ephemeral printed matter as well as patent medicines; that he often went to considerable trouble over his appearance and the spectacular elements of his oration, with crowd-pleasing set pieces involving dangerous animals, chemicals, or weapons; that, although troupes could number from one to eight or more, he tended to have two or three companions, among whom he favored inclusion of a zanni and a woman; and that his oration was supported by a whole range of performative elements. Pictures which can be reliably associated with mountebank activity tend to place a markedly more pedestrian emphasis on these indications than does the written evidence, barely touching on such aspects as the spectacular and acrobatic elements of mountebank entertainment but giving a much more detailed impression of others, such as the typical construction of the trestle and the costume of the mountebank and his assistants.

Some authorities have questioned the links between early modern mountebank troupes and theater, in its narrowest sense. Close comparative analysis of a wide selection of documentation leaves no doubt that some troupes did stage full-length plays, and that the theatrical costumes so widely recorded in mountebank iconography are not always merely borrowed from stage or carnival. The conventions which became established by the written documentation concerning mountebanks are not precisely mirrored in the pictorial traditions evolved by mountebank images. Interpretation of the evidence concerning interaction between mountebanks and the theater involves a comparative approach which contextualizes the iconography within diverging textual and pictorial traditions.

Notes

1. The Italian physician Mercurio defines *charlatans* as follows: "Per Ciarlatani intendo saltainbanco, bagattellieri, buffoni, & universalmente qualunque persona in piazza stando in banco, o in Terra, ò à Cavallo, vende medicine, polveri composti, oglij per guarir alcune infermità, predicando con mille giuramenti, e buggie, mille meraviglie delle cose, che vendono" (Scipione [=Fra Girolamo] Mercurio, *De gli errori popolari d'Italia* [Venice: 1603], fol. 176v).

2. E.g., Piermaria Cecchini [=Fritellino] (1620), in K. M. Lea, *Italian Popular Comedy: A Study in the Commedia dell'Arte, 1560–1620* (Oxford: 1934), 1:60, n.2.

3. E.g., in a Milanese order of state of 1566 (in Natsu Hattori, "Performing Cures: Practice and Interplay in Theatre and Medicine of the English Renaissance" [Ph.D. diss., Oxford University, 1995], 22); a Mantuan *decreto* conferred on Tristano Martinelli in 1599 and renewed in 1613 (in Alessandro D'Ancona, *Origini del teatro italiano* [Rome: 1891], 2:474; Siro Ferrone, ed., *Comici dell'Arte. Corrispondenze;* [Florence: 1993], 1:365).

4. David Gentilcore, "'Charlatans, Mountebanks, and Other Similar People': The Regulation and Role of Itinerant Practitioners in Early Modern Italy," *Social History* 20 (1995): 297–314 (298).

5. J. Knepper, "Ein deutscher Jesuit als medizinischer Satiriker: Zum Jubiläum Baldes am 4. Januar 1904," *Archiv für Kultur-Geschichte* 2 (1904): 38–59; Karl Sudhoff, "Philipp Begardi und sein Index Sanitatis: Ein Beitrag zur Geschichte des Ärztestandes und des Kurpfuschertums in der ersten Hälfte des 16. Jahrhunderts," *Archiv für Geschichte der Medizin* 1 (1907): 102–21; Andrea Corsini, *Medici Ciarlatani e Ciarlatani Medici* (Bologna: 1922); Grete de Francesco, *Die Macht des Charlatans* (Basel: 1937); John H. McDowell, "Some Pictorial Aspects of Early Mountebank Stages," *Publications of the Modern Language Association* 61 (1946): 84–96; P. G. Phialas, "Massinger and the Commedia dell'Arte," *Modern Language Notes* 65 (1950): 113–4; Leslie Matthews, "Licensed Mountebanks in Britain," *Journal of the History of Medicine and Allied Sciences* 19 (1964): 30–45; Claire Jakens, "The Figure of the

Charlatan in the Theatre of the Italian Renaissance" (master's thesis, Warburg Institute, 1977); Carol Clark, "'The Onely Languag'd-men of All the World': Rabelais and the Art of the Mountebank," *Modern Language Review* 74 (1979): 538–52; Sandra Billington, *A Social History of the Fool* (Brighton: 1984); Kitti Jurina, *Vom Quacksalber zum Doctor Medicinae, die Heilkunde in der deutschen Graphik des 16. Jahrhunderts* (Wien: 1985); Petra Schramm, *Die Quacksalber, Heilkünstler, und Scharlatane* (Taunusstein: 1985); Alison Lingo, "Empirics and Charlatans in Early Modern France: The Genesis of the Classification of the 'Other' in Medical Practice," *Journal of Social History* 19 (1986): 583–603; Jill Bepler [=1988a], *Ferdinand Albrecht, Duke of Braunschweig-Lüneburg (1636–1687): A Traveller and His Travelogue* (Wiesbaden: 1988); Roy Porter, *Health for Sale: Quackery in England, 1660–1850* (Manchester: 1989); Kenneth Richards and Laura Richards, *The Commedia dell'Arte: A Documentary History* (Oxford: 1990); Katrin Kröll, "'Kurier die Leut auf meine Art . . .' Jahrmarktskünste und Medizin auf den Messen des 16. und 17. Jahrhunderts," in *Heilkunde und Krankheitserfahrung in der frühen Neuzeit: Studien am Grenzrain von Literaturgeschichte und Medizingeschichte*, ed. Udo Bezenhöfer and Wilhelm Kühlmann (Tübingen: 1992), 155–86; David Gentilcore, "'All That Pertains to Medicine': Protomedici and Promedicati in Early Modern Italy," *Medical History* 38 (1994): 121–42; Gentilcore 1995; Hattori 1995; Roger King, "Curing Toothache on the Stage? The Importance of Reading Pictures in Context," *History of Science* 33 (1995): 396–416; Robert Henke, "The Italian Mountebank and the Commedia dell'Arte," *Theatre Survey* 38 (1997): 1–29; Vivian Nutton, "Idle Old Trots, Coblers, and Costardmongers: Pieter van Foreest on Quackery," in *Petrus Forestus Medicus*, ed. Bosman-Jelgersma et al. (Amsterdam: 1997): 244–54; Margaret Pelling, "Unofficial and Unorthodox Medicine," in *Western Medicine: An Illustrated History*, ed. Irvine Loudon (Oxford: 1997), 264–76; M. A. Katritzky, "Was Commedia dell'Arte Performed by Mountebanks? Album Amicorum Illustrations and Thomas Platter's Description of 1598," *Theatre Research International* 23 (1998): 104–26, plates 2–7; Jonathan Marks, "The Charlatans of the Pont-Neuf," *Theatre Research International* 23 (1998): 133–41; M. A. Katritzky [=1999b], "Mountebanks, Mummers, and Masqueraders in the Diary of Thomas Platter (1595–1600)," in *English and Italian Theatre*, ed. Christopher Cairns, vol. 1 of *The Renaissance Theatre: Texts, Performance, Design* (Aldershot: 1999), 12–44; M. A. Katritzky [=1999c], "Hippolytus Guarinonius' Descriptions of Commedia dell'Arte Lazzi in Padua, 1594–97," *Quaderni Veneti* 30, 1999 (2000), 61–126.

6. George Whetstone, *An Heptameron of Civill Discourses: Containing the Christmass Exercise of Sundrie well-courted Gentlemen and Gentlewomen* (London: 1582); see also Diana Shklanka, ed., *A Critical Edition of George Whetstone's 1582 "An Heptameron of Civill Discourses"* (New York: 1987); Johann Christoph Ettner von Eiteritz, *Des getreuen Eckharts Medicinischen Maul=Affens Erster Theil / oder der Entlarvte Marcktschreyer / In welchen vornehmlich der Marcktschreyer und Quacksalber, Boßheit und Betrügereyen / wie dieselben zu erkennen und zu meiden; Hernach bewertheste Artzney=Mittel in allerhand Kranckheiten und Zufällen Menschlichen Leibes zu gebrauchen?* . . . (Frankfurt: 1694).

7. *Les souhaits des hommes*, early sixteenth century, in *Recueil de poésies françaises des XVe et XVIe siècles: Morales, facétieuses, historiques*, ed. Anatole de Montaiglon (Paris: 1855–78), 3:138; Jakob Balde, *Medicinae gloria per satiras XXII asserta* (1651), trans. German Johannes Neubig (München: 1833).

8. Rutebeuf, *Li diz de l'erberie & De la goutte en l'aine* (circa 1250), quoted in Émile Picot, "Le monologue dramatique dans l'ancien théâtre français," *Romania* 16 (1887): 438–542 (Rutebeuf quoted on pp. 492–6).

9. Flaminio Scala, "Giornata Seconda: La Fortuna di Flauio Comedia," *Il teatro delle*

Fauole rappresentatiue [. . .] *divisa in cinquanta giornate*, Venice 1611 (see also Vito Pandolfi, *La Commedia dell'Arte: Storia e Testo* [Florence: 1957], 2:180–6).

10. Tommaso Medio, *Fabella Epirota* (Venice: 1483); *Farce nouvelle très bonne et fort joyeuse à troys personnages d'un pardonneur, d'un triacleur et d'une tavernière*, in *Recueil de Farces, 1450–1550*, ed. André Tissier, (Geneva: 1989), 5:229–73; John Heywood, "The play called the four PP," circa 1545, in *Medieval and Tudor Drama*, ed. John Gassner (New York: 1963), 232–62; Vincenzo Braca, *Primo Sautabanco*, circa 1596; "Il Resoluto" (of the Rozzi di Siena), *Il ciarlone / Cio è uno che canta in banco e canta come ha medicine, e rimedi a mote infirmità, e come cava un dente a un Villano / Opera molto dilettevole e onesta da recitare alle veglia* (Siena: 1546), in Pandolfi 1957, 1:123–30; Ben Jonson, *Every man in his humor* (circa 1598), 2.1.120–3, *Volpone* (1606), *The masque of flowers* (1614), second antimasque, *The masque of mountebanks* (circa 1618): Shakespeare, *The Comedy of Errors* (circa 1591), 1.2.101–2, 5.1.238), *Hamlet* (circa 1602), 4.7.141, *Othello* (circa 1604), 1.3.61, *Coriolanus* (circa 1608), 3.2.132; D[?Tabarin], *Recueil General des Rencontres, Questions, Demandes, & autres oeuvres Tabariniques, Avec leurs Responses*, (Arras, France: 1626), "question 49," 137–9; Inigo Jones and William Davenant, *Brittania triumphans* (masque of 1638; see Stephen Orgel and Roy Strong, *Inigo Jones: The Theatre of the Stuart Court* [London: 1973], 2:661–704); Aphra Behn, *The Second Part of the Rover* (London: 1681).

11. Thomas Coryat, *Coryat's crudities. Hastily gobled up in five Moneths travells in France, Savoy, Italy, Rhetia commonly called the Grisons country, Helvetia alias Switzerland, some parts of high Germany and the Netherlands; Newly digested in the hungry aire of Odcombe in the County of Somerset, and now dispersed to the nourishment of the travelling Members of this Kingdome* (1611; reprint, 2 vols., Glasgow: 1905). Parts 1–3 of Fynes Moryson's multivolume account of his European travels in the 1590s (*An Itinerary* [London: 1617; facsimile reprint, Amsterdam: 1971]), contain only a brief mention of "Mountibankes" (1:160). Part 4 (*The fourth part of an Itinerary written by Fynes Moryson gent. . . . Continuing the discourse uppon severall heads through all the Dominions he passed in his travell described in the former three parts* [1595], MS CCC.94, Corpus Christi College Library, Oxford [paginated]), which contains extensive references to mountebanks, has achieved only relatively recent and partial publication in Charles Hughes, ed., *Shakespeare's Europe: Unpublished Chapters of Fynes Moryson's Itinerary* (London: 1903). Ferdinand Albrecht I, Herzog von Braunschweig-Lüneburg, *Wunderliche Begebnüssen und wunderlicher Zustand In dieser wunderlichen verkehrten Welt . . . Erster Theil. Begreiffend des Wunderlichen Lebens-und Reisen-beschreibungen* (Bevern: 1678), his own heavily adapted edition from his handwritten travel diaries [WoBüHAB Cod.Guelf.42.19 Aug.2*]; critical facsimile ed., Jill Bepler [=1988b], [Bern: 1988]).

12. Thomas Platter's travel account (MS.Aλ7&8, fols. 262r–265v, University Library Basle; also in Rut Keiser, ed., *Thomas Platter d. J.: Beschreibung der Reisen durch Frankreich, Spanien, England und Die Niederlande 1595–1600* [Basel: 1968]; for English translation of section describing mountebanks in 1598 [fols. 262r–265v] see Katritzky 1998, appendix A); diary of an unnamed Englishman's visit to Italy (British Library MS Sloane 682: fol. 20v is dated 1610); memoranda of Sir Robert Southwell, 1660–1 (British Library MS Eg. 1632, fols. 12r–v); *Diary. Now first printed in full from the manuscripts belonging to Mr. John Evelyn*, ed. E. S. de Beer 6 vols., (Oxford: 1955); Johann Wrage's travel diaries [WoBüHAB Cod.Guelf.267.1 Extrav.]; Thomas Alcock, "The famous pathologist or the Noble Mountebank" (1687; Nottingham University Library MS 1489; also in Vivian de Sola Pinto, ed., "*The famous pathologist or the Noble Mountebank*" by Thomas Alcock and John Wilmot, Earl of Rochester [Nottingham: 1961]).

13. Letter dated March 11, 1602, from the Florentine P. Vinta to his brother Belisario (in Lea 1934, 2:361; translation in Henke 1997, 24).

14. Such as wardens' or chamberlains' accounts, court documents, licenses, edicts, council meeting minutes (see nn. 4, 55, 59, 80, 83, 141, 161, 191).

15. Nicolò Barbieri [=Beltrame], *La supplica discorso famigliare a quelli che trattano de' comici* (Venice: 1634; Ferdinando Taviani, ed. [Milan: 1971]).

16. Philip Begardi, *Index Sanitatis. Eyn Schöns und vast nützlichs Büchlin, genant Zeyger der Gesundtheyt*... (Worms: 1539); William Clowes *The Selected Writings*, ed. F. N. L. Poynter (London: 1948); Petrus Forestus, *De meerto fallaci iudicio* (Leiden: 1589); Mercurio 1603; Thomas Sonnet de Courval, *Satyre contre les charlatans, et pseudomedecins empyriques* (Paris: 1610); Hippolytus Guarinonius, *Die Grewel der Verwüstung Menschlichen Geschlechts* (Ingolstatt: 1610); J.D.P.M.O.D.R., *Discours de l'origine des moeurs, fraudes, et impostures des ciarlatans avec leur descouverte* (Paris: 1622) (Bernier [1688–9, 417] identifies the author as Ambroise Calepin; de Francesco [1937, 253] as Jean de Gorris; Lingo [1986, 599, n.32] as Jean Duret, and notes that Matthew Ramsey has identified the book itself as a free translation of Mercurio's *Errori popolari* [1603], book 4, chap. 1–8); J[ohann] Günther Himantomus, *De incerto urinarum judicio; et intolerabili circumforaneorum impostura, libellus. Das ist: kurtze Beschreibung der heutigen vermeynten Harn-Kunst / und Quacksalberey* (Quedlinburg: 1657); Jean Bernier, *Essais de médecine, où il est traité de l'histoire de la médecine et des médecins* 3 vols. (Paris: 1688–9); Tho[mas] Brian, *The Piss-Prophet, or, certaine pisse-pot lectures*, trans. Johann Reinhard Stolberg (London: 1637), *Der Englische Wahrsager Aus dem Urin*... (Hamburg: 1693).

17. John Rastel, *The third booke, declaring by Examples out of Ancient Councels, Fathers, and Later writers, that it is time to beware of M. Iewel* (Antwerp: 1566); Stephen Gosson, *The Schoole of Abuse* (London: 1579); Tommaso Garzoni, *La Piazza Universale di tutte le professioni del mondo* (Venice: 1586); Lewes Lewkenor, *The commonwealth and Government of Venice* (London: 1599), 182 (In *Volpone* [4.1.40], Jonson's Sir Politic Wouldbe consults "Contarine," from whom Lewkenor draws much of his material on Venice); Tommaso Garzoni, *The Hospitall of Incurable Fooles* (London: 1600); Thomas Winyard, *An owle at Athens: Or A true relation of the enterance of the Earl of Pembroke into Oxford, April xi.1648* (1648); Theodorus Verax [=Clement Walker], *Relations and Observations, Historicall and Politick, upon the Parliament* (London: 1648); *Les sanglots de l'Orvietan sur l'absence du Cardinal Mazarin, et son adieu, en vers burlesques* (Paris: 1649) (one of numerous mazarinades which refer to mountebanks); Giovan Domenico Ottonelli, *Della Christiana Moderazione del Theatro*, 5 vols. (Florence: 1648–52), in Ferdinando Taviani, ed., *La Commedia dell'Arte e la Società Barocca: La Fascinazione del Teatro* (Rome: 1969), 320–526; [Christoph Friedrich Plathner], *Der juristische und medicinische Charletan, entworfen von Xenagogo*, (Frankfurt: 1763).

18. Material of this type forms the basis for Anon., *The harangues or speeches of several famous Mountebanks in town and country* (London: n.d., reprinted 1762 [Billington {1984, 130 n.23} dates the first edition to circa 1700; King {1995, 405} to circa 1725]).

19. Katritzky 1998.

20. Giovanna Botti, ed., "Immagini di Teatro," *Biblioteca Teatrale* 36/37 (1996); R. L. Erenstein and Laurence Senelick, ed., "Theatre and Iconography," *Theatre Research International* 22 (1997); Thomas F. Heck, ed., *Picturing Performance: The Iconography of the Performing Arts in Concept and Practice* (Rochester, N.Y.: University of Rochester Press, 1999).

21. M. A. Katritzky [=1999a], "Aby Warburg's 'Costumi Teatrali' (1895) and the Art-Historical Foundations of Theatre Iconography," *Theatre Research International* 24 (1999): 160–7; idem, "Aby Warburg and the Florentine Intermedi of 1589: Extending the Boundaries of Art History," in *Art History As Cultural History: Warburg's Projects*, ed. Richard Woodfield, Critical Voices in Art, Theory, and Culture series (Amsterdam: G+B Arts International, 2001), 209–58.

22. E. H. Gombrich, *Ideals and Idols: Essays on Values in History and in Art* (Oxford: 1979), 152; Francis Haskell, *History and Its Images: Art and the Interpretation of the Past* (New Haven, Conn.: 1993), 6.

23. Pace Keith Moxey, who suggests that the way forward for visual studies is to make aesthetics their "keystone of disciplinary focus" (in a contribution to Rosalind Krauss et al., ed., "Visual Culture Questionnaire," *October* 77 [1996]: 25–70 [58]).

24. Aby Warburg, "I costumi teatrali per gli intermezzi del 1589. I disegni di Bernardo Buontalenti e il libro di Conti di Emilio de' Cavalieri," *Atti dell'accademia del Regio Istituto Musicale di Firenze, 1895: Commemorazione della Riforma Melodrammatica* 23 (1895): 133–46 (reprinted in Aby Warburg *Gesammelte Schriften* ed. Getrud Bing [1932], 1:259–300, 394–438 [423–4]).

25. The apparent portrait of the mountebank Hans Buling, at the top of his handbill, discussed later in this chap. (p. 262), offers a clear example of this.

26. E.g., a painted cassone panel of circa 1418, in the Museo Nazionale, Florence (Corsini 1922, fig. 3).

27. E. H. Gombrich, *Symbolic Images: Studies in the Art of the Renaissance II*, (Oxford: 1972), plate 128.

28. E.g., Jurina 1985, figs. 155–70.

29. M. A. E. Nickson, *Early Autograph Albums in the British Museum* (London: 1970); J. L. Nevinson, "Illustrations of Costume in the Alba Amicorum," *Archaeologia* 106 (1979): 167–76. Further references: Katritzky 1998, n. 25; 1999b, n. 8.

30. Katritzky 1998, 1999b, c; idem, "Carnival and Comedy in Georg Straub of St. Gallen's Printed Album Amicorum of 1600," in *Künste und Natur in Diskursen der Frühen Neuzeit* (Wolfenbüteer Arbeiten zur Barockforschung, 35), ed. Hartmut Laufhütte (Wiesbaden: Harrassowitz, 2000), 1:603–33. idem, "Franco Bertelli's 'Carnevale Italiano Mascherato' of 1642 and Other Printed Influences on Theatrical Pictures in Alba Amicorum," in *Klovićev Zbornik: Minijatwa-crtež-grafika 1450.-1700.*, ed. Milan Pelc (Zagreb: Croatian Academy of Arts and Sciences, 2001, 216–29).

31. Katritzky, "Straub," 2000.

32. E.g., Susanne Gatineau-Sterr, *Die Trachtenbücher des 16. und 17 Jahrhunderts* (Ph.D. diss., Bern University, 1996).

33. Nickson 1970, 13; Nevinson 1979.

34. E.g., de Francesco 1937; McDowell 1946.

35. Peter Burke, *Popular Culture in Early Modern Europe* (Ashgate: Aldershot, 1996), 80; idem, "The Invention of Leisure in Early Modern Europe," *Past and Present* 146 (1995): 136–50 (146); King 1995.

36. A. Heppner, "Jan Steen and the Rederijkers," *Journal of the Warburg and Courtauld Institutes* 2/3 (1939/40): 46–7; W. Hummelen, "Doubtful Images," *Theatre Research International* 22 (1997): 202–18 (206–7).

37. See Katritzky 1999c.

38. *Farce nouvelle*, sixteenth century, vv.158, 255 (Tissier 1989, 258, 268).

39. *Les souhaits des hommes*, early sixteenth century (Clark 1979, 551).

40. Platter 1598, MS.Aλ7&8, fol. 263r.

41. Jonson, *Volpone*, 1606, 2.2.196.
42. MS Sloane 682, fol. 19r, circa 1610.
43. Coryat 1611 (1905, 1:410).
44. Scala 1611, fol. 6r.
45. Ottonelli 1648 (Taviani 1969, 395).
46. Platter 1598, MS.Aλ7&8, fols. 264v–265r; Moryson 1590s, MS. CCC.94, 600.
47. Rastel 1566, fol. (Aiv)v.
48. Braca, circa 1596 (Jakens 1977, 106, 120).
49. Platter 1598, MS.Aλ7&8, fols. 262r–265v.
50. Jonson, *Volpone*, 1606, 2.2.166.
51. Himantomus 1657, 82.
52. Katritzky 1998, plate 3, 1999b, plate 10.
53. Gentilcore 1995, 304–5.
54. Gosson 1579, 53.
55. Bolognese edict of 1594 (Gentilcore 1995, 302 [in translation]).
56. Begardi 1539 (Sudhoff, 1907, 112–3); Porter, 1989, 111.
57. Heywood, circa 1545, 591–2, 606–7, 612–3, 616–23.
58. Jonson, *Volpone*, 1606, 2.2.90–110.
59. Gentilcore 1995, 304 [in translation].
60. Himantomus 1657, 90–1.
61. *Il ciarlone* 1546 (Pandolfi 1957, 1:126).
62. Guarinonius 1610, 214.
63. Scala 1611, fol. 6r.
64. Lewkenor 1599, 182.
65. Garzoni 1600, 7.
66. Rutebeuf, circa 1250 (Picot 1887, 493–4).
67. Medio 1483 (Jakens 1977, 59 [original and translation]).
68. Garzoni 1586, 763–4.
69. Moryson 1590s, MS. CCC.94, 469, 600.
70. Braca, circa 1596 (Jakens 1977, 106 [original and translation]).
71. Jonson, *Volpone*, 1606, 2.2.6, 16, 59, 74, 90–1, 129, 141, 222–3.
72. Sonnet de Courval 1610, 102, 123.
73. MS Sloane 682 fol. 19r, circa 1610.
74. Ottonelli 1648 (Taviani 1969, 357, 361).
75. Himantomus 1657, 80, 82, 91–2.
76. Bernier 1689, 418.
77. Jonson, *Sejanus*, 1603, 2.78–81, 121, 124–5, 128–31.
78. *Farce nouvelle*, sixteenth century, vv.74, 157, 228 (Tissier 1989, 250, 258, 266); Clark 1979, 547.
79. Rastel 1566, fol. (Aiii)v.
80. Platter 1598, MS.Aλ7&8, fols. 263v–265v.
81. Mantuan *decreto* conferred on Tristano Martinelli in 1599 (Ferrone 1993, 1:365).
82. Mercurio 1603, fol. 178r.
83. Coryat 1611 (1905, 1:410–2).
84. *Decreto* conferred on Martinelli in 1613 (Ferrone 1993, 1:395).
85. *Les sanglots de l'Orvietan* 1649, 5.
86. Garzoni 1586, 757.
87. Moryson 1590s, MS. CCC.94, 631.

88. Guarinonius 1610, 214.
89. Sonnet de Courval 1610, 81, 93, 94, 97.
90. Coryat 1611 (1905, 1:409–10).
91. Ferrone 1993, 1:391.
92. M. A. Katritzky, "Scenery, Setting, and Stages in Late Renaissance Commedia dell'Arte Performances: Some Pictorial Evidence," in *Scenery, Set and Staging in the Italian Renaissance: Studies in the Practice of Theatre*, ed. Christopher Cairns (Lewiston: 1996), 209–88, plates 29, 30.
93. Rastel 1566, fol. (Aiii)r.
94. Whetstone 1582, fol. (Aiii)v [preface], fol. (Liii)v.
95. Platter 1598, MS.Aλ7&8, fols. 262r, 263r, 265v.
96. Vinta 1602 (Lea 1934, 2:361; Henke 1997, 24 [in translation]).
97. Jonson, *Volpone*, 1606, 2.2.48–9.
98. Coryat 1611 (1905, 1:410).
99. Rastel 1566, fol. (Aiii)r.
100. Moryson 1590s, MS. CCC.94, 415, 469, 600, 631.
101. Jonson, *Volpone*, 1606, 2.2.1–2, 69.
102. MS Sloane 682, fol. 19r, circa 1610; Coryat 1611 (1905, 1:267).
103. Coryat 1611 (1905, 1:410).
104. Scala 1611, fol. 6r.
105. Bernier 1689, 418.
106. W. M. H. Hummelen, "The Boundaries of the Rhetoricians' Stage," *Comparative Drama* 28 (1994): 235–51; John Rudlin, *Commedia dell'Arte: An Actor's Handbook* (London: 1994), 49–50.
107. Platter 1598, MS.Aλ7&8, fol. 263r.
108. Coryat 1611 (1905, 1:411).
109. John Granger, *A biographical history of England from Egbert the Great to the Revolution* (London: 1824), 6:169. Marcellus Laroon's "The mountebank" (from his late seventeenth-century series *London Cries* [reproduced in Pelling 1997, 268]) formed the basis for the portrait of Buling in the illustration at the top of his handbill: *The Infallible Mountebank, or Quack Doctor*, circa 1685 (reproduced in Matthews 1964, 29), which in turn provided the basis for an early eighteenth-century frontispiece (to *The harangues or speeches of several famous mountebanks in town and country* [London: n.d., circa 1700–25] King 1995, fig. 3).
110. Rutebeuf, circa 1250 (Picot 1887, 493).
111. Rastel 1566, fols. (Aiv)v, (Aiii)v–(Aiv)r.
112. Lingo 1986, 586; Tommaso Bovio, *Flagello de' Medici Ratimali . . .* (Venice: 1683), fol. 47r.
113. Brian/Stolberg 1693, 164–5; Mercurio 1603, fol. 177r; Himantomus 1657, 56, 81.
114. Lingo 1986, 586; Nutton 1997, 245 (in translation); Hattori 1995, 32.
115. Sonnet de Courval 1610, 93–4.
116. Himantomus 1657, 54–6; [Plathner] 1763, 12, 82.
117. Moryson 1590s, MS CCC.94, 600. Many of the fools shown as or with mountebanks in German woodcuts have an allegorical rather than a literal significance (e.g., Jurina 1985, fig. 168).
118. Hattori 1995, 40; Gentilcore 1995, 297–8 (in translation).
119. Brian/Stolberg 1693, 164–5.
120. Mercurio (1603, fol. 188r) comments on the considerable fortune amassed by Scoto in a decade of activity. Henke 1997, 7.

121. Jonson, *Volpone*, 1606, 2.5.11–15.
122. Coryat 1611 (1905, 1:412).
123. Platter 1598, MS.Aλ7&8, fols. 262r–265v; Katritzky 1998, plate 2.
124. Marks 1998, 137.
125. Jones and Davenant (1638 and 1640: Orgel and Strong 1973, vol. 2, 664, figs. 343, 356, 419, 420).
126. Balde 1651 (Knepper 1904, 40–2 [in German translation]).
127. Ettner von Eiteritz 1694, 93–117 (a seventh novel was planned but not published).
128. Alcock 1687, MS. 1489, fols. 18r, 19r.
129. M. A. Katritzky [=1987a], "Lodewyk Toeput: Some Pictures Related to the *Commedia dell'Arte*," *Renaissance Studies* 1 (1987): 71–125, figs. 18, 25–7; Katritzky 1996, figs. 7, 19, 23, 27.
130. Jonson, *Volpone*, 1606, 2.2.9–17, 50–2; Shakespeare, *Comedy of Errors*, circa 1591, 1.2.101–2; idem, *Coriolanus*, circa 1608, 3.2.131–7.
131. *Les souhaits des hommes*, early sixteenth century (Clark 1979, 551).
132. Medio 1483 (Jakens 1977, 60 [original and translation]).
133. Moryson 1590s, MS. CCC.94, 600.
134. Whetstone 1582, fol. (Liv)r.
135. Garzoni 1586, 758–63.
136. Braca, circa 1596 (Jakens 1977, 93).
137. *Farce nouvelle*, sixteenth century (Tissier 1989, 249).
138. Begardi 1539 (Sudhoff 1907, 113); Himantomus 1657, 87–8. *British Airways Business Life* (October 1998): 30, quotes as follows from Kansas city statute 1923, section 21–2426: "It shall be unlawful for any person to exhibit in a public way within the state of Kansas, any sort of exhibition that consists of eating or pretending to eat of snakes, lizards, scorpions, centipedes, tarantulas or other reptiles."
139. Sonnet de Courval 1610, 98–100, 103–4, 106.
140. Coryat 1611 (1905, 1:411–2).
141. Wardens' or Chamberlains' Accounts, November 27, 1616 (Lea 1934, 2:361).
142. Barbieri 1634 (Taviani 1971, 126–7).
143. Evelyn (February 20, 1645, August 4, 1681).
144. Bepler 1988a, 201; on flying charlatans, see also Kröll 1992, 178 ff.
145. Jonson, *Every man in his humor*, circa 1598, 2.1.120–3.
146. Gentilcore 1994, 133 [in translation]; see also idem 1995, 309–11.
147. Gentilcore 1995, 299–300.
148. Coryat 1611 (1905, 1:412).
149. Ottonelli 1648 (Taviani 1969, 346).
150. MS Sloane 682, fol. 19r, circa 1610.
151. Moryson 1590s, MS. CCC.94, 600.
152. Braca, circa 1596 (Jakens 1977, 63).
153. Jonson, *Volpone*, 1606, 2.2.28, 110, 176–9.
154. Scala 1611, fol. 6r.
155. Jones and Davenant (1638; Orgel and Strong, 1973, vol. 2, 664, figs. 344, 357–8, 367).
156. Behn 1681, act I, scene 2.
157. Guarinonius 1610, 214.
158. Mercurio 1603, fols. 177r, 181r–v, 189r.

159. Verax [=Walker] 1648, 23.
160. Evelyn (August 4, 1681).
161. Winyard 1648 (*Oxford English Dictionary*: "Zany").
162. Bernier 1689, 420.
163. Zürich, Protokollen des Ratshandbuches, 1699 (Schramm 1985, 52).
164. Platter 1598, MS.Aλ7&8, fols. 262r–265v.
165. Phialas 1950, 113. In London again in August 1661, when John Evelyn records going to see "that famous Mountebank, Jo. Punteus."
166. Henke 1997, 26–7.
167. Sonnet de Courval 1610, 94–5.
168. Whetstone 1582, fols. (Liii)v, (Mi)v.
169. Vinta 1602 (Lea 1934, 2:361; Henke 1997, 24 [in translation]).
170. Coryat 1611 (1905, 1:410).
171. *Les sanglots de l'Orvietan* 1649, 3.
172. M. A. Katritzky, "Harlequin in Renaissance pictures," *Renaissance Studies* 11 (1997): 394.
173. Rutebeuf, circa 1250 (Picot 1887, 493, 495).
174. Clark 1979, 550 n.2.
175. Rastel 1566, fols. (Aiv)v–(Av)r.
176. *The Harangues or speeches of several famous mountebanks in town and country*, circa 1700–25.
177. Claire Sponsler ("Writing the Unwritten: Morris Dance and the Study of Medieval Theatre," *Theatre Survey* 38 [1997]: 73–95) highlights "the gap that is opened up between medieval [performance] practices and modern historiography" by archival projects which "inadvertently erase the intricate connections linking a specific performance with surrounding events and practices."
178. *Il ciarlone* 1546 (Pandolfi 1957, 1:130).
179. Rastel 1566, fol. (Av)r.
180. Braca, circa 1596 (Jakens 1977, 93, 120).
181. MS Sloane 682, fol. 19r, circa 1610.
182. Scala 1611, fol. 6r.
183. Moryson 1590s, MS. CCC.94, 600.
184. Coryat 1611 (1905, 1:410, 412).
185. Garzoni 1600, 6.
186. Jonson, *Volpone*, 1605, 2.2.70–1; 110–26, 177–94; 2.5.2; 2.6.14–5.
187. Phialas 1950, 113.
188. Gentilcore 1995, 309.
189. Bernier 1689, 416, 418, 420.
190. Sonnet de Courval 1610, 103.
191. Coryat 1611 (1905, 1:410–2).
192. Ottonelli 1648, 1652 (Taviani 1969, 327, 341, 361, 385, 504. [For shorter extracts in translation, see Gentilcore 1995, 309; Richards and Richards 1990, 28]).
193. Medici documents of 1616 (Henke 1997, 27 [in translation]).
194. Garzoni 1586, 761.
195. Marks 1998, 134–5 D[?Tabarin] 1626.
196. Vinta 1602 (Henke 1997, 24 [in translation]).
197. Evelyn (August 4, 1681).
198. Moryson 1590s, MS. CCC.94, 415, 469, 600, 631; Andreini (Henke 1997, 18 [in translation]); Richards and Richards 1990, 17, 28–30, 85–6, 245; Henke 1997, 17–8.

199. Mercurio (1603; e.g., fol. 177v: "comedie, ò intermedij di suoni, e canti"; fol. 189r: "i giuochi scenici, ò rappresentazioni rappresentate da zanni").

200. MS.WoBüHAB Cod.Guelf.42.19 Aug.2*, fol. 89v, September 23, 1658; Ferdinand Albrecht I, 1678, 26; Bepler 1988a, 199.

201. Guarinonius 1610 (see Katritzky 1999c).

202. Platter 1598, fols. 262r–265v. Raymond Lebègue ("La Comédie Italienne en France au XVIe Siècle," *Revue de Litterature Compareé* 24 [1950]: 15) quotes from a publication of 1669 which notes a conversation between Cardinal du Perron (d.1618) and Jacques Gillot (d.1619) concerning a visit to their town, Langres, by "le Braghetta (*corriger en* Brighella) Italien avec sa compagnie" to perform plays.

203. These include a group initiated by a conference in Venice in 1991, which led to the NIAS 1994–5 Theatre Iconography research group and their June 1995 conference at NIAS, Wassenaar (selected papers in *Theatre Research International* 22 [1997]). Two further conferences in May 1996, at Wimbledon School of Art, London (Selected papers in *Theatre Research International* 23 [1998]) and the University of Prato, led to the formation of the European Science Foundation Theatre Iconography Network 1997–2000.

7 Schubert *Lieder* and the Guitar
Musicological Evidence and Inference

Thomas F. Heck

▋ THE FOLLOWING IS A transcript of a fictional legal inquiry. It is in the form of a nonadversarial encounter between a contemporary European legal magistrate and an expert witness in musicology, in this case the author. The aim of the inquiry is to apply norms and methods common to current legal investigation to a question which is essentially historical and musicological: the legitimacy of performing German songs (*Lieder*), originally composed by Franz Schubert in versions for voice and piano, in arrangements for voice and guitar.

MAGISTRATE: This inquiry is now in session. The court will hear from Thomas F. Heck, who has established his credentials as a musicological expert witness in matters of Schubert *Lieder* performances with guitar accompaniment. Mr. Heck, a complaint has been filed with this court by representatives of the Franz Schubert Society (*Franz-Schubert Gesellschaft*),[1] who contend that a number of guitarists and singers of recent date are besmirching the memory of Franz Schubert, belittling his true worth and falsifying the historical record by attributing to him and performing certain unauthorized and/or inaccurate transcriptions of his *Lieder* for voice and piano. They are allegedly substituting the guitar for the piano in accompaniments. They request that this court issue a restraining order. Just what are the facts with respect to these guitar accompaniments? Did Schubert in fact write guitar accompaniments to his songs? Was the guitar even in existence in the earliest decades of the nineteenth century, when the composer was actively writing for voice and piano?

THOMAS HECK: The guitar rose to considerable musical prominence in Vienna around 1807, when Franz Schubert was still a child and Beethoven a successful and recognized composer. The latter's song, *Adelaide*, transcribed for voice and guitar by Wenzel Matiegka (a guitarist and Kapellmeister of high repute in Vienna), was published that year by the prestigious house of Artaria,[2] as were solo guitar works of Mauro Giuliani, Simon Molitor, and Ferdinando Carulli. Many hundreds of editions of "classic" guitar music, including songs with both guitar and piano accompaniment in parallel staves, appeared in Vienna as well as in many other European capitals over the following two or three decades.[3] So the evidence is clear that the classic, six-string guitar was in existence and was quite popular in Vienna during Schubert's youth and adulthood, when he would have been composing his hundreds of *Lieder*.

M: And did Schubert himself ever have any contact with a guitar? What are the facts in this regard?

TH: Indeed he did. It was undoubtedly the current vogue of the guitar that attracted the young Schubert to the instrument. He set to a guitar accompaniment of his own making a "cantata" (D. 80) which he wrote in honor of his father's name day in October 1813—a fact which assures us, at least, that the young composer knew (and presumably played) the guitar well enough to write for it. We also now know that in early 1814 Schubert reworked, either for his own enjoyment or for that of his guitar-playing friends, Wenzel Matiegka's *Notturno* for flute, viola, and guitar, adding a violoncello part. The manuscript of this work, in Schubert's hand, led Otto Erich Deutsch to assign it D. 96 in his original thematic catalogue of Schubert's works,[4] but the latest Schubert thematic catalogue gives it the designation D. Anhang II,2, in deference to its now-ascertained authorship by Matiegka. Still, it is another instance of Schubert's involvement with the guitar. There is even iconographic evidence, in the famous "Ballspiel in Atzenbrugg" etching, that Schubert's circle of friends included at least one guitar player, for a guitarist is shown in the foreground of this picture seated right next to Schubert, who is congenially depicted puffing a pipe.[5]

M: But let us return to the *Lieder* specifically. Are there any surviving manuscripts of such songs with guitar accompaniment in Schubert's hand?

TH: No. And here we are confronted with the obvious truism that the lack of evidence proves nothing either way.[6]

M: But the converse is also true: Why pretend to base something, in this case modern performances and transcriptions, on nothing?

TH: If we counted as authentic only the works of older composers such as Bach, Haydn, Mozart, and Schubert, for which autograph manuscripts survive, the official canon of their music would be only fraction of what is accepted by scholars today. Experts all agree that the task of establishing authenticity is done by weighing various kinds of evidence, including early catalogues, early editions, transcriptions, and surviving manuscripts (whether autograph or scribal). Each work is handled on a case-by-case basis in this process, one work at a time.

M: Then what other evidence do you propose that the court consider?

TH: While manuscript evidence is altogether lacking on the point of whether Schubert ever arranged his own Lieder for guitar accompaniment, there exists a remarkable publication trail of these songs, arranged for guitar, and appearing in Vienna during the composer's short lifetime (he died in November 1828). I would like to submit as evidence table 7.1, which lists twenty-three such songs, identifies their publishers and plate numbers, and shows how closely the first editions of the guitar versions are associated in time with the first editions of the same works with piano accompaniment.

M: How do you know that these so-called "guitar versions," or the published "piano versions" for that matter, date from the times proposed in table 7.1? What is your evidence? Were they dated on their title pages or elsewhere?

TH: If it please the court, the custom of Viennese and European publishers in the early nineteenth century was *never* to inscribe dates on the plates of music which they engraved and published. Engraved music plates were considered a long-term investment subject to repeated reuse and eventual barter with other publishers. Hence the only way that musicologists can ascertain when they were brought out, aside from the fortuitous mention of their publication in surviving dated letters, is by tracking down their first mention in advertisements in the *Wiener Zeitung* and similar dated newspapers. We infer publication dates, in effect, from the evidence of newspaper advertisements, fully realizing that the actual publication dates could have been somewhat removed (one presumes by up to a week or two) from the respective ads. So far, this is the best the musicological profession can do on the dating of undated early-nineteenth-century printed music.

TABLE 7.1 A List of Schubert *Lieder* Transcribed for Guitar and Published in Vienna during the Composer's Lifetime

Opus No., Title, Deutsch No. Publisher, **Plate No.** (p.n.)	Date First Advertised in the *Wiener Zeitung*
1 Erlkönig, D. 328 (fourth version)	
First ed. for piano: Cappi & Diabelli, publisher's no. **766** (on title page)	2 April 1821
First ed. for guitar: Cappi & Diabelli, p.n. **C. et D. no. 676** as *Philomele (Gesänge . . . mit Guitare)*, no. 106. Source of date for g. version: Weinmann ii/23	12 September 1821
3/1 Schäfers Klagelied, D. 121	
First ed. p.: Cappi & Diabelli, initially no p.n., then **768**	29 May 1821
First ed. g.: Cappi & Diabelli, p.n. **680** as *Philomele (Gesänge . . . mit Guitare)*, no. 110. Source of date for g. version: Weinmann ii/23	12 September 1821
4/1 Der Wanderer, D. 493 (third version)	
First ed. p.: Cappi & Diabelli, p.n. **C. et D. No. 773**	29 May 1821
First ed. g.: Cappi & Diabelli, p.n. **C. et D. No. 678**	12 September 1821
4/2 Morgenlied, D. 685	
First ed. p.: Cappi & Diabelli, p.n. **C. et D. No. 773**	29 May 1821
First ed. g.: Cappi & Diabelli, p.n. **C. et D. No. 679** as *Philomele (Gesänge . . . mit Guitare)*, no. 110. Source of date for g. versions of opp. 4/1–2: Weinmann ii/23	12 September 1821
20/1 Sei mir gegrüsst, D. 741	
First ed. p.: Sauer & Leidesdorf, p.n. **231**	10 April 1823
First ed. g.: Sauer & Leidesdorf, p.n. **278**	10 April 1823
20/2 Frühlingsglaube, D. 686	
First ed. p.: Sauer & Leidesdorf, p.n. **231**	10 April 1823
First ed. g.: Sauer & Leidesdorf, p.n. **278**	10 April 1823
20/3 Hänflings Liebeswerbung, D. 552	
First ed. p.: Sauer & Leidesdorf, p.n. **231**	10 April 1823
First ed. g.: Sauer & Leidesdorf, p.n. **278** Source of date for g. versions of opp. 20/1–3 (p.n. 278): Weinmann ii/15	10 April 1823
21/1 Auf der Donau, D. 553	
First ed. p.: Sauer & Leidesdorf, p.n. **276**	19 June 1823
First ed. g.: Sauer & Leidesdorf, p.n. **277**	not adv. (probably pub. June 1823)
21/2 Der Schiffer, D. 536	
First ed. p.: Sauer & Leidesdorf, p.n. **276**	19 June 1823
First ed. g.: Sauer & Leidesdorf, p.n. **277**	not adv. (probably pub. June 1823)

21/3 *Wie Ulfru fischt*, D. 525
    First ed. p.: Sauer & Leidesdorf, p.n. **276**   19 June 1823
    First ed. g.: Sauer & Leidesdorf, p.n. **277**   not adv. (probably
        Source of date for g. versions of opp. 21/1–3 (p.n. **277**):   pub. June 1823)
        Weinmann ii/15

22/1 *Der Zwerg*, D. 771
    First ed. p.: Sauer & Leidesdorf, p.n. **337**, later corrected   27 May 1823
        to **357**
    First ed. g.: Sauer & Leidesdorf, p.n. (?) **358** (copy not   not adv. (probably
        located)   pub. May 1823)

22/2 *Wehmut*, D. 772
    First ed. p.: Sauer & Leidesdorf, p.n. **337**, later corrected   27 May 1823
        to **357**
    First ed. g.: Sauer & Leidesdorf, p.n. (?) **358** (copy not   not adv. (probably
        located)   pub. May 1823)
        Sources of information about g. versions of opp. 22/1–2:
        W/H 1828 and Weinmann ii/15

31   *Suleika II* (Goethe), D. 717
    First ed. p.: Pennauer, p.n. **133**   12 August 1825
    First ed. g.: Pennauer, p.n. **185**   12 August 1825
        Source of date for g. version: Weinmann ii/20

36/1 *Der zürnenden Diana*, D. 707
    First ed. p.: Cappi & Co., p.n. **60**   11 February 1825
    First ed. g.: Cappi & Co., p.n. **82**   not adv. (probably
            pub. March 1825)

36/2 *Nachtstück*, D. 672
    First ed. p.: Cappi & Co., p.n. **60**   11 February 1825
    First ed. g.: Cappi & Co., p.n. **82**   not adv. (probably
        Source of date for g. versions of opp. 36/1–2:   pub. March 1825)
        Weinmann ii/11, which situates p.n. 75 and
        p.n. 88 in March 1825

37/1 *Der Pilgrim*, D. 794 (second version)
    First ed. p.: Cappi & Co., p.n. **71**   28 February 1825
    First ed. g.: Cappi & Co., p.n. **113**   not adv. (probably
            pub. July 1825?)

37/2 *Der Alpenjäger*, D. 588
    First ed. p.: Cappi & Co., p.n. **71**   28 February 1825
    First ed. g.: Cappi & Co., p.n. **113**   not adv. (probably
        Source of date for g. versions of opp. 37/1–2:   pub. July 1825)
        Weinmann ii/11, which dates p.n. 110 to 9 May 1825,
        and p.n. 116 to 16 August 1825. Guitar versions of
        opp. 37 and 38 were featured in a large ad in the *WZ*
        of 16 August 1825.

continued

TABLE 7.1 continued

Opus No., Title, Deutsch No. Publisher, **Plate No.** (p.n.)	Date First Advertised in the *Wiener Zeitung*
38 *Der Liedler*, D. 209	
First ed. p.: Cappi & Co., p.n. **110**	9 May 1825
First ed. g.: Cappi & Co., p.n. after **122** (poss. **123**?)	16 August 1825
Source of date for g. version: Weinmann ii/11	
(see comments to op. 37/2)	
39 *Sehnsucht* (Schiller), D. 636	
First ed. p.: Pennauer, p.n. **207**	8 February 1826
First ed. g.: Pennauer, acc. to W/H, 1828; Diabelli & Co.,	12 August 1825
acc. to Weinmann	
Note: Weinmann reckoned that this might have been	
no. 67 of the series *Selige Gesänge für eine Baßstimme*.	
A copy has not been located. Source of date for	
g. version: Corresp. with A. Weinmann	
43/1 *Die junge Nonne*, D. 828 (second version)	
First ed. p.: Pennauer, p.n. **136**	25 July 1825
First ed. g.: Pennauer, p.n. **169**	25 July 1825
43/2 *Nacht und Träume*, D. 827 (second version)	
First ed. p.: Pennauer, p.n. **136**	25 July 1825
First ed. g.: Pennauer, p.n. **169**	25 July 1825
Source of date for g. versions of opp. 43/1–2:	
Weinmann ii/20	
60/1 *Greisengesang*, D. 778 (second version)	
First ed. p.: Cappi & Czerny, p.n. **192**	10 June 1826
First ed. g.: J. Czerny, p.n. **701**	not adv. (probably pub. June 1828)
60/2 *Dithyrambe*, D. 801	
First ed. p.: Cappi & Czerny, p.n. **192**	10 June 1826
First ed. g.: J. Czerny, p.n. **701**	not adv. (probably pub. June 1828)
Source of date for g. version: Weinmann ii/11,	
which dates surrounding plate numbers at	
11 April and 12 June 1828.	

Notes: The Weinmann references are to the respective Viennese publishers' plate-number catalogs in his *Beiträge zur Geschichte des Alt-Wiener Musikverlages*, ii series.

Schubert died in Vienna on November 19, 1828. Between circa 1828 and 1833, as reported in Hofmeister's *Handbuch der musikalischen Litteratur* (W/H) of 1834, sixteen more of his Lieder were brought out by Josef Czerny in first editions for both guitar and piano: opp. 65, 1–3; opp. 105, 1–4; opp. 111, 1–3; and opp. 118, 1–6. During the same period Diabelli published guitar versions of several selections from *Die schöne Müllerin* (D. 795): "Das Wandern," "Wohin," "Ungeduld," and "Morgengrüss." He also brought out *Ständchen von Shakespeare*, D. 889, and *Der Einsame*, D. 800, with guitar accompaniment.

M: The court will take note of the margin of error that may apply to such dates. Acknowledging that a comparable degree of uncertainty would apply equally to the dating of either the piano-accompanied or the guitar-accompanied *Lieder*, what do you infer from table 7.1?

TH: A simple numerical count shows that most of the guitar versions were either advertised simultaneously with the first editions for piano or their plate numbers are so close that it is risky to attempt to establish precedence.[7] The piano version would have noticeably preceded the guitar version into print in the case of six of the twenty-three works copublished in this way during Schubert's lifetime.[8] But what is most fascinating is that, judging from the publishers' own plate numbers (not exclusively the dates that these works were first advertised in the *Wiener Zeitung*), *the guitar versions may have preceded the piano versions into print* in up to four instances where there is a relatively wide differential between the guitar version's earlier plate number and that of the piano version, namely:

	Guitar version plate no.	Piano version plate no.
op. 1	676	766
op. 3/1	680	768
op. 4/1	678	773
op. 4/2	679	773

M: Does this bibliographic evidence then imply that the guitar versions were the *first* published editions of these particular songs?

TH: The numerical evidence itself is quite provocative in this regard. But in my experience, it was not uncommon for publishers to set aside limited ranges of plate numbers for certain kinds of series, and thus break the normatively chronological progression of their plate numbers. Indeed, the four works in question are part of Diabelli and Company's "songs with guitar" series called *Philomele*. But they still could have been engraved and released early, perhaps weeks or months before the publication of the voice-and-piano versions of the same songs, as "trial balloons" in a market where Schubert's name was unknown. Whatever the case, these guitar arrangements would have been among Schubert's first works to appear in print.

M: May the court assume that plaintiffs have had access to this evidence in preparing their complaint?

TH: Not necessarily. These surprising discoveries might have been better known long ago, had Otto Erich Deutsch been receptive to the inclusion of information on the early arrangements and transcriptions of Schubert's works in his own "Deutsch" thematic catalogue. Likewise, the compilers of the new German-language edition of this famous catalogue, complementing the new *Neue Ausgabe* of Schubert's works, could have done us all a service in citing them, if for no other reason than to show how Schubert was popularized and performed during his own lifetime.[9] By systematically excluding this hard bibliographic evidence from the official thematic catalogues of Schubert's oeuvre, the publishers in question have done posterity, notably the plaintiffs, no favors.

M: Why do you think Deutsch and his successors rejected the guitar versions? Surely they must have known about them!

TH: Yes, they knew about them. I even corresponded with the editors of the new Schubert thematic catalogue about them. But it is by no means certain that they took full stock of their nature and extent. In 1950 the most knowledgeable scholar in the field of Viennese publishing, Alexander Weinmann, had barely begun his real life's work, the systematic inventory of the output of the major early-nineteenth-century Viennese music publishers (the *Beiträge zur Geschichte des alt-Wiener Musikverlages* series). It was only the following year, 1951, that Deutsch's original *Schubert Thematic Catalogue* appeared. Even the revised, and essentially final, German-language edition of this catalogue, which came out as part of the *Neue Schubert Ausgabe* in 1978, could not have taken into account all the evidence, because Alexander Weinmann and his brother Iganz were still tracking down various "lost" Diabelli editions for their *Verlagsverzeichnis Peter Cappi und Cappi und Diabelli (1816 bis 1824)*, which came out only five years later, in 1983. I am not suggesting that the Weinmanns did not collaborate with the editors of the *Neue Schubert Ausgabe*; they may well have told them all they knew. But I am questioning whether all the evidence was in when these same editors decided once again to ignore, in 1978, as Deutsch had done in 1951, the perplexing fact that nearly two dozen of Schubert's *Lieder* appeared in versions for guitar accompaniment in his hometown, Vienna, during his lifetime.

M: Did the editors in question really just ignore them? Or do you think there might have been other considerations at work?

TH: No, and yes. One very important Schubert scholar, Walther Dürr, editor of the *Lieder* volumes in the *Neue Schubert Ausgabe*, did not ignore them. He recognized in them evidence of the flexibility that obtained in the earliest performances of Schubert Lieder. Here are his words:

> The piano accompaniment ultimately could not only be modified according to the accompanist's capabilities, but could also, as necessary, be performed not on the pianoforte, but on related instruments, and be adapted to them. Thus numerous Lieder . . . were brought out in arrangements for voice and guitar, *which most probably did not originate with Schubert himself, yet were probably sanctioned by him* . . . In one instance, too, a report of the harp being used in place of the piano has come to our attention. . . .[10]

Now, as to any other considerations at work in the decision to exclude mention of the guitar-accompanied Lieder from the 1978 official Schubert thematic catalogue: One can only infer that the decision was consistent with editorial policy. Apparently, if the editors were not convinced that the arrangements were attributable to Schubert himself, they were simply excluded rather than (as was the precedent for the thematic catalogues of other composers, like Mozart, Beethoven, and Haydn) listed as arrangements (*Bearbeitungen*) under the heading of their respective "authentic" works.

M: Then the consensus of Schubert scholars today is, as Walter Dürr stated, that the arrangements probably did not originate with Schubert himself, but were probably sanctioned by him.

TH: Yes.

M: And the evidence for the "probable approval" is what?

TH: First, the very fact of the repeated publication of Schubert's songs in guitar arrangements by *five* different publishing firms in Vienna in the course of the years 1821 through 1828, when Schubert would have been alive and able to intervene to stop such practices if they did not have his approval.

M: Is this another instance of the lack of evidence proving nothing? In other words, does the apparent silence of the historical record with respect to Schubert's attitude or actions toward the practices of his publishers necessarily imply his tacit agreement?

TH: Taken alone, as a historical fact (or more properly a nonfact), certainly not. But when combined with knowledge of the historical circumstances surrounding the appearance of these guitar-accompanied Lieder in Vienna, then Schubert's apparent silence can certainly be seen as assent, if not cooperation.

M: And what do you contend were the historical circumstances surrounding the publication of Schubert's Lieder with guitar accompaniment?

TH: Schubert was born in 1797, when Beethoven was a rising star in Vienna's music world. Destined to live nearly all his life in the shadow of Beethoven, Schubert had considerable difficulty establishing a public musical identity of his own. For instance, he was not listed among the known composers of solo song in Vienna, as reported in the "Referirende Üebersicht des Musikzustandes in Wien . . ." of March/April 1818. The list of "Tonsetzer . . . im Gesang" (in no. 28, of April 8, 1818) included, in alphabetical order, "Hrn. van Beethoven, Graf von Dietrichstein, Fusz, Giuliani, Henneberg, Kanne, Freyh. von Krufft, von Mosel, Salieri, von Seyfried, and Abbé Stadler, among others." But no Schubert![11] By this time he had already composed more than three hundred fifty Lieder, many of which were beginning to be somewhat known from their manuscript copies, at least in his immediate circle of friends.[12]

Finally in 1821, when the Cappi & Diabelli publishing house took the risk of buying, engraving, and publishing what were to be the first songs of the young Schubert in print, op. 1 through op. 7, the partner Anton Diabelli elected to issue four songs from this group in versions with guitar accompaniment—arrangements for which he alone, as a guitarist of some repute at the time, appears to be responsible. These are evidenced in the Whistling/Hofmeister *Handbuch der musikalischen Litteratur* of 1822 (hereafter W/H, 1822), which supposedly listed all such works brought out the previous year.[13] The four songs in question were (and the first one may come as a surprise to many), to quote W/H, 1822:

> Erlkönig, von Göthe, arr. Wien, Cappi et D. 45 Xr.
> Schäfers Klagelied, von Göthe, arr. Ebend. 24 Xr.
> Morgenlied, von Werner, arr. Ebend. 30 Xr.
> der Wanderer, von Schmidt von Lübeck. Ebend. 30 Xr.

Taken as a whole, these 1821 publications mark the beginning of Schubert's slow rise to public recognition as an important composer of Lieder. During the next few years, he sold still more songs to Cappi & Co. and to at least four other rival or successor firms.[14] In each case the publishing pattern established by Cappi & Diabelli in 1821 repeated itself. Certain Lieder would appear concurrently in guitar versions.

M: So the principal factors leading to the publication of concurrent guitar-accompanied versions of Schubert's songs were promotional and financial. Can we know whether this was done at Schubert's request, or was it simply par for the course—the normal way song properties were handled by the Viennese music publishers of that era? Or was it perhaps a special promotional treatment accorded to newcomers, such as Schubert, to help them become better known?

TH: While we may never fully be able to answer all these questions, we can and should at least be aware of the extent to which Schubert's *Lieder* were treated to popular voice-and-guitar arrangements. Here is what the W/H *Handbuch* (the official *Music in Print*) of 1828 listed as being available (in 1827) by Franz Schubert under the heading *Songs with Guitar*. Remember that this is merely an annual snapshot of a practice which had been going on for at least five years (as evidenced in table 7.1):

- Schubert (Frz.) *Erlkönig v. Göthe* arr. op. 1. Wien, Diabelli & Co. 30 Xr.
- *3 Lieder*, arr. op. 20. Wien, Leidesdorf 10 Gr.
- *3 Fischerlieder für Bass*, arr. op. 21. Ebend. 10 Gr.
- *Der Zwerg u. die Wehmuth*, arr. op. 22. Ebend. 10 Gr.
- *Suleika's zweiter Gesang, aus Göthe's westöstlichen Divan*, arr. op. 31. Wien, Pennauer 8 Gr.
- *Sehnsucht, von Schiller, für Bass*, arr. op. 39. Ebend. 8 Gr.
- *Die junge Nonne, und Nacht u. Träume*, arr. op. 43. Ebend. 8 Gr.
- *Morgenlied (Eh' die Sonne)*, arr. Wien, Diabelli et C. 30 Xr.
- *Der Wanderer, von Schmidt*, arr. aus op. 4. Ebend. 30 Gr.

M: This list includes prices. Was the practice of issuing these arrangements purely a matter of money?

TH: This *Handbuch* was a trade catalog, but its entries are not merely evidence of commercial activity. Common sense suggests that something deemed to be of value was obtained for the money—something of musical value to those who had both the means to buy the editions and the skill to read and perform them. Aesthetic considerations therefore would have entered the picture; Schubert songs with guitar accompaniment must have sounded pleasing to fresh, innocent, unjaded, early-nineteenth-century ears. But by all means, let us not overlook the pricing of these editions. There must also have been an affordability factor driving the issuance of guitar-accompanied *Lieder*. Listings in the W/H *Handbücher* show that the piano versions of Schubert's *Lieder* were always more expensive than the corresponding guitar versions. In the W/H of 1826, for example, we find Pennauer bringing out the piano-accompanied version of op. 43 (*Die jünge Nonne, Nacht u. Träume*) for 12 Gr., and the guitar-accompanied version for 8 Gr. It stands to reason, therefore, that the latter were more accessible to more people than the former.

M: The court would like to move on now to the plaintiff's allegation that the guitar accompaniments of Schubert's Lieder besmirch the historical record by being "inaccurate." Please enlighten us on the matter of accuracy: How carefully were the first editions of Schubert's Lieder with guitar prepared?

TH: A close examination of the surviving first editions of Schubert Lieder with guitar reveals many discrepancies between them and their presumed models, most likely the actual Schubert autograph manuscripts for voice and piano. Perhaps the guitar versions were simply done in haste. But it is more likely that they were prepared by "house" guitarists whose modus operandi routinely involved simplification and adaptation. This is why it is more prudent to call them *versions* than *transcriptions*. Unfortunately they often contained serious distortions of what Schubert wrote, both textual and musical. These few examples will make the point:

- The text of Greisengesang (op. 60/1) should begin "Der Frost hat mir bereifet des Hauses Dach" (allegorically speaking, "Frost has whitened the roof of my house"). The guitar version incorrectly reads "Der Ernst hat . . ." (Sternness, seriousness has turned my hair white).
- The first Viennese guitar transcription of Nachtstück (op. 36/2), by F. Pfeifer (exhibit A-1 [fig. 7.1]), begins in a murky bass range rather than in the midrange which the original music requires (exhibit A-2 [fig. 7.2]). Worse, it fails to effect the suspensions which are so important to the mood of the "sehr langsam" introduction, and misses Schubert's whole musical point in creating it: to weave a musical fabric which would persist, repeated an octave lower, as a counterpoint to the vocal line. Pfeifer changes the guitar accompaniment to a trite arpeggio when the voice enters, utterly destroying the intended musical effect. My own published transcription (exhibit A-3 [fig. 7.3]), incidentally, avoids both these musical betrayals of Schubert's compositional genius. Admittedly it is, however, a bit more demanding to play than Pfeifer's version.

Issues of the thinning (or "downsizing") of Schubert's piano accompaniments to fit them to the guitar's more limited resources

FIGURE 7.1. Schubert Lieder inquiry, exhibit A-1: the first Viennese guitar transcription of Nachtstück

FIGURE 7.2. Schubert Lieder inquiry, exhibit A-2: the original Nachtstück

FIGURE 7.3. Schubert *Lieder* inquiry, exhibit A-3: Author's transcription of Nachtstück, published by Tecla Editions (1980), based on the best critical edition of the piano-accompanied version

aside, there are violations of the very musical fabric of his original accompaniments, comparable to the foregoing, to be found in the majority of the other still-extant early Viennese guitar versions.

M: What good are these editions, then?

TH: It may be argued on purely historical grounds that what these versions lacked in musical and textual fidelity to the composer's known manuscripts they made up through their unquestioned proximity in time to the originals for voice and piano. Their pride of historical place is significant. Some of them even have plate numbers, after all, which precede those of their presumed pianistic models.

M: If you, as the court's expert witness, acknowledge the inaccuracies in the earliest *Lieder* of Schubert's transcribed for guitar, what is the point of resurrecting them from historical oblivion?

TH: In the field of music, or in the arts in general, any simplification can be labeled a distortion; yet no reasonable person would deny musicians the right to transcribe or arrange suitable material for their favorite instrument, even a modest little six-string guitar. What these early guitar arrangements *don't* tell us about Schubert's musical thought, one might argue, they *do* tell us about his musical environment. Indeed, the very existence of simplified (let us resist the temptation to dismiss them as simplistic) guitar versions of Schubert *Lieder* during his lifetime can be taken to mean that there was, as Walther Dürr mentioned earlier, a much more liberal—perhaps more cavalier—attitude toward *Lied* accompaniment in old Vienna than has ever been the case since, at least in traditional art-song circles.

M: So you are saying that there is still a musical lesson to be learned from these guitar versions, issues of fidelity aside.

TH: Precisely—but not, obviously, in the area of establishing musical texts or readings. Schubert's own manuscripts for voice and piano must be the defining documents where that is concerned. Rather, it is in the field of "performance practice" that the real significance of the early guitar versions is to be found. But one can go overboard here, too.

M: Kindly explain to the court what you mean by "performance practice."

TH: Historical performance practice is the study of *how* early music was performed in its own time and place, with a view toward recreating such performances today inasmuch as possible. Naturally, advocates of historically informed performance seek out the very editions that Beethoven or Schubert and their circle played from, and try to use them in their efforts to rediscover the performance realities of those bygone days. The growth of interest in historical performance practice, incidentally, has spawned a minor industry of facsimile and reprint publishing houses.

M: And is it your contention that knowledge of the early-nineteenth-century Schubert editions you list in table 7.1 might contribute to a better understanding of Schubertian performance practice?

TH: Yes. These editions (or photocopies of such of them as survive) have not infrequently been used in modern, historically informed performances of the type I just described.

M: And what do musicians who perform from these early Schubert editions do about the errors they contain?

TH: Those who are aware of the errors tend to insert spot corrections where needed to improve fidelity, while still performing substantially from the earliest editions (or facsimiles thereof).

M: But doesn't such tampering with the historical sources, such as they are, violate the spirit of the exercise?

TH: Arguably it does. The use of facsimiles of flawed historical editions in performance places one in a dilemma, because (a) if one does not correct the errors one will be severely criticized for not knowing enough to make things right, and (b) if one does correct them, one can be accused of distorting historical evidence. This leads us to the crux of the problem: When is too much historicity at the expense of the right notes perhaps not such a good idea? A close look at Schubert's famous and dramatic Erlkönig ballad should provide an object lesson in this regard. May it please the court to accept my analysis of the ineffectiveness of Diabelli's transcription of Schubert's Erlkönig as a prepared statement.

M: The court will adjourn for a few minutes to consider Mr. Heck's statement. Will the bailiff please hand out copies of the statement to those in attendance?

Deposition by Thomas Heck

THE CASE OF ERLKÖNIG: ERRORS COMPOUNDED BY INCOMPREHENSION?

There are certainly objective mistakes, chiefly sins of omission, in Diabelli's version for voice and guitar of Schubert's opus 1, a set-

FIGURE 7.4. Schubert Lieder inquiry, exhibit B-1: a facsimilie of the first edition for guitar of Erlkönig

FIGURE 7.5. Schubert Lieder inquiry, exhibit B-2: a page from the Neue Schubert Ausgabe

ting of Göthe's famous *Erlkönig* ballad. The most obvious (see exhibit B-1 [fig. 7.4], a facsimile of the first edition for guitar, in Diabelli's series *Philomele*) is the omission of the repeated triplets in measures 2, 4, 9, 11, and so on—that is, wherever the characteristic bass-line runs in Schubert's accompaniment occur (clearly visible in exhibit B-2 [fig. 7.5], a page from the *Neue Schubert Ausgabe*). Continuity of the repeated triplets is easily maintained in the piano accompaniment, the right hand working independently of the left, but not so with the guitar, because it most often requires the simultaneous use of two fingers (one from each hand) to produce a single tone.

Note that soon after the entrance of the vocal line, Diabelli allows the guitar accompaniment to revert to a simple arpeggio pattern (at the words "reitet so" and "Nacht und,"etc.) instead of maintaining the repeated triplets established in the introduction, and now fully fledged chords in the pianist's right hand. Where repeated-note triplets do occur in this Diabelli transcription, they dribble along on one of the weakest inner strings of the classic guitar, the thick and relatively dull-sounding G string. Much of Diabelli's guitar adaptation lacks the octave reinforcement—hence the punch—of the piano version.

The objective shortcomings of Diabelli's transcription effort aside, the advisability of transcribing *Erlkönig* for guitar in the first place must have been open to question even in Schubert's day. Knowing what we now know about the risk Cappi & Diabelli took in buying and bringing out op. 1 through op. 7, the first works in print by this young, unknown composer, we can reasonably infer that the guitar-playing partner in the firm, Diabelli, had motives other than artistic excellence in mind when he brought out his feeble voice-and-guitar version of *Erlkönig*. Undoubtedly he was seeking the greatest possible return on his investment, perhaps even counting on his own name's prominent size on the title page of the edition (Schubert's is given only on the inside) being a decisive factor in "moving the music."

It is also probable that, since there could not yet have been a spellbinding performance tradition for Schubert's *Erlkönig* (fourth version) in 1821, Diabelli conceived of the setting as a much more intimate musico-poetic account of the ballad than we (admittedly influenced, perhaps adversely, by the late-nineteenth-century "grand" performance tradition) might today. Perhaps he sincerely believed that the humble, gut-string guitar was an appropriate accompaniment medium for even the sometimes frantic and desperate emotions expressed in Schubert's setting of the ballad; the early-nineteenth-century guitar was, after all, not that much softer than its cousin, the wood-framed fortepiano. (Steel-frame pianos had not yet been invented.) It is even conceivable that there was a prevailing expectation in Diabelli's day that it was the singer's business, not the accompanist's, to express the emotions of the song. Finally, being primarily a businessman with a publication series (Philomele, eine Sammlung der beliebtesten Gesänge mit Begleitung der Guitare . . .) to shepherd along, Diabelli might simply have been insensitive to issues of musical appropriateness altogether.[15]

M: [to the public]: The court has taken due note of Mr. Heck's deposition regarding the Diabelli version of Erlkönig for guitar accompaniment. We find that the additional factors, often stylistic and subjective, introduced by his deposition go well beyond what this court can competently rule on. [Turning to Heck] While we may not strike the deposition from the record, given its pertinence to the issues, we must return to the plaintiff's essential grievances. We shall enumerate these grievances and request your conclusions with respect to each.

One: In the matter of certain guitarists' and singers' falsifying the historical record by attributing to Schubert certain guitar-and-voice versions of his Lieder which he did not compose, how say you?

TH: The evidence supports the conclusion that Schubert himself did not make the voice-and-guitar arrangements in question. But it also is clear that Schubert knew about the first two dozen or so of them and did nothing to prevent their repeated publication and circulation in Vienna. Also, it was not false to attribute the songs themselves to Schubert, which was consistently done, despite the fact of their being arranged. The publication of arrangements is as old as the art of music publishing itself, centuries old by the time Schubert Lieder began to be arranged this way.

M: *Two:* Has the reputation of Schubert been besmirched by such arrangements?

TH: The historical record shows that Schubert's reputation was minimal in the eyes of the Viennese public prior to his first being published in 1821. It is therefore very likely that his reputation was significantly enhanced by having his Lieder made available to the many singers-to-the-guitar who lived in Vienna at the time.

In our era, however, with the benefit of hindsight, we would have to acknowledge that the earliest arrangements of Schubert's *Lieder* for voice and guitar misrepresented sometimes what the composer wrote. When compared to the originals for voice and piano, these arrangements can be seen to have introduced avoidable errors of range, of text, of texture, and even sometimes of actual harmonies. Yet there is no question that they give us recognizable versions of Schubert's own compositions. They are still Schubert, in other words, not Salieri.

Perhaps the best answer to your question, then, as regards current editing and publishing practices, is the following:

First, much depends on the quality of the modern edition. Most modern editors seem to do much better than the earliest ones did.

Second, much also depends on how the songs are presented. If they are published or performed simply as "songs by Schubert for voice and guitar," then truth is not well served and, indeed, Schubert's reputation could come under a cloud. If, on the other hand, they are presented as versions or transcriptions of Schubert *Lieder* by a named editor, then it is clear who is responsible for what. Not all the Schubert editions, early or latter-day, respect this notion of truth in advertising.

M: *And finally:* Your closing testimony with respect to the legitimacy of performing Schubert *Lieder* with guitar in the first place?

TH: As a performance practice issue, it is clearly sanctioned by historical precedent dating to Schubert's very time. But here too, one must wrestle with the trade-offs of using the earliest editions, with all their faults, or more critical modern editions, which correct those faults. It is a fact that a number of historically aware guitarists today are still playing selectively from the earliest Viennese editions of Schubert *Lieder*, despite the errors that they contain.[16] Even Diabelli's guitar version of *Erlkönig* has a current exponent, who evidently performs it with great success.[17] It is also a fact that good, reliable, critically acclaimed modern transcriptions (real transcriptions, not just versions) of the repertoire represented in table 7.1, and of many other suitable Schubert *Lieder*, have found their way into print in recent years, in part to enrich the repertoire (such as John Duarte's transcription for guitar of the complete *Schöne Müllerin* cycle), and in part as a corrective to the mistakes of substance, not just of accident, found in the first Viennese editions for guitar.[18] So the choices are clear, and each in its way is "legitimate."

The performance-practice issues and the aesthetic considerations framing this debate will certainly not evaporate with the passage of time. In the end, perhaps, it will be the market forces, just as it was in the beginning, that will determine which older facsimiles and which modern editions of Schubert *Lieder* with guitar survive. But the need for reliable modern editions, for both practical reasons (a number of the earliest guitar versions have never been located) and out of respect for Schubert's original musical intentions, can no longer be questioned. Even a good, modern, guitaristic, idiomatic transcription of *Erlkönig*, if such an adaptation is indeed playable, would be a useful contribution to the present inquiry. Please, can someone do better than Diabelli?

Notes

1. Any resemblance between the fictitious Franz Schubert Society in this essay and an actual society is purely coincidental and unintentional.

2. See plate no. 1853 in Alexander Weinmann, *Vollständiges Verlagsverzeichnis Artaria & Comp. 2. erg. Aufl.* (Wien: L. Krenn, 1978). The first edition of this work, with piano accompaniment, was brought out by Artaria in 1797 (plate no. 691). The publisher must have felt that the time was right in 1807 to introduce the song to the growing guitar-playing public with an appropriate transcription. We know, too, that *Adelaide* was publicly performed with guitar accompaniment on the October 24, 1818. On that occasion, Mme. Milder-Hauptmann sang it, accompanied by the guitarist Franz Mendl, Mauro Giuliani's student. See the AmZ XX/45 (November 11, 1818): 791.

3. Mauro Giuliani's *Sechs Lieder*, op. 89, published in Vienna by Riedl in 1817, is a case in point. It offers settings of *Lieder* of Goethe, Matthisson, Steigentesch, Tiedge, and Reissig set in parallel staves for guitar, voice, and pianoforte, thus allowing the buyer to use either instrument to accompany the voice. A modern (1976) facsimile of the edition is available from Tecla Editions of London.

4. Otto Erich Deutsch, in collab. with Donald R. Wakeling, *Schubert: Thematic Catalogue of All His Works in Chronological Order* (London: Dent, 1951).

5. The etching in question, now in the Gesellschaft der Musikfreunde, Vienna, is often found reproduced in Schubert biographies. It also appears on the cover of the author's edition, *Franz Schubert: Sixteen Songs with Guitar Accompaniment, Containing a Selection of Lieder Published in Guitar Transcription during the Composer's Lifetime, Newly Edited for Performance, with Historical Notes* (London: Tecla Editions, 1980).

6. Cf. David A. Schum, chap. 1, p. XX–XX, and p. XX and following.

7. Simultaneous publication, according to advertisements in the *Wiener Zeitung*, happened with op. 20/1–3, op. 31, and op. 43/1–2 (total six). Very proximate plate numbers (or release dates) characterize the guitar and piano versions of op. 21/1–3, op. 22/1–2 (guitar versions not located), and op. 36/1–2 (total seven).

8. See op. 37/1–2, op. 38, op. 39, and op. 60/1–2.

9. The Beethoven, Bach, and Mozart thematic catalogues delight in passing on such information, which makes it all the more regrettable that Schubert has not been similarly documented. It is therefore with no thanks to either the first (1951) or the new (1978) edition of the Deutsch thematic catalogue that table 7.1,

with its documentation of the plate numbers and dates of the Schubert *Lieder* published with guitar accompaniment during the composer's lifetime, exists.

10. Emphasis mine. See Dürr's foreword to the *Neue Ausgabe sämtlicher Werke Franz Schubert*, Serie IV, Lieder (Kassel, 1970). All translations are also mine.

11. *Intelligenzblatt zu den Vaterländischen Blättern* no. 27–29 (March/April 1818).

12. If January 1818 is taken as a cutoff date for this survey (corresponding to around D. 600), then by my count, not including variant versions of the same *Lied*, nor choral songs, Schubert had already composed 377 *Lieder* when the survey was published. As far as is known, none was yet in print.

13. See, respectively, p. 62 ("Ges. u. Ball. f. eine Singst. m. Pfte.") and p. 64 ("Gesänge mit Guitarre").

14. Sauer & Leidesdorf, Pennauer, Cappi & Czerny, and J. Czerny.

15. He would neither have been the first nor the last music publisher affected with such insensitivity.

16. Usually one corrects audible mistakes in pencil when playing from photocopies of the first editions. I have done the same on numerous occasions. But I have found that only *Nacht und Traüme* is accurately enough transcribed in the Pennauer first edition to justify playing that version virtually in the manner that it has come down to us.

17. Richard Savino, a classical guitar teacher at California State University in Sacramento, reports much success performing the Diabelli version in question. Another guitarist, Frank Wallace, performs his own transcription, which he and soprano Nancy Knowles have recorded on album Gyre 10022, "Schubert and Mertz."

18. My edition, *Franz Schubert: Sixteen Songs with Guitar Accompaniment* (see n. 5), is a case in point.

8 Historical Evidence and Dutch Colonial Labor Relations

V. J. H. Houben

THIS ESSAY EXPLORES the ways in which a historical explanation can be given for a particular string of events that took place around eighty years ago in Indonesia. It is set in the colonial era, on the island of Sumatra, on one of the large plantations that were under European management and worked by Asians, particularly Javanese. Indenture under colonialism is a history of power differences, harsh labor conditions, and a high degree of inter-ethnic violence. Because of the singularity of the historical case studied here, the nature of the inferential analysis made is in part unique, although set within a wider historical context. Various interconnected levels of evidence are taken into account. On the other hand, constructing inferences is a common pursuit by historians. Any historian dealing with a particular period, place, and subject matter cannot provide pure description but needs to offer clues as to why certain events or developments took place. In this way the problem of inference as reflected in this case study may help to produce some generalizations on the way historians collect and present their evidence.

The history of colonial labor relations is presented here in a highly condensed form. My study starts with one detailed record of violent confrontation, including an explicit, contemporary stance toward the cause of this case. Secondly, the wider context of coolie labor and the reasons for the frequent occurrence of conflicts are discussed. Finally, an attempt is made to link the kind of evidence produced in this case study with the nature of historical explanation in general.

The Case of Si Doel

In the Dutch colonial records we can find a report by an assistant inspector of labor named Deibert to his superior in Medan on a violent attack by a Javanese contract laborer who wounded three people with a knife. The report, dated May 23, 1918, offers an interesting, firsthand account of what happened on May 1 on the Asiloem enterprise near Pematang Siantar, on the east coast of Sumatra.

Let us follow in detail what the report tells us of a particular sequence of historical events and the possible reasons for it. The attacker was Si Doel, a soldier who had deserted from the colonial army. His real name was Mahat, and he was a Javanese born in Bondowoso (central Java). He had worked on the Asiloem plantation for about three and one-half months as a night watchman before the incident occurred. On the whole, Doel had apparently been very loyal and polite and was much liked by the manager, Mr. C. de Koningh. In the few days preceding May 1, however, Doel had not been so attentive as normal. On the May 1 itself, a holiday, Doel was found in the gambling shed instead of watching over the telephone, as he had been instructed by the manager.

In the afternoon, at around 5:00, De Koningh and his two European assistants, Serlé and Linkens, were sitting in the front gallery of the manager's house. The manager called out for Doel but, contrary to the latter's usual response, he did not show up immediately. The call was then carried further by the servants, and after about half an hour Doel showed up. Then the following conversation, in a mixture of Malay, Javanese, and Dutch, took place, translated from the report by the author (the intricacies of the use of various languages by people of different cultures in a conflict situation will not be discussed here):

> MANAGER (angry): *Dari mana kowe?* (Where do you come from?)
> DOEL (very polite): *Doel tidoer, toean.* (Doel was asleep, my lord.)
> MANAGER: *Oppas matjem begitoe tida bisa dipake, misti besok tjangkol, panggil mandoer besar.* (Such a behavior by a guard cannot be tolerated; thus tomorrow you have to do digging. I will call the general overseer on this matter.)

Then Doel retreated and returned with the foreman (*hoofdmandoer*) Hardhosoemarto, whereupon a second conversation took place (note that the last two sentences appeared in the report only in Dutch, translated into English by the author):

MANAGER: *Apa kowe maoe, poekoel atau besok pagi tjankol?* (What do you prefer, being beaten or to do digging tomorrow?)
DOEL (answering with pleading voice): When my lord wants to beat me, please go ahead; in that case it is better that I die.
MANAGER: Well, then, you die!

After having said this, the manager instructed the foreman to go and get his rattan stick. Doel and the foreman went away together, the latter collected his rattan walking stick, and both arrived again in front of the gallery.

DOEL (to the manager): *Toean lebih baik Doel, besok pagi tjangkol.* (My lord, it is better that I do the digging tomorrow.)
MANAGER (to foreman): *Nou, mandoer, besok pagi Doel kasih tjangkol, tetapi sekarang kasih djoega sedikit poekoel.* (Indeed, foreman, tomorrow morning Doel can do the digging but right now he has also to receive some beating.)

Next, the foreman started beating Doel but the victim defended himself with his hands. Shortly thereafter, however, those present heard the foreman shout, "*Dia maoe melawan*" ("He wants to have a fight"), upon which the assistants Serlé and Linkens jumped off the stairs of the front gallery. Linkens saw the foreman in a state of fury and beating Doel wildly, Doel still trying to fend off the blows. Serlé asked the foreman to give Serlé the stick but the foreman refused to relinquish it, whereupon Serlé beat Doel with his left hand. At the same moment, however, the foreman called out, "*Djangan deket, dia ada pisau*" ("Don't come near, he has got a knife"). Assistant Serlé grabbed Doel by the throat and forced him down, holding Doel's head to the ground. Assistant Linkens saw a knife in Doel's right hand, tried to hold him by his wrist, but had to let go after being bitten in the right leg by the manager's dogs.

Shortly afterward, Doel was able to free himself of Serlé, too, and ran away toward the coolie shed (*pondok*) and then into the forest, chased by the dogs, although, while still on the premises of the enterprise, Doel had managed to wound three of them. Only after Doel ran was Serlé made aware by the manager that Serlé had been wounded as well. It appeared then that he had been stabbed in the belly and the ribs.

This concludes Assistant Inspector of Labor Deibert's report as far as it renders an account of what happened. However, based on interviews with all those involved, the assistant inspector also added a number of inferences leading up to the single conclusion that it had been the manager and not so much the committer of the crime, Doel, who had really caused the trouble. Apparently, in earlier days De Koningh had thought Doel had a very nasty look on his face and, thinking of the proverb that one has to catch thieves with thieves, had made Doel night watchman. Although this manager did not undertake a single act in the incident himself, the assistant inspector argued that he was the main person to blame. Despite Doel's having submitted himself by accepting the punishment of digging, the manager instructed the overseer immediately to give Doel additional corporal punishment. The intervention of Serlé was also a consequence of this order by the manager, because this order, once given, had to be executed, and Doel was not allowed to resist.[1]

The consequences for De Koningh were severe. The colonial administration decided to enforce a ban on recruitment of new laborers for the Asiloem enterprise unless the manager were fired. The company gave in and dismissed the manager. On the fate of Doel we are not informed, but we can assume that he was sentenced by a court for committing violence against the supervisory staff of the Asiloem enterprise.

When we limit ourselves to the case itself, several features seem to warrant historical comment. What strikes us first, of course, is the inequality of colonial labor relations at that time. Seen from a European perspective, the European manager wielded almost absolute power over his employees. He was able to determine what labor tasks had to be undertaken (e.g., working on a holiday) and what sanctions (including corporal punishment) were to follow when employees did not do their jobs satisfactorily. The sudden and incongruous twist in the sanction to be administered to Doel was possibly a demonstration of absolute power: The overseer had to execute this; the assistants had to tolerate and uphold this unwise decision by the manager.

At the same time, the incident clearly illustrates that intercultural communication had radically gone wrong. From a Javanese cultural perspective, Doel rightly felt that he had lost dignity in having to demean himself, first by accepting inferior work as a punishment, and then by suddenly facing another, even more humiliating correction. Therefore he decided to defend himself, although he might have been aware that this would be interpreted as resistance against the colonial order itself, thus making things even worse. Key inferences from a contemporary point of view seem thus to be the extreme inequality of labor relations and the cultural insensitivity of the European supervisor giving rise to immediate physical violence by the suppressed worker toward his superiors. In this connection, the assistant inspector of labor refers to the cultural notion of *mata gelap*, which alludes to sudden outbreaks of extreme rage on the part of Javanese; such outbreaks were much feared at that time because they often led to the untimely death of the European(s) involved.

Coolie Labor and Violence in Colonial Indonesia

Seen from the standpoint of a present-day historian, what is of interest is not so much the question of who was to blame for the Asiloem incident, but rather the clues it offers about working relationships on an agricultural enterprise in late colonial Indonesia. Inferences of a broader kind thus come into play.

THE CONTEXT OF COLONIAL LABOR

Colonial superiority and its ramifications for labor relations, including violence, have to be set into a wider inferential context: that of coolie labor in general and of the apparently increasingly violent nature of labor relations in late colonial Indonesia in particular. The modernization of the economy there coincided with major changes. The core of the colonial economy, which until 1870 had been centered on the island of Java, moved away to the outer islands, Sumatra and Kalimantan in particular. This shift was accompanied by a change in the nature of output. New products such as oil, coal, rubber, and tobacco were produced first and foremost on the islands beyond Java. Whereas in Java the existing village economies had accommodated production for the world market to a substantial degree, large-scale agricultural and mining enterprises in the thinly populated areas of the outer islands required a different setup. Their sustenance required, besides capital and land, a very considerable input of labor from elsewhere. The increased geographical mobility of labor became the prerequisite for repairing the imbalances between Java and the outer islands (abundance of labor and scarcity of land, versus scarcity of labor and abundance of land), thus contributing to the commercial success of the modern colonial economy in the Dutch East Indies.

The colonial state actively intervened in order to supply the enterprises in the outer islands. It established formal power in remote areas and provided the physical and administrative infrastructure needed by Western entrepreneurs to run their businesses. A regular labor supply was guaranteed by the creation of a system of indentured labor. This system, which bound a worker by written contract for a period of up to three years to a certain enterprise, was put into effect from 1880 onward by means of the so-called Coolie Ordinances. The labor contract contained a penal clause, which made breach of the contract (e.g., through running away) a criminal offense punishable by law. At the time, such systems of forced labor were found throughout the whole of colonial Asia and Africa. For the colonial powers involved, this labor system was an acceptable halfway solution between slavery, which had been abolished around 1860, and free labor, which would not produce enough workers. Seen from a contemporary legal point of view, the penal sanction constituted a curious injection of public law into the domain of private law, which can be explained only by the historical circumstances just outlined.[2]

Before 1900, Chinese coolies (a general term for anyone performing unskilled physical labor) constituted the main labor stock in East Sumatra, but afterward migrants from the overpopulated Java became predominant. The majority of them originated from the poverty belt of southern-central Java, where the ecological balance between the productive soil and the number of people to be supported had already been upset by the end of the nineteenth century. Thus powerful incentives existed that ensured that especially young males were willing to sign up for work in *tanah sabrang* (lands overseas). They were easy prey for henchmen of commercial recruiting agencies, who provided for an immediate advance on future wages and who promised a land of opportunity. After a medical checkup and some formalities, the workers were put onto ships and transported to the enterprises in the outer islands. In Sumatra alone, the number of Javanese coolies rose from a little under 80,000 in 1911 to almost 235,000 in 1929.

Labor relations on the colonial plantation were, however, different from those the Javanese had known in their home region. Plantations in the outer islands were very large enterprises, covering wide tracts of land and involving a complex organization of personnel. Around the turn of the century an average plantation in East Sumatra employed about 630 full-time workers;[3] later, this number increased markedly. The labor regime at the plantation was very strict, forcing the coolies to work outdoors for ten hours a day, under strict supervision. The majority were housed in large sheds that precluded any privacy. Only basic amenities and food were supplied to the labor force. A complex system of bonuses and wage deductions was necessary to motivate those concerned to carry out their work efficiently and in a docile manner. Sanctions ranging from overwork and wage deduction to corporal punishment were meant to reduce resistance as much as possible. The plantation as a social system was marked by hierarchical and depersonalized relationships, instrumentalizing racial distinctions among the Europeans, Chinese, and indigenous workers of various ethnic backgrounds by giving them different tasks in the production process.

An inherent component of the contract labor system was the threat of violence. In recent years there has been a debate involving several social scientists and historians on the twin themes of racism and violence in capitalist enclaves in the colonies. Anticolonial researchers have argued that colonial regimes were exclusively geared toward profit maximization, letting Western economic interests prevail over indigenous demands. They attack "accommodationist" history, which they allege downplays the conflict and violence accompanying European colonialism. Racism and violence as methods of labor control are seen as the benchmarks of the colonial system as a whole. Other researchers tend to dismiss such a deterministic approach. Although they would acknowledge that violence was an integral part of labor relations within plantation society, the unequal colonial relationship as such did not preclude differences over time or even changes for the better.

RISING VIOLENCE IN EAST SUMATRA

The issue of violence as an important element in labor relations may be highlighted by a second case study, one more general than the Doel incident described above. In the late 1920s the economic activity in the outer islands of Indonesia was booming. At the same time violence by coolies toward their overseers rose sharply. In 1929 and 1930, in East Sumatra alone 10 plantation supervisors were killed and 146 wounded as a result of coolie assaults. This was a cause for great alarm among the European community and they called for measures to curb the attacks. A highly politicized debate among several parties ensued in which a great number of reasons for the increased violence were brought forward. From our perspective today, we can observe that several changes occurred simultaneously in East Sumatra at the end of the 1920s. There was a heightened influx of contract laborers from Java, whereas the number of inexperienced European overseers rose as well. Also in the same period the Labor Inspectorate, for reasons explained below, turned to a more scrupulous survey of labor relations.

In 1926 several severe cases of coolie maltreatment came to light on enterprises in Bengkulu and Sumatra's east coast. The Labor Inspectorate was unfavorably affected by these cases, because nothing of the existing abuses had apparently been noticed during previous inspections. In the subsequent political and administrative handling of the two affairs the effectiveness of the Labor Inspectorate was put into jeopardy. Inside the colonial administration the exposed cases of coolie brutalization led to a sincere self-analysis of the functioning of the Labor Inspectorate. There was internal agreement that labor inspectors should be allowed the opportunity for closer contact with the workers without undermining the prestige of the planters. A great multitude of propositions were advanced to realize this aim, of which the most important were inspection of each enterprise three times a year, inspections without prior notice to the staff of the enterprise, a greater number of interpreters, and the gathering of coolies in groups to record complaints. As a result, in April 1927 a general instruction to the labor inspectors was issued that ordered them to implement the main points raised earlier.[4]

From the available figures on violence by European and Asiatic overseers against plantation laborers, it can be observed that under tightened supervision of the Labor Inspectorate these kind of instances effectively declined after 1927. On the other hand, statistics from different sources pinpointed a simultaneous steep rise in the number of cases of violent acts by coolies against the overseers. This rise was so remarkable that it attracted widespread attention among the public and the government both in the Indies and in Holland. Even if the number of attacks was related to the growing number of coolies, there was a disproportionate rise in the official yearly statistics from one attack per every six to eight thousand coolies to one per every five thousand.

The problem of coolie attacks was not confined to East Sumatra or to Europeans alone. Those attacked were, however, mostly young, relatively inexperienced European assistants. Two-thirds of the assaults in East Sumatra in 1926 were made on assistants with less than three years' working experience. The phenomenon of rising violence by coolies coincided with a steep increase in the size of the coolie population in the outer islands in general, and in East Sumatra in particular.

Rising coolie violence triggered a complex debate among the several parties concerned. Most of the discussion was not focused on the exact magnitude of the problem but on its causes. There are several methodological problems concerning the sources on this matter. On the whole, in the contemporary documents immediate and more fundamental causes were not clearly distinguished. To take an example, the behavior of an overseer immediately before an assault should be regarded an immediate cause, whereas defective recruitment can be seen as a fundamental cause. On immediate causality the Labor Inspectorate produced its own statistics: A blow or comment on work performance seemed to be the most frequent. Other immediate causes of coolie attacks were untactful behavior (knocking off the head covering of a coolie; challenging him with utterances like "Come on if you dare!"; enlargement of the previously assigned task) or calling a coolie names.[5]

The discussion on the fundamental causes of coolie violence was much more complex because it involved a charged debate among several interest groups. It involved basically two parties, the employers and the colonial government. In the official documents produced on this issue, three institutions stand out: the employers' associations DPV (*Deli Planters Vereeniging*) and AVROS (*Algemene Vereeniging van Rubberplanters ter Oostkust van Sumatra*), the Labor Office, and the Permanent Labor Committee (*Permanente Arbeidscommissie*, or PAC). The PAC was a standing body existing since 1925 that united representatives from government, employers, and (although limited to one person) workers. The exchange of ideas involved at least thirty-two different items, brought forward by one or more of the parties involved. The causative items mentioned throughout the debate, and the party that brought it forward, are listed below (see table 8.1).

From this table it can be observed that all three parties agreed on only a small number of issues. These included the shortcomings in the administration of law, the quality of the Asian overseers (*mandur*), the changed mentality of the coolies, and the impact of political propaganda. The Labor Office and PAC agreed on a number of points, which the employers failed to note. These concerned the wrongdoings of European assistants, unlawful measures by the plantation managers, deficiencies of recruitment, pressure of the management on assistants, and a change of mentality among the coolies.

TABLE 8.1 Causes of Coolie Attacks Mentioned by PAC, DPV, and Labor Office (1929–30)

Causes	PAC	DPV	Labor Office
Staff behavior			
1. Maltreatment (blow, kick)	■■		■■
2. Rude behavior (calling names)	■		■
3. Untactful behavior	■■		■
4. Remarks on work performance	■■		
5. Remarks on the work of wife of the attacker	■		
6. Non-work-related remarks	■		
7. Incorrect order	■		
8. Misuse of power			■
9. Provocation of the attack			■■
10. Refusal of admission into hospital	■		
11. Unlawful measure by plantation manager	■		■
12. Wage issues	■		
13. Unfounded request by a coolie	■		
14. Sending off to the magistrate	■		
15. Lack of knowledge of Javanese customs			■
16. Inexperience of the assistant			■
17. Insufficient quality of the *mandur*	■	■	■
18. Women *perkara*			■
Coolie-related issues			
19. False suspicions by a coolie	■		
20. Criminal behavior by a coolie		■	■
21. Provocation in order to be sent back to Java			■
22. Drinking habits			■
23. Failure to understand orders given			■
24. "Bad elements" among those recruited		■	■
25. Changed coolie assertiveness	■■	■	■
26. Communist/political propaganda	■■	■	■

Causes	PAC	DPV	Labor Office
Enterprise/government-related			
27. Recruitment deficiencies	■		■
28. Shortcomings in the administration of law	■	■	■
29. Shortage of police	■	■	
30. Way of inspections by the Labor Inspectorate	■	■■	
31. Insufficient quality of the labor inspectors	■	■	
32. Pressure within the organization (on the assistant)	■		■

Notes: DPV (Deli Planters Vereeniging) was a major employers' association. PAC (Permanente Arbeidscommiserie) was the Permanent Labor Committee. See text for more detail. ■■ = strongly positive; ■ = positive.

The employers stressed several factors that were only partly recognized by the Labor Office or the PAC. These comprised criminal coolie behavior, shortage of police, the way in which inspections by the Labor Inspectorate were done, the insufficient quality of European assistants, and the existence of "bad elements" among the coolie population.

To what extent is it possible to systematize the discussion of causes of coolie violence? It is clear that three parties had a major influence on the labor situation in East Sumatra between 1927 and 1930. These were the colonial government, the enterprises, and the coolies. It is within the interplay of these three forces that the rising incidence of coolie attacks should be interpreted. A memorandum by the Labor Office produced in 1930 for the People's Council (Volksraad) offers the main clues to the issue as it was seen at that time.[6]

With regard to the role of the colonial administration, two items provoked intense discussion. First, the malfunctioning of the administration of law was brought up by the employers and confirmed by both the PAC and the Labor Office. The complaint was that once a coolie was brought to trial, the verdict took too long to be issued and the severity of the sentence was often considered to be insufficient. In response, the director of justice promised in the Volksraad on August 10, 1929, that, although no tougher sentences could be agreed upon, experienced judges would be transferred to East Sumatra. Furthermore, the number of country policemen would be increased.

The second issue related to the functioning of the colonial government was the system of inspection by the Labor Inspectorate. Objections were raised against the unannounced inspections, the rounds of inspection without the presence of the plantation manager, the independent behavior of interpreters, and the assembling of workers in groups to question them on labor conditions. Unannounced inspections, which were said to undermine the prestige of the plantation supervising personnel, became the object of an intense debate between employers on the one hand and the Labor Inspectorate on the other. In May 1929 and at the end of November 1929, large meetings were held with representatives of all European parties concerned. The result was that in 1930 the old inspection method was resumed, although inspection without prior notice was still explicitly open as an option. On the issue of questioning the laborers (in groups of twenty to thirty persons) on the maintenance of the conditions of the labor contract, the government defended its position. Good functioning of the Labor Inspectorate made direct contact with all coolies, if possible, a necessity. Collective questioning was thus continued even if it caused loss of working time, which could occur especially during the tobacco harvest or when rubber-tapping coolies who were working at different locations were involved.

The next category of factors believed to affect coolie behavior were those pertaining to the management of the enterprises. According to the Labor Office, remarks could be made with regard to the functioning of *mandur/tandil*, European assistants and local managers. The major blame was, however, put on the centralized management system of plantation firms. As far as Asian overseers were concerned, the quality of these was cast in doubt. Often people were selected as overseers solely because of their personal authority but without consideration of their "civilization" and sense of justice.

The problems with regard to European assistants were manifold. On the whole the assistants were considered to be too young, and lacking proper experience and knowledge of the Javanese language and customs. Often assistants were charged with the independent management of a section (*afdeeling*) within less than a year after their arrival in the Indies. Next, the great many transfers of postings obstructed a personal contact between the assistant and his *mandur* and laborers. *Mandur* themselves were often transferred without the consent of the assistant. On the whole, the position of the assistant in the production process was very precarious because his job and chances of promotion were dependent on production figures, which had to be realized by the coolies. In this respect the head of the Labor Office, Vreede, observed:

> If the assistant—or mandur—finds a number of people that make his life sour, that prevents him from delivering the amount of work of good quality demanded from him; then it is very understandable that he comes to acts or ways of behaviour which he would have avoided under different circumstances.[7]

Yet at the same time, Vreede continued, the coolie demanded humane treatment, which he deserved even if firm treatment was needed in certain cases. A stop must be put to demanding a subservient attitude from the coolie to a larger degree than was necessary for the maintenance of authority, and the use of brutal language without any reason also had to be abandoned.

A very critical judgment was made of the commercialized and centralized management system prevalent in East Sumatra. The remarks made by J. I. J. M. Schmutzer, an agricultural economist and member of the *Volksraad*, were quoted with approval. This man stated the following in the *Volksraad* session of July 22, 1929:

> The large entrepreneur in Amsterdam, Brussels, London or Paris manages his enterprises in the Indies from behind his desk in a way that resembles an army commander who deals with his army units in a situation of war; they set their goals and try to realize these, without being witness to the human or superhuman efforts these cost to their subordinates and without noticing the grief that is often felt by these.[8]

Finally, a number of key factors pertaining to the coolie population itself were brought forward in order to explain the rising estate violence at the end of the 1920s. The major issue here was the changed mentality of the coolie compared to what it had been in earlier days. Coolies were supposed to have become more self-conscious and no longer readily accepted all sorts of circumstances. This change of mentality was believed to be a result of three factors. In general, modernization through education and travel with modern means of transport had diminished the number of workers that had never experienced anything outside their own villages. Second, the more worldly-wise coolie was confronted with a system of compulsory labor in which little room existed for relaxation, in stark contrast to the increasingly colorful life in Java. Also, living in a coolie shed without females around to marry did not contribute to the sense of well-being. Third, according to the Labor Office, political propaganda of "communist" organizations in East Sumatra had to be taken seriously. Among other manifestations of a communist "presence," many members of the PKI (Partai Kommunis Indonesia—the communist party) could be found on the big plantations near Pematang Siantar, and the *Komintern* was reported to have a representative in the Dutch East Indies. This threat had to be warded off by a purge of the enterprises, to be put into effect by the plantation management, political intelligence, and the intelligence of the planters' organization.[9]

Looking back on this discussion of causality at the end of the 1920s, it is abundantly clear how difficult it was for those concerned to draw credible inferences about the highly complex problem of coolie violence. Of course, all three parties involved had their own agenda or standpoints, which heavily influenced the way things were perceived. Still, the problems of explanation faced by the present-day historian studying these documents are in no way easier to solve. How can the multitude of factors involved be systematized? The kinds of causal factors to be brought forward are different from those explaining Doel's violent acts of 1918, although at the bottom level both case studies seem to support the obvious truth that people may resort to violence when they are put in a particularly tight corner.

As proposed elsewhere, one could construct a model-like chart to show that the quality of coolie life was determined by a specific pattern of multiple causality. The sets of preconditions that shaped the conditions under which the individual indentured laborer had to work could be put in a sequential order. Moving from the general to the specific, labor relations constituted an interplay among four main clusters of causal factors: the coolies themselves, the policies of the colonial government, the situation in the region and locality where one was employed, and finally, the kind of enterprise where one was working (see table 8.2).[10] Most likely to be prone to violence were coolies who had been recruited on the basis of misleading information by the recruiting agencies and those who had been too short a period in the outer islands to adapt to the unfamiliar, difficult working regime. The role of the colonial state consisted of two contrasting kinds of interventions at the same time: protecting the worker from abuse and facilitating the large-scale movement of labor from Java to the outer islands. Labor circumstances also differed across regions (malaria-ridden or rela-

TABLE 8.2 Structural Causes That Influenced the Quality of Coolie Living Circumstances

Positive Tendency	Negative Tendency
Coolie Recruitment	
Voluntary	Nonvoluntary
Motivated by push factors	Motivated by pull factors
The Colonial State	
Protection by the Labor Inspectorate	Compulsion upheld by law
The Region	
Relatively healthy; near major centers	Unhealthy; isolated
The Enterprise	
Branch; profit margin favorable	Branch; profit margin unfavorable

tively healthy; isolated or near major towns) and periods (e.g., determining the proportion of demand versus supply). Some sorts of enterprises had better labor conditions to offer than others, depending on the kind of work (oil drilling versus rubber tapping) and the profit margin (a large profit margin allowing for more coolie facilities).

East Sumatra in the late 1920s was indeed an area of very high pressure. Booming world prices for rubber led to a rapid adjustment of productive capacity involving the massive inflow of inexperienced workers and supervisors. The size and quality of coolie facilities, such as housing and medical care, were hardly capable of keeping up with the increased pressure they were subjected to. Working relationships became even more profit-oriented and impersonal than before. The intensive surveys carried out by the Labor Inspectorate brought more mismanagement to light than was the case before 1927. Also, possibly, the coolie population was more aware of their rights than before; accordingly it is not entirely impossible that violent opposition followed an (earlier) improvement in labor conditions rather than its nadir.

On the Nature of Historical Evidence

The famous English historian E. H. Carr had already in 1961 put forward the following plain truth: "The study of history is the study of causes."[11] The finding of historical evidence can be considered a core activity of the historian when he or she tries to give a rendering of the human past. Even in the description of a simple historical event or sequence of events, the historian deploys a number of procedures to corroborate the chosen chain of reasoning. Historical description therefore necessarily involves selection of those pieces of information that are considered to be relevant. Historical description also automatically involves comparison, since specific or even unique phenomena are presented in a form of general templates. Since the historical narrative is delivered using language, the result presented to the reader has a bias and does not produce objective knowledge.

With regard to historical explanation there exist basically two theories: positivistic and hermeneutic. The *positivistic* approach seeks a general correlation among certain facts which is then posited as a cause-effect relationship. A softened variation of this explanatory strategy seeks the correlation of "probability" among certain historical circumstances. The *hermeneutic* approach tries to explain human acts by the intentions of the actors. Through this approach the historian tries to explain certain acts or events "from within." Pure narrativists, meanwhile, reject both these methods of historical explanation. According to them, history should be seen only as a story, which can be explained only within the text itself, interlocuting parts of the text within the textual whole.[12] In this essay bits and pieces of all three methods of historical explanation can be found.

Why did Si Doel attack his foreman and two European assistants on May 1, 1918? To give a satisfactory explanation one needs to distinguish several layers of inferences. The incident itself resulted from a confrontation between the European manager of the plantation and the Javanese worker over the worker's unpermitted absence. The immediate cause was the execution of a humiliating sentence, but the acts by Doel can also be interpreted as a response to a general system that was abusive. At least by pointing toward the manager as the one to blame, the assistant labor inspector, who reported in detail on the incident, addressed the problem of misconduct by an empowered person operating in a system of indentured labor relations.

The colonial system of unfree labor and its linkages with the occurrence of violence constitute a second, more general layer of inference that has been addressed in this essay. Here it proved to be extremely difficult to establish whether violence by coolies against their white superiors really increased over time in East Sumatra or whether it merely reflected better record keeping. If we assume that violence did increase, then a whole range of possible causes, both immediate and more general, were already brought to the fore at the time. As a historian, I would be inclined to link it with the coinciding of several changes in the coolie system: more new contract laborers pouring into the region; a scaling-up of the enterprises, which involved many new inexperienced European assistants; and, possibly, more intervention on the part of the Labor Inspectorate. The pressures resulting from these changes increased the likelihood of conflict and thus of the occurrence of violence. The so-called J-curve—people protesting more as things get relatively better—might also have been a factor of some importance.

Causality in history, as exemplified in this short study, thus seems to be a matter of layers of meaning, different points of view on the part of both contemporaries and later researchers, and conflation of changes in structure. Historical evidence is therefore often built around probabilistic constructs that place events in the context of temporal and situational change. It involves nonlinear causal explanation of complex events.

Notes

1. General State Archives, The Hague, Archive of the Ministry of Colonies, Verbaal, (January 28, 1919), no. 19.
2. On labor relations in late colonial Indonesia, see Vincent J. H. Houben, J. Thomas Lindblad, et al., *Coolie Labour in Colonial Indonesia: A Study of Labour Relations in the Outer Islands c. 1900–1940.* (Wiesbaden: Harrassowitz, 1999).
3. J. Breman, *Koelies, Planters, en Koloniale Politiek: Het Arbeidsregime op de Grootlandbouwondernemingen aan Sumatra's Oostkust in het Begin van de Twintigste Eeuw* (Coolies, Planters, and Colonial Policy: The Labor System on Large Agricultural Enterprises on the East Coast of Sumatra at the Beginning of the Twentieth Century), 3rd rev. edition (Leiden: KITLV Uitgeverij, 1992), 258, table 12.
4. ARA Mailreport 1927, no. 675; ARA Mailreport 1927, no. 1783.
5. ARA Mailreport 1930, no. 91 x.
6. "Nota Kantoor van Arbeid over de Aanslagen op Personeel van in Ondernemingen in de Buitengewesten" ("Memorandum of the Labor Office on the Attacks on Employees of Enterprises in the Outer Regions"), in ARA Mailreport 1930, no. 91 x.
7. ARA Mailreport 1930, no. 91 x.
8. Ibid.

9. Ibid.

10. Discussed in more detail in Houben and Lindblad, *Coolie Labour in Colonial Indonesia*, 113–8.

11. E. H. Carr, *What is History?* (Harmondsworth: Penguin, 1977), 87.

12. C. Lorenz, *De Constructie van het Verleden: Een Inleiding tot de Theorie van de Geschiedenis* (The Construction of the Past: An Introduction to the Theory of History). (Amsterdam/Meppel: Boom, 1994).

9 Evidence and Inference in the History of Political Thought
The Case of Locke's Theory of Property

Iain Hampsher-Monk

Evidence and Inference in the History of Political Thought

HISTORIANS OF POLITICAL thought seek to interpret and establish the development over time of political thinking, as embodied in everything from philosophical treatises to fly-sheets and pamphlets and even the creative arts. Interpretation comprises a range of activities. At its most (deceptively) simple level it involves the explication of a text by a familiar to an unfamiliar reader. It may involve the attempt to demonstrate intellectual debts which are not obvious on the surface or to establish a coherence which is apparently lacking in the text. This in turn can involve the demonstration of assumptions on the part of the author which are not shared by present-day readers, but which can complete an otherwise incomplete or even apparently contradictory chain of reasoning. It may also involve bringing to light a lost controversial context in which the text may be located and which explains various, otherwise puzzling, features of its treatment. One school, that of Leo Strauss, claims true meanings often lie concealed within a text containing coded clues to enable initiates to recover them. This may be a particularly relevant approach in the case of subjects which could not be treated openly in particular historical circumstances, such as unbelief in early modern Europe or political dissent under communist regimes.[1] One common underlying assumption is usually that the authors under consideration aspire to some degree of coherence and that a principle of "interpretive charity" should predispose us to recover that coherence. Esoteric meanings, however, must be rendered plausible, and while the pursuit of theoretical coherence provides one of the shaping constraints on interpretation, the possibility must be borne in mind that the coherence aspired to by the author was never in fact achieved.

The history of political thought, unlike (for the most part) the history of the natural sciences or the history of economics, stands in a quite intimate, if tense, relationship with contemporary political theory and the study of politics itself. Although the fact that it is *history* necessarily distances its subject matter from the contemporary world, the fact that human practices, institutions, and belief systems themselves exist in, and are products of, historical time makes them dependent on historically given conceptual and linguistic resources. Thus, while we make our own politics, we do not do so under circumstances of our own choosing but in circumstances, and with a repertoire and vocabulary, given by our pasts. The need and impulse to invoke, recycle, or appropriate the past is thus much more insistent in politics than it is in subjects (e.g., some economics) which may conceive of their subject matter as atemporal categories on the model of natural science. The *ways* in which past thought is seen to be related to the present, however, differ greatly from school to school.

What all historians of political thought share, however, is a belief that, even if a definitive interpretation is unlikely to be arrived at, there are nevertheless criteria available which render some interpretations more eligible than others and which, indeed, rule out some interpretations altogether—as historical accounts. Postmodern interpretative schools dominant in literary studies commonly reject the idea of any generalized methodological propriety and deny the notion that texts or discourses have any external referent (and hence any external standards by which they might be appraised).[2] The writing of history—that is, a history which could claim to be a history *of* something outside its own text—is impossible under such circumstances.[3] Historians of political thought, self-consciously and often assertively, reject such positions.[4] They insist that all interpretative efforts rely on, and are to be assessed in terms of, the evidence advanced for them.[5]

The idea of a development in political thought also takes a number of forms. In the nineteenth century, Hegel developed an account in which the history of political (and other) thought was driven by an underlying need to overcome internal (conceptual) tensions. The resolution of these was logically implicit in earlier forms of thinking and thus the whole had a movement which could be represented as one of increasing rationality and necessity (in a logical sense). Other variations of this eschew Hegel's transcendental overtones but nevertheless subscribe to a Whiggish view of political development, according to which histories of individual political concepts—"liberty," "toleration" (Hendryk van Loon), or the social contract (Gough)—could be written as a progression culminating in modern political enlightenment. At the end of a century which has savaged belief in the idea of progress, few now subscribe to these views. Nevertheless, in identifying a subject matter as historical we are interested in the vicissitudes it undergoes in passing from its state at t 1 to its state at tN, and not, except in passing, to some imaginary state it might have reached at some point in an alternative present. Some degree of teleology is thus inescapable. Teleology, however, while explaining the present in terms of historical *process*, need not imply *progress*. Modern historians recognize the role of ambiguity,[6] misconception, and opportunism in the process of the evolution of ideas, without relinquishing the notion of interpretative standards. In particular, the so-called "Cambridge School" has stressed that developments in the history of political thought can be seen as innovative political moves within a language, moves designed rhetorically to secure support for the position advanced. This throws the spotlight on the context, intellectual and historical, which enables such moves to be plausibly reconstructed.

There is thus a variety of questions admitting a variety of sources of evidence for historians of political thought to address—the political situation addressed, the motives of the writer, his or her conception of the audience, the available ideas and arguments, and their positive or negative valencies. Because my main discussion will involve one of the most exciting areas of postwar scholarship—the political thought of John Locke—let me take an example from Locke scholarship. Some evidence is internal to the text under consideration—calling attention to, or inviting reappraisal of, unnoticed aspects of a text can transform the way we understand it. For example, early in Locke's *Second Treatise on Government* we find the following passage:

> For men being all the workmanship of one omnipotent and infinitely wise Maker; all the servants of one sovereign master, sent into the world by his order and about his business, they are his property, whose workmanship they are, made to last during his not one-another's pleasure. . . . Everyone as he is bound to preserve himself, and not to quit his station wilfully; so by the like reason, when his own pres-

ervation comes not in competition, ought he, as much as he can, to preserve the rest of mankind, and may not unless it be to do justice on an offender, to take away, or impair the life, or what tends to the preservation of the life, liberty, health, limb or goods of another.[7]

If we think of Locke (as for long, many did) as providing an ideological basis for modern secular liberalism, it is all too easy to read this as a somewhat platitudinous religious aside, rather than as a more or less formal premise of his argument. However, Locke's claim that, because we are God's workmanship, we are therefore under obligations to Him to use our lives properly and to "preserve ourselves—and others" is, as is made clear by the points in his argument at which he reminds us of it, advanced by him as a logical foundation of his claim that we have a duty to establish only those political institutions which do not threaten us with arbitrary power—even if democratic majorities wished to do so.[8]

Other evidence relies on establishing some new relationship between that text and others, or on demonstrating some historical facts surrounding the composition of the text. The role of evidence in this is largely, although not completely, intertextual. For example, John Locke's clear claims of universal natural right in his *Second Treatise* have been taken as grounds for his commitment to a recognizably modern, democratic form of government, but this seems at odds with his apparent acceptance of slaveholding, and the very limited franchise provided for in the constitution he wrote for Carolina. Was Locke a champion of individual rights or not?

Often these issues do not seem to admit of definitive resolution in the form in which they are posed. However, this does not necessarily condemn us to indeterminacy or render futile the attempt to deploy evidence in support of interpretation. The relationship between evidence and hypothesis seems, in the case of interpretative sciences, to be more fluid and interactive than in some other areas of knowledge. Even if the initial interpretations cannot be confirmed or rejected, the process of investigation often leads to a more subtle reconceptualization of the probandum, one which perhaps involves acknowledging the unhistorical and therefore unanswerable form in which the question was originally posed.

To illustrate how evidence is deployed in interpretative sciences, let us review two different views which constitute a major interpretative controversy in Locke studies—namely the character of his account of the origins and justification of private property—

and consider how, and what, evidence might affect our understanding of that account.

Locke on Property: The Context

The political context in which Locke outlined his theory of property in *Two Treatises of Government* (1690) was that of the opposition to what was perceived as the absolutist pretensions of Charles II. The work was later published in justification of the overthrow of James II.[9] One of the issues surrounding the absolutist pretensions of Charles—as it had been for his father, Charles I—was the right of the monarch to raise taxation. In effect, it amounted to the question whether private property rights were absolute and so held against the king, or whether the rights of the king overrode those, as they did other forms of right. Locke, as an apologist for the Whig opponents of the last two Stuarts, sought a theory of private property right which, consistent with ensuring material support for government, was sufficiently strong to deny to government arbitrary rights of taxation or other imposition on the property of its subjects. He devoted one of the two longest chapters of his book to the subject. In providing an account whereby political authority could be established consistent with the guarantee of individual property right, it has been argued, Locke first clearly articulated the basic elements of a liberal political order; and on such grounds, furthermore, any evasions or biases traced in his work, can, by implication, be attributed to that liberal social order, the theory of which he supposedly presaged.

The more immediate and "ideological" context in which Locke wrote was his concern to rebut the arguments of the major apologist of absolute monarchy, Sir Robert Filmer, whose works were persistently republished in the late 1670s and 1680s. Filmer had been a Civil War publicist and was recruited posthumously as champion of the later Stuarts' apparent bid for absolute monarchy. His opponent was not Locke, then a schoolboy, but the parliamentarians, and his argument was against contractualists and natural-rights theorists of an earlier generation, in particular Grotius and Selden. Hugo Grotius, in *De Jure Belli et Pacis*, and his antagonist John Selden, in his *Mare Clausum*, had argued that rights to the earth derived from a Divine grant, were once common, and had become private as a result of convention or agreement among humans.[10]

Filmer's case rested not merely on the Biblical, fundamentalist argument that God gave the world to Adam as an individual (and his descendants), not to mankind in general (thus differing from his opponents in his reading of Genesis). He advanced a more abstract argument against any contractualist account of the origin of private property, and in doing so shaped the grounds on which Locke had to construct his reply.

If all were once common, Filmer questions, how could things now, rightfully, be private? Even granting that there may once have been a universal and unanimous agreement (for such it would have to have been) to assign privately what was held in common—"a rare felicity," he notes ironically, and one for which there is no evidence—even granting that, "how the consent of mankind could bind posterity when all things were common, is a point not so evident."[11] Indeed it is so inevident, Filmer argues, that it effectively disqualifies the contractualists' claim that both kingly rule (also a result of a grant) and private property "depend perpetually on the will of them that constitute, and upon no other necessity." The implications of such positions are to him clearly "desperate inconveniences," leading to anarchy in politics, and to instability and communism in economics.[12] Filmer thus seeks to impale his opponents on the horns of a dilemma: Either God's grant was to Adam as an individual and thus the archetype (if not the ancestor) of all kings, or, as Grotius and his followers say, it was a grant to Adam as the representative of mankind, in which case community of goods follows. Then (*per impossibile*) it must be explained how property could legitimately come to be privately owned in perpetuity. Since it is impossible to overcome the problems involved in the second position, Filmer argues we must revert to the first: Private property must have derived from the grant of a monarch, descended from or representative of Adam, and inheritor of his *dominium*. What a monarch could grant, however, he could recall. If private property existed, Filmer concluded, it must derive from, and be susceptible to, political authority. The two forms of dominion, over men and over goods, were ultimately indivisible.[13] This proposition formed one of Locke's central targets.

That Locke accepted Filmer's formulation of the problem, we can see from his acknowledgment that his task was to "shew, how Men might come to have a property in several parts of that which God gave to Mankind in common, and that without any express Compact of all the Commoners."[14] Moreover, having accomplished the task to his satisfaction, Locke pressed the point that he believed he had shown that such private property legitimately emerged prior to, and thus independently of, political authority: "This partage of things, . . . men have made practicable out of the bounds of Society, and without compact. . . ."[15] Locke achieved this intellectual feat by combining an assertion of original *common* right with an *individual* right of appropriation through the "mixing of one's labour" with what was common, thus individuating property claims out of an entitlement originally held jointly.

This much, I think, would be agreed by all Locke scholars. But from here on matters become more contentious however, for there is wide disagreement as to just how absolute and individualist are the entitlements so established. Scholars' positions on these disagreements largely coincide with differences between those who read Locke through a broadly Marxist lens, seeing him as an ideological apologist for an emergent capitalist order, and those who do not. The Marxist interpretation received its classic statement in the treatment by C. B. Macpherson in his study *Possessive Individualism*.[16] At the end of his discussion of Locke's account of property he concludes:

> The traditional view that property and labour were social functions, and that ownership of property involved social obligations is . . . undermined. In short, Locke has done what he set out to do. Starting from the traditional assumption that the earth and its fruits had originally been given to mankind for their common use, he has turned the tables on all who derived from this assumption theories which were restrictive of capitalist appropriation. He has erased the moral disability with which unlimited capitalist accumulation had hitherto been handicapped.[17]

Macpherson's claims did not go unchallenged, but neither has his broad interpretation lacked support over the last four decades of Locke scholarship. Since we are here discussing the issue of evidence in a dialectical forensic tradition, let us first review the case in favor of Macpherson's characterization (the case, if you like, for the prosecution), and then hear the best defense that can be made.

The Case for Locke as an Apologist for Capitalism

In the original state of nature, the right of individuals to appropriate what was held in common derived, Locke thought, from the basic right of survival. Whereas Filmer had seen the condition of original communism *precluding* the development of private property, through the impossibility of collecting the necessary consent from all rightsholders, present and future, Locke turns this impossibility into a *reductio ad absurdam* which subverts Filmer's argument. "If such a consent as that was necessary, Man had starved, notwithstanding the Plenty God had given him."[18] In short, God's common grant to mankind of the fruits of nature would have been void and empty, if there had not been (and God had not intended there to be) some way of making use of it: "[T]here must of necessity be a means to appropriate them some way or other before they can be of any use, or at all beneficial to any particular Man."[19] That means of appropriation is insinuated by Locke into the very act of "making use" of God's grant to ensure our survival. Consuming what we need from nature both turns what is natural into us (biologically) and follows morally (since "ought" implies "can") from the right and duty of self-preservation.[20] Thus the two conditions of property—"right" and "possession"—are both fulfilled.

The act of consumption is, however, invariably preceded by an act of abstraction, performed by our hands upon external nature. It is this that proves crucial in establishing the right: "'tis the taking any part of what is common and removing out of the state Nature leaves it in, which begins the Property without which the Common is of no use."[21] This action—an act, if only a minimal one, of labor—is presented by Locke as the more generalized source of individual proprietary right. It derives from that part of the world which is not, even under God's original grant, common, namely our selves: "every Man has a property in his own Person. This no Body has any Right to but himself. The Labour of his Body, and the Work of his Hands we may say are properly his. Whatsoever then, he removes out of the State that Nature hath provided, and left it in, he hath mixed his Labour with, and joyned to it something that is his own, and thereby makes it his Property."[22]

That this "right of appropriation" is held to establish an *unencumbered* right is immediately made clear by what, paradoxically, has often been viewed as a condition applied to it. For Locke sums up the argument thus far by insisting that what is appropriated through labor is "the unquestionable property of Labourer, no man but he can have a right . . . at least where there is enough, and as good left in common for others."[23] So, first, not only does Locke insist on the absolute and exclusive nature of the right established by labor, but, second, far from (as many commentators suggest) stipulating the only condition under which the right obtains, he specifically opens up the possibility that the right might obtain *in any case*. For "at least where" should be read as "certainly under the following conditions, and possibly in other circumstances, too," and not, as it has been commonly (if perversely) understood to mean "if and only if the following conditions are met."[24] There is, however, one clear limitation to private appropriation, and that is that we may take only "as much as any one can make use of to any advantage of life before it spoils."[25] This limitation follows, for Locke, from God's intention in granting the world to mankind for the survival of all, because taking more than one needs would be to waste God's provision.

The right so established applies both to consumed goods of nature—Locke gives instances of wild fruit, game, and water—and to the land itself. Thus the private appropriation of the soil is legitimate as long as the appropriator labors on it, and does not take more than he can use without its going to waste (i.e., lying uncultivated). Not only do property rights arise from labor, but so does value itself, or at least "the far greatest part of the value of things we enjoy in this World."[26] There is, then, both a labor theory of property *and* a labor theory of value to be found in Locke's account.

These conditions outline the limits of legitimate appropriation, true "property." It follows that if these constraints are observed, the rights consequently established are absolute and enduring. No individual (or group) can rightfully lay claim to another's private property right once it has been legitimately established in this way. By implication, the right, once rightfully established, continues inviolable even if the title is transferred, through trade, inheritance, or donation, to another. Indeed this was an essential point of the political context of the *Two Treatises*, since it was the disastrous effects of insecurely held property rights on trade and economic growth that was one of the reasons for wanting to oust the absolutist and crypto- or openly Catholic Stuarts.[27]

This original limited right of appropriation applied, however, only in "the first Ages of the World." Although Locke writes that it would hold still "had not the Invention of Money and the tacit Agreement of Men to put a value on it, introduced (by Consent) larger Possessions, and a Right to them; which, how it was done, I shall, by and by shew more at large."[28] His demonstration involves showing that the invention of money—"some lasting thing that men might keep without spoiling, and . . . take in exchange for the truly useful, but perishable Supports of Life"—overcomes the spoilage limitation.[29] In this way, it is claimed, Locke "removed the previous natural limitations of rightful appropriation, and in so doing invalidated the natural provision that everyone should have (only) as much as he or she could make use of."[30] This leads to and justifies the possibility—indeed, the likelihood—of an extremely inegalitarian society.

Locke acknowledged that from the earliest times men have had "different degrees of industry."[31] The original, natural limitations on acquisition, however, come into play long before that differential could create any significant variations in property right: "As much land as a Man Tills, Plants, Improves, Cultivates, and can use the Product of, so much is his Property."[32] The operation of this original limitation "did confine every Man's Possession, to a very moderate proportion."[33] The invention of money, however, gave men not only the possibility to acquire more, but an interest in using their differential industry to do so.[34] Indeed it may even have changed men's psychology, for the invention of money accompanies, if it does not in fact cause, "the desire of having more than Men needed [and] altered the intrinsick values of things."[35] The introduction of money, in sum, through a "tacit and voluntary consent" effectively constituted an agreement to a "disproportionate and unequal Possession of the Earth, . . . an inequality of private possessions."[36]

The invention of money drives the acquisition of larger possessions via the development of trade. Without an imperishable store of value, why accumulate more than one could consume? Even with that store, what would one use it for? Without money, "What would a man value Ten Thousand, or an hundred Thousand Acres of excellent Land, ready cultivated, and well stocked too with cattle, in the middle of the in-land Parts of America, where he had no hopes of Commerce with the other parts of the World, to draw money to him by the Sale of his Product?"[37]

However, there is another aspect to the story, perhaps only partly expressed, but clearly implied, by Locke. Originally a man might only take as much land as he can work and use the product of, without its lying waste. Money overcomes the problem of spoilage, but labor remains as a kind of limitation, for "it was a foolish thing as well as dishonest to hoard up [or enclose] more than he could make use of."[38] Labor is the cost of meeting human wants;[39] it is imposed on mankind by God and "the penury of his Condition."[40] Enclosing is an act of labor, and enclosing more land than we can work is not only dishonest, but foolish, for it is a cost with no return—unless, that is, we can command the labor of another to work the land so acquired. Locke clearly assumes this to be a possibility. The references to "larger estates" intensively cultivated (and justified as being more productive for this reason) reveal his assumption that the introduction of money and inequality brings about, or at the very least is accompanied by, the emergence of wage labor.[41] There is, moreover, a famous reference to the alienation of the right otherwise accruing to employed labor. Locke, in exemplifying his claim that labor establishes a property right, gives three instances: "Thus the Grass my Horse has bit; the Turfs my Servant has cut; and the Ore that I have digg'd in any place where I have a right to them in common with others, becomes my Property." "My servant's labour" is then immediately described as "the labour that was mine. . . ."[42]

Thus, from an initial situation where all is held in common, Locke demonstrates, first, a right to individual sustenance, then an equal right to property in land, established by and also held under the condition of labor, and limited by a prohibition on waste. Then he demonstrates how the invention of money overcomes the wastage limitation (and by implication, too, the limitation of personal labor) through allowing the institution of wage labor. This vastly increases the possibilities of wealth accumulation, a motive for which is also provided by the opportunities for trade that are also opened up by a money economy.

Once again we may need to supply some of Locke's assumptions here. For there would be wage laborers only if there were a shortage of land. Why would anyone work for another for less than the value they could gain in working for themselves? Moreover, who would employ someone who demanded the whole of their product? If access to land were unimpeded, no one would work for less than the value of what they produce. There is an internal dynamic to this, however; for even while assuring us that there is still land available in many parts of the world, Locke points to localized scarcity as a factor in bringing about enlarged estates, and stresses that the persistence of free land can "scarce happen amongst that part of Mankind that have consented to the Use of Money."[43] The emergence of wage labor requires the very landlessness which the increasing inequality of property itself brings about.

This argument presupposes some lowering of the rate of return on labor to the employee, a consideration of which Locke is clearly aware in his economic writings.⁴⁴ Yet this does not matter. The crucial point for Locke is to justify "the preservation of mankind." This is assured in the unequal, wage-labor economy, by its much greater productivity. Land subject to the intensive cultivation which only large estates under wage labor can generate is 10, 100, or even 1,000 times more productive.⁴⁵ As a result, claims Locke, however close to subsistence they are, English wage laborers live better than aboriginal kings.⁴⁶

Thus on both the specific grounds of the law of nature and on more general utilitarian considerations, Locke takes care to demonstrate that property rights, once established, are inviolable. It is the circumstances surrounding the establishment of property right that determine its legitimacy once and for all, not those in which it is exercised once established. This is shown by the notorious care Locke takes to exclude political interference in property rights. As he famously puts it: "The great and chief end therefore, of Mens uniting into Commonwealths, and putting themselves under Government, is the Preservation of their Property."⁴⁷ As a consequence, it is an absolutely fundamental rule of legitimate government that a ruler cannot "have Power to take from any private Man what part he pleases of his Property without his own consent." This is a definitional point about the very meaning of property: "For I have truly no Property in that, which another can by right take from me, when he pleases, against my consent," for "this would be in effect to leave them no Property at all."⁴⁸

This is not only a very strong practical claim, it also emphasizes what a conceptually strong right property is. A property right that was in any way susceptible to other claims would not actually count as a property right at all. Thus the preservation of rights claiming to be property rights entails their absolute inviolability. Even the acknowledged material needs of a contractually established government can be met only through taxation specifically agreed to by the individual or his representative. Locke's conception of property, then, seems indeed an absolute and highly individualist one. In common with others of his time, he recognized property as "the highest right a man can have to a thing."⁴⁹

Thus, although Locke recognized communal limitations on the circumstances surrounding the original appropriation of property, once these had been successfully complied with, or circumvented by the development of institutions such as money, the resulting rights were unencumbered by any social considerations. Locke's argument virtually encapsulates the historical movement from a medieval, morally responsible, socially embedded, and essentially limited conception of property, to the modern, irresponsible, individualistic, and emancipated conception, according to which the continued and unlimited appropriation of property (irrespective of the consequences to others) is not only permitted but seen as rational. This in turn grounds an economic system based on and justified by capital accumulation drawn from the wage labor of the unpropertied—in all but name, capitalism.

Locke's Argument as a Case for Socially Limited Property Right

However, in opposition to the interpretation outlined above is the view that Locke's theory of property right is, like all his thought, permeated throughout by the moral requirements of the law of nature: that man is to be preserved. The responsibility given to each of us for our own preservation is only marginally more salient a moral consideration than what must follow closely behind it: our concern for the preservation of our fellows.[50] Since our right of self-preservation derived from the fact of our having been created by God, we are duty-bound to be concerned about the preservation of others who are also His creations. Such a natural-law morality provides a *continuing criterion* of all human action and institutions and is not at all left behind once the institutions of civil society or a more complex economy emerge. As Locke says:

> The Obligations of the Law of Nature, cease not in Society, but only in many Cases are drawn closer, and have by Humane Laws known Penalties annexed to them, to inforce their observation. Thus the Law of Nature stands as an Eternal Rule to all Men, Legislators as well as others. The Rules that they make for other Men's Actions, must . . . be conformable to the Law of Nature, i.e. to the Will of God, of which that is a Declaration, and the fundamental Law of Nature, being the preservation of Mankind, no Humane Sanction can be good, or valid against it.[51]

On this view, however immaculately conceived a property right may originally have been, its integrity is not guaranteed in the face of others' subsequent need.

It is against this moral backdrop that we must now assess the implications of Locke's arguments about property rights. The law of nature's fundamental preoccupation with the survival of all mankind clearly underlies both the individuality of the original rights of appropriation and the communitarian constraints placed on them. The moral permission to appropriate follows from the need and duty of survival; the—or as we shall see, perhaps it is only one—means of actualizing that duty is labor. The labor provision might best be seen in origin as a practical way of enacting what is effectively a preexisting right to subsistence.[52] True, it is normally labor that "put a distinction between them and common" (i.e., that designates what has been individually acquired), but the right of subsistence is clearly there already—for example, in the case of children.[53] Even in the extreme case of a justly defeated enemy, the subsistence rights of defeated belligerents' dependents override the undoubted property rights of the wronged party to reparations.[54] Since this right to reparations is presented by Locke as an absolutely fundamental and explicit clause of the basic law of nature, we may be assured that the right to subsistence—here, clearly irrespective of labor—is even more so.[55] The uncontentious "spoilage limitation" is a clear recognition that we must not thwart the provisions God has made for our collective survival.[56]

Finally, although the "enough and as good" clause may be infelicitously phrased, it is perverse to read it permissively. If Locke meant "at least where . . ." to be construed in the strictly logically permissive way that Waldron, for example, suggests (meaning "and in other cases, too"), it becomes impossible to understand why Locke should continually mount arguments to show how it could be legitimately overcome, a preoccupation which undoubtedly reveals an intention to construe it restrictively.[57] Thus the development of original property rights is described as taking place in such a way that "in effect there was never the less left for others. . . ," or again, "his Neighbour . . . would still have room for as good, and as large as Possession . . . as before . . . without straightning any body, since there is enough Land in the World to suffice. . . ."[58] Yet again the appropriation of more land "does not lessen but increase[s] the common stock of mankind."[59]

The original appropriation of property, then, takes place against a series of restrictions which express the general injunctions of the law of nature to preserve human life by ensuring there are appropriate rules regarding the distribution of the means of survival to all. Individualist property rights should be read only as one possible second-order specification of this higher-order law, a specification which (Locke seems to believe) is, as a matter of empirical fact, consistent with the more general rule.

On this view, the distributive outcome of private property appropriations is and remains crucial to the legitimacy of the individual property rights comprising that distribution, and cannot be absolute against the claims of the indigent. For the whole rationale of the institution of private property rights is to provide specifications of the law of nature which would enable *each one of us* to discharge our duty of survival.[60] This is not an occasional view, adopted for the purposes of the *Two Treatises*; it is worked out in detail in Locke's *Essays on the Law of Nature* and *Thoughts Concerning Education*.[61] In the *Two Treatises* Locke keeps this broader goal in sight, frequently asserting that as a matter of fact the development of a more complex economy and unequal property rights does indeed fulfill this ultimate goal—in particular stressing the greater productivity of enclosed land, and the continued existence of unclaimed land.[62] However, the very care he takes to argue this is further testimony to the fact that he regarded the background requirements of the law of nature as a *continuing criterion* of legitimate proprietorship, and not just a condition of its creation. Greater productivity (and its appropriate distribution) and the continuing availability of unowned land are clearly recognized as contingent facts; and if they once fail to obtain, the legitimacy of current holdings (no matter how scrupulously they were originally acquired) is impugned. Distributive outcomes as well as origins of title are morally relevant to Locke. He considers the extreme case: It is "a most specious thing" to suggest that if someone were to become "the Proprietor of the whole World, [they] may deny all the rest of Mankind Food . . . God never gave any such Private Dominion."[63]

Since the continuing law of nature commands human survival, and since "the conditions of human life require labour and materials to work on,"[64] any set of property institutions (or the distribution of holdings derived from them) that resulted in some human beings' being in a position to deny others the opportunity to labor or the materials needed for life contravenes the law of nature. Moreover, conceding the needs of the indigent is emphatically not a question of charity, in the sense of being an act of supererogation by property owners. It is a question of the very definition of *property*. Proprietors simply do not have any property in that which their fellows need for their survival. This is straightforward, scholastic property theory, available to Locke in any number of books and tracts in his library:

> God the Lord and Father of all, has given no one of his Children such a Property, in his peculiar Portion of the things of this World, but that he has given his needy Brother a Right to the Surplusage of his Goods; so that it cannot justly be denied him when his pressing Wants call for it . . . 'twould always be a Sin in any Man of Estate, to let his Brother perish for want of affording him Relief out of his Plenty.[65]

This has implications—which Locke is at pains to draw out—for economic and other contracts. Coerced agreements are void. However, if the indigent have a right to subsistence which the property owners' (invalid) claims deny them, it is a fortiori illegitimate to threaten to withhold that right from the poor in order to coerce them into servitude or employment. Thus, "a Man can no more justly make use of another's necessity, to force him to become his Vassal, by withholding that Relief God requires him to afford to the wants of his Brother, than he that has more strength can seize upon a weaker . . . and, with a Dagger at his Throat offer him Death or Slavery."[66] The implications of such a practice would be to sanction coercion as a foundation of human relations and society, a position which, needless to say, Locke rejects out of hand.[67]

Although Locke is indeed concerned to show that political authority plays no role in the *establishment* of private property right, he does not draw from this fact the implication that political authority, once rightfully constituted, has no role to play in *regulating* it. The Marxist interpretation depicts Locke claiming that governments are faced with a distribution of possessions, established *ex ante*, with which no interference is possible without the express consent of the possessor. However, Locke clearly presumes, and in various places describes, a more active role for government. It can establish common ownership where this serves the common good.[68] It is a residuary legatee.[69] More particularly, once an individual joins a commonwealth, his land becomes inextricably a part of its territory—"Commonwealths not permitting any part of their Dominions to be dismembred."[70] All of which represents a considerable restriction on absolute individual property right: "By the same Act therefore, whereby any one unites his Person . . . to any Commonwealth; by the same he unites his Possessions . . . to it also; and they become, both of them, . . . subject to the Government and Dominion of that Commonwealth, as long as it hath a being."[71]

The entry of property rights into political society is not a passage through a transparent medium. The establishment of governments requires them to "regulate the Properties of the private Men of their Society, and so by Compact and Agreement settle the Property which Labour and industry began."[72] If it is unclear at this point quite what "regulation" would involve, Locke's phrasing suggests more than the mere positive endorsement and legal specification of existing titles. Could "regulation" involve acts of redistribution?

This might seem an outrageous suggestion. The overriding duty of government, Locke continually insists, lies in the protection of property. Just so. The question, however, is not "Can a government take it on itself (or be delegated) to redistribute private property rights among its subjects?" For, on Locke's understanding of the concept of property, the answer is, by definition, "No." The true question is: "What is the extent of the citizens' property rights? And if individuals' conventional holdings of goods fall out of line with their true entitlement, is there anything government may or should do to rectify the situation?" Here, I suggest the answer is much more permissive. As we have seen, according to natural law, a man or woman has no property in that which another needs for his subsistence, and legitimate political power is duty-bound to uphold the law of nature. Private property is a means of discharging the requirements of the law of nature—but only a means, and a potentially fallible one. Inasmuch as conventional property holdings depart from the requirements of the law of nature, those holdings cease to be "property," and, to that same degree also, legitimate government, committed to the implementation of the natural law, might have a duty to redistribute to the indigent.

Ironically, the very passage cited to deny this is at least presumptive evidence for its possibility.[73] Section 139, it is claimed, reveals Locke at "great pains to distinguish the regulation of property from its confiscation or redistribution." It reads, in relevant part: ". . . the Prince or Senate, however it may have the power to make Laws for the regulating of Property between the Subjects one amongst another, yet can never have a Power to take to themselves the whole or any part of the Subjects Property without their own consent."

This passage will not do as evidence that Locke allows "regulation" only where that is understood not to allow redistribution. For, first, the passage follows straight on from a section discussing the danger posed to property rights by absolutist rulers. So the danger envisaged here is that of absolutist rulers' appropriating citizens' *property for themselves*, which is of course ruled out. Second, though, the exception made to this—"however it may have the power to make Laws for the regulating of Property between the Subjects one amongst another"—is precisely the case in point. "Regulation" is here being discussed in the context of transferring entitlements, in between a passage denying absolute rulers rights of appropriation and one discussing how property could legitimately be taxed for the support of government. The distinction being made is not between *transfer* and *regulation* in the mere sense of establishing legal conventions (why would anyone think of that in the context of such a discussion?), but between transfer to the personal estate of the ruler (or even legitimate public uses of the government), and authoritative transfer between the members of the commonwealth. Locke's insistence on the stability of individuals' property rights invariably opposes their appropriation, "arbitrarily," "willfully," or "at pleasure."[74] Yet the whole point about transfers to meet subsistence needs is that they are neither arbitrary nor made to serve a willful ruler's pleasure. They are based on a fundamental law of nature, and directed not only toward the benefit of a needy fellow being, but to the meeting of his or her rights.

To clinch such an interpretation would require evidence of Locke in the act of asserting that this was what governments, by positive law, were required to do. This is a stern test, for there is little evidence for Locke's seeking such statutory articulation of other, much better established political principles, such as the need for all to consent to their governments. Yet it is to be found, and in an unlikely source. One of the most difficult documents for those seeking to present a collectivist Locke is his "Memorandum to the Board of Trade on the Poor," which recommends very harsh treatment indeed. This is cited to devastating effect by Macpherson and Wood, and acknowledged as damaging to his own interpretation of Locke by Ashcraft.[75] Yet however severe an attitude to social discipline Locke reveals there (and it is unclear how much allowance should be made for the sensibilities of the times), his proposals as to what those needy poor are entitled to *as a right* are crystal clear: "Everyone must have meat, drink, clothing and firing. So much goes out of the stock of the kingdom whether they work or no."[76] Moreover, parishes were to be made collectively responsible for poor-law administration, and were criminally liable "if any person die for want of due relief in any parish in which he ought to be relieved."[77]

Locke is, therefore, not only insistent on the continuing limitation of individual right by the natural-law claims of others, but, unusually in his case, we even have evidence of his seeking to incorporate this in positive law.[78]

The ambiguity of Locke's account of property right derives from the ambiguity of the context in which he articulated it, not merely in the sense that Ashcraft has brought out—the need to appeal widely to the whole spectrum of interests in the revolutionary movement—but also in a more theoretically specific sense. Locke indeed seeks to defend property from arbitrary intervention by the monarch. To do so, he must stress its inviolability. However, Locke's more general theory of property rights locates them within the law of nature, which stresses the mutuality of all claims and their vulnerability to others' needs. Government, as long as it acts legitimately, is duty-bound to enforce these natural-law criteria. Although in doing so it may invade conventional "property rights," it will be enforcing those which are morally defensible. Thus, to claim the inviolability of property rights against an invasive and arbitrary sovereign is quite consistent with a definition of property rights which incorporates the needs of the indigent. Property rights are inviolable—but there simply is no property right if natural law duties concerning the welfare of others are not being discharged.

Consideration and empirical identification of the socio-economic circumstances under which such duties may be said to be fulfilled is, of course, entirely another matter, and one which was to provide ample scope for both conservative apologists and radicals working within Lockean parameters for the succeeding three centuries.

Conclusion

In seeking to understand (or write) the history of political thought, some aspects, at least, of the evidence seem unproblematic—"evidence" is there on the pages of the texts we study. Yet the claims that are advanced on the basis of such evidence often involve inferring, or ascribing to thinkers, positions which are not made fully explicit by the authors under discussion. There are two approaches to this, one broadly philosophical and one historical. Both are practiced in political theory and, for me at least, the enduring fascination of the subject depends on the tension between the two.

One ground on which an interpretative position can be put forward is through the exegete ascribing to a thinker further premises to which the theorist under study "must have" subscribed, since they are logically entailed or (more weakly) implied, by the premises which *are* explicit. This is a philosophical argument, and philosophers doing political theory tend to want to argue in such a way. However, historical experience shows that what seems to be logically compelling (or even merely *obvious*) at one time and place is often not so at another. It is, on this view, dangerous to ascribe to historical agents positions which depend on their having been aware of what seem to us to be entailments between those positions and others which they undoubtedly did hold. Historically minded political theorists therefore prefer to try to find textual or other independent historical evidence for what other beliefs thinkers did or did not have. This might include the thinker's expressed opinions or beliefs as known from other works, evidence about what kind of knowledge was or was not generally available at the time, and so forth.

If we take Macpherson's position, we can see some of these issues exemplified. From the fact that Locke undoubtedly moves in his theory from a situation of common ownership to one of private, Macpherson infers an intention on the part of Locke to undermine the connection between property and social obligations. Macpherson further infers an intention on Locke's part to emancipate the accumulation of wealth from social or moral considerations—and to do so as part of a project "to provide a positive moral basis for capitalist society."[79]

Now, it is true that in order to establish a capitalist social order as Marx theorized it, it would be necessary to disentangle both property rights and labor from the duties and obligations in which they were characteristically enmeshed in pre-capitalist societies. However it is unclear that support for such a capitalist order is *logically entailed* by the move from communal to private property, as it would have to be to claim that such a move could be grounded only in a desire to establish a capitalist order. While the evidence is consistent with such an inference, it simply does not compel acceptance of it. Moreover, at least a part of Macpherson's claim is very vulnerable indeed to the second set of historians' questions mentioned above, namely, "What kind of knowledge was available to Locke?" For Locke to have been intending to provide a moral basis for a capitalist society, he would have had to know what a capitalist society was, or at least had a conception of something which we came to know by that term. The earliest use of the term *capitalist* in this adjectival sense dates to the middle of the nineteenth century, while even the use of the noun *capitalist* did not come about until a century after Locke wrote. Only the term *capital* in the limited sense of "wealth, worth, or substance" was in use at Locke's time.[80] Even if we assume that the emergence of the concept anticipates that of the word, it is not until Adam Smith's *Wealth of Nations* (1776) that we get the first defense of a *system* of free trade, in which the advance of capital to employ labor for profit is understood to play a central role. The question therefore arises whether Locke could have set out to provide a justification for a system for which he had no name, and which had not been described as an entity at the time he wrote.[81] If the answer to this is "no," then it would be wrong to infer, purely from Locke's desire to emancipate property from moral or social restrictions imposed by an arbitrary monarch, an intention to provide a defense of a capitalist system.

While in a forensic context we tend to be interested in whether evidence supports an inference and ultimately proves or fails to prove a case, in interpretative studies we may be more interested in the way evidential failure or conflict reshapes the charge (or the question). In a trial (plea bargaining apart), the case to be proved is fixed at the start and not renegotiable. Evidence is sifted and inference is deployed so as to bear on this fixed question. By contrast, in the case of the interpretation of Locke—as in many interpretive sciences—what the evidence deployed in the debate has done is continually to refine and force reformulation of the nature of the claims being advanced. Few scholars would now pose the question about Locke's relationship to capitalism quite as baldly as it emerged from Macpherson's study, important and challenging as it was. Another way of expressing this is to say that we have become more careful about the relationship between our evidence and the inferences we draw from it. Jeremy Waldron, for example, in reviewing Jim Tully's collectivist interpretation of Locke, restated the case for unconstrained individual property right in Locke without any reference to the more tendentious question of Locke's relationship to an emergent capitalism.[82] Claims about Locke's individualism, it seems, can be investigated without the burden of that massive and potentially anachronistic issue hanging over the scholar. On the side of the Marxist scholar, too, the claims have become more refined and specific. Reference to Locke's apologetic support for a generalized capitalism has been replaced by more cautious claims about his relationship to aspects of the particular, agrarian form in which it began to emerge in early modern England.⁸³ For Neal Wood,

> Locke's thought was in part expressive of certain basic social changes occurring in England, of a transition to the early stages of capitalism, and . . . he began to conceive of the social relations of production in a manner suggestive of an embryonic capitalist outlook. . . . some of Locke's ideas symbolize or represent the 'formal' subjection of labor to capital, and perhaps the beginnings of the real subjection. . . . Locke's thought testified to important changes in agriculture and the social relations of agricultural production, the necessary conditions for the eventual emergence of English industrial capitalism.⁸⁴

Yet on the other hand, Richard Ashcraft's massive study of Locke's political life and contacts showed him working with classes and groups which cannot be exclusively identified in any simple way either with a generalized "bourgeoisie," or indeed, with an "agrarian capitalist" class:

> by framing his argument in such a way as to knit together 'labor,' 'cultivated land' and 'the common good' Locke produced a powerful natural law critique of those individuals in society who neither laboured nor contributed to the common good of society. Indeed Locke's chapter on property is one of the most radical critiques of the landowning aristocracy produced during the last half of the seventeenth century.⁸⁵

The political theorist, synthesizing these two quotations through Marxist categories, will perhaps see less conflict between them than might appear to the innocent reader. After all, if—as an orthodox Marxian schema would suggest—"agrarian capitalist" is regarded not as a synonym for, but as the dialectical negation of, "landowning aristocracy," then the critique of the latter is indeed consistent with the recognition or celebration of the former. The support for an emerging order of capitalist property is not only consistent with, but requires a critique of, its precapitalist forms, a fact which few of the protagonists in the debate seemed willing to acknowledge. This issue, however, turns out to be beside the point, or at least beside one of them. For Locke is mainly concerned to defend property rights *against absolutist rulers* and is, not surprisingly, lax about discriminating among the different kinds of proprietors whose rights such a ruler might offend. This issue of the "identity" of Locke is not resolved, but the role of evidence and inference has been to generate a more subtle, more sensitive set of questions, rather than to prove or disprove a fixed case.

Notes

1. On writing while concealing unbelief, see David Berman, *A History of Atheism in Britain: From Hobbes to Russell* (London: Routledge, 1990), and "Deism, Immortality, and the Art of Theological Lying," in *Deism, Masonry, and Enlightenment*, ed. J. A. Leo Lemay (Delaware: Delaware University Press, 1987).

2. Radical deconstructionism draws on the hermeneutics of Heidegger and Gadamer, but its principal exponents have been the French writers Foucault, Derrida, and Lacan.

3. For an attempt to intrude deconstructionist "standards" on the new history of political thought pioneered by Pocock and Skinner, see David Harlan, "Intellectual History and the Return of Literature," *American Historical Review* 94 (1989):

4. This is true of writers as different as Quentin Skinner (who rejects Derrida), John Pocock (contra Fish), and Reinhardt Koselleck (who rejects Gadamer's enclosed hermeneutics).

5. In contrast to some postmodern literary theorists who celebrate the death of authors (and thus of the possibility of recovering a specific meaning which the authors intended to embody in the text) and insist there is no reading more authoritative than another to be discovered. There are only "readings."

6. See, e.g., Conal Condren, *The Status and Appraisal of Classic Texts* (Princeton: Princeton University Press, 1985).

7. John Locke, *Two Treatises of Government*, ed. P. Laslett, 2nd ed. (Cambridge: Cambridge University Press, 1967), ii, 2, 6.

8. This was made clear in one of the most influential studies of Locke, John Dunn's *The Political Thought of John Locke* (Cambridge: Cambridge University Press, 1969).

9. The second treatise was composed in the context of the early 1680s when Charles II dismissed the Oxford Parliament, staged mock treason trials against prominent Whigs, overrode the elected sheriffs in the City of London, and revised the charters pertaining to parliamentary elections so as to secure amenable parliaments. So severe was the repression that Locke fled to Holland for his life. The book, comprising the second together with the first treatise (probably written in 1679), was published in 1690 in the aftermath of the Glorious Revolution in which the protestant William of Orange and Mary were invited to take the throne following the Catholic James's flight to France.

10. Sir Robert Filmer, *Patriarcha and Other Political Works*, ed. Peter Laslett (Oxford: Blackwell, 1949), 63–4.

11. Filmer, *Patriarcha*, 65; idem, "Observations on H. Grotius," in *Patriarcha*, 273.

12. Filmer, *Patriarcha*, 70, 71.

13. Ibid., 78.

14. Locke, *Two Treatises: Second Treatise*, §25; and having shown it he reiterates the point in §39.

15. Locke, *Second Treatise*, §50.

16. C. B. Macpherson, *The Political Theory of Possessive Individualism* (Oxford: Oxford University Press, 1962).

17. Ibid., 221.

18. Locke, *Second Treatise*, §28.

19. Ibid., §26.

20. "turns nature into us": "he that is nourished by the Acorns he pickt up

under an Oak, or by the Apples he gathered from the Trees in the Wood, has certainly appropriated them to himself. No Body can deny but the nourishment is his." This follows . . . since "ought" implies "can": "If such a consent [the consent of all mankind] as that was necessary, Man had starved, notwithstanding the Plenty God had given him." Locke, *Second Treatise*, §28.

21. Ibid., §28.
22. Ibid., §27.
23. Ibid., §27.
24. See Jeremy Waldron, "Enough and As Good Left for Others," *Philosophical Quarterly* 29 (1979): 321–3.
25. Locke, *Second Treatise*, §31; see also §37, "if they perished in his Possession, . . . he offended . . ."; §46, "*the exceeding of the bounds of his just Property not lying in the largeness of his Possession, but the perishing of any thing uselessly in it*"; etc.
26. Locke, *Second Treatise*, §42; in §40 commodities are reckoned to have 99/100ths of their value imparted by labor; in §43 the product of cultivated land is reckoned at 1,000 times that of its natural product.
27. Richard Ashcraft, *Revolutionary Politics and Locke's Two Treatises of Government* (Princeton, N.J.: Princeton University Press, 1986) 230 ff.
28. Locke, *Second Treatise*, §36.
29. Ibid., §47.
30. Macpherson, *Possessive Individualism*, 204.
31. Locke, *Second Treatise*, §48.
32. Ibid., §32, and see §38.
33. Ibid., §36.
34. Ibid., §46, 47.
35. Ibid., §37; see also the reference at §111 to the "*Golden Age* (before vain Ambition, and <u>amor sceleratus habendi</u>, evil Concupiscence, had corrupted Men's minds . . .)." Cf. Macpherson's famous but incautious claim that "Locke has evidently started from the position that accumulation is morally and expediently rational *per se*," in *Possessive Individualism*, 235.
36. Locke, *Second Treatise*, §50.
37. Ibid., §48.
38. Ibid., §46.
39. Ibid., §35.
40. Ibid., §32.
41. The central passage (Locke, *Second Treatise*, §37, lines 10–29) justifying this increased productivity was inserted by Locke into the fourth edition; see Laslett's edition, 476; and see Macpherson, *Possessive Individualism*, 211.
42. Locke, *Second Treatise*, §28. The significance of the passage was first stressed by Macpherson, *Possessive Individualism*, 215.
43. Locke continually insists that there is still enough land available for those who wish to work it as subsistence peasants. Locke, *Second Treatise*, §36, §45.
44. ". . . the labourer's share, being seldom more than a bare subsistence. . . ." *Some Considerations of the Consequences of the Lowering Interest and Raising the Value of Money*, in *Works of John Locke*, vol. 2 (London: 1759), 36.
45. Locke, *Second Treatise*, §40 (10, 100), §42 (1,000).
46. This not only contradicts Locke's own views in his economic writings (see nn. 44, 75), but the anthropological evidence is against Locke on this. See Marshal Sahlins, *Stone Age Economics* (London: Tavistock, 1974).

47. Locke, *Second Treatise*, §124, and inter alia §85, 134, 138.
48. Ibid., §138, 139.
49. *An English Dictionary* (1676).
50. "Every one, as he is bound to preserve himself, . . . so by the like reason when his own Preservation comes not in competition, ought he, as much as he can, to preserve the rest of Mankind. . . ." Locke, *Second Treatise*, §6; see also §159, 183.
51. Ibid., §135.
52. The right of subsistence, irrespective of labor, is explicitly claimed on behalf of children, with a correlative duty in parents, (Locke, *First Treatise*, §89), and the right of subsistence is asserted again, more generally, at §87, with a promise that Locke will show how individuation can be established, a promise realized with the "labour theory" in Chapter 5 of the *Second Treatise*, which opens by again referring to "a right to . . . [what] Nature affords for their subsistence" (§25).
53. Locke, *Second Treatise*, §28; the ref. to children is at *First Treatise*, §87. I am indebted to correspondence with the late Richard Ashcraft for this understanding of the importance of the right to subsistence. But see his *Locke's Two Treatises of Government* (London: Allen and Unwin, 1987), 88.
54. Locke, *Second Treatise*, §183.
55. Ibid., §10.
56. Ibid., §37: perishing "without their due use . . . offended against the common Law of Nature."
57. Even the most individualistic modern exponent of Locke's argument reads it this way. See Robert Nozick, *Anarchy, State, and Utopia* (Oxford: Basic Books, 1974), ch. 7, esp. "the Lockean Proviso."
58. Locke, *Second Treatise*, §36.
59. Ibid., §37.
60. "else man had starved notwithstanding the plenty God had given him" (*Second Treatise*, §28). If this argument justifies the institution of the conventions of private property in the state of nature, it can also justify the suspension of them in that form when, as in the commercial economy, there is a danger of man "starving in the midst of plenty."
61. See the discussion in Ashcraft, *Locke's Two Treatises*, 132–3.
62. Locke, *Second Treatise*, §37, 45.
63. Locke, *First Treatise*, §41.
64. Locke, *Second Treatise*, §35.
65. Locke, *First Treatise*, §42, and see *Second Treatise*, §183. This is a fairly standard late scholastic position; cf. St. Thomas Aquinas, *Summa Theologica*, II-II, Qu. 66, art. 8: ". . . human right cannot derogate from natural right . . . the division and appropriation of things which are based on human law do not preclude the fact that men's needs have to be remedied by means of those very things. Hence whatever certain people have in superabundance is due, by natural law, to the purpose of succoring the poor." On the availability of this tradition to Locke, see Janet Coleman, "Dominium in Thirteenth- and Fourteenth-Century Political Thought and its Seventeenth-Century Heirs: John of Paris and John Locke," *Political Studies* 33, no. 1 (1985), 73–100.
66. Locke, *Second Treatise*, §186.
67. "Any thing by this Rule that may be an occasion of working upon anothers necessity . . . may be made a Foundation of Sovereignty, as well as property." Locke, *First Treatise*, §43. Neal Wood's refutation of Tully on this point is—to put it charitably—misleading. Tully quotes the passage, cited above, denying the

right to make use of another's necessity in establishing contracts. Wood rejects this as a "misreading" and quotes from *First Treatise*, §43, that "the Authority of the Rich Proprietor, and the Subjection of the Needy Beggar began not from the Possession of the Lord, but the Consent of the poor Man, who preferr'd being his Subject to starving." Wood presents this as though Locke endorsed the situation. However, Locke's point is directed *against* the possibility of Filmerian absolutism, and he is saying that even such a "perverse use of God's blessings . . . [as the conditions described above by Locke]" does not establish Filmerian subjection; it would all depend on the contract. Neal Wood, *John Locke and Agrarian Capitalism* (Los Angeles: University of California Press, 1984), 91; cf. James Tully, *A Discourse on Property: John Locke and His Adversaries* (Cambridge: Cambridge University Press, 1980), 137.

68. Locke, *Second Treatise*, §35; the point was first made, to my knowledge, by Ruth Grant, *John Locke's Liberalism* (Chicago: University of Chicago Press, 1987), 113.

69. Locke, *First Treatise*, §90.

70. Locke, *Second Treatise*, §117.

71. Ibid., §120.

72. Ibid., §45. Once again, a refutation of Tully relies on imprecision. It is not all, but only part, of this section that refers to the establishment of the territories of *nations* (as claimed by Jeremy Waldron, "Locke, Tully, and the Regulation of Property," *Political Studies* 32 [1984]: 103).

73. Waldron, "Locke, Tully, and the Regulation," 104.

74. Locke, *Second Treatise*, §138, has all three.

75. The *Memorandum* is quoted at length in H. R. Fox-Bourne, *The Life of John Locke*, vol. 2 (London: H.S. King and Co., 1876), 377–91.

76. Ibid., 382.

77. Ibid., 390. It's worth remarking that this degree of accountability (and even, latterly, provision) goes well beyond that which applies in the administration of welfare in the modern British state. Moreover, the degree of responsibility allocated to the Parish goes some way in explaining the severity of the application of the rules to the recipients.

78. There is no evidence of Locke's political attempts to seek statutory articulation of other, supposedly better established of his principles, such as the need for the active consent of all citizens to government.

79. Macpherson, *Possessive Individualism*, 221.

80. *Oxford English Dictionary* s.v. "capitalism" (first use Thackeray, *The Newcomes*, 1854), and s.v. "capitalist" (first use Arthur Young, *Travels in France*, 1792).

81. The notion that intention can play a role in excluding implausible candidate interpretations by drawing our attention to the range of intentional possibilities available within a given cultural repertoire has played a huge role in the methodological revolution championed by Quentin Skinner. See the essays collected in James Tully, ed., *Meaning and Context: Quentin Skinner and his Critics* (Cambridge: Polity Press, 1988), especially "Meaning and Understanding in the History of Ideas," originally published in *History and Theory* 8 (1969): 3–53.

82. Waldron, "Locke, Tully, and the Regulation."

83. Wood, *John Locke and Agrarian Capitalism*.

84. Ibid., 92.

85. Ashcraft, *Revolutionary Politics*, 275.

Notes on Contributors

Terence J. Anderson is a professor at the University of Miami School of Law. As an NIAS Fellow in 1994–5 he applied the method of analysis described in this book to cases decided in the Netherlands criminal justice system, as reported in *Complex Cases*, ed. M. Malsch and J. F. Nijboer (Amsterdam: Thela Thesis, 1999). In June 1995 he delivered the thirteenth annual Uhlenbeck Lecture, "The Battle of Hastings: Four Stories in Search of a Meaning" (Wassenaar: NIAS, 1996), based upon a unique case of impeachment in which he had served as principal counsel for the accused.

M. J. Geller is Professor of Semitic Languages at University College London. Having studied at Princeton, Brandeis, and the Hebrew University, he has been Alexander von Humboldt Fellow in Munich, Berlin, and Leipzig. He spent 1994–5 at NIAS in a research group on "Magic and Religion in the Ancient Near East." While at NIAS, he delivered his inaugural lecture at UCL on the survival of cuneiform, benefitting from discussions with NIAS colleagues working on *Evidence and Inference*.

Iain Hampsher-Monk is Professor of Political Theory at the University of Exeter. He is co-founder and co-editor of the journal *History of Political Thought*. His books include *A History of Modern Political Thought* (Oxford, U.K.: Basil Blackwell, 1992), which won the Political Studies Association McKenzie Book Prize; *Defending Politics: Essays in Honour of Bernard Crick* (London: British Academic Press, 1994); and, as joint editor, *Conceptual History: Comparative Perspectives* (Amsterdam: Amsterdam University Press, 1998), *The De-*

mands of Citizenship (London: Continuum, 2000), and *The History of Political Thought in National Context* (Cambridge: Cambridge University Press, 2001).

Thomas F. Heck (Ph.D., Yale University, 1970) has served as a scholar-librarian and professor at The Ohio State University for much of his career. His research has ranged from guitar history and literature to the Italian commedia dell'arte. He launched a collective study at NIAS on how the graphic arts relate to the performing arts, leading to their collection *Picturing Performance: The Iconography of the Performing Arts in Concept and Practice* (Rochester, N.Y.: University of Rochester Press, 1999).

V. J. H. Houben studied modern history and Indonesian languages at Leiden University, acquiring his Ph.D. in 1987 on the basis of a history of central Java, published in English in 1994. From 1997 until 2001 he was professor of Southeast Asian studies at Passau University, Germany, and now is professor of Southeast Asian history and society at the Humboldt University in Berlin. During his stay at NIAS he prepared a part of a textbook on Indonesian economic history, which has recently been published (Howard Dick, Vincent J. H. Houben, J. Thomas Lindblad, and Thee Kian Wie, *The Emergence of a National Economy: An Economic History of Indonesia, 1800–2000.* (Honolulu, Hawaii: Allen & Unwin/University of Hawaii Press, 2002).

M. A. Katritzky is the Wilkes Research Fellow in Theatre Studies at The Open University, Milton Keynes, U.K., and a research associate of St. Catherine's College, University of Oxford. She has published extensively on theater iconography, festivals, and medical, theatrical, and gender-related issues concerning itinerant mountebanks and commedia dell'arte troupes, and is currently researching "English" actors in early modern Europe. She has held fellowships at the NIAS, Wimbledon School of Art, the Herzog August Bibliothek, and the Universities of Southampton (Hartley Institute Visiting Fellow) and Munich (Alexander von Humboldt Fellow), and is a recent recipient of the Kathleen Barker Award of the Society for Theatre Research, as well as awards from the British Academy and the Harold Hyam Wingate and Leverhulme Foundations.

David A. Schum is a professor in the School of Information Technology and Engineering and in the School of Law at George Mason University in Fairfax, Virginia. His major research interests have involved the properties, uses, discovery, and marshalling of evidence in probabilistic reasoning. He is the author or coauthor of several books and many papers on these subjects.

William Twining, F. B. A. is Research Professor of Law at University College London. His books include *Karl Llewellyn and the Realist Movement* (London: Weidenfeld and Nicolson, 1973); *Theories of Evidence: Bentham and Wigmore* (Stanford: Stanford University Press, 1986); *Rethinking Evidence* (Evanston, Ill.: Northwestern University Press, 1994); *Analysis of Evidence* (with Terence J. Anderson; Northwestern University Press, 1998); *Law in Context: Enlarging a Discipline* (Oxford: Oxford University Press, 1997); and, most recently, *Globalisation and Legal Theory* (London: Butterworth, 2000; Evanston, Ill.: Northwestern University Press, 2001). As an NIAS Fellow in 1994–5 he was a member of the team studying criminal justice in the Netherlands; the study resulted *Complex Cases*, ed. M. Malsch and J. F. Nijboer (Amsterdam: Thela Thesis, 1999). With Terry Anderson he initiated the Evidence and Inference Group, which is responsible for the present volume.

René Weis is Professor of English Literature at University College London, where he has taught since 1980. He has twice been a visiting professor at Dartmouth College in New Hampshire. He is a Shakespearean scholar whose publications include editions of *King Lear*, *The Plays of John Webster*, and *Henry Fourth Part 2*. He is also the author of *Criminal Justice: The True Story of Edith Thompson* (London: Hamish Hamilton, 1988) and *The Yellow Cross: The Story of the Last Cathars, 1290–1329* (London: Viking, 2000).